ANALYTICAL MODELS IN EDUCATIONAL PLANNING AND ADMINISTRATION

EDUCATIONAL POLICY PLANNING AND THEORY

Series Editor
DON ADAMS
University of Pittsburgh

EDUCATION IN DEVELOPING AREAS
Don Adams and Robert M. Bjork

SCHOOLING AND SOCIAL CHANGE IN MODERN AMERICA
Don Adams with Gerald M. Reagan

EDUCATION AS CULTURAL IMPERIALISM
Martin Carnoy

SCHOOLING IN A CORPORATE SOCIETY: THE POLITICAL ECONOMY OF EDUCATION IN AMERICA
Martin Carnoy

A TAXONOMY OF SOCIAL PURPOSES OF PUBLIC SCHOOLS
Richard L. Derr

CONTEMPORARY EDUCATIONAL THEORY
Robert E. Mason

EDUCATION AND EMIGRATION: STUDY ABROAD AND THE MIGRATION OF HUMAN RESOURCES
Robert G. Myers

THE POSSIBILITIES OF ERROR: AN APPROACH TO EDUCATION
Henry J. Perkinson

THE PUBLIC SCHOOL MOVEMENT
Richard Pratte

Analytical Models in Educational Planning and Administration

Edited by
HECTOR CORREA
Graduate School of Public and International Affairs and International and Development Education Program, University of Pittsburgh

David McKay Company, Inc., *New York*

Analytical Models in Educational
Planning and Administration

INTERNATIONAL STANDARD BOOK NUMBER: 0-679-30254-9

Library of Congress Catalog Card Number: 74-15541
MANUFACTURED IN THE UNITED STATES OF AMERICA

Design by Bob Antler

PREFACE

The science of educational planning, and in particular the use of mathematical methods for this purpose, has developed only in the last few years. Nevertheless, many different conceptual frames of analysis are available, and they have been operationalized with many different mathematical methods. Thus, it seems an appropriate time to systematize these developments.

This book presents such a systematization. The emphasis is neither on novelty nor on complete coverage; rather, it focuses on some representative studies in the more substantive areas, and does so at an intermediate level of mathematical sophistication.

In order that the reader may locate the relevant studies in the wide perspective of the field as a whole, chapter 1 offers a critical survey of the present state of knowledge. This survey also makes a somewhat detailed presentation of topics not covered elsewhere in the book.

The main body of the book is divided into two parts. Chapters 2 to 6 consider planning at the level of a country or region. The problems of planning in individual institutions—mainly universities—are studied in the remaining chapters.

Chapter 2 presents the standard model for forecasting flows of students in an educational system and extends it in such a way that it can be applied to the planning of technologically assisted education, in particular TV and computer-assisted education. Applications to Puerto Rico and Brazil are given as examples.

Chapter 3 studies the question of the integration of models for forecasting flows of students and network models of administrative activities. The methods developed are applied to Pakistan.

These two chapters consider the educational system by itself. The remaining chapters of part 1 focus on models for the integration of education and economic planning. Chapter 4 analyzes the question of forecasting manpower requirements for economic growth and applies it to an international sample. Chapter 5 describes the use of economic benefits of education to evaluate improvements of quality in the schools and applies it to several countries, including the United States and Tunisia. Finally, chapter 6 presents a complete model for the integration of economic and educational planning and applies it to Chile.

The first two chapters of part 2 deal with the problem of admission of students to a university. Chapter 7 considers the question of forecasting university attendance and applies it to the University of Minnesota. The somewhat aggregate results obtained could be used for administrative purposes, but not for selecting the specific students that should be admitted to a university department. Chapter 8 discusses this second problem.

Chapter 9 presents, from a mathematical point of view, many problems familiar to chairpersons of university departments. Chapter 10 provides an econometric analysis of the production function of education as applied to university education.

As noted, no attempt has been made to cover all aspects of macro or of institutional educational planning. Each aspect of educational planning and administration can be analyzed using mathematical techniques. The examples presented here should suggest some of the many possibilities that are open.

The selection of the examples was made in terms of their relevance for students and practitioners. Both should find in this book an easy reference to the most frequently used tools.

The editor of this book wishes to thank Don Adams, editor of the Educational Policy, Planning, and Theory Series and Edward Artinian, director of the college department of David McKay Company. Their interest in the book has greatly contributed to its final publication and to the quality of its presentation.

—Hector Correa

CONTENTS

ANALYTICAL MODELS IN EDUCATIONAL PLANNING AND ADMINISTRATION

Hector Correa

1 INTRODUCTION: A SURVEY OF MODELS IN EDUCATION AND EDUCATIONAL PLANNING AND ADMINISTRATION

CONCEPT OF MODEL

This chapter reviews the studies made of education and educational planning and administration with the aid of scientific models. Thus, a more precise delimitation of the concept of model and of the types of models to be considered is essential.

Elsewhere (Correa 1967b) I have defined a model as (1) a set of variables classified as endogenous and exogenous; (2) the cause-effect relationships among these variables; and (3) the consistency of these relationships. By "consistency" I mean that, whenever the values of the exogenous variables are specified, the values of the endogenous variables can be determined in one *and only one* way. This definition can be extended to include stochastic models, in which case the values of the exogenous variables specify only a probability distribution of the values of the endogenous variables.

Models are attempts to "explain" the phenomena characterized by the endogenous variables. By definition, a phenomenon is explained when a model of it is constructed, that is, when the values of its endogenous variables can be determined, given those of the exogenous variables.

The analysis of a model is the determination of the behavior of the endogenous variables in the light of specific changes in the exogenous variables. It is characterized by such statements as: given that the exogenous variables satisfy these conditions, the endogenous will have the following properties.

Models are used in most "sound" scientific thinking. Purely descriptive presentations, whether or not they include comparisons of conditions in several research units, fall short of being models. Even though they use variables to characterize the process studied, they cannot be considered models because they do not include cause-effect relationships and the explicit verification of consistency among those relationships. Thus, descriptive studies, with or without comparisons, are not commented on here, despite the fact that this type of study is the initial indispensable step toward the construction of a model.

Other studies fall short of using models, despite their attempt to explain actual phenomena, because the cause-effect relationships appearing in them do not satisfy the consistency condition. Again, this type of study is not considered here.

Unfortunately, many excluded studies do not fall within either of the two classifications mentioned. To a large extent their exclusion is a matter of personal preference with respect to form of presentation and method of analysis.

The most common form of model presentation uses a common language such as English or Spanish, and the most common method of analysis uses general principles of logic. On the other hand, many models use mathematical notation to complement language for presentation purposes, and mathematical results are used as complements to general logic in the analysis.

Mathematical results are helpful in the analysis of models for the simple reason that some branches of mathematics are in reality nothing more than the analysis of special forms of cause-effect relationships. For instance, in linear algebra, the properties of linear cause-effect relations—called linear transformations—are studied. In mathematical analysis, the properties of cause-effect relationships called functions are studied. In functional analysis, the properties of cause-effect relationships characterized by the properties of their rates of change are studied. As a consequence, once a scientific model is identified, say, with a mathematical function, at least part of the problem of explaining the endogenous variables is solved.

There is no reason why mathematics *must* be used in scientific models. (Actually, the basic ideas of a model cannot be mathematical.) It is simply a question of convenience. Mathematics provides a means of expressing and analyzing the cause-effect relationships that are one element in a model. The distinction between thought itself and the expression of a thought is crucial at this point.

Despite the fact that mathematics is not necessary to models, as a matter of personal preference special emphasis is placed on "mathematical models" in this chapter. I want to reiterate that this unfortunately leaves out many worthwhile models in education and educational planning and administration written by educationists and scientists in related fields who are not well versed in mathematics. Additionally, many studies not published in English are also excluded from this chapter, even though they employ mathematics. I apologize to their authors for my linguistic limitations.

Models in Education and in Educational Planning and Administration

A second delimitation of this chapter involves the definition of "education." The time-honored approach of identifying education with what educationists study and educators do is used here. The same idea can be expressed more elegantly by saying that the intuitive idea of education commonly accepted is used to delimit the area to be considered.

It should be observed that many topics under discussion here fall rather into the more general concept of socialization, which can be defined as the systematic attempt to transmit a culture. Education, in particular formal education, is only a part of the socialization process.

The distinction between models in education and models in educational planning and administration appears at first glance to be more clear. The main objective of the former is to explain educational variables, for example, why students learn or do not learn, and how the interests and preferences of society, parents, and children influence the educational process. Models in planning and administration attempt to specify the requirements that must be met in order to achieve efficiently specific educational targets. The key word in this definition is "efficiently." Targets should be achieved without waste of resources. In order to do this the cause-effect relationships between resources and targets (i.e., between inputs and outputs) have to be known. In other words, scientific models form the basis for planning and administration models.

Unfortunately, a closer look blurs the distinction just stated between scientific and planning models. The problem appears because in many models of human behavior rationality is assumed: that individuals or societies attempt to achieve certain goals by minimizing the inputs that they use for this purpose, or vice versa, that they seek to maximize the goals they achieve with a fixed amount of inputs. This is particularly true of economic models. Nevertheless, the point of view also appears in purely psychological models such as those of achievement motivation.

When this is the case, the distinction between scientific and planning models becomes quite vague. A model is purely scientific when, on the basis of an assumption of rationality, it describes how people behave. A model for planning specifies what people *ought* to do in order to behave rationally.

In spite of this confusion, the subdivision is maintained here. Those models that seem more oriented toward explanation are considered educational models, while those that specify what should be done to achieve goals efficiently are classified as planning models.

MODELS OF THE EDUCATIONAL PROCESS

The common objective of models of the educational process is to explain why students learn. Many answers to this question are possible, ranging all the way from descriptions of biochemical and neurological changes in the students (Russell 1959) to descriptions of teacher and student behavior that have as their final effect the adoption by the students of learned forms of behavior. Here the models are classified as either behavioral or mechanistic, depending upon whether the assumption of goal-oriented behavior is or is not present in them.

Mechanistic Models

In the simplest form of mechanistic model, the educational system is represented as a ladder which students climb, with fixed probabilities of passing from one rung to another, remaining on the same rung, or falling off the ladder. No attempt is made to specify what determines the transition probabilities. These assumptions greatly simplify the computation needed to forecast the flows of students in the educational system (Armitage and Smith 1967; Correa 1967a, 1967c, 1969a; Davis 1966; Fox 1971; Gani 1963; Ministerio de Educacion 1970; Thonstad 1968; Zabrowski and Zinter 1968).

A more systematic attempt to analyze processes conducive to learning has been made in the mathematical models of learning (Atkinson, Bower, and Crothers 1965; Burke 1959; Bush and Estes 1959; Bush and Mosteller 1955; Estes and Burke 1955; Miller and McGill 1952; Restle 1964; Suppes and Atkinson 1960). In their simplest form (Goldberg 1961, 105) these models take the form

$$p_{n+1} = p_n + a(1 - p_n) - bp_n \qquad n = 0, 1, 2 \ldots \tag{1}$$

where

- p_n = probability of a specific response during a specified time interval following the stimulus in the nth trial run
- a = parameter representing positive reinforcement since $1 - p_n$ is the maximum gain that the probability of response may have
- b = parameter representing negative reinforcement since $-p_n$ is the maximum reduction that the probability of response may have.

The parameters a and b usually take the form of probabilities of reward and punishment for specific actions. They could represent teachers' behavior; however, they are not the result of interaction between teachers and students.

The theory attempts to predict how changes in the values of the parameters a and b influence the limiting value of the probability p_n. The predictions of the theory and the results of experimental studies give rather close fits.

Important limitations of these theories are that they do not attempt to explain how the parameters a and b are specified in an actual learning situation, and why the learner adopts a specific pattern of responses. As a consequence, their application to actual practice is rather limited. One manifestation of this is the difficulty of using them as a framework for statistical analysis of the teaching/learning process. They do not specify the characteristics of teachers or students that will influence the educational outputs. Clearly, if this is the case, the practical use of these theories for teaching/learning purposes is very limited.

Mechanistic models of the learning process have been extended with the assumption that specific actions by the students determine the probability of reactions by the teachers. In other words, the parameters a and b in equation (1) are determined, not arbitrarily outside the model, but as functions of the p_n (Burke 1959, Suppes and Atkinson 1960). A basic limitation of these models as tools for the analysis of classroom interactions is that they do not explicitly divide teachers and students into two separate categories. They simply deal with interactions among persons who play more or less identical roles.

A more specific attempt to study actual classroom interaction is found in Flanders (1960). In this approach, statistical recording of the characteristics of classroom interaction is emphasized. A detailed theoretical framework for the analysis of the data selected is not presented.

A combination of the approach in the learning models with or without social interaction with Flanders' technique might produce useful insights. Such a combination would provide an actual testing ground for the model, and a theoretical structure for Flanders' method.

The final group of mechanistic models includes the attempts to relate, using statistical methods only, socioeconomic and psychological characteristics of the school-age population and of the students, teachers, and facilities in an educational system to indices of student participation in the educational process (e.g., probability of remaining in the system) and indices of their school success (e.g., scores on achievement tests). These models take many forms and many names, such as models of the demand for education (Campbell and Siegel 1967; Correa 1967a, 1969a; Dyer 1971; Guthrie et al. 1971; Reif 1965; Ruiter 1963; Sloan 1971), models of student achievement (Bowles 1968, Coleman et al. 1966, Mood 1969), production functions of education (Bowles 1970; Correa 1967a, 1969a; Guthrie et al. 1971; Hause 1972; Tuckman 1971), etc. Numerous statistical studies have been made under these names, but their results have been disappointing thus far.

It might be useful to observe that the terms "demand for education function" and "production function of education" are not appropriate for the models described. As will be seen in the next section, demand functions are derived from very specific behavioral assumptions that are not used in the models commented on above. Production functions in economic theory are technical relationships between inputs and outputs. They determine the maximum output that can be obtained from *well-specified* inputs. Perhaps the closest real counterpart of the idea of well-specified inputs would occur in a completely automated factory. In economics, labor is usually included in a production function. However, the influence on output of human reactions to the process itself, to other workers, and to management is excluded from the concept of production function. Each type of labor is an homogeneous good of constant quality. Production functions of the type just described could possibly be defined for education; the operation of the actual educational processes might be at levels quite different from their technological optimum, however, due to the influence of human factors explicitly excluded from the concept of production function. From this it follows that statistical studies of actual educational processes are far from being studies of the educational production function.

In general, the mechanistic models, as a consequence of the lack of a conceptual framework, do not help to understand education, even if they are validated by statistical analyses.

Behavioral Models

Behavioral models are based on the assumption that the basis for the behavior of students, teachers, and administrators is an attempt to achieve efficiently well defined objectives.

The simplest form of these models is a modification of the mechanistic models described above. As observed, the probability of a specific behavior on the part of a learner is determined by the relative frequency of positive and negative rewards. Behavioral models can be said to assume that the learner is playing a game against nature (Rapaport 1963) and that he selects his acts because he prefers a specific outcome. Mathematically, the two statements of the problem are closely related. The game-theory solution is different from that of the purely stochastic model, however, and the latter is in better agreement with experimental results. Attempts to apply the concepts of game theory to the interaction mechanistic models have also been made (Suppes and Atkinson 1960), but they have not been particularly successful.

Alternate approaches based on the assumption of utility maximization come from economic theory. In Adelman and Parti (n.d.) it is assumed that a student's utility function has as arguments both the satisfactions derived from school achievement, and those derived from nonschool activities. Both satisfactions are functions of the time the student spends in school-related and nonschool-related activities. It is assumed that the student attempts to distribute the time available to him in such a way as to maximize his utility. With this, the effect of a wide variety of student utility functions can be analyzed.

Extending this approach, it would be fruitful to use, instead of a deterministic utility function, a probabilistic one of the type suggested by Von Neumann and Morgenstern. Nevertheless, it is also possible that this extension would simply reduce the problem to that of game theory which has already been studied.

In a more common version of the utility-maximization models (Ben-Porath 1967, 1970; Blaug 1966; Razin 1972; Thurow 1970) it is assumed that students behave like investors who wish to specify the characteristics of the education they receive in order to maximize their lifetime returns minus their costs. This is the standard human-capital approach that has produced valuable insights into the behavior of students and has permitted the exploration of several problems in education and economics.

There is no reason why, in the human-capital approach, only received or paid financial returns and costs should be considered. Actually, emphasis has been placed in this approach on the use of indices of nonreceived or paid financial returns and costs such as external benefits of education and income foregone, and also on nonfinancial returns and costs such as the social and psychological advantages and disadvantages of additional education. Further references to this model will be made when studying the cost-benefit analysis of education.

An important limitation of the two models just mentioned is that they consider only students' optimizing behavior. A conceptual framework for the study of education as an interaction process between teachers and students is presented in Correa (1969b). An attempt to analyze this model using mathematical methods appears in Correa (1973). There it is assumed that students' achievement depends upon the time used by teachers and students, and that it contributes to the well-being of both teachers and students. Their well-being also depends upon the result of their other activities. It is assumed that each of them, teacher and student, maximizes well-being, having as a parameter the contribution of the other to achievement. In this way it is possible to specify functions stating how teachers will react to the behavior of the students and vice versa. These functions can be used to specify school learning functions that will describe actual learning processes and not theoretical production functions of achievement. Finally, from the school learning function, cost functions can be determined. In these cost functions, cost would depend upon the characteristics of the interaction between teachers and students.

Extensions of this model which would also consider the behavior of school administrators would provide a more solid basis for defining school learning functions, cost functions, and so on. Further extensions would make it possible to consider institutions where education is only one of several activities. This would be the case, for instance, in industrial firms that provide large-scale training programs for their workers.

The models described would help to build a bridge between economists' and organization theorists' approaches to education. A description of these approaches appears in Nelson and Besag (1970); it does not appear to have been formalized in mathematical models, however, and for this reason it will not be discussed here.

COSTS AND ECONOMIC RETURNS OF EDUCATION AS AN INDUSTRY

Concepts of Economic Contribution

The expressions "economic contribution of education" and "contribution of education to production" are considered here as equivalent. For the purposes of this study, the concept of economic contribution must be analyzed first.

Any industry, regardless of whether its output is a consumption or an investment good, makes an economic contribution. This is equal, by definition, to the value added by the industry. Basically, the value added is equal to the value of the output minus the value of raw materials. This difference is equal to rents, plus profits, plus wages. It is closely related to the costs in the production of a good.

In the case of a capital good (i.e., of a good used for further production), its contribution is defined to be equal to the present value of its future returns. At first glance it might appear that the first definition of contribution to production is not related to the second. This is not the case. Under the assumption of perfect competition and equilibrium, the following relationships hold: the marginal cost of producing a good is equal to the minimum average cost and to the selling price of a good, and the selling price of a capital good is equal to the capitalized value of its future returns.

The approaches mentioned above to evaluate the contribution of an industry and of a capital good to production can be applied to education. Since detailed studies appear in Machlup (1970), Schultz (1963), and Weisbrod (1962), only the highlights and the controversial points are mentioned. This section analyzes the cost and the economic contribution of education as an industry. Later in the chapter (see pp. 9–21) the contribution of education as an investment good will be studied.

Economic Contribution of the Educational Industry and Costs of Education

The first method for evaluating the contribution of an industry to production, that is, the difference between value of output and raw materials, cannot be applied to education. In most countries education is gratis, and as a consequence, all that can be done is to measure the contribution from the total of rents, profits, and wages. As observed, this total is closely related to the costs paid for education.

A limitation of the method just described is that, by convention, only the expenditures paid are included as part of the contribution. A classical example is that the unpaid work of housewives is not included in the national accounts. This brings up some conceptual problems.

First, if students act in such a way as to maximize their lifetime income, they will be paid after the completion of their studies for the time they spent on their education. In other words, some of the students' future income should be considered as a deferred present cost. Another way to evaluate this deferred present cost is to consider the income the students forego when they use their time as students rather than as members of the labor force. In either case, the empirical evaluation of this economic contribution of education presents serious problems, because there is little basis for establishing the amount of change in present and future wages if present students become workers. Actual present and likely future wages are a poor guide. Whatever method is used in evaluating these costs (i.e., in the evaluation of this form of economic contribution of education), they do not appear in the national accounts.

A similar problem exists regarding the contribution of parents to the education of their children. If parents behave rationally, the marginal utility they derive from the time spent assisting their children in their education must be equal to the marginal utility of the present value of the future income of the children. In this sense, the payment to the cost of parents' time is also deferred to the future. This point has an additional variation. Usually most of a child's formal education takes place in schools rather than at home. As a consequence, no postponement of costs occurs until the time the child receives an income. The educational costs are actually paid to teachers and schools. As observed, these costs do appear in the contribution of the educational industry to production in the national accounts.

In addition, the fact that the children remain in school gives many parents—mainly mothers—the opportunity to become members of the labor force. This possibility cannot be included among the costs of education, and because of this, it cannot be included among the contributions of the educational industry to production. Nevertheless, its inclusion as a return of education is, on the basis mentioned above, somewhat attractive. Another conceptual problem can be conveyed with the following question: Automated farming releases a part of the labor force from agricultural production. Is the production of manufacturing and services (made possible because automated farming releases the required labor force) an economic contribution of farming? If this observation is used as a basis, it follows that the custodial services of education should be included among the contributions of education to production.

EDUCATION AS AN INVESTMENT GOOD

Education can be considered an investment if, after its own production is completed, it contributes to further production. This section attempts to determine whether this is the case, and if so, the value of the contribution of education to further production.

In order to accomplish this, the outputs of education measured, for instance, in terms of behavioral changes of the educated individuals have first to be specified.

Next, the question of whether the output of education contributes to the physical capacity to produce goods and services is analyzed. This capacity, even if actually realized in goods and services, is not identical to economic production. Only the physical production of goods and services demanded in the market are economic production. For example, waste is physical production; unless a recycling firm demands it, however, it is not economic production.

An attempt is made below to study the influence of education, first on the physical capacity to produce, and then on economic production. It should be kept in mind that the data used for the analysis to be mentioned refer to actual production processes (i.e., to economic production).

Outputs of Education

The outputs of education can be classified in the following ways: (1) those affecting the personality of the students, (2) custodial care, (3) certification, and (4) new knowledge.

The Personality of the Students

Adopting the point of view of the theory of learning, it can be said that education is expected to increase the probability that the students will adopt specific forms of behavior. In order to do this, education attempts to change the students' capacity to act and to specify the goals of their actions. Among the determinants of the capacity to act, abilities, motivation, and knowledge are considered here. The goals of a person's actions are assumed to be determined by his values and beliefs. The reasons why education does not attempt to produce the desired forms of behavior in the student through, say, conditioning of reflexes, is that the detailed circumstances of the desired behavior are not known. Education normally takes place long before the actual behavior is required. This means that education has to emphasize general methods and principles that can be applied in many different situations.

Only two abilities are considered here: intelligence and creativity. Some evidence of the existence of these two abilities as separate entities is presented in Getzels and Jackson (1962).

Tests of the hypothesis that education "causes" increments in intelligence are difficult, because another reasonable hypothesis is that high IQ is a cause of educational advancement. Some support for the former relationship comes from the fact that changes in mental age are associated with remaining in school, even when the influence of differences in the initial mental age is eliminated (Green 1964). It should be observed that this result does not imply that the latter relationship is not valid.

Evidence regarding creativity is less conclusive. Getzels and Jackson (1962), Heist (1971), and Snyder (1967) suggest that lack of creativity might be a precondition for success in school. This could lead to the conclusion that education tends to reduce creativity. On the other hand, evidence that will be commented upon later suggests that the probability of producing a patentable invention increases with education.

The results in McClelland et al. (1953) support the hypothesis that education influences motivation in general, and achievement motivation in particular.

It has been stated that knowledge influences the probability that a person will adopt a certain type of behavior. This is so because, with knowledge, a person becomes aware of possibilities that would otherwise have been unknown to him, and has the basis for selecting the actions needed to achieve a desired end in the most efficient way. An educated person will thus select objectives from a wider range of possibilities, and, given the ends, the tested forms of behavior become more likely.

Doubtless some memorization or an effort to increase the ability to reproduce specific information takes place in an educational institution. On the other hand, some doubt exists about whether education makes it possible for the students to apply the information memorized. In other words, little evidence exists that students can transfer the knowledge they acquire. This means that the input of education through knowledge will tend to be reduced to specific activities.

The lack of a well-defined classification of the terms "values" and "beliefs" is a serious handicap to studying them and the influence that education has on them. A summary of the results up to 1957 appears in Jacob (1957). The conclusions reached there, and which are supported by later studies (Lehmann, Sinha, and Harnett 1966), are that:

1. Students tend to become less stereotypic in their beliefs, less dogmatic, and more receptive to new ideas.
2. This does not imply that individual characteristics of the students develop. On the contrary, there is more homogeneity in values at the end of the college experience than at the beginning.
3. The influence of the college curriculum on values and beliefs is rather limited. The changes that occur may be more closely related to the participation of the student in a particular subculture.

Little information exists on the relationship between education and the value attached to self-determination, to work in general as a means of achieving that self-determination, and to work in specific occupations. The values attached to these three concepts might have important economic implications. Let us assume here that education tends to increase the value attached to the first two, and that through education, persons tend to rank low in their scale of preference occupations requiring knowledge below that which corresponds to the level of education they have attained.

Also, little information seems to be available about the relationship between values and behavior. We will assume that individuals tend to behave according to their values.

Custodial Care and Certification

As a consequence of their organization, educational institutions provide custodial care of the students.

The certification function of the educational institution is the warranty they provide that the student has achieved a certain educational level.

Research

New knowledge, in addition to the diffusion of that already existing, is another output of educational institutions, in particular those of higher learning. However, the evidence that new knowledge is actually produced is rather limited. Substantial differences also exist between institutions.

Education and the Capacity to Produce Goods and Services

Economics holds that the physical capacity to produce goods and services is determined by (1) the quantity and quality of the factors of production, namely labor and capital; and (2) their combination in a production function.

Education will influence the physical capacity to produce if it modifies any of the elements mentioned above. The only way to establish whether this is the case is to specify a link between some behavioral characteristic attributed to education and the quantity or quality of the factor of production or the characteristic of the production function. We will attempt to follow this approach, despite the fact that it has not been used frequently and that, with the information available, it is not always possible to do so. Most studies of the influence of education on the physical capacity to produce are based on simple statistical correlations.

Size and Quality of the Labor Force

A negative correlation seems to exist between level of education and rate of population growth. An increase in education tends to reduce the rate of population growth, and consequently, other things held constant, the size of the labor force. In this sense, education has a negative effect on the physical capacity to produce.

A statistical association has also been observed between level of education and migration. Education influences the regional capacity to produce. Clearly, in this case there is no change in the production capacity of the labor force as a whole. Migration might influence the way in which factors of production are combined, however, and thus influence physical capacity to produce at the level of the production function.

Another set of hypotheses deals with the influence of education directly on the would-be workers, through its influence on their personalities.

From the observations that there is a positive correlation between education and achievement motivation, the value attached to work and to economic self-determination, it follows that education is likely to increase the desire for an income-producing occupation. Evidence in favor of this hypothesis is found in the positive correlation between level of education and rate of participation in the labor force (Bowen and Finegan 1969). At this point, however, it is appropriate to emphasize that only certain types of education are likely to produce these effects. Other types might produce opposite effects. This possibility is strongly implied in Lewis (1961), and McClelland (1961, 1966) and might help to explain the unemployment of educated people that affects many developing countries.

Another possible explanation might be that, even if education increases the desire to work, it is likely to restrict the occupations an individual would be willing to accept. Specialization in knowledge frequently accompanies higher levels of education, as does consciousness of status.

In summary, even if education increases the desire for an income-producing occupation, since it also restricts the types of occupation that could be accepted, it is not possible to specify its total effect on the size of the labor force. Whenever the desired occupation can be obtained, education tends to increase the labor force. Otherwise, it might even reduce it.

Education has also been said to contribute to the size of the labor force because it releases parents from the need to educate their children and to provide custodial care for them. As observed earlier, however, any industry releases part of the labor force from the need to produce the goods and services that are the output of the industry in question. This is a general consequence of the division of labor. Since no attempt is made to estimate the contribution to the size of the labor force of an industry by the number of workers it releases, it does not seem appropriate to do so in the case of education. On the other hand, the observation that one of the costs of education is the income forgone by students shows that education tends to reduce the size of the labor force by the size of the student body.

It can also be said that education through certification reduces the amount of work needed for personnel management, because the search for workers is made only among those who have a specific level of education, instead of among all persons offering their services. Certification also reduces the areas in which a person would search for work. The magnitude and implications of this contribution of education have not been explored in detail.

The possible contributions of education to the quality and intensity of work are more difficult to specify. The same factors that tend to increase participation in the labor force may also tend to increase the intensity of work and the number of hours worked.

Some clear correlations exist between occupation and type of education, suggesting that certain types of knowledge are actually required for certain occupations. The basic problem is that few studies seem to be available on the relationship between the actual content of the education included under a professional title and the skills used by workers in those occupations. An exception is found in some studies on the education of managers of production firms, as related to the characteristics of their performance. Newcomer (1955, table 33) studied a sample of executives from firms classified as fast or slow growing. He found that a smaller proportion of executives in the fast-growing companies had had graduate training. This result should be considered together with the observation that education might have a negative effect on creativity.

A final possible contribution of education to the intensity of work is through the influence of education on the health of the workers. Education can influence workers' health, first by its influence on discovery and innovation in the health field, and second by its influence on the adaptation and use of health procedures. These possible influences of education are quite similar to those of education on the quality of capital goods, and for this reason, they will not be studied in more detail here.

Size and Quality of the Capital Stock

If education contributes to the production of goods and services in general, it is also likely to contribute to that of capital goods. The object of capital goods is to contribute to further production. This brings up the question of whether part of the production due to capital goods should be attributed to education. Whatever the decision, it points to the fact that an evaluation of the contribution of education to production is somewhat arbitrary. This could be explained better by looking backward instead of forward. Let

$$Y_t = f_t(R_{t-1}, E_{t-1}, K_{t-1})$$

where

Y_t = output period t
R_t = human and physical not-produced resources
E_t = human resources produced through education
K_t = produced physical capital

from the definition,

$$E_t = g_t(R_{t-1}, E_{t-1}, K_{t-1})$$

and

$$K_t = h_t(R_{t-1}, E_{t-1}, K_{t-1}).$$

When the last two equations are placed in the first one, Y_t appears as determined by R_{t-1}, R_{t-2}, E_{t-2} and K_{t-2}. Further replacements would make Y_t depend upon earlier periods. The final form would show that Y_t depends upon R_{t-j}, $j = 1, \cdots, \infty$. In other words, present production depends on the human and physical resources available in all past periods. The amount that is contributed to education and physical capital depends on the arbitrary decision of where the replacement of the appropriate E_t and K_t in Y_t is stopped.

The contribution of education to the creation of new and improved capital goods can be studied on a somewhat firmer basis. It could be concluded, on the basis of the material in an earlier section ("Outputs of Education"), that since education stifles creativity, it will also reduce inventiveness. The scarce evidence available, while not conclusive, shows that this is not the case (Schmookler 1957, 221–33).

Finally, a potential influence of education is in the diffusion and acceptance of new and better capital goods. There are two areas for this influence. The first is through the additional receptivity that education might create in managers. The results quoted in discussing the contribution of education to the quality of labor suggest that education might have a negative influence on receptivity. The second influence that education might have is through the need for a qualified labor force to operate capital goods. This question is studied in the next section.

Production Function

So far, we have made no specific test of the question of whether education influences the physical capacity of the factors of production to produce, and if so, whether its influence is positive or negative.

An analysis of this type could be made, using as a framework the production function of goods and services. A production function is a theoretical construct that specifies the maximum output that can be obtained with different amounts of inputs. Only through the production function is it possible to determine the output that could be obtained with the existing stock of labor and capital, and the increment that could be obtained with additions to those stocks.

This is so because only the interaction between inputs can cause output. Two main types of interaction are considered in economics: complementarity and substitutability. Factors of production are completely complementary when the increment in the quantity of one or several (but not all) of them is a necessary but not a sufficient condition for an increment in outputs. Only with an increment of all inputs in specific proportions will output increase and inputs be efficiently used. With less complementarity—whenever only one or several factors of production are increased while others are held constant—a point is reached where further additions of the former do not contribute to output. In other words, with complementarity, when some factors of production are held constant, there is a point where output does not increase with increases in the other inputs. This means that, technologically speaking, the inputs fulfill completely different functions. The opposite is true when the factors of production are substitutable. The factors being increased replace those held constant, and production increases without bounds when one or several inputs (but not all) increase without bounds.

A point to be emphasized is that conditions of complementarity and substitutability among inputs are not a consequence only of the nature of the inputs, but also of the relative amounts of each that are available.

From the previous observations it follows that, if a production function of goods and services relating all possible inputs to output were available, it would be possible to specify without hesitation which factors influence physical capacity to produce, which are the relative proportions of the inputs needed, and finally, in what proportions the inputs are substitutive and in what proportion they are complementary. To do so it would be sufficient to check the production function, and this information could be read from it. No such dictionary-type production functions are available, however. Production functions must be estimated from actual data. If one wants to determine whether a particular entity influences production, an index of its quantity must be included among the data used in the estimation. The results of the estimation would indicate whether or not any entity included influences production, whether it is complementary or substitutive with other inputs, and the ranges of relative scarcity when this is the case.

The proper data for this type of analysis would be obtained from experiments in which different types of entities are used in different amounts as inputs, and the outputs obtained are recorded. Such experiments are not possible for large economic units or countries. In this case actual inputs and production have to be used for the estimation of production functions. From this it follows that some way must be found to relate economic to physical production, a topic we will take up in the next section.

Education and Economic Production

As observed in the previous section, the outputs of education may influence the physical capacity to produce goods and services of labor and capital. To test this hypothesis, the characteristics of the production function of goods and services must be analyzed. On the basis of the data available, however, it is not possible to do this in terms of physical capacity to produce goods and services. Only data on economic production are available. The first question to be considered, then, is how to use these data. Another problem that must be considered here is whether education has any influence on the conditions needed to pass from the capacity to produce goods and services to actual economic production.

Contribution of Education to Physical Capacity to Produce Goods and Services

The simplest way to evaluate this contribution, using data on economic production, is to assume perfect competition, equilibrium, and constant returns to scale. Under these assumptions, all physical production is also economic production and vice versa. In addition, the total amount supplied of each input is used in the most efficient way. Finally, all inputs are paid exactly for their contribution to production. In other words, the assumptions of perfect competition, equilibrium, and constant returns to scale provide a basis for using actual data to estimate the production function. The assumption also makes it possible to use wages paid to the workers as the value of their contribution to production. These two approaches, estimated production function and analysis of wages, have been used to study whether education contributes to production, and if so, how much.

Studies by Bensen (1968), Griliches (1963a, 1963b, 1964, 1967, 1969, 1970), Hildebrand and Liu (1965), Scully (1969), and Welch (1970) use the first approach. The coefficients of production functions are estimated using overall indices of outputs (e.g., valued added), together with indices of several inputs (e.g., number of workers or value of capital), and including one or several indices of the education of the labor force (e.g., average number of years of education). The results obtained can be commented upon briefly. Welch (1970) reports inconsistencies between two different estimates of the contribution of education to agricultural production. The educational index introduced in Harberger (1965) did not perform as desired in their study of the manufacturing industries, and they do not discuss it in detail. Griliches (1967, 293) says, "All the coefficients of the labor-quality variables have the expected signs and are in general significant at the conventional levels, but the contribution of these variables becomes small if all the between-industry and between-regions variance is eliminated using the dummy variables procedure." Finally, the educational index used in Bensen (1968) was significant at a 5 percent confidence level in only 6 of the 18 industries studied, and in 7 industries is not significant even at a 10 percent level. Scully (1969), studying interstate wage differentials by industry, reports that education appears as a significant factor at a 5 percent confidence level in only 10 out of 18 manufacturing industries that he studied, while in 5 industries, education of the labor force is not significant even at a 10 percent confidence level. Thus the evidence provided on the contribution of education to production, based on the analysis of production functions, can be considered inconclusive.

A basic question to be considered in the study of production functions is whether workers with different levels of education are complementary or substitutable among themselves and with capital. Some evidence of complementarity with capital is presented in Correa (1963, 1973) and Griliches (1969, 1970). Correa (1973) shows statistically that there is complementarity in some industries and substitutability in others.

As observed, the second approach is based on a logical consequence of the assumptions of perfect competition, equilibrium, and constant returns to scale: that workers are paid for their contribution to production. As a result, the wage differentials for workers having two different levels of education is equal to the value of their different contributions to production. The only problem is to specify how much of this difference is directly due to inequality in education and how much is due to other factors (e.g., innate ability). In the simplest form of this analysis, a more or less arbitrary amount of income differential is attributed to innate ability, and the rest to education (Correa 1963, 1970; Denison 1966, 1967). An immediate result of this approach is an estimate of the contribution of education to production.

A criticism of this approach is that education might only be a proxy for some other variable that actually determines income differentials. To test this point, many studies (Ashenfelter and Mooley 1968; Carnoy 1967; Corazzini 1968; Griliches and Mason 1972; Harberger 1965; Hu, Lee, and Stromsderfer 1971; Lassiter 1965; Lindsay 1971; Morgan and David 1963; Morgan and Sirageldin 1968; Renshaw 1960; Taussig 1968; Thias and Carnoy 1969; Tolley and Olson 1971; Weiss 1972; Welch 1970) use income as the endogenous variable, and as exogenous variables those describing several personal characteristics of the recipients of that income such as age, sex, race, and personal ability, together with quality, quantity, and content of education. The usual result of these studies is that quantity, quality, and content of education have a positive effect on income. It is more difficult to derive from this analysis an estimate of what part of the income differential can be attributed to education.

The results obtained are valid only if the assumptions of perfect competition, equilibrium, and constant returns to scale are valid. A step logically required before the studies on production function and income can be performed is a test of the basic assumptions. As frequently happens in science, the basic assumptions are tested after their consequences have been used as first approximations.

Several possibilities are available to test the basic assumptions. Discrimination for whatever reason is a form of deviation from equilibrium conditions in perfectly competitive markets that has been widely documented. Detailed studies appear in Thurow (1968). These studies take for granted the assumption that the number of workers employed and their wages are consequences of supply, demand, and market conditions, and simply attempt to evaluate the resulting relationship. Correa (1973) and Dougherty (1972) multiple equation models are used to determine explicitly whether this is the case in the United States. The results of the analysis show a greater influence from supply conditions than that accepted in the one-equation models. On this basis, Correa (1973) studies the substitutability of labor and capital, and Dougherty (1972) the substitutability of different types of educated labor.

Comparisons of direct estimates of the marginal contribution of workers to production and their wages appears in Psacharopoulos (1970) and Thurow (1968). The latter study indicates that, on the average, in the United States between 1960 and 1965 wages seem to be only 63 percent of the marginal productivity of the workers. No indication exists of the difference between productivity and wages, say, for workers classified by level of education. The estimate prepared for Greece in Psacharopoulos (1970) shows that there can be wide variations in the income-productivity relationship from one level of education to another. Although the methods used in these two studies are completely different and are applied to different countries, the conclusions derived are the same in both cases: a loose relationship, at best, can be discovered between the theoretically estimated contribution of workers to production and their actual wages.

The reasons that have been suggested to explain the difference between the facts and the conditions predicted with the model of perfect competition can be classified in two groups: (1) slow adaptation to equilibrium conditions, and (2) nonperfect competition.

The general-equilibrium model assumes that the supply of goods tends to increase if prices increase and decrease if they decrease. These changes in the supply take place simultaneously with changes in prices. Since some evidence suggests that the demand for education is related to the income that workers having that type of education receive, the only question that must be analyzed is whether the supply of educated labor can adapt instantaneously to changes in prices. However, a strong positive correlation exists between years of schooling, level of education, and narrowness of specialization. Hence the supply of people having a high level of education is likely to respond with a substantial lag to changes in their wages. In other words, wages of workers with high levels of education might be different from those of equilibrium during substantial periods of time, and, what is equivalent, workers with a high level of education might be paid more than their contribution to production (Arrow and Capron 1959).

An important consequence of these adaptation lags is that equilibrium might never be reached, even if the economic forces that determine it are constant. If this is the case, oscillations between under- and oversupply of labor, and wages both smaller and larger than their equilibrium values, are likely to occur.

Market imperfections are another factor in considering why wages might differ from the workers' contribution to production. They include, among others, monopolic conditions of both firms and unions, lack of information on market conditions, and uncertainty about the future.

No studies seem to attempt to explain the differences between marginal productivity and wages in terms of adjustment lags toward equilibrium and market imperfections.

Market Conditions for Efficiency

So far, the possible contribution of education to the capacity to produce goods and services has been analyzed. This is true even in the preceding section where the influence of market conditions is considered only because the data available deal with economic and not physical production. The likely influence of education on the economic conditions that make it possible to use efficiently the resources available has not been considered.

Some of the reasons why education could have this type of influence have already been suggested. They are mentioned again below, together with several other reasons that could be considered.

As noted earlier, educational certification provides some of the information needed in the labor market. In this way it provides a service similar to that of money. The seller of A and buyer of B eliminate the search for a seller of B and buyer of A. Educational certification for A-level workers limits the search only for certain jobs, and for the employers eliminates from consideration a large number of alternatives.

In a similar line, whatever influence education can have on the flows of information that improve the competitiveness of the markets can be considered influence on conditions that determine the efficiency of the production process.

Finally, a similar statement can be made on the influence of education on the rational behavior of persons. A specific case could be the influence of job discrimination. If job discrimination is defined as exclusion of a worker from a job for reasons not related to his contribution to production, and if education tends to reduce such discrimination, then it contributes to production. Evaluation of this type of contribution of education does not seem to be available.

Consequences of the Economic Contribution of Education

From the analysis made thus far, it can be concluded that there is no definitive answer to the question of whether education can be considered as an investment, and if so, what returns it produces. Nevertheless, available evidence suggests that, at least under certain circumstances, the first part of the question should be answered positively.

Three immediate consequences of this can be considered here: (1) the accumulated stock of education is a part of the total capital stock available; (2) education, like any other capital good, influences economic growth; and (3) the ownership of education, like that of any other capital good, influences income distribution.

It should be observed that there is no particular need to test whether education has these three economic consequences, because they follow from the question previously analyzed of whether education has a return as investment. At that point, it was relevant to test the hypothesis. Now, accepting it on whatever basis, its consequences can be explored.

Education as Capital

If education is an investment, an accumulated stock of education is capital. However, education by itself cannot be accumulated; it is always embodied in human beings. Education thus contributes to the economic value that can be placed on a human being. This value can be estimated in a way similar to that of estimating any other capital good.

There are two possible ways to estimate the value of a stock of capital. The first is based on the cost of producing new capital. (The method for doing so appears on pp. 7–8.) Once this is known, it is possible to compute the value of a stock of capital at a fixed date by adding all past net investments. In the case of education, this approach has been used by Schultz (1960).

On the other hand, the value of capital for the person who purchases it is all its future returns. The methods to estimate these future returns have already been explained. To obtain a figure that represents their value as capital, the returns at different dates must be made comparable. Their present or future discounted value is used for this purpose. This second approach is particularly emphasized by Becker (1964).

In principle, the two methods for estimating the value of human capital attributable to education should produce identical results. This is the case if the rate of return to educational investments is used to compute the future value of the returns to education. In other words, if future returns due a stock of education are discounted at their rate of return, their present value will be equal to the cost of producing that stock.

The rate of return on several investments can be used to compare their profitability. The investment with the higher rate of return is the most profitable. On this basis, the computation described above performed for several possible investments can be used to choose the most profitable one.

Contribution to Economic Development

If education contributes to the workers' productivity, it is clear that increments in the educational stock embodied in the population will contribute to increments in total production (i.e., in economic growth).

The question of measurement of this contribution has received a great deal of attention. Several approaches have been used. Schultz (1960) assumes several rates of return to educational investment. With these figures, and the estimates of the total stock of educational capital, it is possible to evaluate the total return to education. Increments to this total return are estimates of the contribution of education to development. Schultz's estimates are integrated in a macro-production function in Correa (1973). This step makes it possible to compare their impact on growth with that of other factors.

Correa (1963, 1970) and Denison (1966, 1967) estimate the contribution of education based on income differentials of workers having different levels of education. These figures, and data on the educational structure of the labor force on different dates, make it possible to estimate the increments in the incomes received by the labor force that can be attributed to the additional education embodied in them. These increments are the contribution of education to economic growth.

Finally, Galenson and Pyatt (1964) estimate the contribution of education to growth by using regression techniques.

The results obtained with the methods described above give widely different results. Correa (1970) and Galenson and Pyatt (1964) indicate that the contribution of education to growth in developing countries might be negligible. Correa (1963), Denison (1966, 1967), and Schultz (1960, 1971) show a positive contribution of education to growth in the United States, but the relative magnitudes are substantially different. Finally, Denison (1967), studying several advanced countries, finds an important positive influence of education on growth.

An important limitation of these estimates is that they are based mainly on the influence of education on human capital or on personal income. The contribution of education to physical capital is completely ignored. The consequences of this fact are not known.

Income Distribution

As with education and economic growth, if education contributes to personal income, then the distribution of educational attainment among the population should influence the distribution of income. But this obvious conclusion does not seem to be supported by the facts. Characteristics of the distribution of income are more or less stable over time, while those of the distribution of education have been substantially modified. More specifically, while the proportion of persons with different levels of income measured in terms of the average has remained approximately constant, the proportion of persons with low levels of education has been substantially reduced, and that of persons with advanced levels of education substantially increased. Several explanations for this fact have been proposed. A complete survey of the literature appears in Mercer (1970).

Becker and Chiswick (1966), Becker (1967), and Mercer (1958) show that the stability in the characteristics of the distribution of income is a consequence of the high correlation between rate of return to education and level of education. However, this simply transforms the question to one of why high rates of return to high levels of education have not been modified by the larger supply of educated persons.

An attempt to integrate both supply and demand of qualified workers in the explanation of the distribution of income appears in Tinbergen (1956).

Education and Well-Being as Determined by Economic Factors

A basic postulate of economics is that economic production is no more than a means for attaining personal well-being. Some observations on this point, which tends to be lost under the details of the analysis just described,

are made in this section. No attempt is made to study the contribution of education to well-being in general, because no method seems to be available for this purpose.

Income per capita is frequently taken as a very primitive and imperfect index of personal well-being. In this sense, a first analysis of the contribution of education to personal well-being is the study of its contribution to income. The analyses in the previous sections will not be repeated here.

Another contribution of education to income per capita must also be considered. Education tends to reduce fertility and, as a consequence, the rate of population growth. This implies that it tends to reduce the rate of growth of the labor force, and as a consequence, of economic growth. If the reduction in population growth is larger than the reduction of income growth, however, the final effect will be an increase in per capita income, or well-being if the index is meaningful. The possible importance of this observation is receiving a great deal of attention.

MODELS OF THE SOCIAL ORGANIZATION OF EDUCATION AND FOR FINANCING EDUCATION

This section summarizes the arguments in Benson (1968), Friedman (1962), Hartman (1972), Heinemann and Sussna (1971), and Nerlove (1972), and analyzes the question of how much education should be produced. This leads to further questions: How to specify the amount of education that should be produced? Who should pay for it? How should resources be obtained? How should resources be used?

Perhaps the most reasonable answer to the first question is that as much education should be produced as is needed to maximize the well-being of the members of the society insofar as this is determined by education. In making this maximization, the fact that resources are used to produce education should be taken into consideration. This means that additions to the education produced and used are equivalent to reductions in the production and use of some other goods or services. Education should be produced until the additions to well-being it produces compensate the reduction in well-being produced by the goods and services forgone.

If exact measurements of the contributions to well being of education and of all other goods and services were available, as well as measurements of their cost of production, the problem of determining the amount that should be produced of the different goods and services and of resources that should be used in producing them would be a simple mathematical problem. The required data are not available, however.

Even if the correct amounts of resources that should be used in the production of all goods and services were known, still the problem of how to allocate them for the correct purpose would remain. Would each individual act in such a way as to maximize collective well-being, or would the authority of a government be needed? This brings up the additional problem that the method used to

allocate the resources to different uses both in terms of the means to obtain them and in their use affects both their contribution to well-being and their cost.

From these observations it follows that, in order to allocate resources to education in such a way as to maximize social well-being, an allocation method not based explicitly on the knowledge of the influence of education on well-being is needed. Two alternatives are used for this purpose: the market mechanism and the political process.

Economic theory shows that, under conditions of perfect competition, the market mechanism will allocate resources in such a way as to maximize well-being. This conclusion is based on the following assumptions, in addition to that of perfect competition: (1) individuals, whether as producers or consumers, behave rationally; (2) all the costs of producing goods and services are paid to those producing them (pollution created by an industrial process is an example of a cost not paid by the producers); (3) the total cost of producing a good or service, at least for some levels of production, increases with total production; and (4) all the benefits of owning or using a good or service accrue completely to the owner or user.

Under these conditions, the market mechanism maximizes social well-being by maximizing the well-being of each member of a society, in such a way that if the well-being of any one of them is increased, that of some other individual has to be reduced.

A limitation of the analysis in economic theory of the optimization of social well-being is that it takes for granted the existing distribution of income. That is, it specifies the conditions for maximizing well-being once the distribution of income is fixed. It provides no information on the effects on well-being of changes in income distribution.

Defects in the market mechanism imply (1) that some persons or institutions are receiving benefits because they are transferring to society some costs they should themselves pay, or are causing some disadvantage to society that could be avoided at a cost; or (2) that some benefit that could increase the well-being of a member of society fails to materialize. The reason for this is that some goods are not produced in the required volume because their producers bear costs not proportionate with the benefits they will receive.

No attempt is made here to analyze whether individuals behave rationally (whatever the expression means), and whether it is possible to increase the rationality of their behavior. However, with respect to this second point, it should be observed that education might be a way to improve the rationality of behavior. If this is the case, the use or lack of use of the market mechanism should be linked with the level of education of the population.

In our analysis, the assumption of rational behavior is accepted. Actually, very little can be done, at least in economics, if this assumption is not taken as a starting point. Below, some observations are made on whether the other conditions needed to maximize social well-being hold true in practice with respect to education.

Little is known about the characteristics of the cost functions of educational institutions. No definitive conclusion exists on whether costs increase or decrease with the size of the institution, despite some evidence which suggests

that the latter is the case. The possible implications of the fact that educational institutions do not pay all the costs of education, or more specifically, that they do not pay the income forgone by the students, have not been explored. If the observations above are accepted, it could be concluded that it would be beneficial for the educational institutions to produce more education than that needed for a social optimum and that educational institutions would tend to become monopolies.

The benefits of education do not affect only the persons who embody that education. One example is the benefits of education through the innovation of capital goods. This observation shows that, if individuals pay for all the education they receive, then the amount of education produced and demanded will fall below the amount needed to maximize social well-being.

The political process that establishes the government is the mechanism expected to correct the defects of the market. However, little is known about the conditions that the political process, whether alone or together with the market mechanism, should satisfy in order to maximize the well-being of the citizens. The assumption of rational behavior must not only be maintained but also extended to include the behavior of government officials.

The several positions taken on the desirability of government intervention are based on different points of view with respect to the level of rationality of the government vis-à-vis the citizens, and the capacity of the government to act in behalf of the citizens, who otherwise could not express their interests. Conceptual frameworks for the analysis of these topics and empirical information for testing them are not known to me.

If a government allocates the resources for the production of goods and services with cost or benefits beyond its political frontier, then the allocation is not likely to maximize the well-being of society as a whole. More concretely, if education produces benefits beyond, say, a country, then the allocations for education of a country's government will fall below the optimal social level. The remainder of this analysis assumes that the government is willing and able to correct the misallocation to education created by a deficient market mechanism.

The policies that can be used to correct these misallocations change, depending upon whether it is possible to specify the individuals who are paying the real or financial costs of not-optimal production of some goods and services. When this is possible, there is no question of the method to solve the misallocation problem: make cost and benefits fall where they belong. For this, first, the scale or magnitude of the correction is specified, and second, the origin of the resources to be used or transferred is clearly identified.

Nevertheless, it is not always possible to make this identification, and education is one example of this. It is impossible to specify who receives some of the benefits of education embodied in a person. This leaves open the questions of determining the amount of education that should be produced and of the sources and uses of the funds needed to produce the amount considered necessary.

A clear method of determining the scale of production is not available. In practice, and in the case of education, it seems to be determined to a large extent by social demand as expressed by elections and pressure groups through

legislators and government officials, who determine the financial assistance the state will provide for education. This assistance determines the amount of education that should be offered above what the citizens are willing to pay for individually.

To obtain the resources needed to increase the production of certain goods and services or to eliminate the disadvantage brought about by the production of other goods, the government has to rely on general or specific taxes and on debt. No attempt is made here to discuss the relative impact of taxes or debt on well-being. A point that should be observed is that human capital seems to be particularly suitable for paying real taxes. This is so with several types of compulsory education. In this case, at least, the earnings forgone by the student are an example of real tax. A possibility that can also be named is that of teaching conscription.

Again, all the implications for well-being of the different alternatives open for the use of government resources cannot be discussed here. Two principal avenues have been suggested for the use of resources in education. The first is that government pays the educational institution directly. This is the method commonly used when compulsory education is also gratis for the students. A criticism of this approach is that, with it, the economic incentives on the educational institutions reflect the preferences of the population only insofar as the government is able and willing to transmit them. Whether or not this is desirable would depend upon whether government or the citizens are assumed to act more rationally.

Vouchers to be given to the students to pay for their education are a second alternative suggested for the use of educational resources. This alternative has been applied in veterans' educational benefits. In this case, the economic incentives on the educational institutions would directly reflect the preferences of the students or their parents. Also, the amount of education that each student should receive remains an individual decision. As observed, this would be considered desirable if the judgment of the citizen is considered "more rational" than that of the government.

Educational loans that are eliminated if the future benefits from education do not materialize are another possibility that gives more weight to individual preferences in education.

MODELS OF THE PLANNING PROCESS

Educational planning is usually restricted to the forecasting of certain characteristics of the educational system, the determination of the resources needed to achieve educational goals, and the specification of the best uses of available resources. An overview of actual planning processes shows that these operations are not the only ones performed, however, and that they may not even be the most important ones (McCarty and Ramsey 1971).

Correa (1971) and Correa and Adams (1972) consider four main functions in planning: decision making, technical planning, implementation, and control. Although a large number of cases and comparative studies of decision making,

implementation, and control have been made, it does not appear that conceptual or mathematical models of them have been prepared. An initial attempt to integrate the technical and implementation functions in educational planning appears in Kleindorfer's chapter in this volume. The planning models to be considered here refer only to models for the performance of the technical function.

MODELS FOR EDUCATIONAL PLANNING AND ADMINISTRATION

One characteristic of the models to be considered in this section is that their object is to assist in the planning or administration of educational units ranging from divisions of single educational institutions (e.g., departments in a university) to the entire educational system of cities, regions, or countries. In these models no attempt is made to describe or explain how other systems, such as the economy, provide the inputs required for education, or how the other systems use the outputs of education. Only the internal characteristics of the educational institutions are considered in detail. Two alternative assumptions are used with respect to the other systems: (1) they will provide whatever inputs are required by education, and (2) the inputs that they provide are fixed and cannot be modified by the educational planner or administrators.

These assumptions represent two unrealistic points of view: (1) the external world does not impose any constraints on education, and (2) the constraints of the external world are absolute. They are used because they eliminate the need to analyze the characteristics of the other systems that influence education and make it possible to study in detail the educational units being planned.

Planning to Satisfy the Social Demand for Education

The methods of planning to satisfy the social demand for education are based on the mechanistic models of the educational process. Several of these models can be used to forecast the number of students who will in the future form a part of the educational unit being planned. Once this forecast is obtained, the required number of teachers, classrooms, financial resources, and the like can be estimated.

In the simplest version of these models, the number of students entering an educational unit is assumed to be a fixed proportion of the eligible population, and the number of students remaining in the educational unit is assumed to be a fixed proportion of those already there. Models of this type appear in Alper (1971), Belford and Ratliff (1972) Clough and McReynolds (1966, 1970), Correa (1966b, 1967a, 1969a), Harden and Tcheng (1971b), Jacobi (1959), Moser and Redfern (1965), Moser and Layard (1964), Solomon and Auerham (1965), Stockwell and Nam (1963), Stone (1965, 1971), Swanson and Lamitre (1971), and Zenach (1968).

An immediate extension of this model can be made by assuming that the number entering and/or remaining is affected by noneducational factors such as income, place of residence, and job opportunities, and by educational factors such as quality of teachers.

Using as data information about the number of students that will demand education, a detailed analysis can be made with respect to use of teachers, facilities, and the like.

Optimal Allocation of Education Resources

These models assume that there are several alternate ways to achieve educational goals or satisfy educational requirements. These have different costs in terms of the human, physical, and financial resources needed. The problem is to specify the alternative to be used, so that the resources needed to achieve educational goals are minimized or the educational objectives achieved are maximized with fixed amounts of resources. It should be clear that a very large number of problems have these general characteristics.

The principles just mentioned have been used to analyze the following:

1. General problems of allocation of resources in education: Bruno 1969a, 1969b; Correa 1964a, 1966c; Fox et al. 1967, 1972; Reisman and Taft 1968; Lemkin 1969.
2. Particular types of education: Arnold and McNamara 1971; Barton 1970; Correa and Reimer 1970; Hopkins 1970; Lannson and Powell 1972; McNamara 1970, 1971, 1973; Plessner et al. 1968; Sisson 1972; Turksen and Holzman 1970, 1972; U.S. Department HEW 1969.
3. Reference to specific problems, such as school location: Clarke and Surkis 1968; Correa 1966a; Eastman and Kortanek 1970; Heckman and Taylor 1969, 1970; Koenigsberg 1968; Newton and Thomas 1969; O'Brien 1969.
4. Classroom use: Graves and Thomas 1971; Harden and Tching 1971a; Harding 1964; Lawrie 1969; Lutz 1970; Schoeman 1969; Sen 1969; Shapley et al. 1966; Smith 1971.
5. Curriculum: Correa (1965b); Taft and Reisman 1967.
6. Student housing and other problems: Cranbull 1969; Hoenack 1971; Mann 1970; Morse 1968; Tanner 1968.

MODELS FOR THE INTEGRATION OF ECONOMIC AND EDUCATIONAL PLANNING

This section is restricted to models for the integration of economic and educational planning, because little formal work has been done on the integration of educational with other types of planning (e.g., population, health). This does not mean that this work could not or should not be done, or that it is less important. Actually, at the present stage of development, it might be more important to proceed with this work than continuously to refine models for the integration of educational and economic planning.

The point of view that the educational system should be adapted to the needs of the economy is also used here. Clearly, there is no reason why this should be the order of priorities. The opposite point of view, that the economy should be adapted to the educational needs of its citizens, is more reasonable, but most if not all the models developed so far for the integration of educational and economic planning give higher priority to the economic system.

Three approaches have been used to integrate educational and economic planning: (1) the manpower approach, (2) the rate-of-return approach, and (3) explicit optimization models.

THE MANPOWER APPROACH

In the manpower approach to educational planning, a target for production is used as a starting point. This target can be specified as a volume of output or as the maximum that can be achieved with fixed resources. Next, it is assumed that a macro-production function summarizes the technical possibilities of an economy. This function can be expressed with the notation

$$Y = f(A, K, L_1, L_2, \cdots, L_N) \quad (1)$$

where

Y = production, say, GNP
A = level of technology
K = capital
L_i = labor with educational level $i, i = 1, \cdots, N$

The production function in equation (1) does not permit, except in particular and unrealistic cases, the specification in a unique way of the quantities of inputs needed to achieve targets for Y, whether determined as specific volumes of output or in terms of maximization of output with given resources. In the case of a target for volume of output, this is not possible because a fixed level of output can be obtained with an infinite number of combinations of technology and inputs, and in the case of the maximization of output, because the constraints on the inputs are not considered in the production function.

It is possible to overcome the indetermination described with the assumption from economic theory that the combination of technology and inputs actually used will be that which minimizes costs.

In the simplest approach, it is assumed that these costs are wages per worker and benefits per unit of capital. With this assumption, and through the process of minimization, it is possible to specify a demand function for labor. This function would have the form

$$DL_i = g_i(A, Y, r, w_1, w_2, \cdots, w_N) \qquad i = 1, \cdots, N \quad (2)$$

where

DL_i = labor type i demanded
r = rent per unit of capital
w_i = wages labor type i

It should be observed that a function similar to equation (2) would be specified for capital from the minimization process.

The fact that r and w_i play a similar role in the demand function is not accidental. Both of them can be considered as the payment for the services of capital, whether physical or human. As observed, the present discounted value of future wages is equal—under certain assumptions—to the value of the educational capital embodied in a worker.

Equation (2) shows that the only way to specify the labor required to achieve targets of production is when the type of technology and the returns for education and physical capital have been specified. Only after this is done does the DL_i become a function of Y and A only.

In more realistic approaches, the fact that equation (2) describes only a static equilibrium would have to be taken into consideration.

The practical applications of the manpower approach have been based—at best—on the static demand functions in (2). For these applications, those functions can be specified in different ways and must be estimated from statistical data. With respect to the form of the functions, in the first applications (Bombach and Riese 1963, 1965; Correa 1962, 1967a, 1969c; Paines 1962; Tinbergen 1964) constant labor-output rations were used. In more elaborate analyses, including the one by Correa and Leonardson in this volume, number of workers has been related to some index of productivity and to output (Bos and Cornelisse 1964; Correa 1964b, 1969a; Tinbergen et al. 1965). However, up to the present, attention has been paid to the influence of wages on the demand for labor by level of education. The main justification for this has been lack of data.

The methods and data commonly used to estimate manpower requirements include implicitly the assumption of equilibrium in the economies that provide the data used. This is so because actual data on the number of workers by level of education is used without verifying that the observed values are the ones that minimize costs. If the economies providing the data are not in equilibrium, however, the integrated plan would contribute to maintain present inefficiencies in the future. A justification for this, in addition to data problems, is the lack of appropriate methods.

The characteristics of the educational system are derived from the estimated values of DL_i. These characteristics are determined with the condition that the educational system must produce an educational structure of the population able to supply a labor force with the required qualifications. For this purpose, an important link is established between the flow of students models used to plan the educational system to satisfy social demands and the models to specify the characteristics of the system needed to satisfy economic requirements. In the initial forms of the models of the manpower approach, extremely simplified models of the flows of students were used (Bos and Cornelisse 1964, Correa and Tinbergen 1962). Several unsuccessful efforts to correct these deficiencies appear in Tinbergen et al. (1965). A critical review of these attempts and a method for eliminating their defects appear in Correa (1967c, 1969a, 1969c).

Several large computer models have been constructed, based on the manpower approach (Armitage and Smith 1966, Balinsky 1970, Clough et al. 1970, Lavasseur 1969).

The Rate-of-Return Approach

The theoretical justification for the rate-of-return approach to the integration of economic and educational planning is found in the economic models of optimum growth in an economy with several capital goods. These models, with the simplifying assumption that there is only one technique for production, show that the allocation among the different types of capital should equalize all their gross returns (Intriligator 1971, Samuelson and Solow 1956). The application of this conclusion to the integration of educational and economic planning is known as the rate-of-return approach.

In the practical applications of the rate-of-return approach, current educational costs and wages are used to estimate the rate of return to investments in education (Blaug 1967a, 1967b, 1972). From this estimate it is concluded that additional investment should be made in the types of education with highest returns. The method, as currently used, does not provide a figure for the amount of investment that should be made.

The most important criticism of this method is that it leaves out the supply, demand, and market mechanisms that determine the costs and returns of education. This limitation is the reason why the method cannot specify the amount that should be invested in education in order to achieve the desired equality among different rates of return.

Another limitation of the method is that it explicitly excludes the influence on the rate of return of planned changes in the output of the economy and the technology used. This exclusion might have important consequences, because changes in technology bring about changes in the demand for labor in such a way as to alter completely the estimates of earnings that determine the rates of returns.

The data used for the practical applications can also be criticized. If the data used do not come from an economy in equilibrium, they do not reflect the actual costs and returns of education. If the labor supply is below its demand, wages will tend to be high and cost lower than that of equilibrium. The opposite is true when there is an excess of educated labor. Nevertheless, this bias will tend to suggest the right decision, so its impact is not too disadvantageous.

Manpower and Rate-of-Return Approaches Compared

A common practice (Blaug 1972, Bowman 1970, Hollister 1964) is to present the manpower and the rate-of-return approaches as two contending views of the world. My opinion is that they are opposite sides of the same coin. The main limitation of the manpower approach is that so far it has not included the influence of wages on the estimation of a demand function for labor, or of the impacts of educational costs on the economy as a whole, in particular on the constraint of investment resources. However, these same points are the strengths of the rate-of-return approach. Actually, as observed, the rate-of-return approach emphasizes *only* these points, excluding the impact of the number of workers on production and wages. In summary, the manpower approach leaves out what the rate-of-return approach includes and vice versa.

This being the case, ideally both approaches should be used simultaneously when integrating economic and educational planning. If both of them suggest the same policy, it is likely that the system being planned is close to its equilibrium. The opposite is true if the two methods give different results. In this case the initial data should be used—as far as possible—to estimate equilibrium values, and any plans should be based on them.

Optimization Models

It is clear that a new model having the characteristics of both the manpower and the rate-of-return approaches to planning should be developed to integrate educational and economic planning.

The conceptual frame used as a starting point for the rate-of-return approach could be used for this purpose. This means that the object of the models would be to optimize the well-being of a society over a period of time, subject to the constraint imposed by the technological relationships summarized in a production function, the structure of the educational system, and the costs of producing human and physical capital.

In theory, there is no reason why the general model of an economy with several capital goods could not be used for this purpose. But analytical, statistical and computational problems make it impossible to do so at the present. Linear programming techniques have been applied to the solution of the problem described above in Adelman (1966), Benard (1967), Bowler (1967, 1969), Correa (1967c, 1969c), Davis (1966, 1968), Golladay (1968), Maki (1970), Mehmet (1971), Psacharopoulos (1970), and Tinbergen (1963). Unfortunately, the computational advantages of these models are obtained at the cost of several assumptions that are considered unacceptable in the manpower and rate of return approaches. For instance, the demand functions for labor are the constant proportions that are used only in the most primitive forms of the manpower approach. Also, costs per student are taken to be constant, an assumption that is accepted only for a short time horizon in the rate of return approach.

It should be observed that the limitations of the general optimization models are by no means unsurmountable with the technology available, both in terms of mathematics and computational facilities. A method that can be used appears in Kendrick and Taylor (1971) and Von Weizsaeker (1966).

REFERENCES

Adelman, I. "A Linear Programming Model of Educational Planning: A Case Study of Argentina." In *The Theory and Design of Economic Development*, edited by I. Adelman and E. Thorbecke. Baltimore, Md.: Johns Hopkins Press, 1966.

Adelman, I., and Parti, M. "The Determinants of Student Achievement: A Simultaneous Equation Approach." Mimeographed.

Alper, P. "Controllability, Observability and Educational Planning." *Socio-Economic Planning Sciences* 25, no. 3 (June 1971).

Armitage, P., and Smith, C. "The Development of Computable Models of the British Educational System and Their Possible Uses." In *Mathematical Models in Educational Planning*. Paris: OECD, 1967.

Arnold, M., and McNamara, F. "A Systems Approach to State-Local Program Planning In Vocational Education." *Socio-Economic Planning Sciences* 5 (1971): 231–53.

Arrow, K. J., and Capron, W. M. "Dynamic Shortages and Price Rises: The Engineer-Scientist Case." *Quarterly Journal of Economics* 73, no. 2 (1959): 292–308.

Ashenfelter, O., and Mooley, D. J. "Graduate Education, Ability and Earnings." *Review of Economics and Statistics*, no. 1 (February 1968): 78–86.

Atkinson, R. C.; Bower, G. H.; and Crothers, E. J. *An Introduction to Mathematical Learning Theory*. New York: John Wiley, 1965.

Balinsky, W. L. "Some Manpower Planning Models Based on Educational Attainment." Technical Memorandum 185, Department of Operations Research, Case Western Reserve University, June 1970.

Barton, R. F. "On Optimization in the American University." Texas Technical University, 25 June 1970.

Becker, G. *Human Capital.* New York: National Bureau of Economic Research, 1964.

Becker, G. S., and Chiswick, R. "Education and The Distribution of Earnings." *American Economic Review Papers and Proceedings* 56, no. 2 (May 1966).

Becker, G. S. *Human Capital and the Personal Distribution of Income.* Ann Arbor: University of Michigan, 1967.

Belford, P., and Ratliff, H. D. "A Network-Flow Model for Racially Balancing Schools." *Operations Research* 20, no. 5 (May–June 1972).

Benard, J. "General Optimization Model for the Economy and Education in Organization for Economic Cooperation and Development." In *Mathematical Models in Educational Planning.* Paris: OECD, 1967.

Ben-Porath, Y. "The Production of Human Capital and the Life Cycle of Earnings." *Journal of Political Economy* 75 (1967): 352–65.

Ben-Porath, Y. "The Production of Human Capital Over Time." In *Education, Income and Human Capital*, edited by W. L. Hansen. New York: Columbia University Press, 1970.

Bensen, S. M. "Education and Productivity in U.S. Manufacturing: Some Cross Section Evidence." *Journal of Political Economy* 76, no. 3 (May/June 1968): 494–97.

Benson, C. S. *The Economics of Public Education.* Boston: Houghton Mifflin Co., 1968.

Blaug, M. "An Economic Interpretation of the Private Demand for Education." *Economica* 33 (May 1966).

Blaug, M. *A Cost-Benefit Approach to Education Planning in Developing Countries.* Washington, D.C.: International Bank for Reconstruction and Development, 1967a.

Blaug, M. "Approaches to Educational Planning." *Economic Journal* 77 (June 1967b): 262–87.

Blaug, M. *An Introduction to the Economics of Education.* Baltimore, Md.: Penguin Books, 1972.

Bombach, G. "The Assessment of the Long-term Requirements and Demand for Qualified Personnel in Relation to Economic Growth for the Purposes of Educational Policy." Processed. Paris: OECD, 1963.

Bombach, G., and Riese, H. "Qualified Manpower and Economic Growth." Paper presented at the 35th Session of the International Statistical Institute, Belgrade, 1965. Processed.

Bos, H. C., and Cornelisse, P. A. "Financial Aspects of the Educational Expansion in Developing Regions." Mimeographed. Netherlands Economic Institute, Amsterdam, 1964.

Bowen, W. G., and Finegan, T. A. *The Economics of Labor Force Participation.* Princeton, N.J.: Princeton University Press, 1969.

Bowles, S. "The Efficient Allocation of Resources in Education." *Quarterly Journal of Economics* 81 (1967); 189–219.

Bowles, S. "The Determinants of Scholastic Achievement: An Appraisal of Some Recent Evidence." *Journal of Human Resources* 3, no. 1 (Winter 1968).

Bowles, S. *Planning Educational Systems for Economic Growth.* Cambridge, Mass.: Harvard University Press, 1969.

Bowles, S. "Towards an Educational Production Function." In *Education, Income and Capital*, edited by W. L. Hansen. New York: Columbia University Press, 1970.

Bowman, M. J. "Education and Manpower Planning Revisited." In *Occupational and Educational Structures of the Labor Force and Levels of Economic Development*. Paris: OECD, 1970.

Bruno, J. E. "An Analytical Approach to Salary Evaluation for Educational Personnel." *International Journal of Educational Sciences* 3, no. 2 (1969a): 161–72.

Bruno, J. E. "An Alternative to the Use of Simplistic Formulas for Determining State Resource Allocation in School Finance Programs." *American Educational Research Journal* 6 (1969b): 479–514.

Burke, C. J. "Applications of a Linear Model to Two-Persons Interactions." In *Studies in Mathematical Learning Theory*, edited by R. R. Bush and W. K. Estes. Stanford: Stanford University Press, 1959.

Bush, R. R., and Estes, W. K. *Studies in Mathematical Learning Theory*. Stanford: Stanford University Press, 1959.

Bush, R. R., and Mosteller, F. *Stochastic Models for Learning*. New York: John Wiley, 1955.

Campbell, R., and Siegel, B. N. "The Demand for Higher Education in the U.S." *American Economic Review* 57, no. 3 (June 1967): 482–94.

Carnoy, M. "Earning and Schooling in Mexico." *Economic Development and Cultural Change* 15, no. 4 (July 1967).

Clarke, S., and Surkis, J. "An Operations Research Approach to Racial Desegregation of School Systems." *Socio-Economic Planning Sciences* 1 (1968): 259–72.

Clough, D. J. "Theoretical and Empirical Aspects of a Constrained Flow Model For Part of the Ontario Secondary School System." Working Paper 36, Department of Management Sciences, University of Waterloo, 1970.

Clough, D. J., et al. "Mathematical Programming Models of a Quasi-Independent Subsystem of the Canadian Forces Manpower System." Working Paper 34, Department of Management Sciences, University of Waterloo, 1970.

Clough, D., and McReynolds, W. P. "State Transition Model of an Educational System Incorporating a Constraint Theory of Supply and Demand." *Ontario Journal of Educational Research* 9 (1966): 1–18.

Coleman, J. S., et al. *Equality of Educational Opportunity*, 2 vols. Washington, D.C.: U.S. Department of Health, Education, and Welfare, U.S. Government Printing Office, 1966.

Corazzini, A. J. "The Decision to Invest in Vocational Education: An Analysis of Costs and Benefits." *Journal of Human Resources* 3 (1968 Supplement): 88–120.

Correa, H. "Quantity vs. Quality in Teacher Education." *Comparative Education Review* 8, no. 2 (October 1964a).

Correa, H. "Ha Prestado la Planificacion Economica Atencia Suficiente a la Educacion." *El Trimestre Economico* (October–December 1964b).

Correa, H. "Optimum Choice Between General and Vocational Education." *Kyklos* 18 (1965a): 700–704.

Correa, H. "Planning the Educational Curriculum." *Kyklos* 18 (1965b).

Correa, H. "Optima for Size and Number of Schools." *Scientia Paedagogica Experimentalis* 3, no. 1 (1966a).

Correa, H. "Basis for the Quantitative Analysis of the Educational System." *Journal of Experimental Education* 35, no. 1 (Fall 1966b).

Correa, H. "More Schools or Better Schools?" *Scientia Paedagogica Experimentalis* 3, no. 2 (1966c).

Correa, H. *The Economics of Human Resources.* Amsterdam: North-Holland Publishing Co., 1967a.

Correa, H. "A Survey of Mathematical Models in Educational Planning." In *Mathematical Models in Educational Planning.* Paris: OECD, 1967b.

Correa, H. *Quantitative Methods in Educational Planning.* Scranton, Pa.: International Textbook Co., 1969a.

Correa, H. "The Psychological and Social Variables Determining Education." *Socio-Economic Planning Sciences* 2, no. 2/3/4 (April 1969b).

Correa, H. "Flows of Students and Manpower Planning: Application to Italy." *Comparative Education Review* (June 1969c).

Correa, H. "Sources of Economic Growth in Latin America." *Southern Economic Journal* 37, no. 1 (July 1970).

Correa, H. "A Systems Approach to Socio-Economic Planning." University Center for International Studies, University of Pittsburgh, 1971.

Correa, H. "An Econometric Model of Supply, Demand and Wages of Educational Workers." In *Studies in Economic Planning Over Space and Time,* edited by G. G. Judge and T. Takayama. Amsterdam: North-Holland, 1973a.

Correa, H. "A Mathematical Model of Teacher/Student Interaction." Mimeographed. GSPIA, University of Pittsburgh, 1973b.

Correa, H., and Adams, D. "A Model for a Comparative Study of the Educational Planning Process." *Educational Planning* 2, no. 3 (December 1972).

Correa, H., and Reimer, E. "Planning a Literacy Campaign and Other Educational Programs." *Scientia Paedagogica Experimentalis* 7, no. 1 (1970).

Correa, H., and Tinbergen, J. "Quantitative Adaptation of Education to Accelerated Growth." *Kyklos* 15 (1962).

Crandell, R. H. "A Constrained Choice Model for Student Housing." *Management Science* 16, B-112-120 (1969).

Davis, R. G. *Planning Human Resource Development: Educational Models and Schemata.* Chicago: Rand McNally, 1966.

Davis, R. G. "On the Development of Educational Planning Models at Harvard CSED." In *Education and Economic Growth,* edited by R. H. P. Kraft. Tallahassee: Florida State University Educational Systems Development Center, 1968.

Denison, E. *The Sources of Economic Growth in the United States and the Alternatives Before Us.* New York: Committee for Economic Development, 1966.

Denison, E. *Why Growth Rates Differ.* Washington, D.C.: Brookings Institute, 1967.

Dougherty, C. R. S. "Substitution and the Structure of the Labor Force." *Economic Journal*, no. 325 (March 1972).

Dyer, J. A. "Assessing the Effect of Changes in the Cost of Higher Education to the Student." *Socio-Economic Planning Sciences* 5, no. 4 (August 1971).

Eastman, C. M., and Kortanek, K. O. "Modeling School Facility Requirements in New Communities." *Management Science* 16, B-784-799 (1970).

Estes, W. U., and Burke, C. J. "Application of a Statistical Model to Simple Discrimination Learning in Human Subjects." *Journal of Experimental Psychology* 50 (1955): 81–88.

Flanders, N. A. *Teacher Influence, Pupil Attitudes and Achievement.* Washington, D.C.: U.S. Department of Health, Education, and Welfare, Office of Education, 1960.

Fox, K., et al. "Formulation of Management Science Models for Selected Problems of College Administration." Final Report Contract OEC-3-068058, U.S. Department of Health, Education, and Welfare, Office of Education, 1967.

Fox, K. A., ed. *Economic Analysis for Educational Planning: Resource Allocation in Non-Market Systems.* Baltimore, Md.: Johns Hopkins University Press, 1972.

Fox, T. G. "Long-run Planning for Undergraduate–Higher Education Capacity Needs: Basing Enrollment Projections on Partial-college Potential vs. Full-college Potential." *Socio-Economic Planning Sciences* 5, no. 1 (February 1971).

Friedman, M. *Capitalism and Freedom.* Chicago: University of Chicago Press, 1962. See chap. 6.

Galenson, W., and Pyatt, G. *The Quality of Labor and Economic Development in Certain Countries.* Geneva: International Labor Office, 1964.

Gani, J. "Formulae for Projecting Enrollments and Degrees Awarded in Universities." *Journal of the Royal Statistical Society*, series A, vol. 126, pt. 3 (1963).

Getzels, J. W., and Jackson, P. W. *Creativity and Intelligence.* New York: John Wiley, 1962.

Goldberg, S. *Introduction to Difference Equations.* New York: John Wiley, 1961.

Golladay, Frederick L. "A Dynamic Linear Programming Model for Educational Planning with Application to Morocco." Ph.D. dissertation, Department of Economics, Northwestern University, August 1968.

Graves, R. J., and Thomas, W. H. "A Classroom Location-Allocation Model for Campus Planning." *Socio-Economic Planning Sciences* 5 (1971): 191–204.

Green, D. R. *Educational Psychology.* Englewood Cliffs, N.J.: Prentice-Hall, 1964. See chap. 6.

Griliches, Z. "Estimates of the Aggregate Agricultural Production Function from Cross-Sectional Data." *Journal of Farm Economics* 45 (May 1963a): 419–28.

Griliches, Z. "The Sources of Measured Productivity Growth: United States Agriculture, 1940–1960." *Journal of Political Economy* 71 (August 1963b): 331–46.

Griliches, Z. "Research Expenditures, Education and the Aggregate Agricultural Production Function." *American Economic Review* 54 (December 1964): 961–74.

Griliches, Z. "Production Functions in Manufacturing: Some Preliminary Results." In *The Theory and Empirical Analysis of Production,* edited by M. Brown. New York: National Bureau of Economic Research, 1967.

Griliches, Z. "Capital Skill Complementarity." *Review of Economics and Statistics* 51, no. 4 (November 1969): 465–68.

Griliches, Z. "Notes on the Role of Education in Production Functions and Growth Accounting." In *Education, Income and Human Capital,* edited by W. L.

Hansen. Papers presented at the Conference on Education and Income held at the University of Wisconsin in November 1968. New York: Columbia University Press, 1970.

Griliches, Z., and Mason, W. M. "Education, Income and Ability." *Journal of Political Economy* 80, no. 3, pt. 2 (May/June 1972).

Guthrie, J. W., et al. *Schools and Inequality*. Cambridge, Mass.: MIT Press, 1971.

Harberger, A. C. "Investment in Man vs. Investment in Machines: The Case of India." In *Education and Economic Development*, edited by C. A. Anderson and M. J. Bowman. Chicago: Aldine, 1965.

Harden, W. R., and Tcheng, M. T. "Classroom Utilization by Linear Programming." Technical Paper, Office of Academic Planning and Institutional Research, Illinois State University, 1971a.

Harden, W. R., and Tcheng, M. T. "Projection of Enrollment Distribution with Enrollment Ceilings by Markov Processes." *Socio Economic Planning Sciences* 5, no. 5 (October 1971b).

Harding, R. E. "The Linear Programming Approach to Master Time Schedule Generation in Education." In *Optimal Scheduling in Educational Institutions,* edited by A. G. Holtzman and W. R. Turkes. Washington, D.C.: U.S. Department of Health, Education, and Welfare, Office of Education, Cooperative Research Project 1323, University of Pittsburgh, 1964.

Hartman, R. W. "Equity Implications of State Tuition Policy and Student Loans." *Journal of Political Economy* 80, no. 3, pt. 2 (May/June 1972).

Hause, J. C. "Earnings Profile: Ability and Schooling." *Journal of Political Economy* 80, no. 3, pt. 2 (May/June 1972).

Heckman, L. B., and Taylor, H. M. "School Rezoning to Achieve Racial Balance: A Linear Programming Approach." *Socio-Economic Planning Sciences* 3 (1969): 127–33.

Heckman, L. B. "Designing School Attendance Zones by Linear Programming." Department of Environmental Systems Engineering, Cornell University, January 1970.

Heinemann, H. N., and Sussna, E. "Criteria for Public Investment in the Two Year College: A Program Budgeting Approach." *Journal of Human Resources* 6, no. 2 (Spring 1971).

Heist, P. "College Transients." In *Education for Creativity in the American College*, edited by P. Heist. Berkeley: University of California, 1971.

Hildebrand, G. H., and Liu, T. *Manufacturing Production Function in the U.S., 1957: An Inter-industry and Interstate Comparison of Productivity*. Ithaca, N.Y.: Cornell University Press, 1965.

Hoenack, S. A. "The Efficient Allocation of Subsidies to College Students." *American Economic Review* 61 (1971): 302–11.

Hollister, R. G. "The Economics of Manpower Forecasting." *International Labor Review* (April 1964).

Hopkins, C. O. "State-Wide System of Area Vocational-Technical Training Centers for Oklahoma." Ph.D. dissertation, Department of Agricultural Education, University of Oklahoma, May 1970.

Hu, T.; Lee, M. L.; and Stromsderfer, M. "Economic Returns to Vocational and Comprehensive High School Graduates." *Journal of Human Resources* 61, no. 1 (Winter 1971): 25–50.

Intriligator, M. D. *Mathematical Optimization and Economic Theory*. Englewood Cliffs, N.J.: Prentice-Hall, 1971.

Jacob, P. E. *Changing Values in College Education: An Exploratory Study of the Impact of College Teaching*. New York: Harper & Row, 1957.

Jacobi, E. G. "Methods of School Enrollment Projections." *Educational Studies and Documents*, no. 32. Paris: UNESCO, 1959.

Kendrick, D., and Taylor, L. "Numerical Methods and Non-linear Optimizing Models for Economic Planning." In *Studies in Development Planning*, edited by H. G. Chenery. Cambridge, Mass.: Harvard University Press, 1971.

Koenigsberg, E. "Mathematical Analysis Applied to School Attendance Areas." *Socio-Economic Planning Sciences* 1 (1968): 465–75.

Lannson, R. D., and Powell, J. H. "An Improved Model for Determining the Input Cost of University Outputs." *Socio-Economic Planning Sciences* 6, no. 3 (June 1972).

Lassiter, R. L. "The Association of Income and Education for Males by Region, Race and Age." *Southern Economic Journal* 32, no. 1, pt. 1 (July 1965): 15–22.

Lavasseur, P. M. "A Study of Inter-relationships Between Education, Manpower and Economy." *Socio-Economic Planning Sciences* 2 (1969): 269–95.

Lawrie, N. L. "An Integer Linear Programming Model of School Time-Tabling Problems." *Computer Journal* 12 (1969): 307–16.

Lehmann, I. J.; Sinha, B. K.; and Harnett, R. T. "Changes in Attitudes and Values Associated with College Attendance." *Journal of Education Psychology* 51 (1966): 89–98.

Lewis, W. A. "Education and Economic Development." *Social and Economic Studies* 10 (1961).

Lindsay, C. M. "Measuring Human Capital Returns." *Journal of Political Economy* 79, no. 6 (November/December 1971).

Lutz, R. P. "A Systems Study of School Desegregation." Research Report R-70-2, School of Industrial Engineering, University of Oklahoma, October 1970.

McCarty, D. J., and Ramsey, C. E. *The School Managers: Power and Conflict in American Public Education*. Westport, Conn.: Greenwood, 1971.

McClelland, D. C.; Atkinson, J.; Clark, R. A.; and Lowell, E. L. *The Achievement Motive*. New York: Appleton-Century-Crofts, 1953.

McClelland, D. C. *The Achieving Society*. New York: Van Nostrand Co., 1961.

McClelland, D. C. "Does Education Accelerate Economic Growth?" *Economic Development and Cultural Change* 14, no. 3 (April 1966).

McNamara, J. F. *A Mathematical Programming Model for the Efficient Allocation of Vocational Technical Education Funds*. Harrisburg: Pennsylvania Department of Education, 1970.

McNamara, J. F. "A Regional Planning Model for Occupational Education." *Socio-Economic Planning Sciences* 5 (1971): 317–99.

McNamara, J. F. "Mathematical Programming Applications in Educational Planning." *Socio-Economic Planning Sciences* 7, no. 1 (February 1973).

Machlup, F. *Education and Economic Growth*. Lincoln: University of Nebraska Press, 1970.

Maki, D. "A Programming Approach to Manpower Planning." *Industrial and Labor Review* 23 (1970): 397–405.

Mann, S. H. "Dynamic Management of Library Size." *Operations Research* 18, no. 2, B-149 (Fall 1970 Supplement).

Mehmet, O. "Efficient Allocation of Public Resources in Manpower Training." *Socio-Economic Planning Sciences* 5, no. 4 (August 1971).

Miller, G. A., and McGill, W. J. "A Statistical Description of Verbal Learning." *Psychometrica* 17 (1952): 369-96.

Mincer, J. "Investment in Human Capital and Personal Income Distribution." *Journal of Political Economy* (August 1958).

Mincer, J. "The Distribution of Labor Incomes: A Survey with Special Reference to the Human Capital Approach." *Journal of Economic Literature* 8, no. 1 (March 1970).

Ministerio de Educacion y Ciencia. *Modelo Espanol de Desarrollo Educativo.* Madrid: Ministerio de Educacion y Ciencia, 1970.

Mood, A. M. "Macro-Analysis of the American Educational System." *Operations Research* 17 (September–October 1969).

Morgan, J. N., and David, M. H. "Education and Income." *Quarterly Journal of Economics* (August 1963): 423–37.

Morgan, J., and Sirageldin, I. "A Note on the Quality Dimension in Education." *Journal of Political Economy* 76, no. 5 (September/October 1968): 1069–77.

Morse, P. M. *Library Effectiveness: A Systems Approach.* Cambridge, Mass.: MIT Press, 1968.

Moser, C. A., and Layard, P. R. G. "Planning the Scale of Higher Education in Britain: Some Statistical Problems." *Journal of the Royal Statistical Society* (December 1964).

Moser, C. A., and Redfern, P. "A Computable Model of the Educational System in England and Wales." Paper presented at the 35th Session of the International Statistical Institute, Belgrade, 1965. Processed.

Nelson, J. L., and Besag, F. P. *Sociological Perspectives in Education: Models for Analysis.* New York: Pitman Publishing Co., 1970.

Nerlove, M. "On Tuition and the Costs of Higher Education: Prolegomena to a Conceptual Framework." *Journal of Political Economy* 80, no. 3, pt. 2 (May/June 1972).

Newcomer, M. *The Big Business Executive.* New York: Columbia University Press, 1955.

Newton, R. M., and Thomas, W. H. "Design of School Bus Routes by Computer." *Socio-Economic Planning Sciences* 3 (1969): 75–85.

O'Brien, Richard J. "Models for Planning the Location and Size of Urban Schools." *Socio-Economic Planning Sciences* 2 (1969): 141–53.

Parnes, H. S. *Forecasting Educational Needs for Economic and Social Development.* Paris: OECD, 1962.

Plessner, Yakir, et al. "On the Allocation of Resources in a University Department." *Metroeconomica* 20 (1968): 256–71.

Ploughman, T., et al. "An Assignment Program to Establish School Attendance Boundaries and Forecast Construction Needs." *Socio-Economic Planning Sciences* 1 (1968): 243–58.

Psacharopoulos, G. "Estimating Shadow Rates of Return to Investment in Education." *Journal of Human Resources* 1, no. 1 (Winter 1970).

Rapoport, A. "Mathematical Models of Social Interaction." In *Handbook of Mathematical Psychology,* edited by R. D. Luce, R. R. Bush, and E. Galanter. New York: John Wiley, 1963.

Razin, A. "Optimum Investment in Human Capital." *Review of Economic Studies* 39, no. 4 (October 1972).

Reif, H. W. "Factors Influencing Enrollment in Primary, Secondary and Higher Education." Processed. Central Planning Bureau, The Hague, 1965.

Reisman, A., and Taft, M. I. "A Systems Approach to the Evaluation and Budgeting of Educational Programs." *Socio-Economic Planning Sciences* 3, no. 3 (October 1969).

Renshaw, E. F. "Estimating the Returns to Education." *Review of Economics and Statistics* 42 (August 1960): 318–24.

Restle, F. "The Relevance of Mathematical Models for Education." *National Society for the Study of Education 1963 Yearbook,* pt. I. 1964.

Russell, W. R. *Brain, Memory, Learning: A Neurologist's View.* Oxford: Clarendon Press, 1959.

Ruiter, R. "The Past and Future Inflow of Students into the Upper Levels of Education in the Netherlands." Processed. Central Planning Bureau, The Hague, 1963.

Samuelson, P. A., and Solow, R. M. "A Complete Capital Model Involving Heterogeneous Capital Goods." *Quarterly Journal of Economics* 70 (1956): 537–62.

Sanderson, R. D. "The Expansion of University Facilities to Accommodate Increasing Enrollments." Research Project 69-8, Office of the Vice President–Planning and Analysis, University of California, July 1969.

Schmookler, J. "Inventors Past and Present." *Review of Economics and Statistics* (August 1957).

Schoeman, M. "Class Scheduling Algorithm." In *University Management Models,* Project GUM, phase 3. Austin: Graduate School of Business, University of Texas at Austin, December 1969.

Schultz, T. W. "Capital Formation by Education." *Journal of Political Economy* (December 1960).

Schultz, T. W. *The Economic Value of Education.* New York: Columbia University Press, 1963.

Schultz, T. W. *Investment in Human Capital: The Role of Education and of Research.* New York: Free Press, 1971.

Scully, G. W. "Interstate Wage Differentials: A Cross-Section Analysis." *American Economic Review* 59, no. 5 (December 1969): 757–73.

Sen, S. "Models of Course-Sectioning and Faculty Assignment." In *University Management Models,* Project GUM, phase 3. Austin: Graduate School of Business, University of Texas at Austin, December 1969.

Shapley, R. P., et al. *A Transportation Program for Filling Idle Classrooms in Los Angeles.* Santa Monica, Calif.: RAND Corporation, P-3 405, July 1966.

Sisson, R. L. "The Design of a National Right to Read Effort." *Socio-Economic Planning Sciences* 6, no. 5 (October 1972).

Sloan, F. A. "The Demand for Higher Education: The Case of Medical School Applicants." *Journal of Human Resources* 6, no. 4 (Fall 1971).

Smith, R. L. "Accommodating Student Demand for Courses by Varying the Classroom Size Mix." *Operations Research* 19, no. 4 (July–August 1971).

Snyder, B. "Creative Students in Science and Engineering." *Universities Quarterly* 21, no. 2 (1967).

Solomon, E. S., and Auerham, J. "Draft Asian Education Model: Methodology and Concepts." UNESCO Monthly Economics Seminar, 15 September 1965. Processed.

Stockwell, E. G., and Nam, C. B. "Illustrative Tables of School Life." *Journal of the American Statistical Association* 58, no. 304 (December 1963).

Stone, R. "A Model of the Educational System." *Minerva* (Winter 1965).

Stone, R. *Demographic Accounting and Model-Building.* Paris: OECD, 1971.

Suppes, P., and Atkinson, R. C. *Markov Learning Models for Multiperson Interactions.* Stanford: Stanford University Press, 1960.

Swanson, A. D., and Lamitre, R. E. "Project 1990: Educational Planning at the Metropolitan Level." *Socio-Economic Planning Sciences* 5, no. 6 (December 1971).

Taft, M. I., and Reisman, A. "Toward Better Curricula through Computer Selected Sequencing of Subject Matter." *Management Science* 13 (1967).

Tanner, C. K. "An Automated Simulation Vehicle for School Business Administration Accentuating Computerized Selective School Lunch Menu Planning." Ph.D. dissertation, Department of Educational Administration, The Florida State University, 1968.

Taussig, M. U. "An Economic Analysis of Vocational Education in the New York City High Schools." *Journal of Human Resources* 3 (1968 Supplement): 59–87.

Temkin, S. "A Cost-Effectiveness Evaluation Approach to Improving Resource Allocations for School Systems." Ph.D. dissertation, University of Pennsylvania, 1969.

Thias, H. H., and Carnoy, M. "Cost-Benefit Analysis in Education: A Case Study on Kenya." Mimeographed. International Bank for Reconstruction and Development Report EC-173, November 1969.

Thonstad, T. *Education and Manpower: Theoretical Models and Empirical Applications.* Toronto: University of Toronto Press, 1968.

Thurow, L. C. "Disequilibrium and the Marginal Productivity of Capital and Labor." *Review of Economics and Statistics* (February 1968).

Thurow, L. C. *Investment in Human Capital.* Belmont, Calif.: Wadsworth Publishing Co., 1970. See chap. 4.

Tinbergen, J. *On the Theory of Income Distribution.* Weltwirtschaptliches Archiv, 1956.

Tinbergen, J. "Introductory Remarks on the 'ization problem.'" *Zeitschrift fur die Gesamte Staatswissenschaft* 119 Band/2 Heft (April 1963).

Tinbergen, J. *Educational Assessment in Economic and Social Aspects of Educational Planning.* Paris: UNESCO, 1964.

Tinbergen, J.; Bos, H.; Emmerij, L. J.; Blum, J.; and Williams, G. *Econometric Models of Education.* Paris: OECD, 1965.

Tolley, G. S., and Olson, E. "The Interdependence between Income and Education." *Journal of Political Economy* 79, no. 3 (May/June 1971).

Tuckman, H. P. "High School Inputs and Their Contribution to School Performances." *Journal of Human Resources* 6, no. 4 (Fall 1971).

Turksen, I. B., and Holzman, A. G. "Micro Level Resource Allocation Models for Universities." *Operations Research* 18, B-39 (Spring 1970 Supplement).

Turksen, I. B., and Holzman, A. G. "Information System Design for Educational Management." *Socio-Economic Planning Sciences* 6, no. 1 (February 1972).

U.S. Department of Health, Education, and Welfare. *Vocational Education and Occupations.* Washington, D.C.: U.S. Government Printing Office, July 1969.

Von Weizsaeker, C. C. "Training Policies Under Conditions of Technical Progress: A Theoretical Treatment." Paper presented at the OECD Meeting on Systems Analysis Techniques in Educational Planning, Paris, March 1966.

Weisbrod, B. A. "Education and Investment in Human Capital." *Journal of Political Economy* 70, no. 5, pt. 2 (1962 Supplement): 206–23.

Weiss, Y. "The Risk Element in Occupational and Educational Choices." *Journal of Political Economy* 80, no. 6 (November/December 1972).

Welch, F. "Education in Production." *Journal of Political Economy* 78, no. 1 (January/February 1970): 35–59.

Zabrowski, E. U., and Zinter, J. R. *Student-Teacher Population Growth Model.* Washington, D.C.: U.S. Department of Health, Education, and Welfare, U.S. Government Printing Office, 1968.

Zemach, R. "A State-Space Model for Resource Allocation in Higher Education." *IEEE Transactions of Systems Science and Cybernetics* SSC-4, no. 2 (July 1968).

PART I MACRO EDUCATIONAL PLANNING

Hector Correa

2 MODELS FOR FORECASTING FLOWS OF STUDENTS AND THE HUMAN AND PHYSICAL RESOURCES REQUIRED WITH AND WITHOUT TECHNOLOGICALLY ASSISTED EDUCATION

Models of the flows of students and of the educational structure of the population are among those most commonly used in educational planning and administration. They make it possible to forecast the number of students in different subdivisions of the system, the personnel and physical facilities needed to attend them, and the financial resources required. Such models are also used to forecast the educational structure of the population. The frequency of their use is reason enough for their inclusion here.

Two extensions of this basic model are also included in this chapter. The first is the integration of the flow of students models with demographic models for forecasting population by age and sex. This integrated model permits a study of the interaction between population growth and number of students in the educational system, and of the impact of educational achievement on mortality and fertility. In the second extension, the method used to estimate teacher requirements is adapted to cases where television and/or computer-assisted instruction are planned or used.

FLOWS OF STUDENTS AND THE EDUCATIONAL STRUCTURE OF THE POPULATION

With models showing flows of students and the educational structure of the population, the problem is to describe the transformation from one year to the next of children outside the educational system, students in the system, and those persons who have completed their education. The initial data needed are:

1. Initial and final age at which a child can enter the educational system. These ages are denoted here as $e + 1$ and $H + 1$. At age e, no child has yet entered the educational system. They begin doing so at age $e + 1$. Children of age $H + 1$ who do not enter the educational system become part of the population without any education.
2. Number of children of ages $h = e, \ldots, H$ who never entered the educational system. These numbers are denoted as $C_{ho} h = e, e + 1, \ldots, H$. These C_{ho} are considered the components of a column vector C_o. The subscript o for the C_{ho} and the C_o denote the initial year for the forecast.
3. A description of the structure of the educational system. The best form for presenting this description is that of a network diagram with nodes showing stages of the system and arcs connecting the nodes describing the alternatives open for the students in one stage. A simple example of such a graph is figure 2.1.

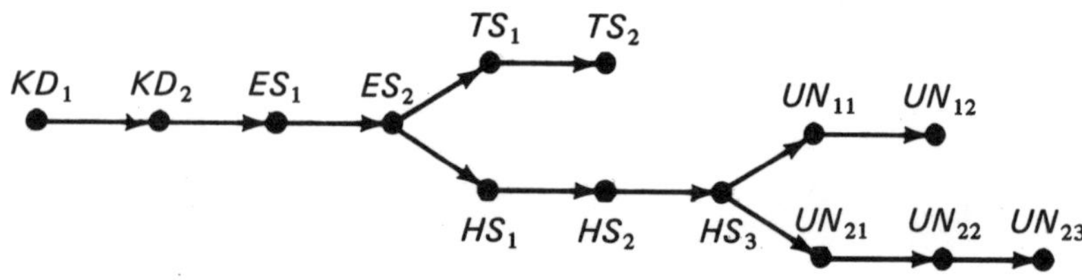

Figure 2.1

KD_i	kindergarten levels: $i = 1, 2$
ES_i	elementary school levels: $i = 1, 2$
TS_i	technical school levels: $i = 1, 2$
HS_i	high school levels: $i = 1, 3$
UN_{ij}	university levels (i career, j course): $i = 1, 2; j = 1, \ldots, 3$

The educational system described in figure 2.1 has two kindergarten levels. Both are points of entrance into the system, as is the first grade in elementary school. After two grades of elementary school there is a choice of continuing in technical school for two years, or in high school for three years. After high school, it is possible to continue in college with two alternatives.

The first step in constructing a model of an educational system is to number consecutively all the subdivisions of the system. For instance, for the system in figure 2.1, the numbering can be that described in table 2.1.

It should be observed that the particular order of the components of the system adopted does not matter. For instance, in table 2.1 the high school grades precede those of technical school.

The different subdivisions of the educational system are identified by the number determined in the procedure just described. It is assumed that these numbers, denoted with a subscript g, range from $g = 1$ to $g = G$.

Table 2.1
Numeration of the Grades in School System in Figure 2.1

Grade	Number
KD_1	1
KD_2	2
ES_1	3
ES_2	4
TS_1	5
TS_2	6
HS_1	7
HS_2	8
HS_3	9
UN_{11}	10
UN_{12}	11
UN_{21}	12
UN_{22}	13
UN_{23}	14

4. Number of students in each of the classifications of the educational system considered. These numbers are denoted by S_{g0} $g = 1, \ldots, G$; where the subscript zero refers to the initial year of the forecasts. They are the components of the column vector S_0.
5. Number of persons outside the educational system, classified in the following way: P_0 persons who never enter the system and have reached at least age $H + 1$ year 0; P_{g0} persons who enrolled in subdivisions g of the educational system and left the system while in the same subdivision or at its termination without proceeding to more advanced subdivisions, in year 0.

   The number P_{g0} $g = 0, \ldots, G$ are the components of the column vector P_0. With the data described in paragraphs 2, 4, and 5, it is possible to form the column vector

$$U_0 = \begin{pmatrix} C \\ S \\ P \end{pmatrix}_0 \tag{2.1}$$

with number $(H - e + 1) + G + (G + 1)$ of rows.

The basic question to be considered here is the transformation of vector U_0 into vector U_1, that is, the transformation of children, students, and population outside the system in year $t = 0$ to those in year $t + 1$. The starting point in this analysis is a set of basic accounting identities, presented in detail in Correa (1966, 1967, 1969) and Stone (1971). They are summarized below.

The identities dealing with the children in C_0 take the following form:

$$C_{h-1,0} = C_{h,1} + \sum_f S'_{f,h,1} + D'_{h,1} \quad h = e, \ldots, H - 1 \tag{2.2}$$

and

$$C_{H,0} = B_{0,1} + \sum_f S'_{f,H+1,1} + D'_{H,1} \tag{2.3}$$

where

$S'_{f,h,1}$ = number of children of age h entering the educational system for the first time in grade f, year 1. The subscript f ranges over all the values of g denoting entrance points in the system.
$B_{0,1}$ = part of the population having no education, and of age $H + 1$ year 1, i.e., the children who can no longer enter the educational system, because of their age.
$D'_{h,1}$ = number of deaths of children ages $h = e, \ldots, H$ between dates 0 and 1.

The basic accounting identity dealing with the number of students in a specific grade g is the following:

$$N_{g,0} + R_{g,0} + M_{g,0} = \sum_j N'_{j,g,1} + B_{g,1} + R_{g,1} + D''_{g,1} \tag{2.4}$$

where

$N_{g,0}$ = number of new entrants, grade g, date 0.
$R_{g,0}$ = number of repeaters grade g, date 0.
$M_{g,0}$ = number of reentrants, grade g, date 0.
$N'_{j,g,1}$ = number of new entrants in grade j coming from grade g of the educational system. The subscript j ranges over all the values corresponding to grades which students from grade g can go.
$B_{g,1}$ = number of dropouts from grade g in period between 0 and 1 when g is not a terminal grade in the educational system, and number of dropouts plus number of students completing their studies successfully when g corresponds to a terminal grade in the system.
D'' = number of deaths among the students.

From the definitions given above, it follows that:

$$N_{g,1} = \sum_{h=e+1}^{H+1} S'_{g,h,1} + \sum_{j=1}^{G} N'_{g,j,1} \quad g = 1, \ldots, G. \tag{2.5}$$

When g in equation 2.5 does not correspond to a grade open to the children outside the educational system, the first sum in the right-hand side of the equation is zero. The second sum is zero for $g = 1$. In any case, many of the terms in these two sums are likely to be zero.

With the terms in N' in equations 2.4 and 2.5, it is assumed that students in one grade can go to or come from several other grades. For instance, in the example in table 2.1, this would be the case if students from both high school and technical school could enter college.

It should also be observed that

$$S_{g,0} = N_{g,0} + R_{g,0} + M_{g,0}. \tag{2.6}$$

The basic identities with respect to the persons outside the educational system can be stated as follows:

$$\begin{aligned} P_{g,0} &= P'_{g,1} + \sum_j M'_{j,g,1} + D'''_{g,1} \quad g = 1, \ldots, G \\ P_{g,1} &= P'_{g,1} + B_{g,1} \end{aligned} \tag{2.7}$$

where

$P'_{g,1}$ = number of persons with education g, date 0 that remain in the class in year 1;
$M'_{j,g,1}$ = number of reentrants in grade j of the educational system from persons in the population presently outside;
$D'''_{g,1}$ = number of deaths among the persons in the population with grade g, between dates 0 and 1.

It should be clear that

$$M_{g,1} = \sum_{j=1}^{G} M'_{g,j,1}. \tag{2.8}$$

Identities 2.2 to 2.8 are to the educational system what the identity assets-equals-liabilities-plus-net-worth is to micro accounting, or income-equals-consumption-plus-savings in macro accounting. They must be satisfied by all educational models. Nevertheless, they do not constitute a model by themselves. The number of variables is substantially larger than that of equations. Below, the identities will be used to construct a linear model of the flows of students in the educational system, making it possible to forecast vector U_0 in equation 2.1 to vector U_1.

The basic matrix equation to forecast the vector U_0 in this equation is the following:

$$\hat{U}_1 = AU_0 \tag{2.9}$$

where $\hat{U}_1$ denotes the column vector with the same components as U_1 except that the number C_{01} of children of age 0 in year 1 is replaced with zero. The reason for this is that from the population U_0 it is possible to pass to all the classes in U_1 except C_{01}. A is a $(H - e + 2G + 2) \times (H - e + 2G + 2)$ matrix to be described below.

As a first step in the study of matrix A as presented in equation 2.9, it is useful to break it down in the columns of matrices A_{ij}.

To do so, the system in 2.9 can be written:

$$\hat{U}_1 \begin{pmatrix} \hat{C} \\ S \\ P \end{pmatrix}_1 = \begin{pmatrix} A_{11} & A_{12} & A_{13} \\ A_{21} & A_{22} & A_{23} \\ A_{31} & A_{32} & A_{33} \end{pmatrix} \begin{pmatrix} C \\ S \\ P \end{pmatrix}_0 \tag{2.10}$$

where $\hat{C}_1$ is the vector with the same components as C_1 except that the value of C_{01} is replaced with zero.

Column A_{i1} describes the transformation of the children in C_0 to children outside the system, students, and population. Column A_{i2} performs the same transformation for students, and column A_{i3} for the population outside the system. A more detailed study of these three columns is made below.

A_{11} is a matrix of dimensions $(H - e + 1) \times (H - e + 1)$ that describes the transformation of the children in C_0 to the children in $\hat{C}_1$, i.e., of the children outside the educational system and age e to $H - 1$ in year zero into the children of age $e + 1$ to H and who remain outside the system in year 1. In this transformation, the children of age H in year 0 are not considered because they do not influence $\hat{C}_1$. The only nonzero components of this matrix are those in the diagonal from second row, first column, to the $H - e + 1$ row, $H - e$ column. These components are defined by

$$C_{e+h+1,t+1} = \alpha_{h+2,h+1} C_{e+h,t} \quad h = 0, \ldots, H - e + 1 \tag{2.11}$$

where α_{ij} is the component in row i, column j.

As mentioned, the last column of A_{11} is composed only of zeros, meaning that $C_{H,0}$ is not transformed into any of the elements of the vector $\hat{C}_1$, because all the children of age H either enter school or become part of the population without school.

A_{21} is a matrix of dimensions $G \times (H - e + 1)$ that describes the transformation of children outside the system in year 0 into students in year 1. The components of this matrix are obtained by combining equations 2.2 and 2.5 in the following way:

$$S'_{g,e+h,1} = \alpha_{H-e+1+g} C_{e+h,0} \quad \begin{matrix} g = 1, \ldots, G \\ h = 0, \ldots, H - e \end{matrix} \tag{2.12}$$

The subscripts of $\alpha_{i,j}$ in equation 2.12 refer to the rows and columns of matrix A in equation 2.9. They should be written $\alpha_{g,h+1}$ when referring to matrix A_{21}.

In general, the coefficients of α_{ij} will be different from zero only for those values of i corresponding to grades open to children without previous education. In addition, if the students of any grade have to be more than $H + 1$ years of age, the corresponding coefficients of α_{ij} would be zero. As a consequence, if the values of g increase with the level of education, the last rows of matrix A_{21} are likely to include only zeros.

A_{31} is a $(G + 1) \times (H - e + 1)$ matrix that describes the transformation of the children in C_0 into the population outside the school system. Since it is assumed that those children of age $H + 1$ who do not enter the school system do not have additional opportunities to do so and must remain without education, the only equation with nonzero coefficients in this matrix is

$$B_{0,1} = \alpha_{H-e+2+G,H-e+1} C_{H,0}. \tag{2.13}$$

Again, the subscripts of α refer to the matrix A. They would be 1 and $H - e + 1$ with reference to A_{31}. The coefficient α in equation 2.13 appears in the upper-right-hand corner of A_{31}. All other coefficients are zero.

At this point, a property of the corresponding columns of the set of matrices $A_{i1}\, i = 1, \ldots, 3$ should be observed. They give, except for the possibility of death, all possible alternatives open for the children in C_0: to remain in C while their ages permit, to enter the educational system, or to become part of the population without education. As a consequence, the sum of all the parameters in any of the columns 1 to $H - e + 1$ of the matrix A is equal to the survival rate of ages from e to H. This explains why the variables D' do not appear explicitly in matrices A_{i1}.

In a detailed study of the matrices in column A_{i2} that describe the transformation of the students, the following observations can be made:

A_{12} is a $(H - e + 1) \times G$ matrix composed only of zeros, as a consequence of the fact that no student can ever return to the group of children without any education.

A_{22} is a $G \times G$ matrix that describes the transition among different grades and levels of the educational system. The components of this matrix are formed by combining equations 2.4, 2.5, and 2.6.

To begin with, it will be assumed that the number of students passing from one grade to another in the educational system is proportional to the number of students in the grade of origin, i.e.,

$$N'_{j,g,1} = \alpha_{H-e+1+j,H-e+1+g} S_{g,0} \quad \begin{array}{l} j = 1, \ldots, G \\ g = 1, \ldots, G. \\ j \neq g \end{array} \tag{2.14}$$

Next, it will be assumed that the number of repeaters is also proportional to the students in the original grade, i.e.,

$$R_{g,1} = \alpha_{H-e+1+g,H-e+1+g} S_{g,0} \quad g = 1, \ldots, G. \tag{2.15}$$

The coefficients α_{ij} in equation 2.15 occupy the main diagonal of the matrix A_{22}.

A_{32} is a $(G + 1) \times G$ matrix that describes the transition from the educational system to the population outside the system. The first row of this matrix contains only zeros because no person passing through the educational system becomes a member of $P_{0,1}$. The only nonzero elements in the rest of the matrix are those in the diagonal going from the second row, first column, to the last row, last column, i.e., from the row $H - e + G + 3$ and column $H - e + 2$ of matrix A to its row $H - e + 2G + 2$ and column $H - e + G + 1$. The components of the matrix $A_{3,2}$ are derived from the equation

$$B_{g,1} = \alpha_{H-e+G+2+g,H-e+1+g} S_{g,0} \quad g = 1, \ldots, G. \tag{2.16}$$

As in the case of the matrices dealing with the C classification, the total of each of the columns $H - e + 2$ to $H - e + G + 1$ should be equal to the survival rate of the students in the different grades of the educational system.

The matrices A_{i3} deal with the elements in equations 2.2 to 2.8 that can be directly related to the number of persons in the population outside the educational system.

A_{13} is a $H - e + 1 \times G + 1$ matrix with only zero components. The reason for this is that no person in the P classification can reenter the C classification.

A_{23} is a $G \times G + 1$ matrix that describes the patterns of return into the educational system of persons who had left it. The elements of this matrix come from equations of the form

$$M'_{j,g,1} = \alpha_{H-e+2+j,H-e+1+G+g} P_{g,0} \quad \begin{matrix} j = 1, \ldots, G \\ g = 0, \ldots, G \end{matrix}. \tag{2.17}$$

The simplest case of equation 2.17 is when $j = g$, that is, only persons who left in grade g can reenter that grade.

A_{33} is a $(G + 1)(G + 1)$ matrix describing the persons who remain in the P classification of the population. Assuming that it is not possible to transfer from one P to another, the only nonzero elements of the matrix are in the main diagonal. They are defined by the equation

$$P'_{g,1} = \alpha_{H-e+2+G+g,H-e+2+G+g} P_{g,0} \quad g = 0, \ldots, G. \tag{2.18}$$

Again, in the case of the matrix dealing with the P classification, the sum of the components of each of the last $G + 1$ columns of matrix A is equal to the survival rate of the population outside the system having P years of education.

So far, the meaning of equation 2.9 has been explained. To obtain the vector U_1 from the vector $\hat{U}_1$ derived with 2.9, it is necessary to use the value of C_{01} given as data. Once this step is completed, and assuming that the coefficients of matrix A in 2.9 remain constant or change in a specified way, it is possible to proceed to compute U_2 and so on up to U_T.

The first use of the models just described is to evaluate the impact of population growth on the number of students in the educational system. The link between population growth and the educational system is provided by the values $C_{e,t}$ of the number of children of age e, i.e., children who have not begun to attend school but will do so the following year, for the values of $t = 0$, to $t = T$, i.e., all the time horizon of the plan. These values are determined by the growth of the population.

FORECASTS OF TEACHERS, CLASSROOMS, AND OTHER IMPLEMENTS

Forecasts of the number of students by grade are useful mainly as a basis for forecasting the personnel and equipment required by the educational system.

In traditional systems, the inputs of teachers and buildings amount to most, if not all, the inputs required. More advanced systems use teaching machines, television, and computers. Thus, methods of forecasting the requirements for this new equipment are also needed and are presented later in this chapter. This section considers only the problem of forecasting number of teachers and classrooms.

The estimates of future requirements of personnel and equipment can be used as a basis for planning teacher education and to estimate the financial resources needed. This section also comments on these points.

The instruments most commonly used to forecast requirements of teachers and classrooms, once the forecast of the number of students are available, are teacher/student and classroom/student ratios. These coefficients are also used in models for determining the optimum allocation of resources in education, and the optimum allocation of resources among education, the economy, and other social sectors.

These ratios have certain limitations. First, they do not reflect the actual number of students a teacher faces in a classroom. Otherwise, teacher/student and classroom/student ratios would always be equal. This limitation gives a theoretical reason why these ratios show a poor performance as indices of the quality of education. Second, these ratios exclude explicitly certain alternatives open to the educational system, such as more intensive use of classrooms, longer hours for teachers, and shorter hours for students. Lastly, it does not seem feasible to adapt these ratios to the study of technologically assisted education.

These limitations suggest that improved coefficients are needed. In Atkinson and Wilson (1969) and Correa (1967) coefficients called weighted teacher/student ratios and weighted classroom/student ratios are introduced. These coefficients do not have the limitations observed for their nonweighted counterparts. What follows is a brief summary of the discussion in those references regarding weighted coefficients.

The elements considered in the weighted student/teacher ratios are number of teachers, number of students, and the average number of hours teachers teach and students attend class. These elements relate in the following way:

$$L = f_s S \tag{2.19}$$

where

L = number of periods of education received,
f_s = average number of periods per student,
S = number of students.

The total number of periods of education offered can be expressed in different ways:

$$F = F_t = f_t T = f_q Q = F_q \tag{2.20}$$

where

F = number of periods of education offered, total without subscript; by teacher, subscript t; or in classrooms, subscript q.
f_t = average number of periods per teacher.
T = number of teachers.
f_q = average number of periods a classroom is used.
Q = number of classrooms.

The reason why it is possible to equate the number of periods of education offered in terms of the number of teachers or classrooms is that the presentation of a class by a teacher and the use of a classroom are simultaneous events.

The average class size (to be denoted as c_t when referring to students per room) is the average number of students receiving a period offered. As a consequence, from formulas 2.19 and 2.20 it follows that:

$$L = c_t F_t = c_q F_q. \tag{2.21}$$

Formula 2.21, when written

$$c_t = \frac{F}{L} = \frac{f_s S}{f_t T} = \frac{f_s S}{f_q Q} = c_r, \tag{2.22}$$

shows that the average class size is a weighted student/teacher or student/classroom ratio, the weights being the average number of hours received by the students, offered by the teachers, or of classroom use. The equality of the ratio with respect to teachers and classrooms has a clear intuitive meaning: the average number of students that a teacher teaches is equal to the number of students occupying a classroom.

The ratios in 2.22 have a much clearer meaning than the S/T or S/Q ratios currently used.

Depending upon the characteristics of the educational system, the elements of formulas 2.21 and 2.22 satisfy several relationships that can be useful for planning purposes.

If each teacher teaches several groups of students,

$$f_s \leqslant f_t. \tag{2.23}$$

This inequality is reversed if several teachers teach one group of students.

Also, in general,

$$f_s \leqslant f_q. \tag{2.24}$$

A problem frequently faced by planners is that of estimating the number of teachers and classrooms to attend fixed numbers f_s^* and S^* of hours per student and students.

To solve this problem, the system of equations

$$\begin{aligned} T &= \frac{f_s^* S^*}{f_t c_t}, \\ Q &= \frac{f_s^* S^*}{f_q c_q}, \\ c_t &= c_q, \end{aligned} \tag{2.25}$$

and condition 2.24 should be used as a starting point.

The conditions in the system are not sufficient to specify the values of the unknowns. This is still the case, even if the following conditions are added:

$$\begin{aligned} f_t &\leqslant f_t^*, \\ c_t &\leqslant c_t^*, \\ f_q &\leqslant f_q^*. \end{aligned} \tag{2.26}$$

Conditions 2.26 can be justified as expressing qualitative constraints for the educational system, and even physical constraints, as in the cases of the limit on the number of hours teachers can work or classrooms be used.

The possibility open at this point is that of determining the unknowns of the system by an optimizing process. One alternative is to maximize quality subject to some resource constraint; this approach is not explored here. Another possibility is to minimize the resources needed subject to constraints 2.24 to 2.26. For this, assume that the cost function is

$$K = k_1 T + k_2 Q \tag{2.27}$$

where

K = cost per period, say, school year.
k_i = unit cost per period: $i = 1$ teachers, $i = 2$ classrooms.

It should be clear that the minimum value of K is obtained when the unknowns of the system are determined from conditions 2.25 and 2.26 transformed into equalities.

APPLICATION TO PUERTO RICO

The Transition Matrix

This section summarizes the results of the application of the model presented in the two previous sections to Puerto Rico. (Correa and Reimer (1968) give a more detailed study.) That this task is particularly simple reflects the characteristics of the system.

It is assumed that all children enter the system for the first time at age 7. As a consequence of this,

$$c = 6,$$

$$H = 7.$$

In the application of the model to Puerto Rico, only the 12 grades of elementary and high school are to be considered. These grades present the simplifying characteristic that a student finishing one grade can continue schooling only in the next grade. There are no alternatives open within the educational system. The graph in figure 2.1 would appear as one straight line with 12 dots. For each grade, a basic accounting identity can be established, as in equation 2.5. These identities for the school year 1966–67 appear in table 2.2. The component S of vector U can be read in column 3 of this table. The index g (for grade) ranges from 1 to 12.

The vector P_0 has 13 components equal to the number of persons outside the educational system classified by level of education. The data for this vector is presented later (see table 2.6).

In summary, the vectors U in equation 2.1 have 27 components.

The 27X27 matrix A in equations 2.9 and 2.10 has the following characteristics:

A_{11} is a 2X2 zero matrix since no 6-year-old children fail to begin school when they reach the age of 7.

A_{21} is a 12X2 matrix with only one nonzero component in the upper-left-hand corner. This component is equal to the survival rate for children aged 6, that is, to the proportion of children aged 6 entering first grade.

Table 2.2
Equation 2.6 for Elementary, Intermediate, and High School Grades in Puerto Rico, 1966-67

grade g	New (1)	Repeaters (2)	Total Enrollment (3)	Promoted (4)	Repeaters (5)	Dropouts (6)
1	77,933	15,794	93,727	77,143	15,414	1,170
2	71,888	8,443	80,301	69,909	8,575	1,847
3	69,727	8,242	77,969	68,524	7,674	1,771
4	68,609	6,331	74,940	66,283	6,135	2,522
5	65,755	4,799	70,554	63,053	4,327	3,174
6	61,746	2,384	64,130	59,280	1,686	3,164
7	55,785	3,142	58,927	51,057	2,963	4,907
8	48,517	1,419	49,936	44,213	1,265	4,458
9	42,080	344	42,424	38,512	364	3,548
10	37,961	1,786	39,747	33,553	1,415	4,779
11	32,714	1,427	34,141	30,054	1,834	2,253
12	26,352	209	26,561	—	10	26,551

Source: H. Correa and E. Reimer, "A Simulation Model for Educational Planning in Puerto Rico" (Department of Education, San Juan, Puerto Rico, 1968). Mimeographed.

A_{31} is a 13X2 zero matrix.

A_{12} is a 2X12 zero matrix.

A_{22} is a 12X12 matrix with a particularly simple structure. In the main diagonal it has the proportion of repeaters in each grade. In the diagonal from the second row, first column, to the 12th row, 11th column, it has the proportion of students promoted from grade g to $g+1$. The values of these coefficients appear in table 2.3, columns 3 and 4.

A_{32} is a 13X12 matrix with zero in its first row and the values of column (7) of table 2.3 in the diagonal from second row, first column, to the last row, last column.

As usually assumed, the matrix A_{13} is equal to zero. In the case of Puerto Rico it was also assumed that none of the persons who had left the educational system returned to it. This means that A_{23} is also equal to zero. With the assumption above, it follows that A_{33} is a 13X13 matrix that has in its main diagonal the survival rates of persons with different levels of education.

Exogenous Forecasts of New Entrants in First Grade

As observed earlier, an exogenous forecast of all the children of an age to enter school is needed. This means, in the case of Puerto Rico, a forecast of the number of 6-year-old children, like that presented for selected years in table 2.4.

Table 2.3
Components of Matrices A_{22} and A_{32} for Educational System in Puerto Rico

Rows A Matrix (1)	Rows A_{22} Matrix (2)	Matrix A_{22} Main Diagonal α_{gg} (3)	Diagonal $\alpha_{g+1,j}$ (4)	Rows A Matrix (5)	Rows A_{32} Matrix (6)g	Diagonal $\alpha_{j,j-1}$ (7)
3	1	0.16445	0.82304	16	2	0.01248
4	2	0.10674	0.87023	17	3	0.02299
5	3	0.09842	0.87882	18	4	0.02271
6	4	0.08187	0.88448	19	5	0.03365
7	5	0.06133	0.89365	20	6	0.04499
8	6	0.02629	0.92435	21	7	0.04934
9	7	0.05028	0.86644	22	8	0.08327
10	8	0.02533	0.88536	23	9	0.08927
11	9	0.00858	0.90777	24	10	0.08363
12	10	0.03560	0.84416	25	11	0.12023
13	11	0.05372	0.88028	26	12	0.06599
14	12	0.00038	0.00	27	13	0.99962

Source: Correa and Reimer, "Educational Planning in Puerto Rico."

Forecasts of Flows of Students and Educational Structure

In this projection, the date $t = 0$ is the beginning of the school year 1966–67. The vector U_0 is obtained from the data on children aged 6 in table 2.4, those for students per grade in table 2.2, column 3, and those on population by level of education in table 2.6, column 1.

For the forecasts, the matrix described earlier was modified year after year. Modification consisted of multiplying the coefficients of the matrix by their rates of change. These rates of change were estimated from data on past experi-

Table 2.4
Projection of Number of 6-Year-Olds in the Population and New Entrants to First Grade, Puerto Rico, 1966–87

Year	Projection
1966–67	77,933
1971–72	80,244
1976–77	87,744
1981–82	93,122
1986–87	97,815

Source: Correa and Reimer, "Educational Planning in Puerto Rico."

Table 2.5
Projection of School Enrollment by Grade, Puerto Rico, 1966-87

Grade (1)	1966-67 (2)	1975-76 (3)	1976-77 (4)	1981-82 (5)	1986-87 (6)
1	93,727	95,189	102,020	106,564	110,507
2	80,331	87,415	95,785	100,981	104,901
3	77,969	84,594	92,440	98,595	102,876
4	74,940	80,417	89,393	96,060	100,294
5	70,554	76,479	86,823	94,201	98,666
6	64,130	71,050	83,647	91,875	96,898
7	58,927	64,503	80,645	93,141	98,364
8	49,936	58,025	72,352	86,017	93,965
9	42,424	52,722	64,087	79,140	90,434
10	39,747	49,561	59,247	74,413	87,733
11	34,141	43,941	53,486	68,429	82,835
12	26,561	37,250	46,550	63,388	78,467

Source explained in text.

ence in the system. In this process, ceilings and floors were given to the values of the modified coefficients.

The other components of the matrices A_{i2} were modified in proportion to their initial values in such a way as to maintain the total of each column equal to

Table 2.6
Educational Structure of the Population Six Years of Age or Older Outside the Educational System, Puerto Rico, 1966-87

Education by Grade Completed (1)	1966-67 (2)	1971-72 (3)	1976-77 (4)	1981-82 (5)	1986-87 (6)
0	372,902	359,879	345,303	331,049	317,149
1	81,900	84,771	82,992	77,464	71,989
2	85,404	85,033	79,751	74,426	69,134
3	115,586	118,592	112,785	106,437	100,137
4	111,421	117,671	112,313	106,046	99,802
5	116,482	124,206	120,662	114,197	107,732
6	120,455	138,970	154,457	155,677	148,300
7	111,930	127,681	139,546	148,690	152,025
8	85,978	98,532	107,580	114,337	117,072
9	48,629	66,754	80,571	91,137	97,511
10	29,302	37,294	43,867	48,941	52,415
11	22,570	27,748	30,868	32,191	31,969
12	229,335	364,294	547,686	780,988	1,150,180
Total	1,531,894	1,751,431	1,958,388	2,181,584	2,515,420

Table 2.7
Projection of Public and Private Enrollment by School Level, Puerto Rico, 1966-87

Year (1)	Organization (2)	Level Elementary (3)	Intermediate (4)	High (5)
1966-67	Public	420,305	135,578	90,223
	Private	41,345	15,708	10,225
	Total	461,650	151,286	100,448
1971-72	Public	448,595	154,847	119,807
	Private	46,548	20,401	10,944
	Total	494,143	175,248	130,751
1976-77	Public	495,351	188,734	148,102
	Private	54,755	28,348	11,179
	Total	550,106	217,082	159,281
1981-82	Public	526,049	221,247	194,109
	Private	62,226	37,049	12,120
	Total	588,275	258,296	206,229
1986-87	Public	546,243	240,346	236,612
	Private	67,898	42,414	12,421
	Total	614,141	282,760	249,033

the corresponding survival rates. The results obtained are presented in tables 2.5 and 2.6.

The forecast of the number of students is used as a starting point to estimate the requirements of teachers and classrooms. For this, it is necessary to determine how many students will be in both public and private schools. Forecasts of these numbers can be obtained with an expanded version of the matrix model on page 49, in which the educational system is subdivided not only by grade but also into public and private schools. For this approach, data on the exchange of students from public to private schools and vice versa are needed. Such information is not available in Puerto Rico. In the method used, the proportion of students in public education with respect to total by level was used as a starting point. This proportion is forecasted according to the change observed in the past. Results appear in table 2.7.

Teacher and Classroom Requirements for Public Education

The forecasts in table 2.7 give the number of students expected in the public schools in Puerto Rico. The next step is to estimate the number of teachers and classrooms required by these students. To specify these requirements, several policy decisions have to be considered.

Table 2.8
Estimated Number of Hours per Student, per Teacher, and per Classroom, Puerto Rico, 1966-87

Year and Level	Hours per Student	Hours per Teacher	Hour per Classroom	Class Size
1966-67				
Elementary	4.042	4.868	5.560	32.644
Intermediate	4.247	4.060	5.218	30.679
High	4.178	3.759	5.242	36.015
1971-72				
Elementary	4.516	4.947	5.244	30.010
Intermediate	4.480	4.394	5.091	26.448
High	4.580	4.070	5.108	32.125
1976-77				
Elementary	4.996	5.010	5.001	27.511
Intermediate	4.998	4.695	5.001	24.503
High	4.991	4.371	5.001	28.701
1981-82				
Elementary	5.0	5.011	5.0	24.874
Intermediate	5.0	4.695	5.0	22.111
High	5.0	4.374	5.0	25.912
1986-87				
Elementary	5.0	5.011	5.0	22.450
Intermediate	5.0	4.694	5.0	19.961
High	5.0	4.374	5.0	23.411

Source: Explained in text.

The educational system in Puerto Rico has three different types of schools: single, double, and interlocking schools. In the single schools, students attend classes five hours per day; in the double and interlocking schools, three hours per day. Educational authorities in Puerto Rico decided to eliminate the double and interlocking enrollment by the school year 1976-77. Since this decision affects mainly the number of hours per day a student attends class, the forecast of teacher and classroom requirements must take it into consideration. The data used to obtain the information appear in table 2.8. This information and the results in table 2.7 on number of students were used to obtain the required number of teachers and classrooms presented in table 2.9.

Financial Resources Needed by the Public Educational System

A first object of this section is to forecast the financial resources needed to pay teachers and to construct and maintain the classrooms that, according to the

Table 2.9
Projection of Teachers and Classrooms Required, Puerto Rico, 1966-87

Year and Level	Number of Teachers	Number of Classrooms
1966-67		
Elementary	10,691	9,630
Intermediate	4,626	3,600
High	2,813	2,017
1971-72		
Elementary	13,645	12,874
Intermediate	5,970	5,152
High	4,197	3,344
1976-77		
Elementary	17,957	17,989
Intermediate	8,200	7,700
High	5,891	5,149
1981-82		
Elementary	21,126	21,169
Intermediate	10,657	10,006
High	8,562	7,491
1986-87		
Elementary	24,277	24,331
Intermediate	12,825	12,041
High	11,558	10,107

estimates, will be required for government-sponsored formal education in Puerto Rico. However, these expenditures are far from representing the total expenditures of the Department of Public Education in Puerto Rico. For administrative reasons, forecasts of the complete budget are needed. They are also presented here.

The method used to forecast resources needed for teachers and classrooms has as a starting point data on unit cost for the initial survey year, 1966-67. These unit costs take into consideration the effect of real per capita income growth on salaries, past experience of real increase in cost of construction, and, finally, the impact of inflation on real values.

Operational expenditures of the Department of Education in the formal educational system include expenditures for classroom materials, books, transportation of students, and student lunches. The first three types of expenditures were included in one group because they had similar rates of growth in the past. Lunchroom expenditures had lower rates of growth, probably reflecting the improved economic situation on the island.

To complete the estimate of the Department's budget, a forecast of expenditures outside the formal educational system are required. The lack of a detailed

Table 2.10
Projection of Budget of the Department of Public Education, Puerto Rico, 1966-87

(1967 dollars)

Year (1)	Teachers' Salaries (2)	Books, Implements, Transportation (3)	Lunchroom (4)	Classroom Construction (5)	Total (6)	Nonformal System (7)	Total (8)
1966-67	64,315	14,731	19,739	15,177	113,962	46,303	160,265
1971-72	113,016	31,781	29,236	33,702	207,735	85,322	293,057
1976-77	203,109	70,409	44,468	45,130	363,116	163,908	527,024
1981-82	341,100	153,359	66,497	62,779	623,735	307,647	931,382
1986-87	548,293	320,939	95,540	88,689	1,053,461	564,948	1,618,409

analysis of these expenditures is a major limitation of the present study. Without such analysis, many alternative uses of resources cannot be considered. The estimates in table 2.10 were obtained using as a starting point the past ratio of total budget to expenditure in the formal system. This ratio was forecast on the basis of its past rate of growth.

INTERACTION BETWEEN EDUCATIONAL ACHIEVEMENT AND POPULATION GROWTH

A method for studying the influence of population growth on the educational system was described earlier in this chapter (p. 47). In that case, population growth was considered the determinant of changes in the educational system. Nevertheless, this is not the only, and perhaps not the most important, relationship between the two. In addition, attention should be paid to the impact of difference in educational level—particularly for women—on fertility rates. As a consequence of this relationship, more education can bring about a reduction in the rate of population growth.

This section describes a model in which the two influences i.e., that of population growth on education and that of education on fertility and population growth, are considered. To do so, either the model for forecasting population by sex and age or that of education (p. 45) can be extended to include the missing links.

With the required changes, to be explained below, the earlier model becomes:

$$\begin{pmatrix} B \\ S \\ P \end{pmatrix}_1 = \begin{pmatrix} B_{11} & B_{12} & B_{13} \\ B_{21} & B_{22} & B_{23} \\ B_{31} & B_{32} & B_{33} \end{pmatrix} \begin{pmatrix} B \\ S \\ P \end{pmatrix}_0 \tag{2.28}$$

where

B = the column vector whose components are the number of children from age 0, i.e., birth, to age H, the last age at which they can enter school.

S, P = the vectors described on page 47.

B_{11} = a $(H + 1)$ $(H + 1)$ matrix that describes the transformation of the vector B_0 to the vector B_1. The first row of this vector includes only zeros because none of the children in vector B_t affect the number of children of age zero in year $t + 1$. (If necessary, this assumption can be modified.) From row 2 to row $e + 1$, the only elements of this matrix different from zero are those in the diagonal from row 2, column 1, to row $e + 1$, column e. These elements give the survival rates for children. The rest of the components of this matrix in columns 1 to e are zero. The remainder is identical to a matrix obtained by deleting the first row and column of matrix A_{11} on page 50.

B_{21} = a $G \times (H + 1)$ matrix, with zero components in its first columns and the rest of the matrix as in matrix A_{21} on page 50.

B_{31} = a $(G + 1) \times (H + 1)$ matrix, with zero components in its first column, and the rest as in matrix A_{31}.

B_{12} = a $(H + 1) \times G$ matrix with zero components.

B_{22} = a $G \times G$ matrix identical to A_{21}.

B_{32} = a $(G + 1) \times G$ matrix identical to A_{31}.

B_{13} = a $(H + 1) \times (G + 1)$ matrix that has nonzero components only in its first row. These components are the educational-level specific birth rates, i.e., the birth rates computed with the following formula: Number of births to persons with educational level i between t and $t + 1$ divided by number of persons with educational level i at date t.

B_{23} = a $G \times (G + 1)$ matrix identical with matrix A_{23}.

B_{33} = a $(G + 1) \times (G + 1)$ matrix identical with matrix A_{23}.

B_{33} = a $(G + 1) \times (G + 1)$ matrix identical with matrix A_{33}.

Finally, it should be observed that the total of each column of matrices B_{ij} for $i = 1, 2$ and $j = 1, \ldots, 3$ (i.e., with matrix B_{13} eliminated) is equal to the survival rate of the corresponding group in the population.

With the assumption of constant coefficients, repeated applications of formula 2.28 permit a forecast of the vector

$$\begin{pmatrix} B \\ S \\ P \end{pmatrix}_0$$

for any year T.

The most important application of the model just described is to illustrate the influence of educational achievement on population growth. Without changing the coefficients of the matrices involved, it will show that an increasing level of education among the population tends to reduce the rate of population growth if more educated people have lower fertility rates. Also, if the coefficients of the matrices B_{2j} j = 1, 3 are changed, it will show how changes in educational policy affect population growth.

A useful modification of this model is to consider a change of the components of the matrices of equation 2.28. This does not present any basic problem in computation. In every case, the control imposed on the totals of the columns should be taken into consideration.

TELEVISION-ASSISTED EDUCATION (TAE)

Television is probably the instrument most frequently used to expand the educational process. Several applications of television in education are presented in Schramm (1962) and Schramm et al. (1967). A particularly useful description of a TAE system is found in Wade (1967). A reading of Wade's paper would be very helpful to persons not familiar with the characteristics of TAE.

At the present time, television seems to be education's most popular technological innovation. With live transmissions, TAE simply multiplies the number of teachers, through the use of a special means of diffusion.

This point will be emphasized below. To do so, straightforward generalizations of the formulas on pages 53–54 are used. These generalizations deal not only with teachers, students, and TV sets as instruments of communication, but also with classrooms, which play in TAE a role as important as that played in educational systems with direct contact only between teachers and students.

In this analysis, little attention is paid to requirements for equipment. The systems considered here can serve one building, one school, one neighborhood, one city, or one country. Different cases do have different equipment requirements, but is neither feasible nor useful to discuss them here. For this, as for many other questions, the planner needs the advice of specialists.

TAE with One Channel, Several Screens, No Teacher Assistants

In order to study TAE, the direct "communication" between teacher and TV receivers must be taken up first. The number of periods of education offered by teachers has already been described in that part of equation 2.20 that is relevant to teachers. The total number of hours of reception on the TV sets can be described with the identity

$$L_v = f_v V \tag{2.29}$$

where

L_v = total hours of reception,
f_v = hours per set,
V = number of sets.

With live transmission, the average time a set is used, i.e., f_v, satisfies the following condition:

$$f_v \leqslant f_t T. \tag{2.30}$$

From formulas 2.20 and 2.29 it follows that the number of sets per teacher is

$$v_t = \frac{f_v V}{f_t T}. \tag{2.31}$$

Equations 2.30 and 2.31 imply that the maximum number of sets to which a teacher can transmit is

$$v_t \leqslant V. \tag{2.32}$$

The next link in the communication chain is the relationship between TV sets and students. From equation 2.19, which gives total number of hours of education received, and equation 2.29, which gives total number of hours of education transmitted through the TV sets, it is possible to determine the number of students per set, i.e.,

$$c_v = \frac{f_s S}{f_v V}. \tag{2.33}$$

At this point, several possible relationships between f_s and f_v must be studied. If $f_s > f_v$, each student receives more hours than each set transmits. This is possible only if each student listens to more than one set at a time. If $f_s = f_v$, each set is used to present all the subject matter required by the students. All the students attend all transmission time on each of the sets. If a student misses a transmission, he misses part of his course. If $f_s < f_v$, not all the students are taking all the subjects transmitted. This could be the case if, say, two grades are taught with TAE. One grade uses the system part of the time, another grade the rest of the time.

As a summary of the previous observations, it can be said that

$$f_s \leqslant f_v$$

and that the actual value of f_v is related to the content of the courses taught with TAE.

The interdependence of f_s and f_v must also be considered when TAE faces a change, say, an increase, in $f_s S$. If this increase reflects only an increase in S, then the television system will usually respond with an increase in c_v or in V while f_v remains constant. This is so because a larger group of students will receive the same educational content. An exception to this rule occurs when the increase in S is large enough to make it possible to establish parallel classes, for instance, to duplicate, triplicate, etc., a course. In this case, f_v will increase as the consequence of an increase in S. On the other hand, an increase in f_s must be met with an increase in f_v. No change in c_v or V will be appropriate in this case.

Finally, the basic relationships referring to classrooms must be considered. The weighted student/classroom ratio introduced in formula 2.22 does not change. The number of sets per classroom (v_q) is given in

$$v_q = \frac{f_v V}{f_q Q}. \tag{2.34}$$

Since a classroom is used whenever a set is receiving, it should be clear that

$$f_q \geqslant f_v.$$

From the above equations it follows that

$$c_t = c_v v_t \tag{2.35}$$

$$c_q = c_v v_q \tag{2.36}$$

i.e., the weighted student/teacher ratio c_t is equal to the weighted students per set c_v X the weighted sets per teacher, and the weighted students per room c_q is equal to the weighted students per set c_v X the weighted sets per room v_q.

The usual planning problem in the case of a single TAE system considered here would be to determine the number of teachers, classrooms and sets needed to attend S^* students receiving f_{s*} hours of class each. To estimate these numbers, the following formulas are appropriate:

$$\begin{aligned} Q &= \frac{f_{s*}}{f_q c_q} S^*, \\ V &= \frac{f_{s*}}{f_v c_v} S^*, \\ f_{s*} &\leqslant f_v \leqslant f_t T. \end{aligned} \tag{2.37}$$

These three expressions include 8 unknown variables and data values for h_{s*} and S^*. This means that the values of at least 6 variables can be determined arbitrarily.

In order to determine the values of the free variables, it is possible to use an optimization process, say, the minimization of costs. In formal terms, the problem takes the following form:

Minimize

$$K = k_f f_v + K_t T + k_q Q$$

where

K = total cost,
k = cost per unit of subscript,
f = hours of TV transmission, excluding teacher costs,
t = teachers,
q = rooms.

subject to equation 2.37 and to the following constraints that can be considered as determined by quality considerations:

$$\begin{aligned} f_q &\leqslant f_{q*} \\ c_q &\leqslant c_{q*} \\ c_v &\leqslant c_{v*} \\ f_t &\leqslant f_{t*} \\ f_v &\leqslant f_{v*} \end{aligned} \tag{2.38}$$

(with $c_{v*} = c_{v*} v_{q*}$ from 2.36).

This problem has a particularly simple solution that can be obtained with the analysis that follows. To minimize K, the variables f_v, T, and Q should be as small as possible.

It follows from the constraints in 2.37 that f_q, c_q, c_v, should be equal to their maximum admissible values, f_v should be equal to the minimum admissible value, and

$$f_v = f_t^* T.$$

It should be observed that in the analysis above, no attention has been paid to the possible limitations of the value of f_v determined by the content of the courses taught.

TAE with Several Channels and Several Curricula

The most restrictive assumption among those in the previous section asserts that there be only one channel. This assumption, together with the one that all education is presented through TAE, results in a restriction to only one curriculum if $f_s = f_v$. If $f_s < f_v$, several curricula are possible, but f_s is likely to be below the normal load, say, mornings for one group of students and afternoons for another. This section modifies these assumptions. The system to be studied includes several groups of students with several curricula, each student being served by a different TV channel. Clearly, in this case the formulas presented in the previous section can be used for each group served by one channel. Despite this, some clarification is necessary with respect to the equipment required. The only point that need be mentioned here, without entering into technical details is that the equipment necessary for one channel does not have to be multiplied by the number of channels when this type of system is used. With several channels, economies of scale can be introduced.

TAE with Teacher Assistants

Earlier sections of this discussion assumed that the students do not have direct contact either with the teachers or with any other person. They attend the TV transmission, and that is the sum of their teaching-learning experience. Clearly a somewhat extreme assumption. Here it will be assumed that the students, in addition to receiving classes transmitted by television, have "live" classes with teacher assistants. In this process, one teacher assistant is assigned to each of several subgroups of students. After all the students attend a TV class, each subgroup continues instruction with a teacher assistant, who extends the explanations presented through television, answers questions, and performs all the other functions usually associated with teachers.

To simplify the presentation, the conditions assumed earlier will be modified only by the introduction of teacher assistants. Several teachers present TV lectures to each grade, and then the assistants for that grade expand and explain the lectures to the students. Thus, the earlier equations need very little modification. Equations 2.29 to 2.33, dealing with the direct communication of teachers to TV sets, do not change at all.

Next, the communication from teacher to assistants through television will be considered. The number of hours of communication, to be designated F_a', is by definition

$$F_i' = f_i' I \tag{2.39}$$

where

F_i' = total number of hours received by assistants from teachers through television. During this time, students are also receiving TV classes from teachers.
f_i' = hours per assistant.
I = number of assistants.

It follows that assistants per teacher is given by

$$i_t = \frac{f_i' I}{f_t T}.$$

It should be clear that

$$f_i' \leqslant f_t T \tag{2.40}$$

and, as a consequence,

$$i_t \leqslant I.$$

From the previous formulas it also follows that the number of sets per assistant is:

$$v_i = \frac{f_v V}{f_i' I}. \tag{2.41}$$

Each period of instruction that the assistant receives together with the students via the TV sets is expanded by the assistant to a longer period for the students. In concrete terms, for each hour of TV class, assistants remain in contact with the students, say, one and one-half hours. The first hour is spent in receiving the teacher's class, and the last half hour in answering students' questions. This means that each F_i' assistant hours is expanded according to the formula

$$F_i = x_i F_i' \tag{2.42}$$

where

F_i = total number of hours offered by assistants,
x_i = expansion factor.

The total time per assistant is

$$f_i = x_i f_i' \tag{2.43}$$

with

$$F_i = f_i I.$$

The number of students per assistant is

$$c_i = \frac{f_s S}{f_i I}. \tag{2.44}$$

It should be clear that each hour transmitted by the TV sets is expanded by x_i to hours offered to the students. So students per set becomes

$$c_v = \frac{f_s S}{x_i f_v V}. \tag{2.45}$$

The condition imposed before that,

$$f_s \leqslant f_v, \tag{2.46}$$

is still valid in the present case.

To establish the basic identities with respect to classrooms, it should be observed that each assistant uses a classroom when he teaches. As a consequence, the total number of hours/classrooms used

(F_q) is

$$F_q = f_i I \tag{2.47}$$

and

$$F_q = f_q Q. \tag{2.48}$$

As before, the number of students per classroom is given as

$$c_q = \frac{f_s S}{f_q Q}. \tag{2.49}$$

From equations 2.41, 2.44, 2.47, and 2.48, it follows that

$$c_q = c_i = v_i c_v. \tag{2.50}$$

Finally, the number of sets per room is given as

$$v_q = \frac{x_i f_v V}{f_q Q}. \tag{2.51}$$

The identities and definitions presented can be used to plan the hours and physical resources needed for a system such as the one assumed here. To describe this application, assume that targets for the number of hours per student and the number of students have been determined. They will be denoted with f_s^* and S^*. To estimate the resources needed to achieve these targets, a system formed by equations 2.40, 2.41, 2.44, 2.45, 2.47, 2.49, 2.50, 2.51, and 2.39, 2.46 must be used. This system has the following 14 variables: f_i, f_t, T, v_i, f_v, V, I, c_i, x_i, c_v, f_q, Q, c_q, v_q. In addition, the following constraints can be added:

$$\begin{aligned} v_i &\leqslant v_i^* \\ c_i &\leqslant c_i^* \\ c_v &\leqslant c_v^* \\ c_q &\leqslant c_q^* \\ v_q &\leqslant v_q^* \\ x_i &\leqslant x_i^* \\ f_q &\leqslant f_q^* \\ f_i &\leqslant f_i^*. \end{aligned} \tag{2.52}$$

The conditions and constraints imposed on the variables are not enough to determine the value of the variables. As a consequence, an optimization process can be used. The cost of the TAE system used in this section is

$$K = k_1 f_v + k_2 T + k_3 Q + k_4 I. \tag{2.53}$$

Reasoning is very similar to that used on page 67, where it can be shown that all the constraints in 2.52 have to be binding, and that $f_v = f_s^*$ for a minimum.

TAE WITH TEACHERS' LECTURES RECORDED ON FILM OR VIDEOTAPE

The starting point for the TAE analysis on pages 64–67 is that the number of hours of transmission is

$$F_t = f_t T.$$

This number indicates the number of teachers and the average number of hours of work per teacher based on the assumption that all transmissions are live transmissions. When this assumption is removed, and it is assumed that all transmissions are based on lectures recorded on film, videotape, and the like, the equation above does not hold, i.e., there is no relationship between number of teachers and hours of transmission. On the other hand, none of the other relationships is modified when F_t is defined only as hours of transmission and not as hours of work per teacher. With this observation, all the formulas presented before can be retained.

TEACHER-STUDENT SYSTEMS VERSUS TAE

No attention has so far been paid to the problem of choosing among the several alternatives considered, such as the choice between teacher-student systems and TAE in any of the forms previously discussed. A general form of this problem would include not only the choice between T/S systems and one type of TAE, but a selection among T/S, all the available types of TAE, and also any other forms of education, such as computer-assisted education. The method to be presented briefly here deals only with T/S and the form of TAE set forth on pages 64–67.

In principle, the statement of the optimization problem does not present any particular difficulty. The objective function in the sum of the function is 2.27 and 2.53, with obvious changes in notation needed to avoid confusion. For instance, the teachers and classrooms in the T/S system should be identified with subscript 1, and those in TAE with subscript 2, and the unit costs k_i should be modified to take into consideration the fact that salaries for teachers in T/S are different from those in TAE.

The constraints used for the minimization of 2.27 and 2.53 do not change, except for the constraint dealing with total number of hours of education received by the students, i.e., equations 2.22 and 2.44, that in the present case become

$$h_s^* S^* = c_i f_i I + c_{t_2} f_{t_2} T_2, \tag{2.54}$$

meaning that the total number of hours of education received by the students can be received either through the TAE system with the help of assistants or directly from the teachers.

In its full generality, the problem as stated is one of nonlinear programming that could be solved using, say, the Kuhn-Tucker methods. However, the quadratic expressions can be eliminated using the fact that costs are reduced if the constraints in 2.26 and 2.52 are transformed into equalities. Once this is done, the problem reduces to one of linear programming.

The approach outlined above can be extended to consider the maximization of an objective function in which the different impacts on the achievement of the student of T/S and TAE are considered. In this case, a limited amount of resources should be also included among the constraints. Again, this problem will not be studied in detail here.

An Example of TAE*

This section studies the TAE system in the city of Sao Luis, in the state of Maranhao, Brazil. In the presentation, a comparison is made of this system with one having the usual interaction between teacher and students.

Present plans call for the use of TAE for the four grades of *gimnasio* (equivalent to junior high school). In 1971, only the first three grades were being served; the fourth was included in 1972. This analysis concentrates on the system as it was in 1970, with television operating only for the first two grades.

The same system is also used for adult education. Adults can obtain certificates of junior high school education by attending evening classes. However, little attention is paid here to these adult courses.

The first step will be to characterize the teachers' work and its relationship to transmission time. The number of teachers in the three years of operation of the system is presented in table 2.11. The teachers are expected to work 5 hours per day, 6 days per week, for a total of 120 hours per month, per teacher; in 1970, this amounted to 2,760 hours for all teachers. Of this total, only 64 hours per month are used in transmission; the rest is used in the preparation of classes.

Table 2.11
Number of Teachers in TAE, Sao Luis, Marahao, Brazil

Year	Teachers
1969	8
1970	23
1971	36

Source: Fundacao Maranhense de Televisao Educativa Caderno Maranhense de Teleducacao, Sao Luis, 1971.

*I am grateful for the cooperation of Miss Maria do Socurro Neiva, Head of Programming and Budgeting of the Department of Education and Culture of the Maranhao State, Brazil.

This description shows that the formulas used in the earlier TAE sections, based as they were on the assumption that hours of transmission and hours of work were equal, have to be modified. For this, let

H'_t = hours of transmission per month (64),
H_t = total hours of work per month (2,760),
x_t = expansion factor defined by

$$x_t = \frac{H_t}{H'_t}. \tag{2.55}$$

This factor influences the quality of the education offered.

According to formula 2.20, it follows that

$$T_1 = \frac{x_t H'_t}{f_{t1}}. \tag{2.56}$$

Each of the components of formula 2.56 is a variable. Below it will be assumed that x_t and f_{t1} remain constant at their levels of 1970. With this, formula 2.56 becomes

$$T_1 = .36H'_t.$$

The next step is to relate hours of transmission to hours of reception on the TV sets. The basic data appear in table 2.12. The reason why only some of the available sets were used in 1970 morning and afternoon is that in the morning the first-grade classes met, and there were more sections of this class, because of the larger number of students. In the afternoon, only second-grade classes met. From these data, it follows that the average number of hours of reception per set is 44.22.

Table 2.12
Hours of TAE Reception on TV Sets, Sao Luis, Marahao, Brazil, 1970

Use of Sets	Number	Hours per Day
Morning only	68	1.33
Morning and afternoon	42	2.67
Total	110	

Source: Elaboration from official data of the program.

The assumption used in formula 2.30, that all sets are used all the time, is not satisfied in the present case. The quotient between hours of reception per set and hours of transmission is an index of the utilization of the TV sets. Below this index will be considered constant, so that

$$f_v = .69H'_t. \tag{2.57}$$

However, it should be observed that the index of utilization of the sets is determined by the distribution of students in grades, and should be taken as a variable in detailed studies of systems having several grades.

Table 2.13
Number of Assistants in TAE, Sao Luis, Marahao, Brazil

Year	Assistants
1969	105
1970	162
1971	214

Source: Fundacao Maranhense de Televisao Educativa.

As the next link of the chain, the assistants in direct contact with the students are considered. The total number of assistants from 1969 to 1971 appears in table 2.13. These numbers also refer to assistants who work with the evening classes for adults, and refer only to physical persons, not to number of positions filled. In 1970 the number of positions filled was 194, with some assistants working double time and receiving double salary. Only 152 of them worked with the day classes. The schedule for the assistants is 5 hours per day, 6 days per week.

The assistants remain in the classes during five 50-minute periods. In four of these periods, 20 minutes are used for reception of a TV transmission and the remaining 30 minutes are used by the assistant. The other 50-minute period is used entirely by the assistants. From these observations it follows that each assistant receives 32 hours of transmission per month, which expands to 120 hours of class, i.e., the expansion factor is $x_i = 3.75$. This factor should be determined by quality considerations, and will be assumed to be constant in the analysis below.

The obligation of the assistants is that of explaining the material presented through the TV sets. The achievement tests are uniform for all the students, and are produced and graded in a central office. In the grading, a computer system is used.

From the data with respect to hours received on the TV sets, hours received by the assistant, and formula 2.41, it follows that the number of sets per assistant is one, and that

$$f_v = \frac{f_i' I}{V} = .291. \tag{2.58}$$

The students of the TAE system are the closing link of the chain. Their numbers are presented in table 2.14. As mentioned earlier, attention will be paid here to the 6,251 students in the regular courses in 1970 only. They were divided into two groups: first grade, with 4,480 students, and second, with 1,701. Each of them received 120 hours of class per month, or a total of 741,720 for the 6,181 students. From formula 2.44, it follows that the average number of students per assistant was 40.04, and from 2.50 that this was also the number of students per set. Below it will be assumed that these values for c_i and c_v are determined by quality considerations and will be considered constants.

Table 2.14
Number of TAE Students, Sao Luis, Marahao, Brazil

Year	Students in High School	Students in Adult Education
1969	1,304	—
1970	6,181	742
1971	9,415	4,200

Source: Secretaria de Educacao e Cultura, Estado do Maranhao, *Projecto "Equipe Sarney"-Reformulacao*, Anexo 2, tables 4 and 6 (n.d.)

The unit costs of the system are presented in table 2.15.

One of the most important reasons for the study of a TAE system is that of determining whether it is more economical than a system with direct teacher/student contact.

According to the forecasts of teachers, classrooms, and other implements section, the main data required for an analysis of such a T/S system are hours per teacher. In Sao Luis, each teacher was expected to work up to 48 hours of class per month, and received a payment of 600 cruzeiros per month. To relate this figure to the hours of education received by the students, it will be assumed that class sizes are fixed at 40.04, observed in the TAE system in 1970.

On the basis of the information presented so far, it is possible to state the following problem:

Minimize costs:

$$K = 21.34\, H_t' + 750\, T_1 + 500\, I + 600\, T_2.$$

subject to

$$741{,}720 = 4{,}804.8\, I + 1{,}921.92\, T_2 \qquad \text{(from 2.54)}$$

$$T_1 = .36\, H_t' \qquad \text{(from 2.56)}$$

$$f_v = .69\, H_t' \qquad \text{(from 2.57)}$$

$$H_t' = .29\, I \qquad \text{(from 2.58)}$$

and nonnegativity of all the variables involved.

Table 2.15
Unit Costs per Month of the TAE System, Sao Luis, Marahao, Brazil, 1970 (cruzeiros 1970)

Concept	Cost
Teachers' salaries	750
Assistants' salaries	500
Hours of transmission	21.34

Source: Elaborated from official data.

The solution of this simple programming problem is that $T_2 = 0$, $H_t' = 64$, i.e., the TAE system is more economical. From the formulation above it is also possible to show that f_{t2} would have to be larger than 116 hours per month for the system direct teacher/student interaction to become more economical than the TAE system.

COMPUTER-ASSISTED EDUCATION (CAE)

Computer-assisted education (CAE) can be considered an extension of TAE in which the lectures of the professor are recorded on film or videotape. In this instance of TAE, the entire contribution of the teacher is recorded and presented to the students through a transmission-and-reception TV system. One limitation of the procedure is that the students cannot influence the presentation of the material in any way. It must be presented strictly in the sequence recorded in the film or videotape. Since the information is always presented in the same way, regardless of the needs of the students, there is no advantage in having one screen per student. This could be done, but individualized instruction would not be obtained.

With CAE, the contribution of the teacher is recorded in a computer program that replaces the film or videotape used in TAE, and presented to the student through a computer terminal. Its use presents many new possibilities.

To operate CAE, a computer system is needed. Such a system is formed by (1) input-output units: usually typewriterlike terminals with or without audiovisual capabilities, (2) a central processing unit that follows the instructions of the program, and (3) a memory where the program and other relevant information are stored. The computer programs for CAE make it possible for the computer system to receive inputs from the students through the terminals. These inputs could be in the form of questions from the students, or their answers to questions recorded in the program and presented to them through the terminals. The presentation of the teacher's contribution is modified according to these student inputs. The teacher can ask questions of the student if he feels that his input is insufficient to decide the next steps, or suggest the revision of certain topics or the study of new information.

In the process described, the contribution of each student is not only useful but necessary. Actually, the computer terminals cannot proceed when a student does not contribute some input whenever the program expects one. Consequently, there is an advantage in giving each student the opportunity to interact by himself with the professor through the computer program. CAE permits individualized instruction.

From the description, it should be clear that the heart of CAE is the program prepared for a course. The teacher who prepares the program is the one who decides the sequencing with which the "new" material will be introduced, the questions to test the understanding of the students, the correct answers to those questions, and where to direct the student following a comparison between his answers and those stored in the computer. These operations to a large extent reproduce the actions of a teacher in class.

It should also be observed that the more narrowly specified the answers to a question, the easier to prepare such a program. For instance, the correct answer to a 2 + 2 = ? is quite well defined, while that for What is mathematics? is quite imprecise. It is not correct to conclude from this observation that certain subjects cannot be adapted to CAE. Nevertheless, there are substantial differences in the difficulty of preparing computer programs for different subjects, and also of the time the computer uses to decide whether an answer is true or false, and to select the appropriate next step for the student. As a consequence, there are substantial differences in the cost of preparing a computer program for the different subjects, and in computer time for actual teacher/student interaction. In certain cases, the costs might reach the level of making CAE uneconomical for some subjects, meaning that the same course could be taught more cheaply using other methods.

CAE can be used in several ways: in combination with regular classes, where the students have some direct contact with a teacher and do part of their work through a computer; or to present the main material of a course, while an assistant gives additional help to the students. Finally, a complete curriculum can be taught using CAE only. However, for economic reasons, the possibilities of this alternative are limited at present. Despite this difficulty, the first model for planning CAE assumes a system where all teacher/student interaction is made through a computer. The next model illustrates the case where the computer facilities are used only to complement and extend the classroom presentation made by a teacher. A third model plans CAE when the computer facilities are used simultaneously with the teacher's presentation. Finally, some comments focus on the problem of choice between direct teacher/student interaction, and interaction through a computer.

CAE When All Teacher/Student Interaction Is Through the Computer

As mentioned, the basic component of CAE is the program used to direct the computer. As with TAE, when lectures are recorded on film or videotape, the time used in the preparation of the program is not directly related to the number of times the program can be used or the number of students who can use it. The cost of the program is a fixed cost of CAE, independent of its utilization.

The direct interaction is between computer terminals and students. Assuming that each student uses one terminal, it is possible to establish the following identity:

$$f_s S = f_z Z \tag{2.59}$$

where

f_z = hours per terminal,
Z = number of terminals.

It should be observed that in formula 2.59

$$\begin{gathered} f_s \leq f_z \\ Z \leq S \end{gathered} \tag{2.60}$$

otherwise, some terminals could be eliminated and f_z could be increased without changing the total time that terminals require the services of the central processing unit and the memories of the computer.

The next step is to relate the total time that terminals are used, i.e., $f_z Z$, to the time the central processing unit and the computer memories are used. Several variables must be considered in this case, such as the time it should take the computer to verify a student's answer, to print directions to the student's terminal, etc. To study these aspects, it is necessary to analyze in detail the technological characteristics of different computer facilities. This is one of many cases where educational planners need the assistance of other experts.

Finally, attention must be given to the requirements for classrooms. The basic identity presented in the Forecasts of Classrooms section still holds, i.e.,

$$f_s S = c_q f_q Q. \tag{2.61}$$

In the present case, an element not considered in identity 2.61 must be considered: the size of the rooms. When terminals are used, rooms have to be larger.

The earlier condition that

$$f_s \leq f_q \tag{2.62}$$

still holds in the present case.

The weighted terminals/classrooms ratio is, in this case,

$$z_q = \frac{f_z Z}{f_q Q}. \tag{2.63}$$

It follows from the assumption that at any time only one student uses a terminal that

$$z_q = c_q. \tag{2.64}$$

It is also clear that

$$f_z \leq f_q. \tag{2.65}$$

At this point, the problem of the computer facilities required to attend $f_s^* S^*$ students must be studied. For this, the system formed by identities 2.59 and 2.61 must be used together with the constraint

$$f_s^* \leq f_z \leq f_q^* \tag{2.66}$$

This system has 5 unknowns, namely Z, Q, f_z, f_q, c_q. An approach to determining these unknowns is to minimize the cost in 2.67.

$$K = k_1 f_z Z + k_2 Z + k_3 Q. \tag{2.67}$$

The first term of the right-hand side of 2.67 reflects the fact that the computer time used is related to $f_z Z$, i.e., the time the terminals are used. This cost is not modified if the product $f_z Z$ is determined from a high f_z and low Z or vice versa.

To minimize K it should be observed that $f_z Z$ is fixed in equation 2.59. As a consequence, $k_1 f_z Z$ is also fixed. The only way to minimize K is to reduce Z and Q. For this, f_z and f_q should be made as large as possible, within the limits of 2.66.

CAE When Computer Terminals Are Used to Complement Direct Teacher/Student Interaction

In this case, an educational system with the characteristics described in the Forecasts section is assumed as a starting point. This means that the weighted student/teacher ratio is as in 2.22

$$c_t = \frac{f_s'S}{f_tT} \tag{2.68}$$

where

f_s' = number of hours per student in direct contact with the teacher.

In addition, each class hour presented by the teacher is assumed to generate the need for x_t hours of interaction between each student and the teacher through the computer. In this interaction it is assumed that each student uses one terminal. This means that the teacher's classes generate

$$f_zZ = (x_tf_tT)S \tag{2.69}$$

hours of terminal use. The relationships between the variables in equation 2.68 observed while discussing equations 2.59 and 2.60 also hold in the present case.

The total number of hours received by the students is, in the present case,

$$f_zS = f_zZ + c_tf_tT. \tag{2.70}$$

An immediate extension of the formulas used before with respect to classrooms makes it possible to write

$$f_s'S = c_{q1}f_{q1}Q_1 \tag{2.71}$$

for classrooms used for direct teacher/student interaction with $c_t = c_{q1}$; and

$$f_zZ = c_zf_{q2}Q_2 \tag{2.72}$$

for classrooms with terminals, with $c_{q2} = c_z$.

The problem in planning is to determine the values that the variables in equations 2.68 to 2.72 should have when the hours per student and the number of students are arbitrarily fixed. Those values of the variables should be fixed to minimize costs, subject to constraints to be described below.

The expansion factor x_t will be assumed to be constant for a desired educational quality, i.e., $x_t = x_t^*$. Also, from equation 2.66 it follows that

$$x_t^*f_tT \leq f_z \leq f_z^*. \tag{2.73}$$

Finally, it will be assumed that

$$\begin{aligned} f_t &\leq f_t^* \\ c_t &\leq c_t^* \\ f_{q1} &\leq f_{q1}^* \\ f_{q2} &\leq f_{q2}^* \end{aligned} \tag{2.74}$$

$$c_{q1} \leq c_{q1}^*$$
$$c_{q2} \leq c_{q2}^*$$

From equation 2.68 and 2.69 it follows that

$$T \geq \frac{f_s^* S^*}{(x_t^* S^* + c_t) f_t^*} \tag{2.75}$$

and that

$$Z \geq \frac{x_t^* f_t TS^*}{f_z^*} \tag{2.76}$$

The cost to be minimized is

$$K = k_1 (f_z Z) + k_2 Z + k_3 T + k_4 Q_1 + k_5 Q_2 \tag{2.77}$$

The procedure described below will be used in this minimization. It is clear from equation 2.69 that $c_t = c_t^*$ for a minimum of 2.77. From equations 2.68 and 2.69 it follows that

$$f_s^* S^* = (x^* S^* + c_t^*) f_t T$$

i.e., that $f_t T$ is a constant. This, together with equation 2.69, implies that $f_z Z$ is a constant. From this it follows that the minimization of K must be obtained through changes in Z, T, Q, and Q_2. This list of variables is further reduced when it is observed that 2.70, 2.71 and the corresponding inequalities in 2.74 fix the values of Q_1 and Q_2.

Finally, the corresponding inequalities in 2.74 and inequalities in 2.75 and 2.76 clearly need to be reduced to equalities for a minimum.

CAE When Students Interact Directly with Teachers and Through Computer Terminals

This section can be described as follows: In a classroom, each student and the teacher have terminals. The teacher completes an explanation, the students answer some questions that appear in the terminal. The teacher receives a feedback in his terminal on which students are not giving correct answers and what types of problems they encounter.

In this case, the direct teacher/student contact is described in the identity

$$f_s S = c_t f_t T. \tag{2.78}$$

During all this time, the teacher *and* the students can be thought of as sitting in front of computer terminals. These terminals will actually be used only when the teacher asks a question of the class. The question is typed by the students' terminals, and when the students type the answers, a summary of them appears in the teacher's terminal.

Each student or small group of students can use one terminal. The relationship describing these conditions is

$$c_z f_{z1} M_1 = f_s S \tag{2.79}$$

where

c_z = students per terminal.

The relationship between hours per terminal and per student in 2.60 holds in the present case.

Assuming that only one teacher is in the classroom at any time, the number of hours of f_{z2} use of the teacher's terminal is

$$f_{z2} = f_t T. \tag{2.80}$$

The minimization to determine the values of the variables is as straightforward in the present case as in the one presented earlier and need not be discussed here.

REFERENCES

Atkinson, R. C., and Wilson, H. A. *Computer Assisted Instruction.* New York: Academic Press, 1969.

Correa, H. "Basis for the Quantitative Analysis of the Educational System." *Journal of Experimental Education* 35, no. 1 (Fall 1966).

Correa, H. "A Survey of Mathematical Models in Educational Planning." In *Mathematical Models in Educational Planning.* Paris: Organization for Economic Cooperation and Development, 1967.

Correa, H. *Quantitative Methods of Educational Planning.* Scranton, Pa.: International Textbook Co., 1969.

Correa, H., and Reimer, E. "A Simulation Model for Educational Planning in Puerto Rico." Mimeographed. Department of Public Education, San Juan, Puerto Rico, 1968.

Coulson, J. E. "Computer Based Instruction." *International Review of Education* 14, No. 2 (1968).

Johnson, F. C., and Dietrich, J. E. *Cost Analysis of Instructional Technology.* Washington, D.C.: Academy for Educational Development, 1970.

Kiesling, H. J. *On the Economic Analysis of Educational Technology.* Washington, D.C.: Academy for Educational Development, 1970.

Republique de Cote-d'Ivoire, Ministere de l'education nationale. *Programme d'education televisuelle.* 3 vols. Paris: Beugnet S.A., n.d.

Schramm, W. "Learning from Instructional Television." *Review of Educational Research* 32, no. 2 (April 1962).

Schramm, W.; Coombs, P.; Kahnert, F.; and Lyle, J. *The New Media: Memo to Educational Planners.* Paris: UNESCO: IIEP, 1967.

Stone, R. *Demographic Accounting and Model-Building.* Paris: Organization for Economic Cooperation and Development, 1971.

UNESCO: IIEP. *New Educational Media in Action Case Studies for Planners, 1, 2, 3.* Paris: UNESCO, 1967.

Wade, S. "Hagerstown: A Pioneer in Closed-Circuit Televised Instruction. In *New Educational Media in Action Case Studies for Planners 1.* Paris: UNESCO, 1967.

*George B. Kleindorfer**

3 EDUCATIONAL PLANNING WITH COMBINED NETWORK AND STATE VARIABLE MODELS

It is common in mathematical planning exercises to build what may be called aggregate dynamic planning models. In order to represent the intertemporal processes of a system, these models contain constraints in the form of difference or differential equations. The planning problem, when viewed in such terms, consists of choosing a sequence of values for decision variables so as to drive the system along a trajectory that is optimal with respect to some chosen criterion. Following the terminology of the control engineers (Tou 1964) and lacking a better term, we will call these models "state variable" models.

By their nature, state variable models do not deal with the many discrete activities that may have to be planned, ordered, funded, and executed in order to affect the factors represented by parameters or decision variables in the models. This being so, we wish to explore the mathematical problems involved in coordinating such aggregate planning models with planning at an operational level. Specifically, we intend to study the combination of state variable planning models with network planning models which derive from industrial project planning and management.

In network models a planned project is characterized as a set of disjoint activities, tasks, or jobs which are ordered with respect to one another. Each activity is assumed to require resources (men, money, etc.) and each may be of uncertain duration. The network conceptualization forces the planner to define in a

*I wish to express my thanks to Charles S. Benson for his helpful comments and discussion throughout this study.

very specific way the reasonably foreseeable work that must be carried out to achieve some desired goal. We are interested in situations in which one purpose of the activities of a network is to affect some significant aspect of a system that is modeled by a state variable model.

Many problems in economic planning, health planning, agricultural planning, educational planning, etc., might be profitably viewed in this light. Consider, for example, an educational planning situation in which a given country desires to plan and implement a policy of universal primary and secondary education. The aggregate dynamic model appropriate for studying such a policy might be a flow model (Correa 1967, 1969), characterizing students coming from the general population and moving through the educational system. In this model there will be admission rates which will have to be increased with time so as to portray the trajectory of the educational system toward the desired goal. Having set or chosen these rates, the model can be used, of course, to generate estimates of the resources needed to sustain such a growth pattern. However, a number of ordered activities may have to be planned, coordinated, and carried out before or simultaneously with a schedule of increased admissions. Examples of such work may be the revision of the system of taxation and distribution of funds for the educational system, the development and specialization of the educational system at certain levels for people in different locales, the creation of on-the-job training programs for people leaving the educational system, and so forth.

In such planning situations, it may be helpful, if not necessary, to use a combined model consisting of state variable and network submodels. The network model may show that operational level work precludes the implementation of certain policies dictated by an aggregate model alone. On the other hand, considerations derived from an aggregate planning model in conjunction with a network model may show that operational level activities should be postponed, diminished, or expanded. The activities represented in the network model may require resources independently of the processes described by the state variable model. If we are given the costs of resources together with time requirements, then a general form of planning problem arises as to how to balance and distribute these resources over the processes and activities represented by the combined model containing state variable and network submodels.

There are difficulties in the mathematical underpinnings of this combined conceptualization, the chief one being that some of the basic problems connected with network methods have never been solved. The content and organization of the rest of this chapter is, for the most part, a reflection of these difficulties in network theory.

The first section presents a short general description of the various ways in which we intend to represent in state variable models the effects of outside activities. The next section reviews the mathematical treatment of network models for project planning. The primary focus is on the problem of uncertainty since this problem naturally arises in any foreseeable application of the proposed combined model. Next, we briefly review the literature dealing with resource allocation in planning networks, the emphasis again being on the practicality of the methods when applied to planning in an uncertain environment. The section following focuses on the problem of combining network models with state variable models and presents a model that incorporates both submodels. Unfortunately, except for certain special cases, this model is not susceptible of exact solution. Heuristic methods are described for effecting this combination in planning practice. These methods amount to simulation of the state variable submodel coordinated with an analytical approach for obtaining bounds on the probabilities associated with the network submodel. A simulation approach to the total model is usually not tractable because of the large combinatorial problem posed by the network. (This last fact is one of the most important points that must be considered in treating the combined model. We deal with it extensively throughout this chapter.) The concluding section sets out an example of the combined approach in a study of vocational education in what used to be called East Pakistan.

STATE VARIABLE MODELS AFFECTED BY EXTERNAL ACTIVITIES

For the sake of convenience, we will consider only state variable models in the following discrete time form:

$$S_{t+1} = F_t(S_t, D_t, E_t) \tag{3.1}$$

$$Y_t = G_t(S_t, D_t, E_t) \tag{3.2}$$

where

t = the discrete time index $t = 0, 1, 2, \ldots,$
S_t = a vector of state variables,
D_t = a vector of decision variables,
E_t = a vector of exogenously determined parameters or variables,
Y_t = a vector of output or observation variables, and
F, G = vector functions which can change with time.

When this model is applied in educational planning, for example, the S_t may be projected enrollments, numbers of teachers, costs, etc. The D_t may be rates of transfer, pupil-teacher ratios, per-pupil costs, etc. The E_t may be population forecasts, exogenously determined rates, etc. The Y_t may be total costs, recurring and capital, etc.

In terms of such a model, planning consists of choosing a sequence of decision variables, $D_0, D_1, \ldots, D_{t-1}$, so as to optimize the expected value of an objective function:

$$\sum_{t=1}^{T} H_t(Y_t, S_t, D_{t-1}). \tag{3.3}$$

The initial state of the system, S_0, is usually given. In addition, both the state variables, S_t, and the decision variables, D_t, may be constrained to be in some specified space.

This form of planning model has been extensively studied in modern control theory (Aaki 1967, Tou 1964). There are two general ways of treating such a model. One alternative is to solve it mathematically. This is the substance of modern control theory. A number of analytical methods exist for the solution, depending on whether the model is linear or nonlinear, deterministic or stochastic. When analytical treatment is not practical for one reason or another, the remaining alternative is to resort to simulation to obtain satisfactory solutions.

Suppose now that we have a network of N interrelated activities, $i = 1, 2, \ldots, N$, which are outside the system of processes modeled by equations 3.1 through 3.3. Let V_i be the time at which activity i will be finished, $i = 1, 2, \ldots, N$. The V_i will, in general, be a random variables.

We are interested in situations in which the completion of the various activities affects the system modeled by 3.1 through 3.3. Thus, a more general form of the state variable model would be to optimize the expected value of

$$\sum_{t=1}^{T} H_t(Y_t, S_t, D_{t-1}, V_1, V_2, \ldots, V_N) \tag{3.4}$$

subject to

$$S_{t+1} = F_t(S_t, D_t, E_t, V_1, V_2, \ldots, V_N) \tag{3.5}$$

$$Y_t = G_t(S_t, D_t, E_t, V_1, V_2, \ldots, V_N). \tag{3.6}$$

This model might appear in several possible ways in practical applications. One way is that the $V_1, V_2, \ldots, V_N$, might be included in 3.5 and 3.6 implicitly because certain of the exogenous parameters E_t depend on the finishing of some or all of the various activities. Thus

$$E_t = C_t(V_1, V_2, \ldots, V_N) \tag{3.7}$$

where 3.7 holds for $t = 0, 1, 2, \ldots, T$. Another way is that the form of the functions F, G, H in the model may change as the various activities are completed. Still another way, which can be written as a side condition to the formulation of 3.4 through 3.6, is that the decision variables, D_t, may be constrained in a space determined by the finishing of the activities; for example,

$$D_t \geqslant C_t(V_1, V_2, \ldots, V_N). \tag{3.8}$$

There are, no doubt, many other possible ways in which it may be visualized that random variables associated with outside activities could affect a model like 3.4 through 3.6.

To take up again our earlier example of educational planning, we can consider the situation in which the admission rates in a flow model are wholly or partially determined by whether or not a network of outside activities is completed. This connection might be represented by whichever of 3.7 or 3.8 is appropriate with the admission rates playing the part of exogenous parameters, as in 3.7, or as decision variables, as in 3.8. The educational planning problem described in the last section of this chapter gives an explicit example of the framing of this connection.

We have not specified anything yet about the random variables, $V_1, V_2, \ldots, V_N$. In order to be able to approach any problem like that of 3.4 through 3.7, at least some statistical properties of these random variables must of course be known. When these random variables are the finishing times of the various activities in a network of activities, the problem of deriving these statistical properties is a complicated one. We consider it next.

PROBLEMS ASSOCIATED WITH NETWORK-BASED PLANNING

In applying network theory to project planning and management it is customary to make the following assumptions (Wiest and Levy 1969):

ASSUMPTION 1. *A project can be broken into a number of ordered separate activities;*
ASSUMPTION 2. *The duration of the activities are independent random variables; and*
ASSUMPTION 3. *The probability distribution for the duration of each activity is known.*

The practical implications of these assumptions have been examined by MacCrimmon and Ryavec (1964). We will assume that they hold throughout.

Let a network be composed of a set of nodes or circles and a set of arcs or arrows. The nodes will correspond to activities, tasks, or jobs* which must be carried out to develop a plan or carry out specific work under a plan. The arcs will be used to order the nodes. As is most common in the literature, we will deal only with acyclic networks; that is, networks that have no feedback loops. Let the nodes be indexed $i = 1, 2, \ldots, N$ so that if node i precedes node j in the network then $i < j$. Let node 1 precede all other nodes. Denote by B_i the set of nodes that immediately precede node i, $i = 2, 3, \ldots, N$. Let U_i and V_i be the starting and finishing times respectively of the ith activity, and let W_i be the duration of the ith activity. By assumption 2 the durations W_i, $i = 1, 2, \ldots, N$, are independent random variables.

The ordering of the activities (nodes) in the network leads to the following inequality for $i = 2, 3, \ldots, N$:

$$U_i \geqslant \max_{b \in B_i} V_b. \tag{3.9}$$

This simply states that activity i will begin only after all its immediate predecessors are finished. In our discussions hereafter, in order uniquely to determine 3.9, we will always utilize the assumption† that activity i starts as soon as possible. Thus 3.9 is changed to 3.10:

$$U_i = \max_{b \in B_i} V_b. \tag{3.10}$$

*We are adhering to what is called the "activity-on-node" convention (Wiest and Levy 1969). The contrary convention, letting the arcs represent activities and the nodes the events of starting and finishing the activities, is also often used.

†This is called the "early start" assumption (Wiest and Levy 1969). It is an artificial assumption in that we can always introduce a "dummy" or "slack" activity into the network representing a delay which is to be imposed in the starting of activity i.

In addition we have for $i = 1, 2, \ldots, N$ that

$$V_i = U_i + W_i. \tag{3.11}$$

Finally, for the sake of convenience in what follows, let

$$U_1 = 0 \tag{3.12}$$

and

$$W_N = 0. \tag{3.13}$$

Corresponding to the starting and finishing times, U_i and V_i, let the following probabilities be defined:

$$P_i(t) = Pr[U_i \leqslant t], \quad \text{and} \quad Q_i(t) = Pr[V_i \leqslant t],$$

$i = 1, 2, \ldots, N$, where t as before is the time index (not necessarily discrete). We will refer to $P_i(t)$, and $Q_i(t)$ as the *starting and finishing time probability distributions* respectively for activity i.

By assumption 3 above, the probability mass functions for the random variables, W_i, for $i = 1, 2, \ldots, N$, are known; that is, we have available the probabilities, $Pr[W_i = t]$. As a shorthand notation, let $a_i(t) = Pr[W_i = t]$.

The central problems associated with the network model we have defined are:

Problem 1. *Given the network geometry and the $a_i(t)$, then what are the $P_i(t)$ and $Q_i(t)$, $i = 1, 2, \ldots, N$?*

Problem 2. *What are the moments of the distributions $P_i(t)$ and $Q_i(t)$, $i = 1, 2, \ldots, N$?*

Problem 3. *Given the resource needs for each network activity, what are the resource needs for the whole network at any given time and over the whole duration of the network?*

Problem 4. *What is the best pattern of resource allocation to the activities in a network when certain of the activities are elastic with respect to resource inputs?*

This section deals with the first three problems; problem 4 is discussed in the next section.

The reader will have noticed that the problems are not independent. The total solution of problem 1, of course, would lead to the easy solution of problems 2 and 3, since the possession of $P_i(t)$ and $Q_i(t)$ allows the simple computation of expectations. Solving problem 1, however, is easier said than done, and no complete solution (for other than certain simple networks) has as yet appeared. For this reason, some studies bypass problem 1 and go directly to work on problem 2 (Elmaghraby 1967, Fulkerson 1962). Let us remain, however, with problem 1 for a while longer.

As a first approach to problem 1, we can write out probability equations associated with the model 3.10 through 3.12.

For $i = 2, 3, \ldots, N$, corresponding to 3.10, we have

$$P_i(t) = Pr\left[\bigcap_{b \in B_i} (V_b \leqslant t)\right] \tag{3.14}$$

where $A \cap B$ denotes the intersection of events A and B. For $i = 1, 2, \ldots, N$, corresponding to 3.11, we have

$$Q_i(t) = \int_{s=0}^{\infty} a_i(s) P_i(t - s)\, ds. \tag{3.15}$$

Finally, 3.12 yields for $t \geqslant 0$

$$P_1(t) = 1. \tag{3.16}$$

The expressions 3.14 through 3.16 completely determine the probabilities $P_i(t)$ and $Q_i(t)$ for $i = 1, 2, \ldots, N$, and $t \geqslant 0$. Unfortunately, the random variables $V_1, V_2, \ldots, V_N$ are, in general, not independent, because they are a function of the interconnected geometry of the network. This dependence prevents 3.14 from being broken up into the product $\Pi_{b \in B_i} Q_b(t)$ so that there is no exact way of combining 3.14 through 3.16. As a consequence of this intractability, as well as the practical importance of the problem, a number of different lines of attack have been proposed. A convenient order in which to discuss and evaluate them is the approximate order in which they appeared.

The first method proposed, called the PERT method (Wiest and Levy 1969), proceeded as follows. Let k_i be defined as

$$k_1 = 0 \tag{3.17}$$

$$k_i = \max_{b \in B_i} \{k_b + \underline{E}(W_b)\}, i = 1, 2, \ldots, N, \tag{3.18}$$

where B_i is again the set of immediate predecessors of activity i, and $\underline{E}(W_b)$ is the expected duration of activity b. k_i is the PERT approximation to the expected early starting time for activity i. Since in 3.13 we have assumed that activity N has zero duration, k_N is also an approximation to the duration of the whole network. A critical path of the network is a path of nodes running from node 1 to node N through the network over which the maxima in the calculation of k_N in 3.18 are attained. Intuitively, the critical path is a path of activities with at least as great an expected duration as any other path through the network. A common extension of the PERT method consists of approximating the variance of the network duration by adding the variances of the activities on the critical path (Wiest and Levy 1969). The probability distribution for the entire network, $Q_N(t)$, is then approximated as a normal distribution with the mean k_N and the described estimate of variance.

The PERT method makes sense when the durations of all activities are deterministic or when the expected duration of every activity on the critical path is much greater than that of parallel activities off the critical path. However, it can be quite erroneous when applied to stochastic networks possessing paths of approximately equal duration (Wiest and Levy 1969). It is well known (Fulkerson 1962) that k_N is always an optimistic estimate of the expected network duration; that is, if m_N is the mean of $Q_N(t)$, then

$$k_N \leqslant m_N. \tag{3.19}$$

Both Fulkerson (1962) and Emaghraby (1967) have given ways to calculate better approximations to m_N than the PERT estimate k_N. Their approximations, however, are also optimistic; that is, they are bounded between k_N and m_N. Neither author attempts to find $Q_N(t)$ or an approximation of it. They also do not suggest any revised approximation or estimate for the variance of $Q_N(t)$.

Early analytical attempts to solve problem 1 by Charnes, Cooper, and Thompson (1964) and Martin (1965) failed to yield methods feasible for large practical networks. As noted by Hartley and Wortham (1966), the former paper presents solutions for assumed distributions of the exponential type and for networks with very simple geometry. The latter paper gives a polynomial approximation method for estimating $Q_N(t)$ for which the computational effort increases exponentially with the number of activities in the network. Hartley and Wortham (1966) give an analytical procedure for reducing a series-parallel network into a successively simpler network. Nevertheless, the method becomes intractable for complicated crossing networks. As an antidote for this difficulty, these authors suggest that Monte Carlo simulation be carried out on a network that has been reduced as far as practical using their analytical techniques.

Van Slyke (1963) presents among other matters a study of what has come to be called the straightforward or crude simulation approach. He suggests taking samples, $W_1^k, W_2^k, \ldots, W_N^k$, $k = 1, 2, \ldots, K$, from the distributions $a_1(t)$, $a_2(t), \ldots, a_N(t)$. These draws for the activities are added together according to the model 3.10 through 3.12 to obtain a realization of network duration, V_N^k. Of course, the V_N^k, $k = 1, 2, \ldots, K$, can then be used to construct a histogram of $Q_N(t)$.

A great deal of the subsequent work (Fulkerson 1962, Hammersley and Handscomb 1967, and Shrieder 1966), nicely presented and described by Burt and Garman (1970), has centered around improving upon straightforward simulation. Among the methods which have been adapted from general Monte Carlo analysis (Naylor 1971) are antithetic variates, stratification, and control variates. The main bent of these techniques is toward improved estimation of m_N or $Q_N(t)$ through more efficient use of the samples, W_i^k; that is, attention is directed toward methods which estimate m_N with smaller variance for the same number of samples.

Another method called "conditional Monte Carlo" has been proposed by Burt and Garman (forthcoming), and extended by Garman (1971). This technique is a combination analytical-simulation method in which "unique" activities are identified which lie at most upon a single path through the network. The distributions of the durations of these activities are entered into an analytical network distribution estimator along with samples from the "nonunique" activities. The result is a more efficient method for estimating m_N and $Q_N(t)$.

The analytical and simulation approaches thus far described are often quite complicated and this, together with their newness, partly accounts for the fact that they seem not to be used much in practice. Other reasons are that simulation approaches are still prohibitively costly in computer time for large networks. The analytical approaches, too, work only for relatively small and simple networks. Thus, despite its shortcomings, reliance is still placed on the original PERT method in most applications.

Kleindorfer (1971) has proposed and explicated a straightforward analytical method for obtaining distributions which bound and approximate $P_i(t)$ and $Q_i(t)$, $i = 1, 2, \ldots, N$, from above and below. Since we intend to use this upper and lower bounding method in what follows, we will describe it in fairly great detail here.

The idea for the upper bounds arises directly from a consideration of 3.14. Note from that equation that at any time t

$$P_i(t) = Pr\left[\bigcap_{b \in B_i} (V_b \leqslant t)\right] \leqslant Pr[V_{b^*} \leqslant t] = Q_{b^*}(t) \tag{3.20}$$

where b^* is any element of B_i. Hence, we see that $Q_{b^*}(t)$ is an upper bound for $P_i(t)$. However, it is easy to obtain a still more stringent upper bound for $P_i(t)$ if, instead of just choosing any $b^* \in B_i$, we choose at any time t the $b \in B_i$ which gives a minimum value of $Q_b(t)$. Thus

$$P_i(t) \leqslant \min_{b \in B_i} Q_b(t). \tag{3.21}$$

The difficulty in applying 3.21 is that for a complicated network we will not possess the $Q_b(t)$ because the nodes in B_i themselves will have followed some intertwined network, which makes the calculation of the $Q_b(t)$ impossible. If we have calculated upper bounds for the $Q_b(t)$, $b \in B_i$, previously, however, then it is possible to use these upper bounds in equation 3.21 in place of the $Q_b(t)$ in order to calculate an upper bound for $P_i(t)$ and, as easily follows, for $Q_i(t)$. The variables $P_i'(t)$ and $Q_i'(t)$ defined in 3.22 through 3.24 allow us to carry out these operations.

For $i = 2, 3, \ldots, N$, $t = 0, 1, 2, \ldots$, let

$$P_i'(t) = \min_{b \in B_i} Q_b'(t), \tag{3.22}$$

and for $i = 1, 2, \ldots, N$, $t = 0, 1, 2, \ldots$, let

$$Q'(t) = \sum_{s=0}^{\infty} a_i(s)\, P_i'(t - s). \tag{3.23}$$

For $t = 0, 1, 2, \ldots$, let

$$P_1'(t) = 1. \tag{3.24}$$

These equations are discretized because this is the most convenient form for application. Expanding upon the intuitive reasoning already set out, Kleindorfer proves that for $i = 1, 2, \ldots, N$

$$P_i'(t) \geqslant P_i(t), \tag{3.25}$$

$$Q_i'(t) \geqslant Q_i(t). \tag{3.26}$$

In order to understand the basic ideas behind the lower bounds, consider the following situation. Suppose that node i has two immediate predecessors, b_1 and b_2. Suppose that b_1 and b_2 satisfy the property that

$$Pr[V_{b_1} \leqslant t \mid V_{b_2} \leqslant t] \geqslant Pr[V_{b_1} \leqslant t] = Q_{b_1}(t) \tag{3.27}$$

where $Pr[A \mid B]$ is the conditional probability of event A given event B. If 3.27 is the case, then from 3.14 we can write

$$\begin{aligned} P_i(t) &= Pr[(V_{b_1} \leqslant t) \cap (V_{b_2} \leqslant t)] \\ &= Pr[V_{b_1} \leqslant t \mid V_{b_2} \leqslant t]\, Pr[V_{b_2} \leqslant t] \\ &\geqslant Q_{b_1}(t) \cdot Q_{b_2}(t). \end{aligned} \tag{3.28}$$

We see that the product of the probabilities of the immediate predecessors, b_1 and b_2, is a lower bound for $P_i(t)$. The inequality 3.27 is intuitively appealing because for an acyclic network the information that activity b_2 is finished should allow us to say that the probability of the completion of activity b_1 is greater than it would be had the information about activity b_2 been absent. More generally, we would expect that the product of the finishing time distributions of the nodes immediately preceding node i would constitute a lower bound for $P_i(t)$. Thus,

$$P_i(t) \geqslant \prod_{b \in B_i} Q_b(t). \tag{3.29}$$

Again, the difficulty in using 3.29 will be that the $Q_b(t)$ will often not be obtainable because the nodes B_i themselves will have followed upon some complicated network. If, however, we have already calculated a lower bound for each $Q_b(t)$, then these may be used in 3.29 in place of the $Q_b(t)$ in order to calculate a lower bound for $P_i(t)$. The following definitions of the variables $P_i''(t)$, and $Q_i''(t)$ embody these ideas.

For $i = 2, 3, \ldots, N$, $t = 0, 1, 2, \ldots$, let

$$P_i''(t) = \prod_{b \in B_i} Q_b''(t), \tag{3.30}$$

and for $i = 1, 2, \ldots, N$, $t = 0, 1, 2, \ldots$, let

$$Q_i''(t) = \sum_{s=0}^{\infty} a_i(s)\, P_i''(t-s). \tag{3.31}$$

For $t = 0, 1, 2, \ldots$, let

$$P_1''(t) = 1. \tag{3.32}$$

The intuitive ideas we have just set out can be expanded (Kleindorfer, 1971) to a rigorous proof that:

$$P_i''(t) \leqslant P_i(t), \tag{3.33}$$

$$Q_i''(t) \leqslant Q_i(t). \tag{3.34}$$

Thus, with respect to $P_i(t)$ and $Q_i(t)$, the $P_i'(t)$ and $Q_i'(t)$ are upper bounds and the $P_i''(t)$ and $Q_i''(t)$ are lower bounds.

Equations 3.23 and 3.31 are convolutions that can easily be converted to difference equations quite suited for digital computation. In order to compute the bounds for each activity, one need only take one pass through each of equations

3.22, 3.23, and 3.30, 3.31 over a time interval at least as great as the maximum possible finishing time of that activity. The computational effort rises roughly in linear proportion to the number of activities in the network.

One advantage of the method, other than its computational ease, is that the bounding distributions are obtained for the starting and finishing time of each activity in a network. Once these bounding distributions are obtained, then bounds for expectations can easily be computed as partial solutions for problems 2 and 3 above.

Simple inductive arguments can be used to show that the upper bound $Q_i'(t)$ can be a much better upper bounding approximation to $Q_i(t)$ than that obtained by the PERT method.* Kleindorfer (1971) sets out also an examination of the stringency of the bounds.

Let l_i, m_i, and n_i denote the means of the distributions $Q_i'(t)$, $Q_i(t)$, and $Q_i''(t)$ respectively. Because of 3.26 and 3.34 it follows that for $i = 1, 2, \ldots, N$

$$l_i \leqslant m_i \leqslant n_i; \tag{3.35}$$

that is, the means of the bounding distributions for a given activity, not surprisingly, bound the actual mean. From what we have said about the PERT method, 3.35 can be expanded to

$$k_i \leqslant l_i \leqslant m_i \leqslant n_i. \tag{3.36}$$

Thus, in addition to providing the better (in general) optimistic estimate l_i than the PERT method, the bounding methods also provide the pessimistic estimate, n_i. A survey of the literature has not yielded another method for obtaining a pessimistic estimate of expected network duration† except for the obvious worst possible network duration.

The PERT method for calculating the network time schedule of expected costs and total network costs is based on the direct use of the PERT scheduled activity starting and finishing times (Wiest and Levy 1969), despite the shortcomings in these estimates that we have pointed out.

Different kinds of costs (Kleindorfer, 1971) can always be associated with the different activities in the network. The total amount of resources used will in general depend on the costs for each activity and the durations as well as the starting and finishing times of the activities. Thus, in terms of the random variables U_i and V_i, the total network cost can be represented as a random variable of the form

$$\sum_{i=1}^{N} K_i(U_i, V_i). \tag{3.37}$$

If we knew the actual distributions $P_i(t)$ and $Q_i(t)$, $i = 1, 2, \ldots, N$, we could straightforwardly compute the expected value of 3.37 for any single time t as

*These arguments were not set forth in Kleindorfer nor is it appropriate to set them out here. They can be obtained upon request from the author.

†This point is of more than theoretical interest and may help to explain many of the overruns in time and costs that have occurred in projects in which network planning techniques have been used (Cleland and King, 1968).

well as over any time interval. Such an expectation would simply be the sum of the products of appropriate probabilities and costs. Since, in general, we do not know the values of these distributions, we must be satisfied instead with bounds on these various expectations. We will not enter into the mechanics of how these bounds are computed. For details see Kleindorfer (1971).

Bounds may also be computed for higher moments of any of the costs or any of the distributions $P_i'(t)$, $P_i''(t)$, $Q_i'(t)$ and $Q_i''(t)$. Again, see Kleindorfer.

RESOURCE ALLOCATION PROBLEMS IN NETWORK PLANNING

Let us now discuss problem 4 that was raised above. We are concerned with resource allocation in a network in which certain activities can be delayed or expedited or in which the durations of the activities can be made to vary with resource inputs. The model for such a situation is a generalization of 3.37 and 3.10 through 3.12 of the last section. Let X_i, $i = 1, 2, \ldots, N$, be decision variables which we must choose to optimize

$$\underline{E} \sum_{i=1}^{N} K_i(U_i, V_i, X_i) \tag{3.38}$$

subject to

$$U_i = \max_{b \in B_i} V_b, \quad i = 2, 3, \ldots, N, \tag{3.39}$$

$$V_i = U_i + W_i + X_i, \quad i = 1, 2, \ldots, N, \tag{3.40}$$

$$U_1 = 0. \tag{3.41}$$

where $\underline{E}$ is the expectation operator. Each decision variable X_i (which may be constrained to some interval) can be viewed as a change in the technology of activity i or simply as a time saving or delay. Let us assume that the W_i, $i = 1, 2, \ldots, N$, are random variables with known distributions. In some applications it may have to be also assumed that the distributions for W_i will depend on X_i, and U_i.

The deterministic form of this problem is the so-called CPM model (*C*ritical *P*ath *M*ethod). When deterministic, the model 3.38 through 3.41 constitutes a regular optimization problem. At the present time, there exist many methods and programs for treating it (Wiest and Levy 1969).

Another version of the problem has been treated under the title Decision CPM, (DCPM) by Crowston and Thompson (1967, 1968, 1970). In their work it is assumed that there is a discrete set of different ways that each activity in a network can be performed. Each way may require different resources, and may be tied to or determine choices for activities elsewhere in the network. The problem is to pick from the sets of possible activities so as to optimize a combined cost and time criterion.

When the resources available to a network at any given time are limited, then the deterministic CPM (and DCPM) problem is much more difficult to solve. So far no tractable optimization method for treating it is available. Instead, heuristic simulation programs have been developed (Levy, Thompson, and Wiest 1962; Wiest, 1964, 1967). In these programs either network duration is taken as a constraint and activities are scheduled so that resource usage over time is smoothed to acceptable levels or else the maximum permissible level of resource usage at any one time is set and activities are scheduled to obtain an acceptable network duration.

There are reasons why the resource allocation methods we have been describing (CPM, DCPM, and heuristic programming) have limited usefulness in many important applications. A primary reason is that these methods do not deal adequately with uncertainty. This criticism is probably not as serious an objection in an industrial production scheduling environment where the nature and duration of activities is more definitely determined. But in most social, and in research and development planning (where uncertainty will be important), problems 1, 2, and 3 that we discussed in the previous section must be treated along with problem 4. It is interesting again to note that the CPM, DCPM, and the extant heuristic methods *still use the PERT method for approximating activity starting and finishing times* (Wiest and Levy 1969). Thus, these methods have the shortcomings described in the last section.

One compensating factor should be mentioned. The average research and development planning network will usually possess a much smaller number of activities than the average network in an industrial production scheduling setting. This smallness together with the political and social sensitivities involved in many planning applications will often dictate "custom tailoring" in the rearrangement of activities in order to achieve acceptable resource allocation patterns. For all these reasons (uncertainty, smallness, political and social sensitivity) the classical methods for treating resource allocation problems in networks are probably not germane for many social applications.

A way that we would like to suggest for handling these problems is as follows. In a given exercise, a network containing the ordered foreseeably needed activities should be developed to meet the given planning goals. The activities' descriptions should include uncertainty in activity duration. This network can then be very easily subjected to the bounding distribution analysis we described above in which upper and lower bounds are obtained for expected costs as a function of time, for total costs, and for expected starting and finishing times for each network activity. If any of these bounds conflict with acceptable thresholds, then the network can be rearranged, deterministic delays inserted for certain activities, or certain activities may be redefined. This process can be repeated until an acceptable network is found. In matching expectations against thresholds, it may be helpful to have at hand the bounds on the variances of each of the costs, and starting, and finishing times. These, too, are available using the bounding methods.

THE COMBINED MODEL

A fairly general version of the combined model containing state variable and network submodels follows. Given S_o, choose D_t, $t = 0, 1, \ldots, T - 1$, and X_i,

$i = 1, 2, \ldots, N$, so as to optimize

$$\underline{E}\left\{\sum_{t=1}^{T} H_t(Y_t, S_t, D_{t-1}, V_1, V_2, \ldots, V_N) + \sum_{i=1}^{N} K_i(U_i, V_i, X_i)\right\} \quad (3.42)$$

subject to

$$S_{t+1} = F_t(S_t, D_t, E_t, V_1, V_2, \ldots, V_N) \quad (3.43)$$

$$Y_t = G_t(S_t, D_t, E_t, V_1, V_2, \ldots, V_N) \quad (3.44)$$

$$U_i = \max_{b \in B_i} V_b \quad (3.45)$$

$$V_i = U_i + W_i + X_i \quad (3.46)$$

$$U_1 = 0 \quad (3.47)$$

where the constraints 3.43 through 3.47 hold over the appropriate times and nodes we detailed in the preceding sections. Left out of this formulation are state variable and decision variable constraints in the state variable submodel as well as resource or time constraints in the network submodel.

Note that in this combined model we must choose decision variables from both the network and state variable submodels. Also, the objective function 3.42 includes costs from both submodels so that we are simultaneously taking into account the costs of the system for which we are planning (represented by the state variable submodel) as well as the costs of our system for effecting the operations of the plan (represented by the network submodel). Unfortunately, while we have here the sought depiction of interaction, it proves, not unexpectedly, to be difficult to treat this combined model analytically.

In order to make our discussion more concrete, let us consider a specialized form of the model. Given S_o, choose D_t, $t = 0, 1, 2, \ldots, T-1$, so as to optimize

$$\underline{E} \sum_{t=1}^{T} H_t(Y_t, S_t, D_{t-1}) \quad (3.48)$$

subject to

$$S_{t+1} = F_t(S_t, D_t, E_t) \quad (3.49)$$

$$Y_t = G_t(S_t, D_t, E_t) \quad (3.50)$$

$$E_t = C_t(V_N) \quad (3.51)$$

$$U_i = \max_{b \in B_i} V_b \quad (3.52)$$

$$V_i = U_i + W_i \quad (3.53)$$

$$U_i = 0. \quad (3.54)$$

In this formulation it is only the total network duration in 3.51 that affects the state variable model through the exogenous parameters. Accordingly, we do not have to deal with the joint distribution of the $V_1, V_2, \ldots, V_N$, although bounds for such a joint distribution are available using the bounding methods. A second feature is that we have left off the decision variables, X_i, in the network submodel. This deletion goes along with our discussion of the heuristic treatment of problem 4 in the last section; that is, we are assuming that a satisfactory network has been already constructed, and the only problem left is to choose a decision sequence in the state variable model. In this special model, 3.48 through 3.54, we are, of course, mathematically assuming away the whole problem of balancing the state variable submodel with the network submodel. This special model will be appropriate only when the work represented by the network model is fixed.

Is it possible to treat even this much simpler form of the combined model analytically? If we knew the probability distribution $Q_N(t)$ for the duration of the network submodel, then based on 3.51 we might be able to derive enough statistical information about the random variables E_t, $t = 0, 1, \ldots, T - 1$, to allow analytical treatment of the state variable submodel constituted by 3.48 through 3.51. This remaining state variable problem is one of optimal stochastic control in which we have a system with random parameters. Such problems have received treatment in the control literature (Aoki 1967). The chances for any tractable analytical attack in most applications are probably small (Aoki 1967).

The next analytical alternative, subject to the usual criticisms (Hadley 1964), would be to use the expected values of as many of the random variables as possible and solve the resulting deterministic problem. For example, if we substitute the network expected duration into 3.51, then the model 3.48 through 3.54 reduces to choosing D_t, $t = 0, 1, 2, \ldots, T - 1$, so as to optimize

$$\sum_{t=1}^{T} H_t(Y_t, S_t, D_{t-1}) \tag{3.55}$$

subject to

$$S_{t+1} = F_t(S_t, D_t, E_t) \tag{3.56}$$

$$Y_t = G_t(S_t, D_t, E_t) \tag{3.57}$$

$$E_t = C_t(m_N). \tag{3.58}$$

Unfortunately, we will be balked here too, since, as already noted, we will not, in general, possess the m_N.

In most cases, then, analytical treatment of the problem represented by 3.48 through 3.54 will not be possible. Instead, we will have to resort to simulation, which can be carried out as follows. As a first step, we can subject the network to the bounding distribution analysis already described. In this way, we obtain the bounds on the time schedules of costs, and the bounds on total costs. This information from the network analysis will allow us to proceed to a simulation of the state variable submodel. We can do this in an approximate mean value sense by substituting whichever of l_N or n_N is appropriate into 3.58 for m_N. By "appropriate" we mean that, for example, in estimating completion times we will want to use the pessimistic bound n_N. On the other hand, when estimating when resources will have to be available, we might use the earlier time l_N.

Since we possess the bounding distributions for the network, another alternative is to use these distributions as a basis for *approximate* Monte Carlo simulation of the state variable model. We can, for example, use the lower bounding distribution $Q_N''(t)$, in order to obtain by simulation a distribution for E_t and from thence, by simulation, the distributions for the values of other variables in the state variable submodel. This can be done in the obvious way, by taking draws from $Q_N''(t)$ (or $Q_N'(t)$) as an independent distribution determining the random parameters, E_t. For each of these draws, we simulate the state variable submodel, and from repeated draws we construct the distributions corresponding to the variables in the state variable submodel. By the appropriate use of $Q_N'(t)$ and $Q_N''(t)$ as sampling distributions, it may be possible and desirable in given situations to carry this treatment out to the point of obtaining bounding distributions for the variables in the state variable submodel.

The results of these simulations will be combined estimates of costs from both submodels. If these estimates or any other factors are beyond desirable limits, then the process will have to be repeated after making changes in either or both of the two submodels.

Suppose we are dealing with a situation in which the arrangement and content of the network submodel is flexible whereas the structure of the state variable submodel is fixed. An important instance will be where we have chosen a long-range aggregate planning goal and the fixed state variable submodel shows that the network duration, V_N, must be less than some target time in order to achieve the goal. In such a case, we would rearrange and redefine the network until, say, n_N is less than the target time. All the remarks made about treating problem 4 in the previous section apply here.

In summary, while it is true that analytical treatment of the combined model will seldom be possible, this should not preclude the application of the model in situations where it provides the desired conceptualization of the planning process. In such situations, a combination of treatment using the bounding methods for the network submodel and simulation or analytical methods for the state variable submodel will always be available.

AN EXAMPLE* OF THE USE OF COMBINED NETWORK AND STATE VARIABLE MODELS IN EDUCATIONAL PLANNING

A proposal that there be a massive development of vocational education was widely debated in Pakistan during the summer of 1969. At the same time, there was a commitment on the part of the East Pakistani government to achieve universal grade 1–5 education by 1980 and universal grade 6–8 education by 1985. Traditionally, in East Pakistan vocational education had been carried out at the grade 9–10 level. At the time (in 1969), only a few small vocational education programs were in existence. It was suggested by some that as much as 60 per-

*The material in this section is a very brief version of a paper by Kleindorfer, White, and Benson (1970).

cent of the grade 9-10 enrollments be converted from general education to vocational education.

We decided arbitrarily and for the speculative purposes of this study to adopt the goal of diverting 50 percent of the grade 9-10 students into vocational education by 1980, while simultaneously adhering to the aforementioned goals of universal education for grades 1-5 and 6-8 by 1980 and 1985 respectively. Part of the reason for the arbitrary selection of this 50 percent level was that the time and resources were not available in order to make possible the detailed economic, political, and social analyses required to determine in a more rigorous fashion what the level should be. Indeed, this is part of the work in the proposed planning network to be described below. Second, we felt that any significant increase in vocational education should be preceded or accompanied by a well-integrated comprehensive planning program so that our exercise might be of value no matter what level was eventually chosen.

Two models were constructed: a flow model and a network model. The flow model was devised in order to forecast the aggregate magnitudes of students, teachers, teacher trainees, construction, and funds associated with or required by the educational system of the country. The network model was devised in order to define and lay out the specific planning tasks the government would have to carry out in order to bring a large adequately designed vocational education program into existence.

For the purposes of the study, it was assumed that the government would start the planning described by the network model in January 1971. During the duration of that planning, it was assumed that the diversion rate into vocational education (hereinafter called simply the diversion rate) would increase at 2 percent per year (the approximate figure proposed by the government's five-year plan). Finally, it was assumed that after the completion of the network planning, the diversion rate would increase in much larger increments in order to attain the 50 percent level by 1980.

The reader who has followed our discussions in the preceding sections can see already that the diversion rate will provide the basis for the connections we will make between the network model and the flow model. Before we discuss this connection, however, let us describe each submodel in more detail.

The Flow Model

The structure of the flow model is extensively set forth in Kleindorfer and Roy (1969). The model deals with grades 1-10 of the East Pakistani school system. These grades are split into three grade levels: primary (grades 1-5), middle (grades 6-8), and secondary (grades 9-10). Provision is made for splitting the secondary level into general and vocational education. The model is divided into four sections which are designed to project (1) student enrollments, (2) teacher needs, (3) teacher training institution enrollments, and (4) costs. Each of these sections is comprised of a set of equations and computer programs. The substance of each section of the model follows.

Enrollments. The assumption is made that the number of students in each grade is the sum of the number of students in each of three groups: (1) first-time enrollees, (2) promotees, and (3) repeaters. The number in each component

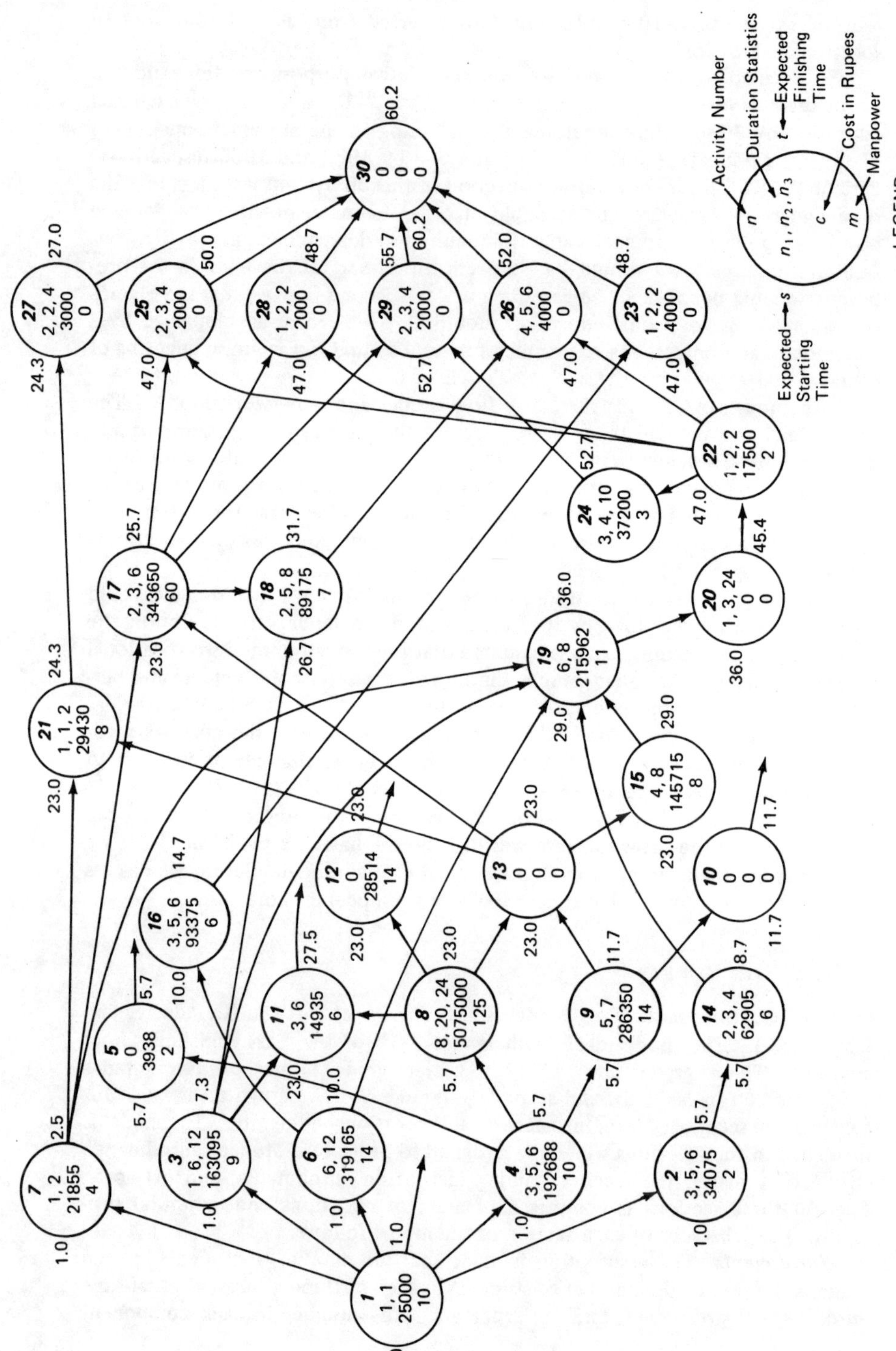
1
1, 1
25000
10
7
1, 2
21855
4
3
1, 6, 12
163095
9
6
6, 12
319165
14
4
3, 5, 6
192688
10
2
3, 5, 6
34075
2
5
0
3938
2
11
3, 6
14935
6
8
8, 20, 24
5075000
125
9
5, 7
286350
14
14
2, 3, 4
62905
6
16
3, 5, 6
93375
6
12
0
28514
14
13
0
0
0
10
0
0
0
21
1, 1, 2
29430
8
15
4, 8
145715
8
19
6, 8
215962
11
17
2, 3, 6
343650
60
18
2, 5, 8
89175
7
20
1, 3, 24
0
0
24
3, 4, 10
37200
3
22
1, 2, 2
17500
2
27
2, 2, 4
3000
0
25
2, 3, 4
2000
0
28
1, 2, 2
2000
0
29
2, 3, 4
2000
0
26
4, 5, 6
4000
0
23
1, 2, 2
4000
0
30
0
0
0
Activity Number
Duration Statistics
Expected Finishing Time
Cost in Rupees
Manpower
Expected Starting Time
LEGEND

Note: An arrow leaving an activity circle without going on to another activity circle (see activities 1, 5, 10, 11, and 12) means that the activity associated with the arrow is an ongoing activity; that is, once that activity starts, it continues for the duration of the project. All costs and men for these activities are assessed monthly.

1. Creation of Technical Education Board
2. Student-body Composition
3. Choice and Channeling Policy for Vocational Education
4. Standard Job Classification
5. Coordination with Ministry of Labour
6. Inventory of Buildings and Equipment
7. Survey of Teachers
8. Training Needed for Each Vocation in Standard Job Classification
9. Inventory of Skills and Enterprises by District
10. Coordination with GSO and National Manpower Council
11. Establish Research and Evaluation Unit
12. Community Information
13. Narrowing of Emphasis
14. Future Student Population
15. Prediction of Future Skill Needs by District
16. Building Methods Research
17. Design Teacher Training Courses
18. Design Headmaster Retraining Course
19. Match Supply and Demand for Technical Education
20. Final Decision on Number and Placement of Vocational Schools
21. Design Training Courses for Agricultural Extension Officers
22. Hire Vocational Education Staff and Plan Timetable
23. Plan Building, Renting, Renovating, and Equipping Program
24. Survey of Availability of Skilled Workers to Be Vocational Teachers
25. Plan General Teachers Training
26. Plan Headmasters Training
27. Plan Agricultural Extension Officers Training
28. Plan Vocational Teachers Training
29. Plan Skilled Workers Training
30. END

Figure 3.1
NETWORK MODEL

group is calculated using admission, promotion, and repetition rates respectively. These rates are supplied to the model exogenously and then applied to population forecasts and projected enrollments for earlier years in order to calculate projected enrollments.

Teacher Needs. Pupil-teacher ratios are used to forecast the total number of teachers that will be needed. Taking into account the rate at which teachers leave the profession, the number of new teachers that will be needed each year is calculated.

Teacher Training Institution Enrollments. The projection of needed new teachers is used to forecast (ahead of time) what teacher training enrollments should be in order to meet teacher needs.

Costs. Total recurring costs are projected using the student enrollment forecasts as data. Projected increases in enrollment are used to calculate the number of pupil places which will have to be constructed each year. Then, from these figures, total capital costs are calculated. Finally, the projected recurring and capital costs are added to obtain the total projected costs.

The Network Model

Most of the information for the network was obtained from the directors of presently existing vocational schools. The network consists of thirty ($N = 30$) interrelated ordered activities dealing with some aspect or other of the following general problems.

The Problem of Selection and Direction. How should students be selected and what programs should the selectees choose?

The Problem of Geography. The course in the schools should bear a relation to the needs of the surrounding areas. What are those needs and how should the vocational program meet them?

The Problem of Curricula. What is a vocational skill? How many such skills are there? What are the components of these skills? What should the vocational programs do to impart these skills to students?

The Problem of Resources. Vocational education is expensive. How should it be planned on both the operating and capital side so as to use as small an amount of resources as possible?

The network of activities designed to deal with these problems is shown in figure 3.1. The detailed nature of the work under each activity is described in Kleindorfer, White, and Benson (1970). The figure is mostly self-explanatory. The statistics for the duration distribution of each activity are written in the line immediately below the number of the activity. All time units are in months. If a single statistic is given, then the activity duration is treated as deterministic with duration equal to that statistic. If two statistics are given, then the activity duration distribution is assumed to be rectangular with outer limits equal to the given statistics. Finally, if three statistics are given, the activity duration distribution is assumed to be triangular, the middle statistic being the mode and the other two statistics being the outer limits of the distribution.

Two kinds of costs were associated with each activity in the network: manpower costs and monetary costs. Each of these costs was further subdivided into permanent and short-term categories. By "short term" we mean that the cost was considered to be incurred only at the beginning or during the duration of the activity and that it ceased being incurred at the completion of the activity.

In accord with our earlier notation, let $Q_i(t)$, $Q_i'(t)$, $Q_i''(t)$ stand for the actual distribution, and the upper and lower bounding distribution for activity i respectively, $i = 1, 2, \ldots, 30$. Let m_i, l_i and n_i respectively denote the means of these three distributions. $Q_{30}'(t)$ and $Q_{30}''(t)$ are the upper and lower bounding distributions for the total network duration. The expected starting and finishing times of the activities shown in figure 3.1 are computed from the lower bounding distributions. Thus, the finishing times are n_i, $i = 1, 2, \ldots, 30$.

Treatment of the Combined Model

The two submodels were viewed as being connected in the fashion of equations 3.49 through 3.54. We will describe explicitly below the form of the constraint 3.51. The bounding distribution analysis of the network showed

Table 3.1
Rate of Diversion of Grade 9 Entrants into Vocational Education

Year	Stage	Fraction of Students Entering Grade 9 Who Are Diverted into Vocational Technical Education	
		Boys	Girls
1969	static	0.003	0.0001
1970		0.003	0.0001
1971		0.003	0.0001
1972	slow growth during planning phase described by network	0.02	0.02
1973		0.04	0.04
1974		0.06	0.06
1975		0.08	0.08
1976		0.10	0.10
1977	rapid growth after planning phase	0.20	0.20
1978		0.30	0.30
1979		0.40	0.40
1980		0.50	0.50
1981	static	0.50	0.50
↓			
1989		0.50	0.50
1990		0.50	0.50

among other things that l_{30} = 56 months and n_{30} = 60 months. The actual expected duration of the network, m_{30}, is, of course, somewhere between these two values. The treatment of the flow model was then carried out in the mean value sense described by 3.56 through 3.58 except that we used the known pessimistic bound, n_{30}, in place of the unknown expected duration, m_{30}.

In effect, then, a target duration for the network was set at 60 months. (In inspecting the network we could find no way to shorten this target duration without changing fundamentally the nature of the planning.) Thus, if the network planning commenced in January 1971, we considered the target time for its completion to be January 1976. Accordingly (see table 3.1), we set the diversion rate in the flow model to increase linearly 2 percent a year up to 1976, and then to increase linearly at 10 percent a year until 1980 at which point the desired 50 percent diversion would be attained. With these diversion rates and other adjustments for grades I through VIII to represent the universal education goals, the flow model was programmed to forecast the corresponding enrollments, teacher needs, and aggregate recurring, capital and total costs.

Table 3.1 shows the diversion rates. Figure 3.2 shows the bounding distributions for the duration of the network. Figure 3.3 contains a summary time schedule for the combined model. The expected manpower needed for the activities in the network is graphed in figure 3.4. The upper and lower bounds for all cost expectations, manpower and monetary, proved identical. Accordingly, no separate notation is shown for them in figure 3.4 or in reporting these costs hereafter. Enrollment projections are summarized in table 3.2. Expected costs from the network model, the flow model, and the combined model are all shown in table 3.3.

Finally, from the material in the example, let us describe in detail the connection which can be made between the network model and the flow model; that is, the exact framing of the connecting constraint 3.51. We have already

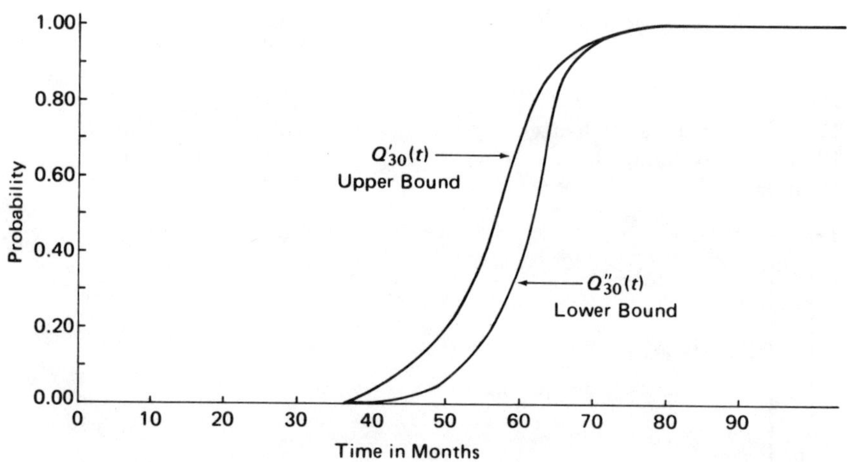

Figure 3.2
BOUNDING DISTRIBUTIONS FOR THE NETWORK DURATION

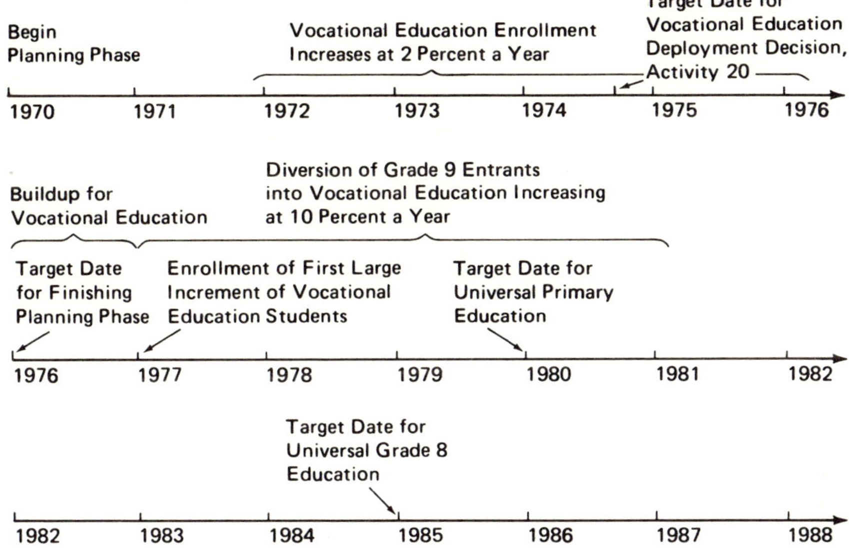

Figure 3.3

TIME LINE FOR THE VOCATIONAL EDUCATION PROGRAM

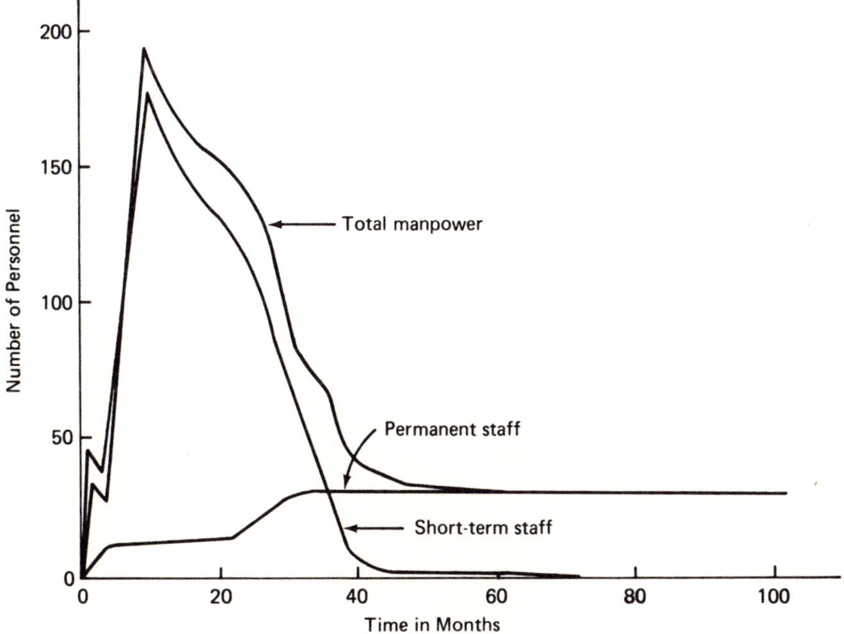

Figure 3.4

EXPECTED NUMBER OF PROFESSIONALS EMPLOYED IN PLANNING THE VOCATIONAL EDUCATION PROGRAM

Table 3.2
Total Enrollment
(figures rounded to thousands)

	Level			
Year	1–5	6–8	9–10 General Education	9–10 Vocational Technical Education
1969	5,504	803	349	2
1970	6,039	908	395	1
1971	6,599	1,044	432	1
1972	7,297	1,209	473	5
1973	8,101	1,353	531	16
1974	8,871	1,582	601	30
1975	9,613	1,888	678	50
1976	10,463	2,261	735	71
1977	11,436	2,675	792	142
1978	12,438	3,131	858	283
1979	13,459	3,688	877	465
1980	14,488	4,322	861	697
1981	15,398	5,035	927	906
1982	16,228	5,826	1,077	1,075
1983	16,891	6,678	1,257	1,257
1984	17,394	7,560	1,458	1,458
1985	17,792	8,397	1,680	1,680
1986	18,228	9,020	1,916	1,916
1987	18,709	9,444	2,159	2,159
1988	19,168	9,727	2,376	2,376
1989	19,594	9,998	2,516	2,516
1990	19,975	10,263	2,602	2,602

discussed the approximate mean value sense in which we treated this constraint in order to construct the table of diversion rates shown in table 3.1. If a more extensive analysis of the combined model than this approximate mean value treatment were required, then an explicit representation of 3.51 might be needed. By "a more extensive analysis" we have in mind the various other methods of treatment described in the last section, such as the use of the bounding distributions in the simulation-flow model.

Let R_y be the diversion rate at year y. R_y is an exogenously determined parameter of the flow model. Let Z be the target year for finishing the network planning. Z is a random variable determined by the network duration. Specifically, let Z be

$$Z = 1971 + [V_{30}/12] \tag{3.59}$$

Table 3.3
Total Costs
(figures given in millions and inflated at 2.5% per annum from 1968)

Year	Cost of Planning Vocational Education Program[1]	Implementation Cost of Vocational Education Program (not including Planning)[2]	Total Cost of Vocational Education Program[3]	Cost of Grades 1-10 Including Vocational Education Program but not Including Planning Vocational Education[2]
1971	7.0	23	30	6,736
1972	.9	62	63	7,942
1973	1.5	97	99	9,641
1974	1.1	138	139	11,524
1975	1.1	172	173	13,509
1976	1.1	497	498	18,562
1977	1.1	1,015	1,016	25,644
1978	1.1	1,434	1,435	31,925
1979	1.1	1,981	1,982	39,561
1980	1.2	2,112	2,113	43,944
1981	1.2	2,101	2,102	47,406
1982	1.2	2,422	2,423	53,821
1983	1.3	2,824	2,825	60,961
1984	1.3	3,269	3,270	68,137
1985	1.3	3,715	3,716	74,030
1986	1.4	4,133	4,134	79,369
1987	1.4	4,323	4,324	82,137
1988	1.4	4,073	4,074	80,343
1989	1.5	3,889	3,891	80,662

[1] network model
[2] flow model
[3] combined model

where $[X]$ is the smallest integer greater than or equal to X. In order to represent the desired 2 percent a year increase in the diversion rate during the network planning period, we can write

$$R_y = .02\,(y - 1971) \tag{3.60}$$

for $1971 \leqslant y \leqslant Z$. In order to represent in large equal increments the increase in the diversion rate required thereafter, we can write

$$R_y = R_Z + (y - Z)\left\{\frac{0.5 - R_Z}{1980 - Z}\right\} \tag{3.61}$$

for $Z < y \leqslant 1980$. Finally

$$R_y = 0.5 \tag{3.62}$$

for $1980 < y$.

The composite of equations 3.59 through 3.62 forms a constraint of the type 3.51. The diversion rates shown in table 3.1 are obtained by letting $Z = 1976$ in equations 3.60 through 3.62.

REFERENCES

Aoki, Masanao. *Optimization of Stochastic Systems.* New York: Academic Press, 1967.

Burt, J. M., Jr., and Garman, M. B. "Monte Carlo Techniques for Stochastic Pert Network Analysis." *Proceedings of the Fourth Conference on Applications of Simulation*, New York, December 1970, pp. 146–53.

Burt, J. M., Jr., and Garman, M. B. "Conditional Monte Carlo: A Simulation Technique for Stochastic Network Analysis." *Management Science* (forthcoming).

Charnes, A.; Cooper, W. W.; and Thompson, G. L. "Critical Path Analysis via Chance Constrained and Stochastic Programming." *Operations Research*, 12, no. 3 (May–June 1964): 460–70.

Cleland, D. I., and King, W. R. *Systems Analysis and Project Management.* New York: McGraw-Hill, 1968.

Correa, Hector. "A Survey of Mathematical Models in Educational Planning." In *Mathematical Models in Educational Planning.* Paris: OECD, 1967.

Correa, Hector. *Quantitative Methods of Educational Planning.* Scranton, Pa.: International Textbook Co., 1969.

Crowston, W. B. "Decision Network Planning Models." Management Sciences Research Report 380, Carnegie Mellon University, Pittsburgh, Pa., May 1968.

Crowston, W. B. "Decision CPM: Network Reduction and Solution." *Operational Research Quarterly*, vol. 21. Oxford: Pergamon Press, 1970. Pp. 435–52.

Crowston, W. B., and Thompson, G. L. "Decision CPM: A Method for Simultaneous Planning, Scheduling, and Control of Projects." *Operations Research* 15, no. 3 (May–June 1967): 407–26.

Elmaghraby, S. E. "On the Expected Duration of PERT Type Networks." *Management Science* 13, no. 5 (January 1967): 299–306.

Fulkerson, D. R. "Expected Critical Path Lengths in PERT Networks." *Operations Research* 10, no. 6 (November–December 1962): 808–17.

Garman, M. B. "A Note on Conditioned Sampling in the Simulation of Stochastic Networks." Working Paper CP-335, Center for Research in Management Science, University of California, Berkeley, May 1971.

Gaver, D. P., and Burt, J. M. "Simple Stochastic Networks: Some Problems and Procedures." Management Sciences Research Report 142, Graduate School of Industrial Administration, Carnegie-Mellon University, Pittsburgh, Pa., July 1968.

Hadley, G. *Nonlinear and Dynamic Programming.* Reading, Mass.: Addison-Wesley, 1964.

Hammersley, J., and Handscomb, D. C. *Monte Carlo Methods.* London: Methuen and Co., 1967.

Hartley, H. O., and Wortham, A. W. "A Statistical Theory for PERT Critical Path Analysis." *Management Science* 12, no. 10 (June 1966): 469–81.

Kleindorfer, G. B. "Bounding Distributions for Stochastic Acyclic Networks." *Operations Research* 19, no. 7 (November–December 1971): 1586–1601.

Kleindorfer, G. B., and Roy, L. M. S. "A Model for Educational Planning in Pakistan." *Pakistan Development Review*, Ford Foundation, Islamabad, Pakistan, December 1969.

Kleindorfer, G. B.; White, M. J.; and Benson, C. S. "A Planning and Implementation Model for Vocational Education in East Pakistan." Ford Foundation, Islamabad, Pakistan, June 1970. (May be obtained from the authors, c/o School of Education, University of California, Berkeley.)

Levy, F. K.; Thompson, G. L.; and Wiest, J. D. "Multi-Ship, Multi-Shop Workload Smoothing Program." *Naval Research Logistics Quarterly* 9, no. 1 (March 1962): 37–44.

MacCrimmon, K. R., and Ryavec, C. A. "An Analytical Study of the PERT Assumptions." *Operations Research* 12, no. 1 (January–February 1964): 16–37.

Martin, J. J. "Distribution of Time through a Directed, Acyclic Network." *Operations Research* 13, no. 1 (January–February 1965): 46–66.

Naylor, T. H. *Computer Simulation Experiments with Models of Economic Systems.* New York: John Wiley and Sons, 1971.

Shrieder, Y. A., ed. *The Monte Carlo Method.* Oxford: Pergamon Press, 1966.

Tou, Julius T. *Modern Control Theory.* New York: McGraw-Hill, 1964.

Van Slyke, R. M. "Monte Carlo Methods and the PERT Problem." *Operations Research* 11, no. 5 (September–October 1963): 839–60.

Wiest, J. D. "Some Properties of Schedules for Large Projects with Limited Resources." *Operations Research* 12, no. 3 (May–June 1964): 395–418.

Wiest, J. D. "A Heuristic Model for Scheduling Large Projects with Limited Resources." *Management Science* 13, no. 6 (February 1967): B359–77.

Wiest, Jerome D., and Levy, Ferdinand K. *A Management Guide to PERT/CPM.* Englewood Cliffs, N.J.: Prentice-Hall, 1969.

*Hector Correa and Gene Leonardson**

4 AN EMPIRICAL TEST OF DIFFERENT METHODS FOR ESTIMATING THE EDUCATIONAL STRUCTURE OF THE LABOR FORCE REQUIRED TO ACHIEVE ECONOMIC TARGETS

A central question in the manpower approach to educational planning is the determination of the number of workers by level of education, i.e., the educational structure of the labor force required to achieve targets for income and productivity. This problem can be described more specifically as follows: Usually, the basic target for an economic plan is the increase of per capita income. This target, plus forecasted or planned information about the size and age structure of the population and the characteristics of the income distribution, makes it possible to determine the target productivity of the labor force. The question, then, is to specify the educational composition of the labor force needed to achieve this target productivity. The three sections of this chapter present a formal statement of the problem just described; several methods of solving it; and, using the data available, the method that is most likely to give satisfactory results.

STATEMENT OF THE PROBLEM

As already observed, a desired level of per capita income at some specific future date is one of the main targets of plans for economic development. In addition, it will be assumed here that the plan for economic development for country i, $i = 1, \ldots, I$ specifies targets for GNP (to be denoted with $\hat{X}_i$) for the

*H. Correa is responsible for the theoretical argument; G. Leonardson, under the direction of H. Correa, collected the data and carried out the required computations.

total number of workers in the labor force (L_i), and for the total energy to be used ($\hat{E}_i$). It will also be assumed that the plan for economic development is consistent with a system of equilibrium prices and wages. For the sake of simplicity, this system will be designated as a target system of prices and wages.

It might appear that too many targets are being assumed for a plan for economic development. In particular, the assumption that both X_i and L_i are available, i.e., that there is a target productivity for the labor force, might be questioned. However, the assumption of a target labor productivity is acceptable because it follows to a large extent from the target per capita income. It should be clear that the rate of growth of per capita income should be proportional to that of labor productivity, unless changes in the participation of the population in the labor force are planned.

The target values of production and labor productivity can be achieved by using any of several alternative educational structures of the labor force, as long as workers with one level of education can be substituted for workers with another level. Nevertheless, it can be said—with some simplifying assumptions—that only one educational structure of the labor force will minimize the cost of achieving the targets of the plan for economic development. Two forms of this minimization problem can be used. In the first one, the costs of producing goods and services and of preparing the required qualified labor are minimized. This approach gives as a by-product "shadow" prices and wages, that could be included among the targets for a plan. In the second approach, a target system of prices and wages is assumed, and the educational structure of the labor force needed to achieve the productivity target is obtained by minimizing costs with respect to the target system of prices and wages.

The first method is better from a conceptual point of view. However, many analytical, statistical and computational problems appear when one tries to apply it in practice. For this reason, the second approach is useful. The manpower approach to educational planning is based on this approach. It will be assumed below that, at least conceptually, the number of workers with educational level $j, j = 1, \ldots, J$ required to achieve the targets of an economic plan is determined by minimizing the cost of achieving the target of the plan, with respect to a target system of prices and wages.

The number of workers with educational level $j, j = 1, \ldots, J$ required to achieve the targets of the economic plan will be denoted here by $\hat{L}_{ij}$. The required educational structure of the labor force is the vector $[\hat{L}_{ij}]$ of dimension J that has the $\hat{L}_{ij}$ as components.

From the definition of $\hat{L}_i$ and $\hat{L}_{ij}$ it is clear that

$$\hat{L}_i = \sum_{j=1}^{J} \hat{L}_{ij}. \tag{4.1}$$

The problem of estimating the required educational structure of the labor force is that of estimating the $\hat{L}_{ij}$ using as data time-series or cross-sectional observations of educational structures, of productivity levels and systems of price and wages, or of related variables. Here it will be assumed that the following data are available:

L_{ijt} = number of workers in country or region $i = 1, \ldots, I$, with educational level $j = 1, \ldots, J$ date $t = 1, \ldots, T_i$ where the same educational classification of the labor force by level of education is valid for all countries. For simplicity, it will be assumed that $T_i = T$ for all i. This assumption could be discarded if needed. Observe that either I or T can be equal to 1, but not both at the same time.

L_{it} = Size of the labor force in country i, year t. Clearly,

$$L_{it} = \sum_{i=1}^{J} L_{ijt}$$

for every i and t.

X_{it} = GNP, country i, date t.

P_{it} = Total population, country i, date t.

E_{it} = Total energy used, country i, date t.

Using these variables, average labor productivity will be defined

$$\pi_{it} = X_{it}/L_{it}.$$

No data on prices and wages are assumed to be available, and none will be used below. This drastic departure from the previous observations is a consequence of the lack of sufficient data for the purpose, and, more important, the lack of appropriate methods for taking advantage of them. We will return to this point later.

A first problem in the use of past educational structures of the labor force $[L_{ijt}]$ to estimate the one required is that the past structures might not be equilibrium structures, i.e., they might not be the ones that minimize the costs of achieving X_{it} with labor productivity.

If this is the case, the estimated required educational structure might not be the one that minimizes the cost of achieving the targets of the economic plan. As a consequence, the manpower and educational plans are likely to perpetuate the inefficiencies that it is assumed they will correct.

These observations show that, before using observed values of the $[L_{ijt}]$ for estimating the required ones, one should verify whether they correspond to equilibrium conditions. To do so, it is necessary to find out whether some wages or prices are changing in relation to others. If this is not the case, the observed $[L_{ijt}]$ do correspond to equilibrium, otherwise, they correspond to disequilibrium conditions.

In theory, if the observed $[L_{ijt}]$ do not correspond to equilibrium conditions, they should be corrected before being used to estimate the educational structure of the labor force required to achieve the targets of the plan.

Unfortunately, the information available—as already observed—is extremely scarce. In addition, even if sufficient data were available, the methods of correcting observed data in order to find the equilibrium values of supply and demand of qualified labor are at best very primitive. For these reasons, existing information without any correction is commonly used. This implies the assumption that the past educational structures are those corresponding to equilibrium. This common practice will be followed here.

SOME METHODS FOR ESTIMATING REQUIRED EDUCATIONAL STRUCTURE OF LABOR FORCE

Regression Analysis

An extremely large number of specific methods can be included in this subsection. For specificity, only the case in which equations of the form

$$Y_j = A_j Z^{bi} \qquad j = 1, \ldots, J \tag{4.2}$$

are fitted will be considered. In these equations, A_j and b_j are parameters to be estimated. The subscript j indicates that these two parameters must be estimated for each level of education. They are specific for each level of education in the sense that they change with them but do not change from country to country or date to date.

The variables Y_j and Z can have many different meanings. Below, Y_j will take the following three forms: L_j/L, L_j/X, and L_j/P, while Z will be made equal to X/L, X/P, L/X, E/L and E/P where the variables have the meaning given in the preceding section. The subscripts i and t for country and for date denote different observations of the variables.

The three alternatives for the dependent variables and five for the independent variables include most of the alternatives considered in Cornelisse (1966), Layard and Saigal (1966), and OECD (1970). These three studies can be considered the most representative statistical analyses of the demand for qualified labor.

A point that does not seem to have been observed is that, since it is possible to pass from some of the regression equations proposed above to others using simple mathematical transformations, the estimated coefficients and estimates derived from the regression equations will present special regularities. Two examples will be discussed. First, since

$$X/L = (L/X)^{-1},$$

the coefficients b_j obtained with L/X as independent variables are equal to those obtained with X/L, multiplied by -1. Second, the coefficient of

$$(L_j/P) = \hat{A}\,(X/P)^{\hat{b}}$$

and

$$(L_j/X) = \bar{A}\,(X/P)^{\bar{b}}$$

are related by the equations

$$\hat{A} = \bar{A}$$

and

$$\hat{b} = 1 + \bar{b}.$$

In addition, the estimates of L_j derived from these two equations will be equal. Other relations of the coefficients A_j and b_j obtained with the different forms of Y_j and Z in equation 4.2 will become evident later.

The regression method used to estimate A_j and b_j is the standard one and no explanation of it is required. Once these estimates—to be denoted as RA_j and Rb_j, the R emphasizing regression—are obtained, the estimates of Y for a specific country i can be obtained with the formula

$$(RY_{ij}) = (RA_j)\,\hat{Z}_i^{(Rb_j)} \qquad i = 1, \ldots, I$$

where the subscript i denotes that the value of the independent variable $\hat{Z}_i$ is evaluated with the target values $\hat{L}_i$, $\hat{P}_i$, $\hat{X}_i$, and for $\hat{E}_i$ for country i. As a consequence, the values of RY_{ij} are specific for country i and educational level j. However, their evaluation is based on the parameters A_j and b_j which are specific only for a level of education and not for a country.

The method used to pass from the RY_{ij} to the estimated required number of workers by level of education does not need any explanation. These estimates will be denoted as RL_{ij}. The quality of these estimates is evaluated in the final section.

Methods Based on Correction of Estimates RL_{ij} Obtained with Regression Equations

A serious limitation of the estimates obtained with the regression equations is that in general they do not satisfy the following conditions:

$$\hat{L}_i = \sum_{j=1}^{J} RL_{ij},$$

i.e., the total of the estimated components RL_{ij} of the educational structure of the labor force needed to achieve the targets of the plan in general is not equal to the size of the labor force $\hat{L}_i$ included in those targets. Clearly, this is a serious limitation of those estimates.

Different methods can be used to modify the RL_{ij} so that the corrected values—to be denoted as CL_{ij}, C for corrected—satisfy the condition

$$\hat{L}_i = \sum_{j=1}^{J} CL_{ij}.$$

The possibility that will be used here is that of applying the formula

$$CL_{ij} = RL_{ij}^{*}\,\hat{L}_i / RL_i$$

where

$$RL_i = \sum_{j=1}^{J} RL_{ij},$$

i.e., in order to obtain the CL_{ij}, the RL_{ij} are corrected in proportion to their value.

Methods Based on Regression Subject to Constraints

From the method of estimation of the coefficients A_j and b_j in equation 4.2, it is clear that they are independent of the natural constraint in 4.1 of equality between the total of the required number of workers by level of education and the planned size of the labor force. In fact, this means that each of the J regression equations is independent of each of the others, and of the fact that

$$L_{it} = \sum_{j=1}^{J} L_{ijt}$$

for every value of i and t.

This limitation is not really overcome with the method presented in the previous subsection. Only one of the most obvious defects of the results obtained is somewhat artificially eliminated. The fact that the A_j and b_j are independent for different values of j still remains.

In the method used in Correa et al. (1964) and Correa (1969), which is also presented here, the constraint imposed by the relationship between estimated required number of workers by level of education and the target total number of workers will be explicitly considered in the estimation of the parameters of the regression equations. To do so, it is necessary to consider simultaneously the regression equations for all levels of education, and not, as before, an independent equation for each level.

To explain this method, some additional notation will be used. First, it will be assumed the $T = 1$ for all countries in the sample. This means pure cross-sectional data are available, an assumption that can be discarded if this is not the case. Also, let

$$N_{ij} = L_{ij}/X_i,$$

$$N_i = L_i/X_i = \sum_{j=1}^{J} N_{ij},$$

$$\hat{N}_{ij} = \hat{L}_{ij}/\hat{X}_i,$$

and

$$\hat{N}_i = \hat{L}_i/\hat{X}_i.$$

Finally, the estimated values of $\hat{N}_{ij}$ will be denoted as EN_{ij}. The E is used to emphasize elasticity, since the estimates are derived using properties of the elasticities of N_{ij} with respect to N_i.

The elasticity e_{hj} of N_{hj} with respect to N_h is, by definition,

$$e_{hj} = \frac{dN_{hj}}{dN_h} * \frac{N_h}{N_{hj}}. \tag{4.3}$$

From 4.3 it follows that

$$\hat{N}_{hj} = N_{hj} + e_{hj}N_{hj}(\hat{N}_h - N_h)/N_h \tag{4.4}$$

It can easily be verified that

$$\hat{N}_h = \sum_{j=1}^{J} \hat{N}_{hj} \tag{4.5}$$

when the elasticities satisfy

$$\sum_{j=1}^{J} e_h N_{hj}/N_h = 1. \tag{4.6}$$

It should be observed that condition 4.5 is equivalent to condition 4.1.

From the previous analysis it can be concluded that the problem of estimating the $\hat{L}_{ij}$ satisfying condition 4.1 reduces to that of estimating the e_{bj} satisfying condition 4.6.

Elasticities are usually estimated by applying regression techniques to the equation

$$N_j = A_j N^{e_j}$$

where the subscript for country has been eliminated to emphasize the fact that the estimates obtained are not country specific. More to the point, the estimates for the e_j are obtained by minimizing

$$F_j = \sum_{i=1}^{I} (n_{ij} - e_j n_i)^2 \tag{4.7}$$

where

$n_{ij} = \log N_{ij} - M(\log N_{ij})$,
$n_i = \log N_i - M(\log N_i)$,
$M(\ )$ denotes mean of ( ).

This usual method of estimating e_j will be modified here to estimate the e_{hj}. The modification consists of minimizing

$$F = \sum_{j=1}^{J} \sum_{i=1}^{I} (n_{ij} - e_{hj} n_i)^2 \tag{4.8}$$

subject to 4.6.

It should be clear that with the procedure outlined, the estimators or the e_{hj} are not independent among themselves for the different values of j, and also that the stimators are not only specific for educational level j, but also for country b.

The minimization of 4.8 subject to 4.6 with respect to e_{hj} is obtained using Lagrange multipliers. The estimators of the e_{hj} are given by the formula

$$Ee_{hj} = S_j + N_{hj}\left(N_h - \sum_j S_j N_{hj}\right) \bigg/ \sum_j N_{hj}^2 \tag{4.9}$$

where

Ee_{hj}, estimator of e_{hj},

and

$$S_j = \sum_{i=1}^{I} n_{ij} n_i \bigg/ \sum_{i=1}^{I} n_i^2, \tag{4.10}$$

i.e., the S_j are the estimators that would be obtained for the elasticities with the minimization of F_j in 4.7. Formula 4.9 shows that the e_{hj} have two parts, one common to all countries but specific to educational level j, and another specific to educational level j of country h. It is interesting to observe that this second part is determined not only by the conditions of the labor force with educational level j in country h, but also all the educational levels in all the countries. This is the consequence of the components $\Sigma_j\ S_j N_{hj}$ and $\Sigma_j\ N_{hj}^2$ in the second term.

To obtain the estimated values of the $\hat{N}_{hj}$—to be denoted as EN_{hj}—formula 4.4 is applied, using Ee_{hj} instead of e_{hj}. The EN_{hj} satisfy the condition

$$\hat{L}_h = \sum_{j=1}^{J} EN_{hj}$$

since Ee_{hj} satisfies condition 4.6.

STATISTICAL EVALUATION OF THE METHODS

To apply the methods described for estimating the required educational structure of the labor force, time-series or cross-sectional data of L_{ijt}, L_{it}, P_{it}, X_{it} and E_{it} and of the target values $\hat{L}_i$, $\hat{P}_i$, $\hat{S}$, and $\hat{E}_i$ are needed. Here, for the first set of data information on 23 countries* for $t = 1950$ will be used. As targets of hypothetical plans for economic development, data for $t = 1960$ for 14 of these 23 countries will be used. In addition, it will be assumed that the educational structures of the labor force required to achieve the targets of the economic plans in these 14 countries are the structures actually observed, i.e., L_{ij1960}. These observed educational structures in 1960 will be denoted with $\hat{L}_{ij}$. Four levels of education are considered: $j = 1$, no education; $j = 2$, from 1 to 6 years; $j = 3$, from 7 to 12 years, and $j = 4$, more than 12 years.

These data are used with each of the variations of the methods presented in the previous section. Fifteen alternative estimates of the required educational structure of the labor force—i.e., 15 vectors, components RL_{ij}—are obtained for each country, using regression methods. Again, 15 estimated educational structures CL_{ij} are obtained with the second method described in the previous section. Finally, one vector EL_{ij} per country is obtained with the third method described. The different estimates will also be denoted with $\overline{L}_{ijg}$, for $g = 1, \ldots, 31$.

A review of the estimates shows that those obtained with the elasticity method used for Greece and Japan are unacceptable, because some estimated components of the educational structure of the labor force are negative. For this reason, in some comparisons between results obtained using different methods, the results for Greece and Japan will not be included.

The data are collected from the UN Statistical Yearbook and UN Demographic Yearbook. The 23 countries with data for 1950 are Argentina, Bolivia, Brazil, Canada, Chile*, Colombia, Costa Rica, Cuba, Ecuador*, El Salvador*, Guatemala, Finland*, Greece*, Japan*, Mauritius*, Mexico*, Nicaragua*, Panama*, Paraguay, Portugal*, Puerto Rico*, United States*, Venezuela. Countries marked with an asterisk also have data for 1960.

This elimination is not completely arbitrary. A technical planner faced with negative $\overline{L}_{ij}$ will not consider them in his work. His problem is to make his selection from among estimates that are not obviously unacceptable.

In order to compare the RL_{ij}, CL_{ij}, and EL_{ij} estimates, they are compared with the observed $\hat{L}_{ij}$, using the following formulas:

$$\overline{W}_{ig} = \sum_{j=1}^{4} \frac{(\overline{L}_{ijg} - \hat{L}_{ij})^2}{L_{ij}} \qquad \begin{array}{l} i = 1, \ldots, 14 \text{ for country} \\ g = 1, \ldots, 31 \text{ for method} \end{array}$$

and

$$\overline{W}_g = \sum_{i=1}^{I} W_{ig} \qquad g = 1, \ldots, 31.$$

The coefficients $\overline{W}_{ig}$ and $\overline{W}_g$ will be called proportional square errors.

A superficial review of the coefficients $\overline{W}_{ig}$ and $\overline{W}_g$ showed that in most cases the estimates obtained with the third method were the most acceptable. For this reason, the analysis below will be reduced to a comparison of the estimates obtained using the first and second methods with those obtained using the third method.

In table 4.1 the minimum values of $\overline{W}_{ig}$ for $g = 1, \ldots, 15$ to be denoted as RW_{ig} and of $\overline{W}_{ig}$ for $g = 16, \ldots, 30$ to be denoted as CW_{ig} and for each i are compared with the value of $\overline{W}_{i31}$, to be denoted as EW_i. This comparison

Table 4.1
Comparison of the Indices of Quality of the Estimate Obtained with the Methods Described

	$(\min RW_{ig})/EW_i$ $1 \leqslant g \leqslant 15$			$(\min CW_{ig})/EW_i$ $16 \leqslant g \leqslant 30$		
Country	Dependent	Independent	Quotient	Dependent	Independent	Quotient
Canada	L_{ij}/X_i	L_i/X_i	.51	L_{ij}/X_i	X_i/P_i	.22
Chile	L_{ij}/X_i	X_i/P_i	7.67	L_{ij}/X_i	X_i/P_i	2.75
Ecuador	L_{ij}/L_i	X_i/P_i	1.05	L_{ij}/X_i	X_i/P_i	1.01
El Salvador	L_{ij}/L_i	E_i/P_i	65.68	L_{ij}/X_i	E_i/P_i	88.80
Finland	L_{ij}/X_i	X_i/P_i	390.16	L_{ij}/X_i	X_i/P_i	1,789.77
Greece	L_{ij}/X_i	E_i/P_i	.01	L_{ij}/X_i	E_i/P_i	1.90
Japan	L_{ij}/L_i	E_i/P_i	2.14	L_{ij}/X_i	E_i/L_i	5.05
Mauritius	L_{ij}/L_i	E_i/P_i	10.16	L_{ij}/X_i	E_i/P_i	5.45
Mexico	L_{ij}/X_i	X_i/P_i	2.85	L_{ij}/X_i	X_i/P_i	4.12
Nicaragua	L_{ij}/L_i	E_i/P_i	6.68	L_{ij}/X_i	E_i/P_i	10.64
Panama	L_{ij}/X_i	E_i/L_i	4.76	L_{ij}/X_i	E_i/P_i	3.49
Portugal	L_{ij}/X_i	L_i/X_i	.19	L_{ij}/X_i	L_i/X_i	.13
Puerto Rico	L_{ij}/P_i	E_i/P_i	.26	L_{ij}/X_i	E_i/P_i	.17
United States	L_{ij}/X_i	X_i/P_i	.79	L_{ij}/X_i	L_i/X_i	.79
Mean			35.21			136.74

shows that in 5 of the 14 cases, some regression estimates performed better than the elasticity estimates. The same is true in 4 of the 14 cases for the corrected estimates obtained with the second method. These observations should not be interpreted in the sense that, by using simple regression, one has a .36 probability of obtaining better estimates than with the elasticity estimates, or that using corrected estimates assures a .29 probability of doing so. The reason for this is that there are 15 alternative regressions and corrected estimates from which the best ones were selected to be compared with the elasticity estimates. When this point is considered, one observes that only two regressions with L_{ij}/X_i as dependent and L_i/X_i as independent give better estimates than the elasticity method. The same is true for two regressions with L_{ij}/X_i and E_i/P_i, and for one with L_{ij}/X_i and X_i/P_i. This shows that the probability of doing better with a regression estimate is only .14 if the researcher knows which regressions equation should be used. In other words, in 86 percent of all cases one would do better using the elasticity estimates. Similar conclusions can be reached from an analysis of the comparison of the corrected estimates with the elasticity estimates.

The results just presented are given in table 4.2, where the quotients 1,000* EW_g/RW_g and 1,000* EW_g/CW_g are presented. These quotients show that, on the average, the elasticity estimates had an average proportional square error for all the countries ranging from 17 per thousand to 3,207 per thousand in the case when Greece and Japan are included. When these two countries are eliminated, these indices range from .27 per thousand to 8.4 per thousand. In other words,

Table 4.2

Comparison of Different Values of EW_{ij} RW_i and CW_i

Dependent Variables	Independent Variables				
	X_i/L_i	X_i/P_i	E_i/L_i	E_i/P_i	L_i/X_i
Values of 1,000 EW_i/RW_i including Greece and Japan					
L_{ij}/L_i	22.77	17.49	875.87	1260.05	22.77
L_{ij}/P_i	45.56	39.62	1746.52	2484.53	45.56
L_{ij}/X_i	22.77	39.62	1885.14	3207.35	22.77
Values of 1,000 EW_i/RW_i excluding Greece and Japan					
L_{ij}/L_i	1.73	5.45	.83	1.27	1.73
L_{ij}/P_i	2.97	8.47	1.42	2.12	2.97
L_{ij}/X_i	1.73	8.47	.16	.27	1.73
Values of 1,000 EW_i/CW_i including Greece and Japan					
L_{ij}/L_i	46.71	43.41	361.20	478.61	46.71
L_{ij}/P_i	46.71	43.31	361.20	478.61	46.71
L_{ij}/X_i	46.71	43.31	361.20	478.61	46.71

Table 4.3
Comparison of Actual and Estimated Educational Structures of the Labor Force in Ecuador and Mexico

Years of Education	j	Ecuador L_{3j}	Ecuador EL_{3j}	Mexico L_{gj}	Mexico EL_{gj}
0	1	446,804	485,611	4,688,088	2,931,000
1-6	2	760,014	958,970	5,375,201	6,922,302
7-12	3	386,745	136,164	562,183	723,332
13+	4	8,979	21,976	144,315	193,153
Totals		1,602,542	1,602,542	10,769,787	10,769,787

the error in the estimated required educational structure with the elasticity method is likely to be less than 1 percent of the error with either of the other methods.

To complete this presentation, in table 4.3 actual L_{ij} and EL_{ij} are compared for Ecuador and Mexico, the countries that rank 7th and 8th in the low-to-high order of values of EW_i. This information is somewhat surprising. It shows that, despite the fact that the method of elasticities gives a substantially lower value for $\overline{W}_{ig}$ and $\overline{W}_g$, the values of EL_{ij} can be quite different from those actually required, i.e., $\hat{L}_{ij}$.

CONCLUSIONS

This chapter attempted to determine how well a technical planner can estimate, with the simple methods commonly used, the required educational structure of the labor force. The first conclusion is that, regardless of which method analyzed here is used, the difference between estimates and actual requirements can be large. On the other hand, the method of elasticities seems to give substantially better results than simple regression methods or methods based on a posteriory correction of the results obtained with regression.

The next problem that would have to be considered is whether the policy decisions based on the estimates described above are better or worse than those made without those estimates or with other types of estimates. This problem, which is one of the most important in planning, has not received the attention it deserves.

REFERENCES

Cornelisse, P. A. "The Educational Structure of the Labor Force: A Statistical Analysis." Mimeographed. Netherlands Economic Institute, Rotterdam, 1966.

Correa, H., et al. "Ha prestado la planificación económica atención suficiente a la educación?" *El Trimestre Económico*, October/December 1964.

Correa, H. *Quantitative Methods of Educational Planning.* Scranton, Pa.: International Textbook Co., 1969.

Layard, P. R. G., and Saigal, J. C. "Educational and Occupational characteristics of manpower: An international comparison." *British Journal of Industrial Relations* 4 (July 1966).

OECD. *Occupational and Educational Structures of the Labor Force and Levels of Economic Development.* Paris: OECD, 1970.

Martin Carnoy

5 THE SOCIAL BENEFITS OF IMPROVING PUPIL PERFORMANCE

As societies begin to concern themselves with equal opportunity, there is increased focus on improving the performance of pupils in school. In the United States, attempts at that improvement are represented by performance contracting, voucher plans, upgrading of teachers through accountability, and technical innovations such as computer-assisted instruction and educational television. In almost all these efforts, evaluation is carried out in terms of school performance rather than in terms of the social benefits that increased performance may or may not produce.

This criterion for educational decision making may make sense to parents, teachers, administrators, and even many pupils, but it stands on very shaky ground. First, in order to compare the improvement in school performance *at different levels of schooling*, we either need a uniform measure of school performance applicable to children at all levels of schooling, or a common social value into which increases on different tests can be translated. Second, the evaluation of investment in improved pupil performance (as compared to other investments) has to be estimated in terms of increased school performance's contribution to social output. This contribution can be direct: increasing performance at a given level of schooling may, for example, cause graduates to learn more than before. It may also be indirect: increasing performance may increase the average number of years that students attend school, and this may increase the average earnings in the economy.

This chapter presents a model for analyzing the social benefits of increasing pupil "quality" and assesses the empirical evidence available on the various components of the model. It is written from an economist's point of view; that is, it focuses on the *economic* benefits of increasing student performance in school. Nevertheless, much of the analysis could be applied to political participation and other benefits associated with schooling. Since most of the empirical work done on the output of schooling measures that output by student exam performance, the analysis' conclusions apply primarily to the relationship between pupils' quality as measured by student exam performance and their income as members of the labor force. Again, the model can be used to relate other measures of school output, such as "modernization," to other measures of social benefits.

On the evidence available, we conclude that economic benefits to increasing aggregate student performance in school are probably higher at lower levels of school than at higher levels. At these lower levels of school, the return to higher performance will be higher if the primary reason that students do not take more school is actually academic performance (urban primary schools, for example) rather than the lack of facilities to accommodate students (rural primary schools in nonindustrialized countries, for example).

A MODEL FOR ANALYZING CHANGES IN SOCIAL OUTPUT RESULTING FROM CHANGES IN SCHOOL PERFORMANCE*

We can build a simple model for measuring the social benefits of any change in pupils' exam score, level of socialization ("modernization"), or other measures of school output. These measures of school output can be considered estimates of "student performance." Social benefits can be measured by economic performance, political participation, and other measures of societal well-being. In the model we express any component of the social benefits of schooling at age i (B_i) as a function of some component of pupil performance j in school (A_j), the grade level attained (G), and the sex (x) of the graduate. (The model assumes that once a student graduates from a certain level of school with a certain level of performance in school, he or she will not be discriminated against on the basis of social class, ethnic identification, or race. Sex has been included in the model because women almost universally receive lower social benefits from schooling than men. Where class, racial, or ethnic discrimination is practiced in labor-force hiring or wages, those variables should also be included in equation 5.1.)

$$B_i = f(A_j, G, X) \tag{5.1}$$

In turn, the grade level attained is also a function of the quality of schooling and the social class of the students.

(Racial and ethnic identification can be added to the function in equation 5.2 if grade attainment is related to such identification as well as to social class):

$$G = g(A_j, S) \tag{5.2}$$

*For research on a similar model, see Johnson and Stafford (1970); for other attempts to estimate the benefits of the "quality" of schooling, see Welch (1966) and Morgan and Sinageldin (1968).

The increase in social benefits of schooling for a given age, sex, and social class of students due to some increase in pupil performance is found by taking the derivative of equation 5.1:

$$dB_{isx} = \frac{\partial B_{isx}}{\partial A_j} + \frac{\partial B_{isx}}{\partial G} \cdot \frac{\partial G}{\partial A_j} \tag{5.3}$$

The change in the particular component of social benefits (dB_{isx}) is therefore a function of the change in social benefits due directly to the change in pupil performance for a *given* school completion level ($\partial B_{isx}/\partial A_j$) plus the change in benefits due to a change in average grade-completion level times the change in average completion level due to a change in school performance (increased retention rate).

In order to measure the increased benefits due to a change in pupil performance, then, we must know not only the direct social benefits of an increase in that indicator, but also the effect that the indicator has on grade-level attainment of pupils and the social benefits associated with increased time spent in school. If we know these three relationships, we can estimate the total effect on social benefits of a change in the quality of schooling. The present value of this increase in benefits (assuming that benefits at various ages represent the expected future benefits of an increase in student quality) equals:

$$P_{sx} = \sum_{k=1}^{n} \frac{dB_{isx}}{(1+r)^k}; \tag{5.4}$$

where r = social discount rate, and k = age i—age at completing school.

In the analysis of schooling benefits, we assume that the benefits of increased investment in human capital accrue to those who take the schooling. The equations above refer only to social product captured by students/workers. However, if the economy is characterized by monopsony or oligopsony capitalism, or by discrimination on sex, ethnic, or racial grounds, part of the product of higher quality schooling will be picked up by owners of physical rather than human capital. From that point of view, since it only measures the return to those taking schooling, equation 5.3 underestimates the social value of improving performance.*

This chapter discusses each component on the right side of equation 5.3 separately, even though they are related to each other. We know most about the social benefits of spending more time in school ($\partial B_{isx}/\partial G$) so the analysis begins with that component. There are also a number of general issues in the estimation of social benefits covered in the discussion of the value of more schooling ($\partial B_{isx}/\partial G$), such as the choice of productivity or income for estimating the economic benefits to society of more schooling and better performance in

*A society should also consider the distributions of product on wage-earners' well-being. The income distribution effect may more than offset the benefits accruing to owners of physical capital from improved schooling.

school and the problem of marginal and average benefits to investment in additional schooling.

THE SOCIAL BENEFITS OF INCREASING THE AMOUNT OF TIME SPENT IN SCHOOL ($\partial B_{isx}/\partial G$)

Observed Income Differentials as a Measure of Social Benefits

Since the mid-1930s (Walsh 1935) a number of studies in the economics of education have equated the benefits of schooling to the increased income earned by those with additional years of school (Schultz 1964, Blaug 1967). In almost every country of the world, and in the United States in all census years for which data are available (1940–70), we observe that those with more schooling earn, on the average, more than those with less schooling within the same sex, racial, or ethnic group. Observed income differences are generally identified as being *caused* by increased schooling. The individual assesses the economic return to going further in school by the additional income he or she expects to earn: the average income at various ages of those with the next highest level of schooling. This is a rational benchmark in choosing whether or not to continue attending school. Of course, other factors may enter into this choice, such as the desire to learn more for the sake of learning, the higher status associated with having a higher level of schooling, the pain or pleasure of sitting in classrooms and taking tests, the fun of organized athletics and other activities, etc. These are the direct consumption components of schooling. But the *individual* does not have to concern himself with the effect his taking more schooling has on other individuals in the society or on the collectivity of society. The private economic benefits of taking more schooling can therefore be measured by the increase in income the individual expects to earn with the additional amount of schooling. In estimating the *social* benefits to increasing the average schooling of individuals, the appropriate measure is subject to much more controversy. This controversy has revolved around the discrepancy between additional income and "productivity" as a measure of the economic contribution to society of investment in schooling.

If there are social costs or benefits to the society from individuals deciding to take more or less schooling which are not borne by or accrue to the individual, average social benefits net of social costs will not equal average net private benefits. Many economists, as well as educators, have argued that not only does an educated society benefit directly from the increased productivity of its individual members, but also that there are "external" rewards to the society from a high average level of schooling which do not necessarily accrue to those who receive more schooling. Thus, it is generally assumed (Agency for International Development 1969) that a more schooled society is a more *stable* and more *democratic* society; that more schooling, especially university training, produces leadership and research which has very high payoffs in better societal management and progress; and that skilled individuals in key positions throughout society teach those around them to be more productive. In all these cases, it is argued, the individual will not capture his entire contribution to society through his increased income; therefore, the social benefits to increased schooling cannot be measured solely by the increased average income of those who get the schooling.*

Differences in wages or income received, therefore, do not necessarily equal "productivity" differences among workers with different amounts of schooling. In the United States, for example, nonwhites, Spanish-surname Americans, and women receive significantly less income on the average than Euro-American males for, in many cases, exactly the same job classification. It would be difficult to argue that the "productivity"—the social contribution—of groups discriminated against is lower than that of other workers. Yet, their observed *incomes* are lower. Furthermore, in many countries, including the United States, a large fraction of the highly schooled labor force is employed by the public sector. This sector includes the public bureaucracy defense industries, and the schools and universities themselves (Thias and Carnoy 1972). Since the public sector produces public goods, whose value is not determined in a competitive marketplace, it is difficult to measure the absolute productivity or market price of labor working in the sector. A discrepancy between productivity and income could bias the estimated social value of schooling.

The criticism by John Vaizey, Thomas Balogh, P. P. Streeten, and others (Blaug 1970) that observed income differences among those with different amounts of schooling are not valid measures of the *social* benefits of schooling attacks the neoclassical assumption of equality between income and marginal product of labor. In addition, these critics argue that a significant discrepancy exists between marginal social product of labor, which would include the external social production and consumption benefits of schooling, and the observed average income of those with a given amount of schooling. The discussion between the critics and the neoclassicists, such as G. Becker (1964) and T. W. Schultz (1964), has therefore centered on the degree of distortion in capitalist economies between productivity and price of labor, and the significance of externalities in social costs or benefits. As already mentioned, price-productivity distortion is a function of monopolization (or monopsonization) of society, discrimination in the hiring of labor, perhaps unionization of the labor force, and the pricing policies of the public sector.

However, the critics of the income-benefits approach avoid the real issue: What, after all, is the meaning of "productivity"? The problem that has plagued traditional economists seeking to apply marginal productivity theory to personal income distribution is that the theory of demand for commodities, including labor services, interrelates the prices and quantities of *homogeneous* goods. But workers do not supply a homogeneous good. Rather, they supply a set of physical and mental attributes such as physical strength, intelligence, submissiveness, dependability, ambition, etc. On the demand side, "What employers seek is

*Such externalities would have to be added to the benefits in equation 5.3 even if the market for labor were perfectly competitive and there were no discrimination.

'productive capacity' which is separated from 'personal attributes' by a thick curtain of socio-phychological variables conveniently labeled incentive, attitude, and experience. . . . It is safe to say that the role of these variables in the theory of wages is not well understood" (Reder 1969).

If we assert that the movement of wages acts to equilibrate the "quantity" of labor supplied to the firm to the "quantity" demanded, then we must formulate a set of transformations between the units of talent that measure ability and the units of productive capacity that measure employer demand. But, as Reder (1969) admits, no one has been able to specify such a set of transformations until now (Gintis 1971). Thus, human capital theory has identified schooling, ability, and on-the-job training as the most important components of "productivity," but it may very well be that these are imperfect proxies for other characteristics supplied and demanded. Schooling itself *may not contribute to productivity* but may merely act as a screening device for those characteristics of workers which do. "It is at least possible that the characteristics employers seek—consciously or otherwise—cannot be transformed into those that workers supply. If this is the case, imbalances between supply and demand . . . have to be adjusted by non-price rationing and/or by adjustments of characteristics offered. . . . If so, institutional rules governing these procedures would have to be built into the theory as an integral part" (Reder 1969).

In the absence of other easily obtainable information on individuals' behavior, employers may use years of schooling as a convenient hiring device. The school system may also weed out those who do not have "productive" traits. If so, there will be a high correlation between income and years of schooling (investment in human capital), but schooling itself does not contribute to production except as an identifier of those who are potentially productive. If the distribution of schooling were made more equal, all that would happen is that employers would have to find a new and more costly screening device (Carter 1972).

Furthermore, productivity is a function of the demand for goods and the supply of people and other inputs to produce them. If certain *kinds* of goods are in demand, the people able to produce these goods will be more highly rewarded than those producing less desirable goods. It is crucial to know who determines *what* goods are desirable and what mechanism is used to *select* those who get to produce the desirable goods. The neoclassical assumption is that the sum of individual consumer choices, made rationally among a whole range of alternative goods produced by freely competing firms, determines the kinds and quantities of goods produced. Similarly, the choice of the amount of schooling to take is also made by the individual, based on both monetary and nonmonetary return. If there are distortions in this system, the neoclassical economist believes that they can be solved through price-alteration mechanisms. For example, it is readily admitted that the market for investing in human capital is very imperfect: even if the return to the investment of poor people in schooling were high, their inability to finance their children's schooling, either through savings or bank loans, would make them underinvest in education. The neoclassical solution would be to perfect the capital market; i.e., make such loans available to all, based on purely economic considerations. Thus, the neoclassical assumptions about choice of goods and services, and the derived demand for inputs (including labor skills) to produce those goods, is based on individual consumer sovereignty. The supply of skills is also based on individual sovereignty to decide how many skills they want to learn. Productivity, if it could be measured properly, reflects these individual choices. The critics of the income-benefit approach do not challenge these basic premises.

The real world, however, cannot be characterized in this way. To some extent, the demand for goods and services is determined *for* consumers and not *by* them. The information needed by consumers to make rational decisions about goods based on *their* preference functions is often not made available by producers. In fact, many of the highest "productivity" people in the business and public sectors of even those countries with highly developed communication and information networks are experts in *obscuring* the truth—in developing products which can be sold to the consumer at a higher price than a different product that does exactly the same thing (Turner 1970). The choice of goods to be produced depends, in reality, as much on the producers of goods as on the consumers; advertising plays a major role in shaping consumer tastes. The public sector attempts, especially through the media, to influence people's view of the world and of problems in their own country. The media, generally, are a powerful factor in determining tastes and styles.

The types of goods produced are, therefore, only in part controlled by autonomous consumer demands, and even these are influenced heavily by information available to the consumer. Moreover, in many countries the percentage of total adult population consuming goods in the market economy is relatively small. This small percentage of the population is the group which, in turn, has only a part in determining what goods will be produced. Producers (the financial institutions, the owners of physical capital and the managers) themselves have a great deal to say about the desirability of goods, and hence, about the "productivity" of different kinds of work. Furthermore, on the supply side of the human capital market, schooling in most countries can be viewed as a convenient screening device which develops skills and attitudes needed by the economic and social system but at the same time controls access to the high "productivity" positions in that system. The same socioeconomic class of people that has a lot to say about the definition of "productivity" strongly supports the school system as a means of ensuring that its children will be the ones to get high "productivity" positions in the next generation. The structure of the schools, the curriculum, and the relationship among teachers and students all reflect the need to develop those characteristics associated with "high productivity" (Bowles 1972, Illich 1971). Those who reach higher levels of school are defined by their certificate as being more "useful" to the economic and social structure; i.e., more "productive than those with a lower-level certificate." The higher the level of "productivity," the higher, on the average, is their income.

To summarize, income (or wages) paid may incorrectly estimate the social value of labor because of distortions in the market for labor. Monopsony and discrimination are clear examples of such distortions. However, "productivity" is not a very useful concept for the measurement of social benefits of schooling either. "Productivity" of labor, like income, is not determined exogenously but by a similar set of forces from both the demand and supply side. What measure of economic benefits can we use, then, to estimate economic benefits of schooling? In any economic system, whether or not the market for labor is competitive, we can assume that the institutional structures which influence that market are part and parcel of the system. If different workers are paid differentially for doing the *same* job because of race, sex, or ethnic differences, we can consider that income is a poor estimate of the value of product produced by those receiving lower wages. Similarly, in a monopsony situation, wages are an underestimate of product. In both cases, "productivity" would be a better measure of labor product. But if racism and sexism are practiced largely by preventing those discriminated against access to higher paying (higher "productivity") occupations, it is unclear whether "productivity" would be any more accurate measure of the value work than income. Since *different* jobs depend so much for their "productivity" on political-economic forces in the society, we could say that, for example, women are paid less not because they are underpaid for doing the same work as men, but because society values women less and places them in jobs that pay less. Therefore, if discrimination is practiced primarily interoccupationally rather than intraoccupationally, and if the institutional structure of the economic system is taken as given, income paid to labor can be defined as the value of the product which the political-economic forces in the society assign to that level of skills, education, socialization, race, sex, ethnic group, and whatever other criteria are used to gauge the value of a person's work. Where distortion is interoccupational, income is therefore the best measure of productivity available, since it reflects the value assigned by the given system to various kinds of work. If we do not accept the political-economic system as given, then even in this case, income becomes a useless measure of the value of labor, since under a new ordering of economic and political power, the value assigned to various kinds of skills, race, sex, etc., could be completely different.

Relationship Between Measured Income and Schooling

People with more schooling earn more income. We have tried to show that this correlation between more schooling and higher income is in part a matter of *defining* income in terms of the requirements of being highly productive. Is there any reason to believe, then, that additional schooling *causes* an increase in income or productivity? Would a policy of increasing the aggregate level of schooling be expected to increase the average income per capita? Since schooling is a form of learning and a more schooled population is complementary in production to modern technology, it is reasonable to assume that investment in schooling produces a positive return, even when the physical capital stock is held constant. Nevertheless, a growing body of literature argues that the contribution of schooling to increased output has been greatly overestimated. We will cite two examples of the kinds of critiques raised. The first concerns the relationship between measured productivity and schooling within occupations. The second deals with the possible correlation between increased schooling in the labor force and lower labor-force participation of the population.

1. Ivar Berg (1970) cites data on productivity of workers with different amounts of schooling within the same occupation as showing that workers with less schooling actually had, on the average, the same or higher productivity. He also shows that employers use schooling largely as a screening device, requiring more schooling for certain jobs in a skill buyer's than in a skill seller's market. Fuller (1970), using data from a sample of Bangalore, India, workers from three factory occupations, also shows much lower correlation between schooling and productivity than is usually found in labor-force survey results relating income to schooling. He finds that rural-born workers with a given quantity of schooling have higher productivity than urban-born workers.

Nevertheless, the results of these productivity studies do not negate results that show a positive correlation between schooling and income. In using samples drawn *within* occupations, both Berg and Fuller have eliminated the much larger variations in "productivity" that occur *between* occupations. Moreover, within a single occupation it is likely that persons with education levels that are higher or lower than the median for that occupation are not representative of persons with higher or lower education in the population at large. That is, the most capable people with less than the average amount of schooling per worker in the occupation, and the least capable people with more than the average amount of schooling for that occupation, are all found in the occupation. A productivity comparison is made among people who are working at a given job, but, except for those with approximately the mean amount of schooling for the occupation, schooling is not the variable that got them the job. For those with less schooling, some other characteristics related to productivity enable them to do the job as well as or better than the people with the average schooling in the group. For those with more schooling, some other characteristic prevents them from moving up to higher paying and higher "productivity" jobs (productivity comparisons *between* jobs are only possible in dollar terms, anyway, not the physical terms used by Berg and Fuller). From these studies, however, we can argue that it is *possible* to do the same job with less formal schooling required of the workers. It would certainly be feasible to substitute other forms of training for formal schooling.

Perhaps the more convincing evidence for the overschooling of the labor force (from the standpoint of increasing productivity) is the change in the schooling requirements of jobs over time. Before World War II, both assembly-line jobs and many professional careers in the U.S. required less schooling than today, even though the nature of the jobs themselves has hardly changed. It is almost impossible to get a job in a factory, or driving a truck, or any other skilled work without a high school degree. Even now, the requirements are rising for these jobs, so that soon junior college training will be a necessary prerequisite for the same work. Similarly, lawyers, engineers, architects, and even doctors once had the option of getting a professional certificate by working as an apprentice for a certain number of years. Training has gradually shifted out of the place of work to the schools, so that employers do not have to bear the cost of general training which could be marketable to other firms (Becker 1964). Under the assumption that higher returns to physical capital are in the national interest, the public sector has undertaken to train workers in schools at public expense. Since trained labor is probably a complementary input to machines, public schooling may subsidize the owners of physical capital.

2. In most countries, urban employment does not grow as rapidly as population. One of the main assumptions of the income-benefits approach is that schooling additional people will lead to the same private and social benefits for the additionally schooled people as the average for those already employed. This implies that, at the margin, the new labor force entrant is *added* to the employed labor force, rather than *replacing* someone else who is, in turn, unemployed.

The economic value of increasing the number of graduates of school has to be measured in terms of the *unemployment-adjusted* income of those in the labor force. If wages are inflexible downward, i.e., do not decrease even in real terms because of labor organizations or other institutional practices, the effect of increasing the number of graduates of a given level of schooling in response to high observed incomes could increase the level of unemployment rather than lowering wages. Graduates would, on the average, not receive the expected observed income at the margin, but that income adjusted by the expected rate of employment. As the number of graduates increases rapidly, the employment rate may drop rapidly as well, even though observed incomes could remain the same or rise for that skill level.

In Puerto Rico, for example, employment did not grow in absolute number between 1940 and 1960. During the same period, the Puerto Rican economy grew very rapidly, at almost 4 percent per capita. Rather than expanding the number of jobs, the growth was accompanied by exogenous minimum-wage increases which kept the number of jobs in the economy almost the same over time. But the average level of schooling of jobholders increased rapidly. In effect, Puerto Ricans competed for jobs by increasing their schooling (Carnoy 1972). At the margin, an entrant into the Puerto Rican labor force "bumped" somebody else from the employed labor force; someone with, on the average, less schooling.

Therefore, if the public sector expands schooling in response to such income differentials, the same differential does not necessarily obtain for new entrants to the labor force. As more graduates enter the labor market, the return to investing in that level of schooling may fall. The return to those who graduate four or five years after the initial decision to invest in expanded primary schooling, for example, may receive a much lower return than observed in the initial year. Even if wages themselves do not fall, the employment rate may fall, so unemployment-adjusted return would be lower.

The rate at which the return falls, or the likelihood that it will fall with a given expansion in the number of graduates from school, depends on the income and wage elasticity of demand for labor with that level of schooling. These, in turn, depend on size and type of the physical capital stock of the country, and the technology employed in expanding production. If the technology is relatively unskilled labor intensive, the income elasticity of demand for unskilled labor will be much higher than if the technology is relatively skilled labor intensive. The imported technology used in developing countries, and the accent by these countries on capital-intensive manufacturing industries, has created a relatively low income elasticity of demand for unskilled or semiskilled labor. Expansion of primary school graduates often leads to a high unemployment rate for that group (Thias and Carnoy 1972, Calloway 1963). On the other hand, the income elasticity of demand for secondary school graduates, as a result of substitution of secondary for primary educated labor (Carnoy 1972) and more complex technology in production, may be high enough to absorb a rapid increase of such graduates. In the United States, we observe that the ratio of wages of secondary school graduates to wages of primary school graduates has risen over time (Griliches 1970), and absolute real income of secondary school graduates (adjusted for unemployment) has also risen (Griliches 1970). In other countries, however, the income elasticity of demand may not be high enough to absorb the rapid increase in graduates at the secondary level (Thias and Carnoy 1972, Blaug 1970).

Empirical Evidence on the Value of Increasing the Amount of Time Spent in School

The benefit of increasing the amount of time spent in school varies with grade level and should be adjusted for the employment rate and for differences in socioeconomic class of those at different levels. As already described, the effect on income of more years in school is generally positive and significant in every study done to date, even when socioeconomic class differences are accounted for. Based on the 1959 U.S. census data, Hanoch (1967) has shown, for example, that earnings of both white and nonwhite males adjusted for socioeconomic class differences between levels rise steadily throughout the schooling range of eight years of primary school to four years of college. Thias and Carnoy (1972) have shown the same results for African males in Kenya in the schooling range of no schooling to completed university. Carnoy's studies of Mexico (1964) and Puerto Rico (1972), Selowsky's (1968) study of Colombia, Castro's (1971), and Carnoy and Katz's (1971) studies of Brazil show increasing incomes over broad ranges of schooling in Latin America. Other studies in Asia and Africa (Psacharoupoulos 1972) confirm these results.

Studies by sociologists using U.S. data, notably Duncan and Blau (1971), also show positive correlations between income and years of schooling and between occupational status and schooling, in each case controlling for the subject's socioeconomic background. A study of the Tunisian labor force (Thias, Carnoy, and Sack 1971) shows that schooling has a positive effect on occupational status at lower secondary school (seventh, eighth, and ninth grades), especially at lower ages, but little effect on income at those grades when socioeconomic class is held constant. The last two years of secondary school have a significant and large effect on both income and occupational status at all age levels.

From the available evidence, then, the effect of increased years in school appears relatively large. Again, however, the size of the marginal effect may be mitigated by a relatively rapid decrease in the marginal return to increased years of school if there is a rapid increase in the number of students graduating from a given level of schooling.

THE DIRECT SOCIAL BENEFITS OF IMPROVED PUPIL PERFORMANCE AT A GIVEN LEVEL OF SCHOOLING ($\partial B_{isx}/\partial A_i$;)

The first term of equation (5.3) refers to the direct increase in social benefits associated with an increase in the performance of students finishing a given level of schooling. How much more do graduates of a certain school level contribute to a society if their performance in that level is improved? Several estimates have been made in the United States of the contribution of "ability" to income, controlling for number of years of school. Ability in these studies is usually measured by a person's achievement on a written test, so we can consider it to be a good proxy for student school performance.

The results of two such studies are shown in table 5.1. The Griliches-Mason study estimates the contribution of ability to income (and occupational status) to be small when schooling completed is held constant. Their sample had a mean schooling level of 11.5 years when they took the Air Force Qualifying Test (AFQT) at about age 18. Griliches and Mason conclude: "If the psychological

Table 5.1
Schooling and Earnings of Low and Average Achievers, United States, Early 1960s

Low Achievers[a]		Average Achievers[b]	
Variable	Regression Coefficient[c] (standard error)	Variable	Regression Coefficient[d] (standard error)
Color	361.7* (63.1)	Color	0.1714* (.048)
Schooling	20.3 (13.2)	Schooling Before Service	0.0328* (.005)
AFQT Score	23.7* (4.5)	Schooling Increment	0.0462* (.007)
Training	291.3* (89.3)	AFQT Score	0.00105* (.0004)

*Indicates statistically significant at 5 percent level of significance.
[a]W. Lee Hansen, Burton A. Weisbrod, and William J. Scanlon, "Schooling and Earnings of Low Achievers," *American Economic Review* 9, no. 3 (June 1970): 409-18, table 1. Dependent variable, annual earnings. National sample of approximately 2,400 men, 17-25 years old (mean age, 21.9 years), rejected for military service because of failure to pass Air Force Qualifying Test (AFQT), 1963.
[b]Z. Griliches and W. Mason, "Education, Income, and Ability," *Journal of Political Economy*, 80, no. 3 (May/June) 1972, 74-103, table 3, equation 4. Dependent variable, log income. National subsample of 1,454 army veterans from 1964 Consumer Population Survey.
[c]Besides variables shown, age, marital status, divorce of parents, family size, and nonsouth held constant. $R^2 = .155$.
[d]Besides variables shown, age, education plus occupation of father, length of military service and where subject grew up held constant. $R^2 = .2159$.

literature is to be believed, both as to the closeness of the AFQT measure to IQ and to the great difficulty of affecting the latter, it should be much easier (less costly) to affect income via changes in schooling than changes in measured ability" (p. 50).

The Hansen-Weisbrod-Scanlon study of low achievers shows the opposite result: higher AFQT score contributes significantly to income, while schooling is a much less important explainer of income variance. They estimate that an additional year of school adds $44 to a person's income ($20 in additional earnings per year of schooling plus $24 from the additional point in AFQT associated with each additional year of schooling) as compared to an increase of $24 from increasing a person's score on the AFQT by one point. "In the light of this finding one may question the wisdom of campaigns to keep teen-agers in school, which do not change their attitudes and motivation, do not improve the quality of instruction offered and do not affect the amount of learning that takes place" (p. 414).

Although apparently contradictory, both results may be valid since their samples are drawn from very different populations. As Griliches and Mason point out, the Hansen-Weisbrod-Scanlon sample is "peculiar in that it concentrates on the very young and on blacks (about half their sample is non-white versus 9 percent in our sample). It is well known that schooling-income differentials are rather low at the beginning of the labor force experience and that there is little evidence for a strong schooling-income relationship for blacks (see Hanoch, 1967). This is also a population where there is likely to be great diversity in the schooling experience and the AFQT may in fact be a better measure of accumulated learning than years spent in a Northern slum or Southern rural school" (p. 48). Also, the average level of schooling in the Hansen-Weisbrod-Scanlon sample is less than 9 years, much lower than the Griliches-Mason sample. And for those with relatively low levels of schooling, whether white or black, the schooling-income relationship is not as strong as for higher levels (Hanoch 1967).

Other studies in other countries seem to corroborate the pattern of the Hansen-Weisbrod-Scanlon and Griliches-Mason results. Thias and I asked labor force members in Kenya with both primary and secondary schooling how they fared on national exams which are given at the end of primary school (Kenya Primary Exam) and at the end of secondary school (Cambridge School Certificate). At the primary level, the income of those who pass the KPE exam (even though they do not go further in school) is significantly higher than of those who fail for age groups 25-29 years old and above (Thias and Carnoy 1972). Both failers and passers have completed 7 years of school. Of course, the pass/fail grade on the KPE was used until 1968 (when the sample was taken) as an important screening device in the Kenyan labor force, so the grade on that exam could be expected to have a significant effect on income. At the secondary level, exam scores on the CSC exam did not have a significant effect on income. At that level, assuming that someone had finished the 7 years of primary school and first 4 years of secondary school, the secondary school attended was the most important variable affecting income. Graduates of the elite secondary schools did significantly better, income wise, than those from other high schools, even if their CSC scores were lower.

In Tunisia, secondary-school-trained members of the labor force were asked, in addition to the grade level attained and socioeconomic background, their class rank in the last grade they completed and attitude questions that make up a modernity index (Thias, Carnoy, and Sack 1971). A subsample (those less than 25 years old) of those interviewed was also traced back to the secondary school attended and their actual grade point average recorded. We estimated the relationship between income, occupational status, and employability (number of months between school graduation and final job) as the dependent variables, and years of schooling, socioeconomic class, rank in class (or grade point average), and other variables as the independent variables. The estimates show that when years of school are held constant, the effect of rank in class on present income, for example, is significant only in the lowest two age groups (⩽20 years old, and 21-25 years old). The coefficient of reported rank is negative for the lowest age group and slightly positive for the 21–25-year-olds. When actual grade point average (GPA) is used as the independent variable rather than reported rank, the coefficient of school performance is positive and significant for both of these age groups taken together (see table 5.2).* However, GPA is not significant in contributing to occupational status. In the Tunisian sample of secondary-trained labor force, therefore, the effect of higher grades on income is significant when the years of schooling are held constant. The Tunisian sample was taken from a population which represents a relatively small proportion of all Tunisians who attended school and are now working. Male secondary-school-trained graduates represent only about 15 to 20 percent of the labor force with *some* schooling, even at lower age groups. There is some unemployment of secondary-school-trained labor, but, in general, the labor market is relatively tight for this level of skills. Therefore, school performance would probably not be as important a criterion for selection into the labor force as it might be at lower levels.

The Tunisian study also analyzes the relationship between earnings, schooling, and "modernity" (a measure of modern attitudes) in the labor force (Inkeles 1973). Modernization is considered as an output of school which might influence social benefits. Unlike grade point average, however, which is measured at the time a person finishes school, modernization of a labor-force member can increase between school completion and the time it was measured by the interview. It was impossible to get a measure of the interviewee's modernity at the time he graduated from school.

The modernization scale is correlated with years of schooling, but even with years of schooling held constant, modernity has a positive and significant effect on earnings. Table 5.3 shows for all age groups taken together an increase of one year of schooling yields an increase of (Tunisian dinars) TD 5.7 per month, while an increase of one standard deviation in the modernity scale (10.1 points) yields a salary increase of TD 1.8. Therefore, with a number of other variables held constant, including schooling, the effect of modernity on salary, while significant and positive, is very small compared to the effect of schooling.

*Grade point average in Tunisia ranges from 0–20 with a mean of about 10. A 2-point increase in GPA (about one standard deviation) would result in a salary increase of about Tunisian dinars (TD) 5.6 monthly. An additional year of school between 9 and 12 years results in a TD 6.3 increase.

Table 5.2

Comparison of the Effect on Salary and Occupation of Reported Rank and Grade Point Average (GPA) (from Ministry Statistics) in Last Grade Attended for a Subsample of 99 Subjects Aged 17-30, Tunisia, 1970

Independent Variable	Using Rank		Using GPA	
	Salary	Occupation	Salary	Occupation
7-8 years of school[a]	-0.555	-1.033	4.212	-0.938
10-11 years of school[a]	7.815	0.833	6.034	0.759
12 years of school[a]	24.247*	0.958	19.901*	0.763**
⩾13 years of school[a]	43.680*	2.126*	44.187*	2.033*
Reported rank	-19.355**	0.674	—	
Grade point average	—	—	2.830*	0.161
Constant	47.061	3.086	8.483	2.104
R^2	0.39	0.18	0.41	0.19

*Significant at 5 percent level.
**Significant at 10 percent level.

Source: Hans Thias, Martin Carnoy, and Richard Sack, "Schooling, Ability, Modernization, and Labor Force Performance of Middle Level Manpower in Tunisia" (IBRD, July 1971). Mimeographed.
[a]Dummy variables for various amounts of schooling. The left-out dummy is 9 years of schooling, so all schooling coefficients represent the salary of those with the given level of schooling *relative* to those with 9 years of school.

Hause (1971) has criticized these types of studies on the grounds that there is an interaction effect between the quantity of schooling taken and ability. People with more ability have, on the average, more schooling. Furthermore, he points out that the effect of ability on earnings may be different at different ages, depending on the learnings-productivity relationship. In order to account for both these factors, he uses Daniel Rogers' longitudinal data *ibid.* to relate earnings, log earnings and discounted lifetime earnings to ability *within* education level, holding some socioeconomic class variables constant. The results show that there is a *tendency* for the coefficient of IQ to *increase* with increased levels of schooling (see table 5.4), and to increase with increased age of the cohort (Hause 1971). The table 5.4 results indicate an interaction between schooling and IQ, but they do *not* tell us that ability is necessarily more important than schooling in explaining income variance at higher levels of schooling than at lower levels. First, as Hause shows, the coefficient of ability is relatively more important at lower levels of schooling in earlier years of the cohort's earnings streams. Using 1955 incomes instead of 1965 incomes would have shown that there is little or no significant difference between the coefficients of

Table 5.3
Schooling, Modernization, and Earnings, All Age Groups, Tunisia, 1970; Dependent Variable, Monthly Salary

Independent Variables	Regression Coefficient	Mean
Socioeconomic background	0.59*	4.49 (scale)
Years in school	5.70*	9.22 (years)
Foreign travel	17.40*	0.35 (percent)
Vocational training	1.39	0.41 (percent)
Job time	1.28*	6.72 (years)
On-the-job training	8.47*	0.38 (percent)
Family geographic background	-0.84*	4.80 (1 = rural, 7 = urban)
Subject geographic location	1.61*	6.22 (1 = rural, 7 = urban)
Modernity	0.18*	60.87 (scale)
R^2	0.45	

*Significant at 5 percent level.

Source: Hans Thias, Martin Carnoy, and Richard Sack, "Schooling, Ability, Modernization, and Labor-force Performance of Middle Level Manpower in Tunisia" (IRBD, July 1971). Mimeographed.

Table 5.4
Earnings, Schooling, and IQ, United States

		1965 Earnings		Discounted Lifetime Earnings	
Education Level	Sample Size N	Coefficient IQ	R^2	Coefficient IQ	R^2
High school dropout (E_1)	60	-3.5 (26.9)	0.16	-115 (367)	.19
High school graduate (E_2)	117	74.6* (35.8)	0.19	756 (592)	.09
College dropout (E_3)	51	-2.2 (127.2)	0.34	-589 (1,606)	.23
College graduate (E_4)	70	132.5 (88.7)	0.31	1670 (2,395)	.23
College, two or more degrees (E_5)	47	223.0 (154.5)	0.19	1968 (1,754)	.19

*Significant at 5 percent level of significance.

Source: John C. Hause, "Ability and Schooling as Determinants of Lifetime Earnings or If You're So Smart, Why Aren't You Rich," *American Economic Review* 61, no. 2 (1971): 289–98. Table 3, p. 294.

ability at different levels of schooling. Although Hause argues that others have misspecified the earnings function by not accounting for the interaction between schooling and ability, Hause himself may have misspecified his functions by not accounting for on-the-job training, which is undoubtedly also correlated with both ability and schooling.

Nevertheless, even if the effect of ability on income is significantly higher for those with more schooling, this does not mean that the effect of ability on income is necessarily greater than the effect of additional years of schooling for those with more schooling. For example, ability differences appear to explain a *higher* proportion of income differences between high school completion and some years of college (E_2 and E_3) than between one college degree and two or more college degrees (E_4 and E_5) even though the coefficient of ability is higher at E_4 than at E_2. Ideally, Hause should have estimated the differential *tradeoff* between years of schooling and ability differences at different levels of schooling.

It is difficult to put all these studies together into some coherent theory of the relationship between income, years of schooling, and school performance. There seems to be an interaction effect between schooling and ability, but the nature of the interaction is not altogether clear. It may be that the effect of ability is relatively more important than years of schooling in explaining income differences for those with low levels of schooling than for those with the mean level of schooling. The labor market may differentiate more on ability among relatively unskilled workers than among skilled workers with more schooling. Below a certain level of schooling, employers consider everyone a "dropout," so the amount of schooling is less important than other qualities in determining what kind of job—if any—a person gets. The "certain level" of schooling obviously varies from country to country. For Kenya and Tunisia it may be completed primary school; in the United States, completed secondary school, etc. This implies a substitution of the schooling criteria for the "ability" criterion in determining a person's learning capacity or occupational opportunities as the individual takes more schooling.

But we also must reconcile the logic and possible empirical evidence that at very high levels of schooling, at least in the United States, there may also be an important effect of ability relative to years of schooling in explaining income differences among individuals. In high-technology countries such as the United States, opportunities for very highly schooled people are varied. In those countries, we would expect that ability differences play an important role relative to schooling in determining income among those with already high average level of schooling and income. However, in low-income countries, a highly schooled person moves directly into the most highly paid position in the society. The kind of high-status positions available to a person with even some years of university may be extremely limited. Thus, performance on tests would not be an important factor compared to years of schooling in explaining income differences even among highly schooled individuals.

These hypotheses rationalize into some coherent whole the various results discussed: school performance is more important relative to schooling in explaining income differences among individuals in high income countries who have very low levels of schooling (compared to the mean level in, say, the urban employed labor force) and very high levels of schooling. In low-income countries, the importance of performance is higher at lower levels of schooling than at higher and does not rise again at high schooling levels. We would also expect that the effect of performance on income is more important for those with lower schooling levels relatively earlier in working life than for those with higher schooling levels. The age of the individuals should therefore be an important factor in determining these various effects.

An *increase* in school performance of pupils related to a change in the nature of schooling can be taken as a proxy for improved "quality of schooling." However, as noted in the beginning of this chapter, other literature has taken expenditures per pupil as the measure of school quality. Johnson and Stafford (1970) estimate the relation between years of schooling, school expenditure per pupil, other variables, and the logarithm of hourly wages. Most of the data is derived from a survey of individuals, but the school expenditure per pupil data comes from state averages. The results show that both years of schooling and expenditures per pupil have a positive and significant effect on earnings (table 5.5). The inclusion of the expenditure per pupil variable has little effect on the size of the coefficient for years of schooling. When the southern states are excluded, both the coefficient of years of schooling and expenditures per pupil fall but remain significant and of the same order of magnitude. The Johnson-

Table 5.5
Hourly Earnings, Years of Schooling, and Expenditures per Pupil, Employed Males, United States, 1964 (dependent variable, log hourly wages)

Independent Variables	Regression Coefficient (all states)	Regression Coefficient (North)
Years of schooling	.0665*	.0614*
	(.0047)	(.011)
Potential job experience	.0126*	.0122*
	(.0020)	(.0048)
Nonwhite	-.311*	-.170*
	(.038)	(.053)
Urban	.284*	.171*
	(.028)	(.029)
Log expenditures per pupil	.182*	.147
	(.048)	(.071)
R^2	.40	.26

*Other variables not shown: education times experience, education times years of experience squared, and grew up in urban area.

Source: George Johnson and Frank Stafford, "Social Returns to Quantity and Quality of Schooling" (Paper presented at the Econometric Society Meetings, December 1970), table 1, p. 7, equations 1-c and 1-d.

Stafford estimates are particularly suited to calculating the rate of return to increasing expenditure per pupil—their proxy for quality of school—and the rate of return to taking additional years of schooling. Their results show that the rate of return to increasing expenditures per pupil is higher at lower levels of schooling. They also show that the rate of return to increasing expenditures per pupil is generally higher than increasing the years of schooling taken: "As a partial equilibrium question, there appear to be clear benefits of reallocating resources in favor of greater school quality and away from years of schooling" (p. 15). But this last conclusion is based on the regression estimate which does not take account of regional differences in expenditures per pupil and in hourly wages. The estimated coefficient in the "North" equation is almost 25 percent lower than the coefficient of expenditures per pupil used to estimate rates of return. The coefficient of years of schooling in the "North" equation, on the other hand, is only 8 percent less the coefficient used to estimate rates of return to years of schooling. If these percentage reductions are applied to the rates of return estimated by Johnson and Stafford, the difference in the rates to quality and quantity are greatly reduced, and except for increasing expenditures per pupil at very low initial levels, the preference for quality over quantity becomes much less clear.

Change in Average Grade Level Completed Due to Pupils' Increased Performance ($\partial G/\partial A_j$)

Of the three variables in equation 5.3, least is known about this last term—$\partial G/\partial A_j$. So many other factors may enter simultaneously to affect retention rates that it is difficult to isolate the effect on retention of some measure which improves the performance of pupils, either on achievement tests or in non-cognitive areas such as political efficacy or modernization. If the function of grading in a particular school system or in part of a school system is to *select* a percentage of students to go on, grading will always be on the curve; i.e., a certain percentage of students will pass and a certain percentage will fail. This percentage will not be a function of the quality of the students necessarily, but of the places available in the next grade or next level of schooling. At levels of schooling that are "compulsory"—that is, everyone in those levels is expected to complete them—improving exam scores may indeed improve retention rates through reducing repetition or increasing student self-esteem and expectations.* Even in the case where schooling at a certain level is supposedly compulsory, however, schools have not been built in many areas of the country, or where built, have a teacher only several days per week. Obviously, the major problem in increasing retention rates is the provision of some form of schooling, not increasing the quality of schooling in areas which already have schools.

*In Venezuela, we found that the most important variable affecting retention rates in primary school among children already in six-year primary schools (many rural primary schools are only three-year schools) is the repetition rate. Now repetition has been abolished in Venezuelan primary schools, as it was long ago in the United States. Retention should therefore increase significantly without any increase in resources per pupil.

Table 5.6
Dropout Rates, Repetition Rates, Enrollment Rates, and Per Pupil Expense, Primary Schools in 42 Countries, 1957-62

Independent Variables	Dependent Variables: Cumulative Dropout Rate[a]	Dropout Rates, After Grade 1[b]
Average repetition rate	0.856	0.832*
Enrollment ratio	—	-0.309*
Per pupil expense	—	-0.231*
R^2	0.64	0.70

*Significant at 5 percent level of significance.

Source: Mildred Levy, "Determinants of Primary School Dropouts in Developing Countries," *Comparative Education Review* 15, no. 1 (February 1971), tables 1 and 2.
[a]Cumulative dropout rate a percent of grade 1 enrollment. 42 observations. Other variables included in equation but not shown: social tension, fertility, modern outlook, traditional elite, and level of overhead.
[b]Dropouts after grade 1 as percent of grade 1 enrollment. Other variables in equation: middle class, fertility, democratic institutions, military, GNP growth, and improvement of overhead.

These difficulties are borne out in research done on dropouts. Levy (1971), using data on dropouts from 42 countries, shows that cumulative dropout rates in the primary cycle are significantly and positively related to repetition rates (table 5.6). A 1 percent decrease in the repetition rate is associated with a 0.86 percent decrease in dropout rate. But this result tells us little about the relationship of quality of schooling in a given system and the retention of students. We cannot assume a priori that lower repetition rate is due to higher performance in school rather than policies which are not necessarily connected with school or student quality. Although dropouts in the second through sixth grades, according to Levy's results, are negatively related to per pupil expenditures with a number of other variables held constant, it is unclear that the decreased level of dropouts associated with higher per pupil costs is the result of higher pupil performance. According to Levy's results, the repetition rate coefficient changes little when expenditures per pupil are accounted for in the estimated equation. This would indicate that the repetition rate is not highly correlated with expenditures per pupil.

The literature on dropouts frequently discusses the need for improved schooling as a key to reducing educational "wastage," but the effect of increased school performance of pupils—assuming that such increased performance will follow from improved schooling—on dropouts has not been adequately tested (Correa, Ordonez, and Sanclemente 1971). Johnson and Stafford (1970) estimate a relationship between school expenditures per pupil and the average number of years of schooling taken, age, father's education, number of brothers and sisters, number of older brothers and sisters, and color held constant. Log expenditures has a positive and significant effect on years of schooling; more specifically, the estimate implies that doubling the expenditures per pupil increases the level of educational attainment by 0.8 years of school. The effect of additional expenditures on educational attainment is therefore not very high in this sample.

Product of Benefits from Increased Schooling ($\partial B_{isx}/\partial G$) and Increased Retention from Increased Performance ($\partial G/\partial A_j$)

Combining terms two and three of equation 5.3 yields the *indirect* effect on benefits from increasing student performance. What can we expect from this combined term? We know that the return from increased schooling is higher at completion levels of school over noncompletion levels than at noncompletion over the previous completion level (Hansen 1963, Hanoch 1967, Thias and Carnoy 1972, and Blair 1971). Logically, the more selective the level of schooling, i.e., the higher the dropout rate, the higher the return to completing that level, everything else equal.

There are three primary reasons why a level of schooling is marked by a high dropout rate: (1) facilities (classroom places and teachers) are limited at that level or the next highest level, so that the dropout rate is "programmed" to meet the availability of scarce resources; (2) the standard of performance in that level is set by society to be higher than the capability of most students; (3) the private benefit-cost ration to investment in that level and higher levels of schooling is relatively low. Reasons 1 and 2 are constraints on the supply side and are probably highly interrelated. In the case where public investment in a level of schooling is a constraining factor, teachers and administrators act as "gatekeepers" on student passage through the level by maintaining high "standards."* But the nature of the system itself can fulfill the same function. Assume that an important reason for completing one level of schooling is to go on to the next level. If a large fraction of children are in rural areas, restricting investment in secondary schooling largely to urban areas insures a high dropout rate in rural primary schools.

Restrictions on the supply side (reasons 1 or 2) can persist in the fact of high benefits to increased quantity of schooling ($\partial B/\partial G$). If the supply restriction is the result of limited school facilities, raising the quality of student performance would have little effect on retention rate since student performance is not the factor causing high dropout rates. ($\partial G/\partial A_j$) would therefore have a value close to zero. If the supply restriction is due to the maintenance of standard, and the number of places or resources per student is not a limiting factor, the retention rate might be rapidly increased through measures which increase student performance. The size of the increase depends on the size of ($\partial G/\partial A_j$). A high dropout rate caused primarily by low private returns to additional schooling implies that student performance is not an important factor

*In the 1970 Tunisian educational reform, for example, the Ministry of Education limited expanded investment in the secondary level with the rationale of maintaining quality of graduates from that level.

in determining retention rate. If the retention rate is mainly a function of economic factors, we would expect $(\partial G/\partial A_j)$ to be small. If the return to taking additional school were sufficiently low, students would not stay in school even if their performance were improved.

Levy's data indicate that economic factors, at least at the primary level, are not as important in explaining dropout rates as academic factors. It is likely, therefore, that at the primary level in most countries and at the secondary level in many countries, improving student performance *could* lead to increased retention rates and higher average levels of schooling attained. This hypothesis is true only if the reason for low retention rates is poor academic performance (reason 2) and not an educational investment policy which restricts the number of places available in schools. When the direct and indirect effects on earnings of expenditures per pupil are combined in the Johnson and Stafford study, the direct effect accounts for about 75 percent of the total. All in all, a 100 percent increase in per pupil expenditure is associated with a 23-25 percent increase in hourly wages, but this does not account for North/South regional differences.

If low academic performance has restricted the supply of graduates, $(\partial G/\partial A_j)$ as well as $(\partial B/\partial G)$ may be high. In that case, the indirect effect on social benefits of increasing the quality of schooling (student performance) would be relatively large. If availability of places is restricting supply or economic factors are most important in affecting dropouts, $(\partial G/\partial A_j)$ would be small and the indirect effect on benefits would also be small.

CONCLUSION

We have discussed two components of benefits from improving the performance of pupils in school: the direct benefits of increasing student performance at a given level of schooling and the indirect benefits which result from the added schooling people would take if they performed better in school.

Most evidence we have for the United States, Kenya, and Tunisia indicates that the direct economic benefits from increased student performance may be relatively important at low levels of schooling. People completing primary or some secondary school are competing in a part of the labor market which apparently differentiates as much on the basis of ability as on the basis of schooling. Ability increases at that level may yield high benefits at the margin. At higher levels of schooling (slightly above the average levels in the United States and secondary schooling in Kenya and Tunisia), ability differences are probably less important than schooling differences in explaining economic performance. Hence, increasing performance, with years of schooling held constant, would probably yield lower benefits at those schooling levels. At high levels of schooling in countries like the United States, the payoff to improved quality of schooling may rise again.

Although we can be even less conclusive about indirect benefits, it seems that the indirect payoff to increased student performance would occur in the situation where poor performance relative to some standard is presently the major factor in causing dropouts, and where the benefits to taking more schooling are relatively high. Urban primary schools and lower secondary schools in many developing countries fit this description. Completion of secondary school in the United States is also marked by such characteristics. The *lowest* indirect payoff to increased student performance would occur in a situation where the dropout rate is largely a function of limited space or teacher availability at higher levels of school rather than academic performance or where dropouts are a function of high foregone income (conversely, a low return) associated with taking more schooling. In both cases, the retention rate would not be increased significantly by increasing the quality of student performance. High dropout rates in developing country rural primary schools are a good example of limited resources-cased dropouts. Most rural schools stop at the third grade and many of those get only part-time teachers. Increasing performance of rural students through increasing the quality of teaching, for example, will do little for retention rates in the last three grades of primary school if these are not available. Likewise, limited access to higher secondary school and university for urban students has little to do with the quality of students applying. Unless the number of places at those levels is expanded, increasing quality of output in the years immediately prior to them would result in little or no increase in the quantity of secondary or higher education taken. It is also likely that economic reasons for dropouts increase as the level of schooling increases. Alternative opportunities became more valuable and to some extent, the marginal private rate of return for the average student falls with increased schooling (Carnoy 1970).

REFERENCES

Agency for International Development, Bureau for Latin America. *A Review of Alliance for Progress Goals.* Washington, D.C.: U.S. Government Printing Office, 1969.

Becker, Gary. *Human Capital.* Princeton, N.J.: Princeton University Press, 1964.

Berg, Ivar. *Education and Jobs: The Great Training Robbery.* New York: Frederick A. Praeger, 1970.

Blair, Philip. "Rates of Return to Schooling of Majority and Minority Groups in Santa Clara County." Ph.D dissertation, Stanford University, 1971.

Blaug, M. "Approaches to Educational Planning." *Economic Journal* 77, no. 306 (June 1967): 267–87.

Blaug, M. *An Introduction to the Economics of Education.* London: Penguin Press, 1970. See chap. 7.

Blaug, M., et al. *The Causes of Unemployment in India.* London: Penguin Press, 1969.

Bowles, Samuel. "Unequal Education and the Reproduction of the Social Division of Labor." In *Schooling in a Corporate Society*, edited by Martin Carnoy. New York: David McKay, 1972.

Calloway, Archibald. "Unemployment Among African School Leavers." *Journal of Modern African Studies* 1 (September 1963): 351–71.

Carnoy, Martin. "The Cost and Returns to Schooling: A Case Study of Mexico." Ph.D dissertation, University of Chicago, 1964.

Carnoy, Martin. "The Rate of Return to Schooling and the Increases in Human Resources in Puerto Rico." *Comparative Education Review* 16, no. 1 (February 1972): 68–84.

Carnoy, Martin. "The Political Economy of Education." In *Education and Development*, edited by Thomas LaBelle. Los Angeles: UCLA Latin American Center, 1972.

Carnoy, Martin, and Katz, Marlaine. "Explaining Differentials in Earnings Among Large Brazilian Cities." *Urban Studies* 8, no. 1 (February 1971): 21–37.

Carter, Michael. "To Invest or Not to Invest." Mimeographed. School of Education, Stanford University, 1972.

Castro, Claudio. "Investimiento em Educação no Brasil." *Pesquisa e Planejamento*, no. 1 (June 1971): 141–52.

Correa, J.; Ordonez, D.; and Sanclemente, J. "Dropouts: The Case of Colombia at the Elementary Level." Mimeographed. Stanford University, July 1971.

Duncan, O. D., and Blau, P. M. *The American Occupational Structure*. New York: John Wiley, 1967.

Fuller, William P. "Education, Training and Productivity: A Study of Skilled Workers in Two Factories in South India." Stanford University (SIDEC-OEI 7), 1970.

Gintis, Herbert. "Education and the Characteristics of Worker Productivity." *American Economic Review* 61, no. 2 (May 1971): 266–79.

Griliches, Zvi. "Notes on the Role of Education in Production and Growth Accounting." In *Education, Income, and Human Capital*, edited by W. L. Hansen. New York: National Bureau of Economic Research, 1970. See table 6.

Hanoch, Giara. "An Economic Analysis of Earnings and Schooling." *Journal of Human Resources* 2, no. 3 (Summer 1967): 310–29.

Hansen, W. Lee. "Total and Private Rates of Return to Investment in Schooling." *Journal of Political Economy* 71 (April 1963).

Hause, John. C. "Ability and Schooling as Determinants of Lifetime Earnings or If You're So Smart, Why Aren't You Rich?" *American Economic Review* 61, no. 2 (1971): 289–98.

Illich, Ivan. *Deschooling Society*. New York: Harper & Row, 1971.

Inkeles, Alex. *Becoming Modern*. Boston: Little, Brown, 1973.

Johnson, George, and Stafford, Frank. "Social Returns to Quantity and Quality of Schooling." Paper presented at the Econometric Society Meetings, December 1970.

Levy, Mildred. "Determinants of Primary School Dropouts in Developing Countries." *Comparative Education Review* 15, no. 1 (February 1971): 45–58.

Morgan, James, and Sinageldin, Ismail. "A Note on the Returns to Quality in Schooling." *Journal of Political Economy* (September/October 1968): 1069–77.

Psacharoupoulos, George. "Rates of Return to Education Around the World." *Comparative Education Review* 16, no. 1 (February 1972): 54–67.

Reder, Melvin. "A Partial Survey of the Theory of Income Size Distribution." In *Six Papers on the Size Distribution of Wealth and Income*, edited by Lee Soltow. New York: Columbia University Press, 1969.

Schultz, T. W. *The Economic Value of Education*. New York: Columbia University Press, 1964.

Selowsky, Marcelo. "The Effect of Unemployment and Growth on the Rate of Return to Education: The Case of Colombia." Economic Development Report, Center for International Affairs, Harvard University, 1968.

Thias, H., and Carnoy, M. *Cost-Benefit Analysis in Education: A Case Study of Kenya.* Baltimore, Md.: World Bank/Johns Hopkins Press, 1972.

Thias, Hans; Carnoy, Martin; and Sack, Richard. "Schooling, Ability, Modernization, and Labor Force Performance of Middle Level Manpower in Tunisia." Mimeographed. IBRD, July 1971.

Turner, James S. *The Chemical Feast.* New York: Grossman, 1970.

Walsh, J. "Capital Concept Applied to Man." *Quarterly Journal of Economics* 49 (February 1935): 255–85.

Welch, Finis. "Measurement of the Quality of Schooling." *American Economic Review* (May 1966): 379–92.

Ernesto Schiefelbein *

6 AN APPROACH TO INTRODUCING QUALITY IN EDUCATIONAL MODELS

Model builders do not include "quality of education," arguing that educational research has not yet provided good measures of learning performance. At the same time all educators agree that quality should be included as a measure of the effectiveness of the system if models are going to be used in decision making. No solution has yet been presented to this problem.

The available set of complex models for the quantitative aspects of educational system provides a partial answer to decision makers in education. A continuous improvement in their design may be expected, but the art of educational modeling is actually constrained by the lack of relevant data.

It is possible to foresee new flows of information on qualitative aspects of education. Interest in the concept of "accountability for the schools" is increasing (Lieberman 1970, ETS 1969). It now seems appropriate to explore the possibilities of designing realistic models. This chapter describes an attempt to take into account some qualitative aspects of the problem through a combined use of the Delphi method for subjective estimates and sensitivity analysis.†

At the outset it is necessary to emphasize that the model to be described herein is not presented as a complete and thoroughly worked exercise. Rather, it is offered to point the way toward further research into the development and

*I am particularly indebted to Drs. David Kendrick, Russell Davis, Richard Durstine, Hector Correa, and John Carroll for their advice and criticism.

†It is hoped that a "quality of education index" will be available in the near future (Tyler 1966). The index does not necessarily have to measure the absolute level of quality but to reflect changes of the quality level through time. Subjective estimates through the Delphi method are used meantime.

use of more comprehensive models than those actually available. The model is designed to become a tool for decision making, i.e., to facilitate reasoning in a complex situation where the "complexity of the web of interdependencies makes any partial analysis misleading" (Bowman 1966). The model, therefore, must be used only by educational administrators who have a thorough knowledge of the situation the model describes.

OUTLINE OF THE MODEL

A basic rule of modeling: the simpler the model, the better it is. Linear models have the virtue of clarity and simplicity together with a well-worked body of numerical techniques for obtaining useful solutions. But, unfortunately, simplicity does not come without cost. When considering quality, certain variables, for example "input per student" and "number of students," would seem to enter into the problem in multiplicative fashion and, hence, suggest quadratic terms. This presents the classic problem that quadratic programming models are more difficult to design and more complicated to work numerically than linear ones.

The assumed character of the educational system is such that various input factors influence its output. The educational system may, therefore, be considered as a set of activities producing educated people of different achievement levels (with respect to a given set of educational objectives). In the process of educating, these activities use human resources (teachers, students, workers) and other resources (buildings and some current expenses) at exogenously fixed rates.

The present model does not pretend to include "quality of education" as a measure of the effectiveness of the system. The model does, however, include some implicit assumptions about quality in the input-output variables. The example includes only three inputs but there may be more relevant inputs than those considered. Food, medical care, transportation, students' clothing, and teachers' housing are included in the total monetary costs, but their effects may be so diverse that one could justify the inclusion of some of them as distinct variables. A number of other factors related to quality are not included at all. For instance, the effects of per capita income, the educational level of parents, the access of population to mass media communications, the access to cheaper sources of energy, and even teachers' expectancies, which may be determinant of student success (Rosenthal and Jacobson 1966), are not considered.

The objective function will be a quadratic cost function. This function must be minimized subject to certain conditions which prevent the objective function to become null. These conditions are expressed as linear equations or inequalities.

Minimizing costs, however, will be only a condition for each solution. The operator must appraise the activity levels of different variables in each trial in a subjective way. The optimum value of a given set of variables may be determined by trying every possible combination of values for the relevant variables and by subjectively estimating the effectiveness associated with each substitution. This type of search for the "best" is too crude to be included in current optimization theory, but it is suitable for helping everyday decision making in a field in which it is very difficult to measure output (Kaufmann 1963). The objective function of the quadratic programming model, therefore, is not the criterion applied by the operator to choose a particular solution among a family of solutions.

THE OBJECTIVE FUNCTION

The criterion in this model is the minimization of the operating expenses for all levels of the educational system (in the numerical example basic and more than basic) while (1) meeting certain desired levels of economic, social, and educational activities and (2) given the relationships defined for the model.

The use of a quadratic function allows the variation of "number of students" and "inputs per student" at the same time. (See equation 6.1, Appendix A.) All linear models force the designer to choose among these two variables. Usually the number of students is selected, thus freezing the technology of the system, and the optimization process cannot select the best levels of inputs per student.

A social-discount rate must be assumed in multiperiod models or there would be stimulus to educate people beyond the economic and social requirements in the initial years (initial costs per students would be lower than future costs per student). Although the design is perfectly general, a one-period model was implemented, because time effects in the Chilean case have already been explored in a large linear programming model (Schiefelbein 1969).

The three terms of the objective function correspond to: (1) current expenditures in the formal educational system, including teachers' in-service training; (2) investment expenditures in the formal educational system; and (3) the cost of on-the-job training the labor force outside the formal educational system.

THE CONSTRAINTS

The analytic expressions of the constraints are presented in Appendix A. A brief description of their role follows. Equations are grouped in four categories, two dealing with the educational system and two with the labor market:

Constraints Dealing with Quality Levels of the Educational System

Equation 6.2 states the relation between quality and inputs per student as a Leontieff-type production function of educational quality. Each input factor is considered as an index of quality being related through a common scale (see s in Appendices). The present input ratios are known, but no empirical estimation has been made of the shape of the function relating the quality level index of education and the magnitude of those inputs. Educators, however, do have subjective estimates of these relationships that are used in the implementation of the model.* The inequality may also be described as an interrelated set of quality indexes (Carroll 1963). Choosing a linear expression means that interactions among input factors are not considered, given the scarce knowledge on the quality aspects of education. Both the quality index and the input factors were defined as teachers usually use them. Thus their estimations were hoped to be reliable.

Equation 6.3 defines the upper extreme of the quality of the educational system. The quality of education variable is introduced as a homogeneous variable described by a univariate scale ranging from 0 to 1. This scale facilitates the quantitative translation of educators' opinions on the qualitative relationships.†

Equation 6.4 establishes (as a constraint) nondecreasing levels of inputs per student from one year to the next. Because of social constraints inherent in educational planning, it was considered impractical to reduce the initial levels of inputs per student. This constraint also ensures that the quality indexes be in date t at least as high as in date $t-1$.

Equation 6.5 puts a limit on increments in quality from period to period. With this constraint it is also possible to represent variations in the number of years in which a given change in quality can be introduced into the system.

Equation 6.6 relates the quality levels of the graduates from different educational levels and the requirements for those who join the labor force.

Equation 6.7 limits the levels of the educational quality indexes. This relation is also used for the simulation of social policies regarding quality of education.

Constraints Dealing with Demand for Labor

Equation 6.8 establishes labor demand (in quantity and quality) as a function of GNP levels (Correa and Tinbergen 1962). A certain degree of substitutability in production between number of workers and their educational levels (quality) may be assumed. This constraint, however, may be replaced by exogenous estimates of the quantitative and qualitative labor requirements.

The model assumes in this equation that the social capital is constant all over the period, i.e., the increments in GNP are only due to changes in the labor force (Denison 1964).

Equation 6.9 defines the additional labor demand of the period. It is implicitly assumed that the workers of the previous period want to continue working at the market salaries and that the current labor force must be at least as large as the previous one. Some flexibility, however, can be introduced by considering death or retirement.

*There was a rapid convergence in the process of estimating these ratios through the Delphi method.

†The known levels of more developed countries were used as references by the experts (judges) providing the information. The upper level of the scale was assigned to the best performance known by each one of the experts. Averages were computed and each judge repeated his estimations later on. This process was iterated several times including some discussion sessions.

Although an increment in the labor force is defined in this equation, the usual Δ sign is not used because the variable we are really working with is the additional labor demand and not total labor demand. Thus the definition of a new variable simplifies symbology.

Equation 6.10 states the educational-quality levels of the additional labor force. These levels depend on the workers' initial educational level and assumed workers' learning-by-doing abilities. The more they learn by doing, the less the increments in average educational quality of the labor force must be accounted for by the new workers (Arrow 1962).

Equation 6.11 establishes nondecreasing levels of educational quality of the labor force. There was no interest in obtaining unrealistic results, and historical trends show continuous increments in educational levels of the labor force.

Equation 6.12 defines the upper extreme of the educational-quality index of the labor force.

Constraints Dealing with Labor Supply

Equation 6.13 defines the increments in educational quality (performance) of workers over the historical trend. In order to define the increments, the educational quality of workers is assumed to increase at a rate similar to productivity. These increments in quality (and the cost of attaining them through on-the-job-training) are included in the third term of the objective function. Equation 6.13, therefore, deals with the increments in the educational-quality levels that can be attained if special training programs are developed. This equation introduces the need for on-the-job training programs into the model.

Equation 6.14 relates the increments in labor supply and demand. The inequality expresses that the supply must be greater than the demand thus, allowing a certain level of unemployment. For the sake of simplicity, special variables are defined instead of using the usual Δ sign.

Equation 6.15 defines the increment in labor-force supply. This equation includes the previously inactive people who want to join the labor force. If the increments in labor-force supply that the model can draw from the available sources do not match those in the demand, the result would not be feasible. The upper bound, therefore, is built into the model.

Equation 6.16 fixes a limit on the number of new workers coming from the inactive population. Thus it is possible to represent the effect of changes in this source of labor supply under different levels of unemployment.

Equation 6.17 defines the students leaving the educational system to join the labor force as a proportion of the total number of leavers.

Constraints Dealing with the Size of the Educational System

Equation 6.18 defines the students leaving the educational system as a proportion of the total enrollment. Equations 6.17 and 6.18 can be combined into equation 6.15. They are included, however, to simplify the operation of the model; it is easier to represent different policies through changes in the parameters of these equations.

Equation 6.19 sets up limits to the enrollment in each educational level according to the age distribution of the population.

Equation 6.20 defines the increments in enrollments from period to period. The transition matrix describes an important aspect of educational technology (Blot 1965). Changes in the quality of education must also affect the transition rates. Iterative procedures may be necessary to obtain adequate solutions.

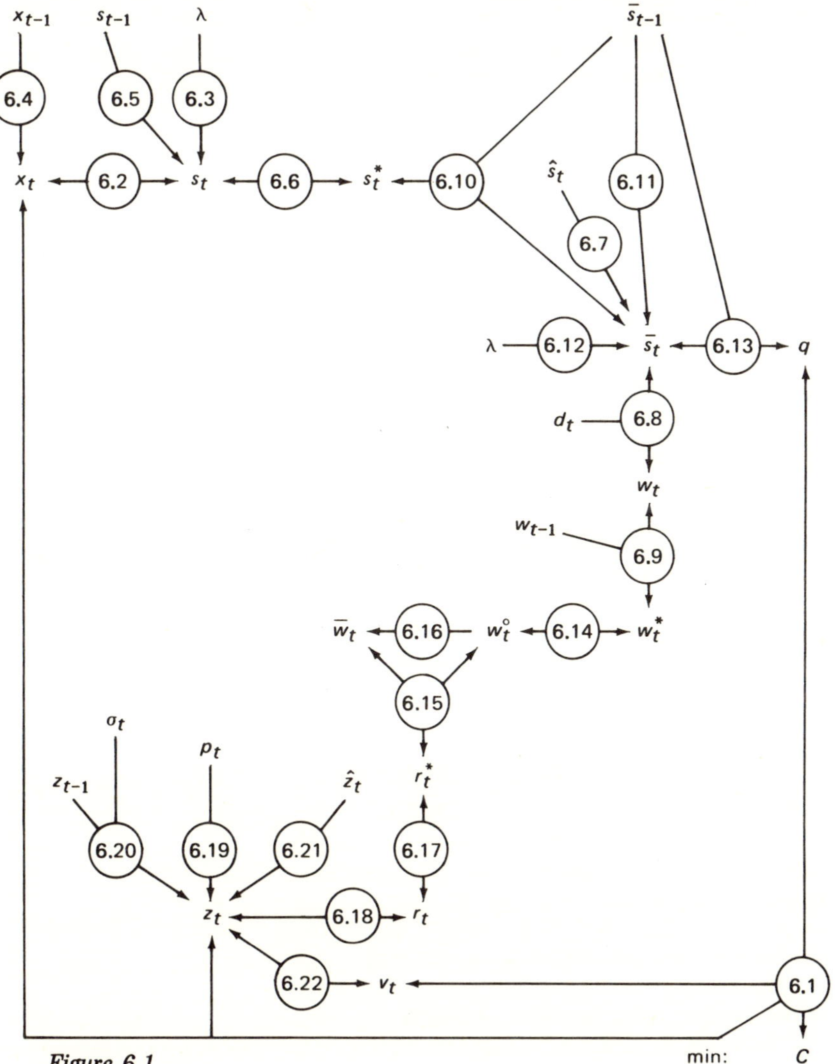

Figure 6.1
FLOW DIAGRAM

NOTE: Equation numbers are shown within circles along the lines representing the relationships.

Equation 6.21 limits the number of students in each level. This constraint facilitates simulation of social decisions in connection with democratization of the educational system.

Equation 6.22 states that the capacity of the educational facilities supplied have to be larger or equal than the demand for them. Thus, required investments to eliminate capacity bottlenecks are computed. However, the true constraint would require a quadratic expression ($x \cdot z$ instead of $\phi \cdot z$). Equation 6.7 being an alternative to a quadratic expression may need the usage of iterative techniques to get values of ϕ similar to those of x in the final solution. If necessary, lagged relations can be established.

The variables included in the previous equations are displayed in figure 6.1. The number of the equations relating to the variables are presented in circles. The arrows indicate the different interactions among variables. Parameters and constraints are joined by lines with the corresponding equations. The four groups of equations described above may be easily identified with the equation numbers.

IMPLEMENTATION

The model is general enough to fit most educational systems. In the implementation described herein, however, only two educational levels (primary and higher than primary) were defined for the educational system and the labor force. The three inputs used were plant space per student, number of teachers per student, and teachers' in-service training per student. Variables, therefore, are very aggregated. Definitions for each variable are presented in Appendix B.

In spite of defining very aggregated variables and dealing with only one period, there are still 45 choice variables, 57 slack variables, 58 equations, and 157 matrix entries in the implemented version of the model. Table 6.1 illustrates the structure of the numerical case.*

There is a large amount of data on educational costs. Little is known, however, about the shape of the cost curves. The shape of the cost curves included in the objective functions were guessed (see equation 6.1, Appendix A). Future research will test this assumption. Meanwhile, the shape of the cost curves used in the example must be considered when choosing among alternative results. In the implementation, a two-piece function was used. The first linear segment corresponded to the present cost value and the second linear segment corresponded to a subjective estimate of the costs required in an optimal educational process. The cost coefficients (present and optimal) actually used for each variable in the numerical case are presented in table 6.2.

The model must include the main relationships of the system. As noted, information on quality is scarce. Four coefficients (η, π, δ and α') in this model will therefore be estimated using subjective judgments which rely upon the experience or intuition of the decision maker as well as on the available data.

*A detailed description of the model and its application to Chile has been presented in my thesis (Schiefelbein 1969).

Table 6.1
Characteristics of the Equations in the Implemented Version of the Model

Type of Equation	Number of Equations
Objective function	1
Functional relations	27
Boundary constraints	25
Identities (definitions)	5
Total	58

Variants of the Delphi method were used for data collection (Helmer 1970). In three to four stages of the algorithm, convergency was attained. Subjective assessments of uncertainty are useful for a study such as this, where the data in itself is not sufficient to enable an objective analysis. In any case, no amount of data will remove all uncertainty in planning.

Coefficients used in the simplified version presented herein are described in table 6.3. The sources for estimating these coefficients are listed in Appendix C.

In order to illustrate the usage of the model, two different examples have been selected. The first one shows the effects of changes on exogenous variables; the second is an example of the advantages of the model in cost-benefit analysis. Additional uses are also mentioned.

Table 6.2
Cost Coefficients Used in the Objective Function

Coefficients		Levels	
Name	Description	First	Second
α_1'	Actual annual cost per teacher (E° millions)	6.1	25.8
α_1''	Optimal annual cost per teacher (E° millions)	12.2	31.9
α_2'	Actual current expenditures per 1,000 classes	.245	4.6
α_2''	Optimal current expenditures per 1,000 classes	1.950	8.63
α_3'	Cost of in-service-training per 1,000 teachers	.10	.20
α_3''	Optimal cost of in-service-training per 1,000 teachers	.30	.50
Δ_1	Construction cost (E° billions) per classroom (1,000 units square)	.01225	.075
Δ_2	Recruiting costs (E° billions) per teacher (millions)	.0005	.005
$\in$	Upgrading costs (E° billions)	1.16	—

NOTE: α parameters are used in a piecewise function, that is, a linear approximation of the estimated cost curve. Two values are presented for each type of cost. See text.

Table 6.3
Coefficients Used in the Constraint Equations

Coefficients		Levels	
Name	Description[a]	First	Second
γ_1	Optimal number of students per classroom	15	10
γ_2	Optimal number of students per teacher	17	15
γ_3	Optimal number of students per teacher-in-training	360	360
ϕ_1	Estimated classroom size per student	.027	.030
ϕ_2	Estimated teacher-student ratio	.030	.030
φ	Dropout rate		.10
ρ	Adjustment of population of the corresponding age	1.01	.877
θ	Rate of substitution between number (millions) of workers and the educational index of workers	1.9	
π_1	Estimated adaptability to technological change	.25	
π	Perfect adaptability to technological change	.50	
ν	One plus the historical productivity rate	1.02	
ψ	Number of workers from the inactive population	.05	
μ	Proportion of "leavers" joining the labor force	.60	
d	Initial value of the GNP level index	3.8	

[a] A more complete description of the coefficients is presented in Appendix C.

ASSESSING THE EFFECTS OF ECONOMIC GROWTH ON THE EDUCATIONAL SYSTEM

It is difficult to relate the effect of assumed changes in the control variables to the final activity levels. It is even more difficult to assess the effect of a change in a single exogenous variable, because many variables change at the same time. On the other hand, the greater the number of relations subjectively estimated, the larger the number of parameters that it would be desirable to vary. In order to simplify the analysis of the results obtained with the model, the changes in only one of the variables that are supposed to have a key role in social development will be plotted.

The economic growth is arbitrarily selected as the exogenous variable and the effect of increasing the GNP target (parameter d in equation 6.8) is traced in three relevant variables of the model. For each value of the parameter, the model gives one *and only one* result.

The initial solution corresponds to the situation computed with actual data (see tables 6.2 and 6.3). The value of parameter d in the initial solution is 3.8. The results of changing parameter d from 3.8 to 4.37 (an increment of 15 percent) are depicted in figure 6.2.

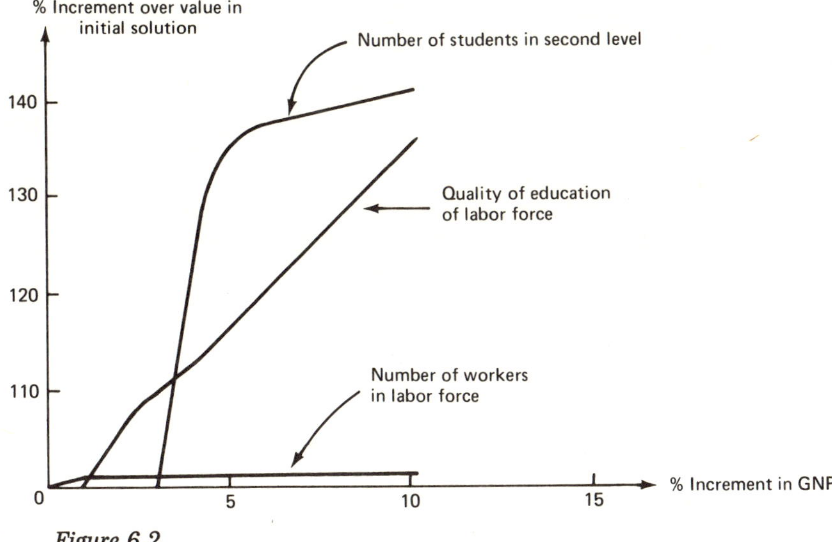

Figure 6.2

Under the assumption of constant capital (see equation 6.8) the graph shows that increments in the number of workers are rather limited. The structure of the system does not permit a substantial increment in the number of workers in the short run. Given the limitations in the number of workers available for future development (above a 3 percent increment in GNP) quality of education becomes the only way to match the new targets. Thus, the qualitative aspects of the problem plays a key role in the search for a feasible short-run solution.

This result implicitly built into the model is intuitively acceptable for semi-developed countries. To attain a slight increment in the labor force beyond a certain threshold induces great pressure on enrollments. But the model takes into account different constraints for increasing enrollments and compensates them with increments in quality.

The graph shows that beyond a 5 percent increment in GNP, the increments of quality in the labor force requires an increment of more than 40 percent in the second level of the educational system. An examination of the model's rationale indicates that this increment is a result of assuming constant dropout rates. In the short run, the amount of leavers with certain minimum educational training is relatively fixed. In order to expand the number of leavers from the second level, it is necessary to expand the whole educational system. This relationship may be unrealistic in certain cases. It is possible to introduce flexibility in the model assuming that an unused amount of educational quality is available. This "stock" could be used when great pressure is exercised in the labor force.

These computations of the model show that changes in quality may be decisive for reaching adequate solutions. If the effects of quality are not duly considered in the decision process, the proposed policies may be misleading. Numerical results also showed that supply shortages could be created by attempting to promote rapid changes in the educational system. The technical coefficients of the educational system are not easy to adapt in the short run. Gaps created by rapid change may be bridged through massive training. On-the-job training, therefore, seems the key variable for tackling the more pressing problems.

Trying to check the effect of changes in the magnitude of coefficients subjectively estimated, and looking for alternative solutions, several sets of parameters were represented. Special attention was paid to simulation of different rates of substitution and input-output ratios. In all trials the changes affected total costs but not the shape of the relationships depicted in figure 6.2. For the sake of simplicity these results are not included in this paper. These additional checks only increase the confidence in the answers provided for the model when the GNP targets were raised.

These complementary trials lead to a better understanding of the process. For example, they show that changes in the educational technology were the only way to reduce the rate of growth of quality depicted in figure 6.2, that is, repetition rates should be reduced in order to graduate more students in the same period. Although more complex models may introduce other relevant variables,* these results show that educational technology plays a role usually forgotten in the theory of human resources.

USING THE MODEL IN COST-BENEFIT ANALYSIS

One of the most difficult problems that planners must face is estimating the amount of resources to be devoted to education. Does it "pay" to expand education assuming that it will help to reach higher GNP levels in the future?

The model may provide an answer, given the built-in assumptions. In other words it may help the decision maker when he faces uncertain decisions and assigns subjective probabilities to different alternative events. The results are presented in figure 6.3

The graph shows that increments of GNP which are less than 6 percent are greater than the costs in education required for the increment. It would be an adequate social policy, therefore, to expand the educational activities in order to provide the human resources required for a targeted increment in GNP not greater than 6 percent. As in the first example, the decision maker may explore the effects on the break-even point of changes in several coefficients. In each case the model would provide a quantitative appraisal of the final result of each set of assumptions. The family of answers thus computed may help the decision maker, at least, to be consistent in his "guesstimates."

The degree on which model results may be relevant for decision making depends on the reliability of the sets of equations and, as usual, on subjective judgment. In this example, further sensitivity analysis showed that only the labor demand (equation 6.8) affected the break-even point substantially. Even slight changes in the slope of the labor-demand equation modified the shape of

*For example, the effect of salary raises on the dropout rates was not considered in this model.

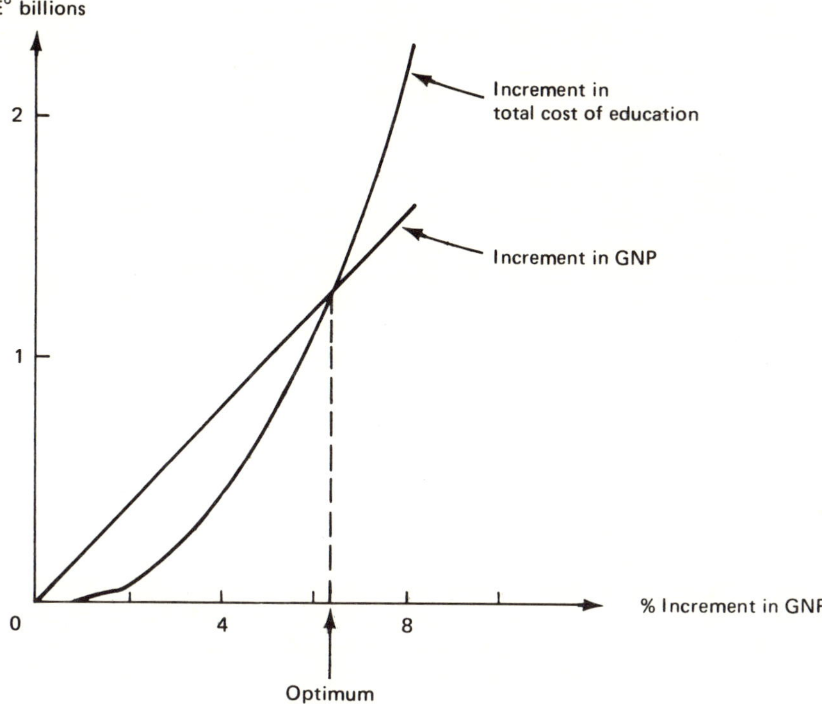

Figure 6.3

the "total cost of education" curve. The slope depends on the rate of substitution between number of workers and quality of workers and the estimation of this parameter is a poor one. Thus, efforts may be devoted toward improving a single parameter. In this case, however, assuming that the model represented reality relatively well, the decision maker focused his attention on a few parameters related to equation 6.8 instead of dealing with the complex web of interdependencies at the same time.

OTHER USES OF THE MODEL

One must be cautious in the use of the model. Previous examples have shown that its application to real situations presupposes the ability of the operator to use it.

Similar graphs to those presented above might be constructed to find the break-even points between different alternatives to train people, to increase production, to reduce unemployment, or to increase the qualitative aspects of education. The effects of many social constraints may also be simulated. Variables may be disaggregated in several dimensions according to the objectives of the analysis. If enough computer time is available and the probability distributions are known, the use of random numbers may help to obtain probability distributions of the results. One must be aware, however, that the computational problem becomes cumbersome if more than one variable is randomly varied at the same time (Madansky 1963).

The lack of objective antecedents for selecting adequate variables, and the need for defining them in order to account for more dimensions of the inputs, has already been mentioned. Many interactions between the variables are not included in the model. For instance, the number of students working with a teacher may be related with teacher training; that is, in a given situation, a certain number of highly trained teachers may be a better solution than a greater number of teachers with less preparation. But we have to wait for results of new research in education before modifying the model. So far, it does not seem worthwhile to make the model more complex.

CONCLUSIONS

The main objective in designing this quadratic model was to develop a tool for improving decision making in an educational system. The numerical example represents a first step toward this goal. Implementation showed how data on quality could be used in models for decisions in education. The use of Delphi methods provided the basic information for sensitivity analysis. The rapid convergence of the educators' estimates was, in itself, an interesting conclusion. The model computed the secondary effects of these estimates, bringing into light unexplored interactions, such as the effects of quality in a rapid development process or the role of on-the-job training in bridging short-term gaps.

The systematic exploration of the relevant alternatives through models may be one of the few devices capable of dealing with the huge problems of decisions under uncertainty facing the educational executive. Interaction between the decision maker and the model is, therefore, taken for granted. Available knowledge about the relevant relationship is scarce; more information is necessary to design more comprehensive models. In the meantime, the model may be used to compute the effects of sets of assumptions, i.e., to provide a test for consistency and to explore the implications of these subjective assumptions.

This type of model cannot be used to provide exact answers. The model provides only a framework for disciplined judgment. The model will not make active manipulation of reality possible nor will it reveal new factors or factor relations. In other words, the model cannot replace the educational executive. The model is only a tool; but the better the set of tools, the easier will be the work of the executive. In this case the model showed that, with the usual assumptions, quality becomes a key factor in educational decision making. Policies should be reviewed with this fact in mind.

The model may be easily improved by adding alternative educational activities and constraints, increasing the number of input ratios and levels of the educational system, or increasing the segments of the piecewise function. The expanded computer capacity enlarges the feasible size of implemented models. It might also be interesting to develop a battery of complementary models. Time and resources, however, are limited. It is necessary to trade larger models for more models and vice versa. The subjective aspects of decision making are present even when selecting the type of model to be implemented.

The case developed in this chapter advocates including some subjective appraisals of educational authorities, especially on quality aspects, in a systematic way. It is pioneer effort in a rapidly changing field of knowledge. I hope it will be soon replaced by more comprehensive schemes.

Appendix A: Equations and Inequations

Serial Number		Brief Description
(6.1)	$\text{Min. } c = \sum_t [x_t' A_t z_t + v_t' \Delta_t v_t + q_t' E_t q_t]$	Objective cost function
(6.2)	$\Lambda s_t \leqslant \Gamma_t x_t$	Relation between quality and input per student
(6.3)	$s_t \leqslant \lambda$	Upper extreme of the quality index
(6.4)	$x_t \geqslant x_{t-1}$	Nondecreasing levels of input per student
(6.5)	$s_{it} \leqslant \eta_{i-1,t-1} s_{i-1,t-1}$	Limit on increments in quality from period to period
(6.6)	$s_t \geqslant s_t^*$	Quality in education system greater than the labor requirements
(6.7)	$s_t \geqslant \hat{s}_t$	Limit on levels of quality in each level of education
(6.8)	$w_t + \theta_t \bar{s}_t \geqslant d_t$	Labor demand for each level of GNP
(6.9)	$w_t - w_t^* = w_{t-1}$	Defining the additional labor demand of the period
(6.10)	$s_t^* \geqslant (1 - \Pi_t) \bar{s}_t + \Pi_t \bar{s}_{t-1}$	Level of education of the additional labor force
(6.11)	$\bar{s}_t \geqslant \bar{s}_{t-1}$	Nondecreasing levels of education of the labor force
(6.12)	$\bar{s}_t \leqslant \lambda$	Upper extreme of the quality index
(6.13)	$\bar{s}_t - q_t \leqslant \tau \bar{s}_{t-1}$	Defining increments in education levels over historical trends

Appendix A (Continued)

Serial Number		Brief Description
(6.14)	$w_t^* \leqslant w_t^0$	Increment in labor demand not exceeding increment in supply
(6.15)	$w_t^0 = r_t^* + \overline{w}_t$	Increment in labor-force supply
(6.16)	$\overline{w}_t \leqslant \psi_t w_t^0$	Limit on number of workers from the inactive population
(6.17)	$r_t^* = M_t r_t$	Proportion of the leavers joining the labor force
(6.18)	$r_t = Z_t z_t$	Number of leavers of each educational level
(6.19)	$z_t \leqslant P_t p_t$	Demographic constraint
(6.20)	$z_t = \Omega_{t-1} z_{t-1} + \sigma_t$	Limit on increments in enrollments from period to period
(6.21)	$z_t \geqslant \hat{z}_t$	Limit on number of students in each level of education
(6.22)	$\Phi_t \cdot z_t \leqslant v_t + v_{t-1} + \cdots + v_0$	Capacity requirements

Appendix B:
Variables

Name	Description	Equations in Which They Appear
c	Cost of the operational expenses of all levels during t periods.	6.1
z	Column vector, $(n \times 1)$, of activity levels z_i. Each z_i denotes the number of students in educational level i.	6.1, 6.18, 6.19, 6.20, 6.21, 6.22
x	Column vector, $(n \times 1)$, of elements x_i. Each x_i is itself a column vector, $(m \times 1)$, of activity levels x_{ji}. Each x_{ji} denotes the amount of input j per student enrolled in educational level i. (It may also be considered as a $(nm \times 1)$ vector.)	6.1, 6.2, 6.3, 6.4
w	Column vector, $(n \times 1)$, of activity levels w_i. Each w_i denotes the number of workers in level i.	6.8, 6.9

Appendix B (Continued)

Name	Description	Equations in Which They Appear
w^*	Column vector, $(n \times 1)$, of activity levels w_i^*. Each w_i^* denotes the number of new workers that have to join the i level of the labor force in order to produce a given level of GNP.	6.9, 6.14
w^0	Column vector, $(n \times 1)$, of activity levels w_i^0. Each w_i^0 denotes the number of people that are available to join the labor force in level i.	6.14, 6.15, 6.16
$\overline{w}$	Column vector, $(n \times 1)$, of activity levels $\overline{w}_i$. Each $\overline{w}_i$ denotes the number of previously inactive people that want to join the i level of the labor force at the market salaries.	6.15, 6.16
v	Column vector, $(n \times 1)$, of elements v_i. Each v_i is itself a column vector, $(k \times 1)$, of activity levels v_{hi}. Each v_{hi} denotes the investment of input h in educational level i.	6.1, 6.22
s	Column vector, $(n \times 1)$, of activity levels s_i. Each s_i denotes the performance of the average student at the end of one period, measured by a weighted battery of tests for level i. It will be referred to as quality of education index of level i.	6.2, 6.3, 6.6, 6.7
s^*	Column vector, $(n \times 1)$, of activity levels s_i^*. Each s_i^* denotes the educational performance of the average new worker joining the labor force level i. It is measured by a weighted battery of tests for educational level i.	6.6, 6.10
$\bar{s}$	Column vector, $(n \times 1)$ of activity levels $\bar{s}_i$. Each $\bar{s}_i$ denotes the educational performance of the average worker in a weighted battery of tests for educational level i.	6.8, 6.10, 6.11, 6.12, 6.13
r	Column vector, $(n \times 1)$, of activity levels r_i. Each r_i denotes the number of leavers that have attained the ith level of education.	6.17, 6.18
r^*	Column vector, $(n \times 1)$, of activity levels r_i^*. Each r_i^* denotes the number of leavers that have attained the ith level of the educational system and want to join the labor force at market salaries.	6.15, 6.17
q	Column vector of activity levels q_i. Each q_i denotes increments in educational performance of workers in level i over the historical trend.	6.1, 6.13
τ_e	Row vector of dual variables, where the index e represents the number of the constraints.	Dual

Appendix C:
Coefficients

Name	Description	Source of Values Used in Numerical Example	Equations in Which Used
A	Diagonal matrix, $(n \times n)$, of vectors α_i. Each α_i is itself a row vector, $(1 \times m)$, of coefficients α_{ji}. Each α_{ji} denotes the current cost of input j in educational level i. (It may also be considered as a $[mn \times n]$ matrix.)	Carrillo 1969	6.1
Δ	Diagonal matrix, $(n \times n)$, of elements Δ_i. Each Δ_i is a diagonal matrix, $(k \times k)$, of coefficients δ_{hi}. Each δ_{hi} denotes the investments costs of input h in educational level i.	Ministerio de Educacion 1966	6.1
E	Diagonal matrix, $(n \times n)$, of coefficients ϵ_i. Each ϵ_i denotes the current cost of improving the education of workers in level i over the historical trend.	Schiefelbein 1969	6.1
Γ	Diagonal matrix, $(n \times n)$, of elements Γ_i. Each Γ_i is a diagonal matrix, $(m \times m)$ of coefficients γ_{ji}. Each γ_{ji} denotes the optimal number of students in level i per unit of input j.	Schiefelbein 1969	6.2
Λ	Scalar matrix, $(n \times n)$, of λ vectors of unit elements.	Definition	6.2
λ	Unit column vector, $(m \times 1)$, of (identical) unit elements.	Definition	6.2
$\eta_{i,t}$	Coefficient of the maximum increment in quality it is possible to attain from level i in year t to level $i + 1$ in year $t + 1$.	Guessed with Delphi method	6.5
Φ	Diagonal matrix, $(n \times n)$ of vectors ϕ_i. Each ϕ_i is a column vector, $(k \times 1)$, of coefficients ϕ_{ji}. Each ϕ_{ji} denotes the amount of input j per student enrolled in educational level i.	Schiefelbein 1969	6.22
θ	Diagonal matrix, $(n \times n)$, of coefficients θ_i. Each θ_i denotes the absolute rates of substitution between number of workers and quality of workers of level i.	Schiefelbein 1969	6.8
Π	Diagonal matrix, $(n \times n)$, of coefficients π_i of learning by doing in the i level. They must be $0 < \pi_i < .5$.	Guessed with Delphi method	6.10

Appendix C (Continued)

Name	Description	Source of Values Used in Numerical Example	Equations in Which Used
I	Diagonal unitary matrix, $(n \times n)$.	Definition	6.10
Υ	Diagonal matrix, $(n \times n)$, of coefficients υ_i. Each coefficient is calculated as the sum of one and the historical productivity rate.	Educated guess	6.9
Ψ	Diagonal matrix, $(n \times n)$, of range coefficients ψ_i. Each coefficient represents the maximum number of workers coming from the inactive population.	Instituto de Economia 1966	6.16
M	Diagonal matrix, $(n \times n)$, of coefficients μ_i. Each μ_i denotes the proportion of the total number of leavers of the i educational level who will join the labor force.	Herrick 1965	6.17
Z	Diagonal matrix, $(n \times n)$, of coefficients ζ_i. Each ζ_i denotes the dropout rates of the i level of the educational system.	Planning Office (unpublished)	6.18
P	Diagonal matrix, $(n \times n)$, of the range coefficients ρ_i. Each coefficient represents the maximum amount of population of the corresponding age.	CELADE 1967	6.19
Ω	Matrix, $(n \times n)$, of transition ratios (probabilities). The ω_{ii} elements of the matrix are the repetition rates of the level i and the $\omega_{i,i+1}$ elements correspond to the promotion rates from level i to the level $i + 1$. (The graduates from the last level are included in equation 6.9d.)	Planning Office (unpublished)	6.20
σ	Column vector, $(n \times 1)$, of σ_i number of students entering the educational system directly into the i level.	Not used in example	6.20
d	Column vector, $(n \times 1)$, of indexes d_j of the GNP level. A Latin letter was used to denote that these parameters were used as an exogenous variable in the numerical example.	Schiefelbein 1969	6.8

Appendix D:
Boundaries, Initial and Terminal Conditions (exogenous variables)

Name	Description	Source of Values Used in Numerical Example	Equations in Which Used
d	Column vector, $(n \times 1)$, of scalars d_i. Each d_i denotes the index of the GNP.	Schiefelbein 1969	6.8
p	Column vector, $(n \times 1)$, of scalars p_i. Each p_i denotes the number of people in the population with the median age of educational level i.	CELADE 1967	6.19
$\hat{s}$	Column vector, $(n \times 1)$, of scalars $\hat{s}_i$. Each $\hat{s}_i$ denotes the minimum levels of quality of education in educational level i.	Guessed with Delphi method	6.7
$\bar{v}$	Column vector, $(n \times 1)$, of scalars $\bar{v}_i$. Each v_i denotes the initial stocks in educational level i.	Ministerio de Educación 1966	6.22
$\hat{z}$	Column vector, $(n \times 1)$, of scalars $\hat{z}_i$. Each $\hat{z}_i$ denotes the minimum levels of enrollment in educational level i.	Guess based on actual enrollment	6.21

Appendix E:
Indexes

Name	Description
t	Time index. The unit used is one year. The initial stocks are denoted by $t = 0$.
i	Educational levels index. For $i = 1, \ldots, n$.
j	Type of input in the educational processes. For $j = 1, \ldots, m$.
h	Type of inputs in the investment processes. For $h = 1, \ldots, k$.
e	Number of the constraints. For $e = 2, \ldots, 22$.

REFERENCES

Arrow, Kenneth J. "The Economic Implications of Learning by Doing." *Review of Economic Studies* 29, no. 2 (June 1962).

Blot, Daniel. "La Deperdition d'Effectifs Scolaires. Analyse Theorique et Aplications." *Revue Tiers-Monde* 6, no. 22 (Paris: Presses Universitaires de France, April–June 1965).

Bowman, Mary Jean. "The Human Investment Revolution in Economic Thought." *Sociology of Education* 39, no. 2 (Spring 1966).

Carrillo, Carmen Julia. "Variables de Costo en la Proyeccion del Gasto en Educación Fiscal." Thesis, Facultad de Ciencias Económicas, Universidad de Chile, 1969.

Carroll, John B. "A Model for School Learning." *Teachers College Records* 64, no. 8 (May 1963): 723–33.

CELADE. "Proyección de la población por años individuales de edad, 1960–1980." Ms. Santiago, Chile, 1967.

Correa, Hector, and Tinbergen, Jan. "Quantitative Adaption of Education to Accelerated Growth." *Kyklos* 15 (1962).

Denison, Edward. "Measuring the Contribution of Education to Economic Growth." In *The Residual Factor and Economic Growth.* Paris: OECD, 1964.

Educational Testing Service (ETS). *Proceedings of the 1969 International Conference on Testing Problems*, Princeton, N.J., 1969.

Helmer, Olaf. "L'utilisation de l'avis des experts dans la planification de l'education." Paris: IIPE, 1970.

Herrick, Bruce H. *Urban Migration and Economic Development in Chile.* Cambridge, Mass.: MIT Press, 1965.

Instituto de Economía de la Universidad de Chile. "Ocupación y desocupación. Gran Santiago." Santiago, Chile, June 1966.

Kaufmann, Arnold. *Methods and Models of Operations Research.* Englewood Cliffs, N.J.: Prentice-Hall, 1963.

Lieberman, Myron, ed. "Eight Articles on Accountability." *Phi Delta Kappan* 52, no. 4 (December 1970).

Madansky, Albert. "Linear Programming under Uncertainty." In *Recent Advances in Mathematical Programming*, edited by Robert L. Graves and Philip Wolfe. New York: McGraw-Hill, 1963.

Ministerio de Educación. "Sinopsis del Programa de Educación 1965–1970 (Versión Preliminar)." Santiago, Chile, 1966.

Rosenthal, Robert, and Jacobson, Lenore. "Teachers' Expectancies. Determinants of Pupils' IQ Gains." *Psychological Reports* 19 (1966).

Schiefelbein, Ernesto. "A Model for Assessing the Quantitative Results of Alternative Educational Policies." Ph.D. dissertation, Harvard University, 1969.

Tyler, Ralph W. "The Objective and Plans for a National Assessment of Educational Progress." *Journal of Educational Measurement* 3, no. 1 (Spring 1966).

PART II PLANNING IN EDUCATIONAL INSTITUTIONS

Byron W. Brown, Jr., and I. Richard Savage

7 STATISTICAL STUDIES IN PREDICTION OF ATTENDANCE FOR A UNIVERSITY*

OBJECTIVES

These studies were motivated by the necessity for making predictions of attendance in planning educational programs of the University of Minnesota. The university's Planning Committee sponsored this work in 1960. This revision condenses the original report (Brown and Savage 1960), tests the 1960 projections against true outcomes, and also reflects some intervening changes. Although we have made no effort to distinguish between text written in 1960 and revisions or new comments added in 1971, we feel that we have been fair in not allowing hindsight concerning forecasts for the 1960s to look like foresight.

The approach was descriptive rather than analytical. Models for the various prediction situations were presented which fit the past data in a satisfactory manner and, barring abrupt changes in behavior, would fit data in the near future. No attempt was made to study the basic socioeconomic problems of why people become students nor were the long-range dynamics of demography and short-range changes of economic level investigated. No attempt has been made to specify which techniques would be most useful in a particular administrative situation and no precise formulation is made of how attendance predictions should be used in administrative decisions.

Although nearly all the data relate to the state of Minnesota, particularly to the University of Minnesota, the methods are applicable to other states and regions.

*In memory of Dean Robert E. Summers whose workmanship provided a solid base for us.

General Summary

Attention was centered on making predictions at various educational levels—primary, secondary, and university—and substantial effort was devoted to collecting data and investigating data sources. The material related to predictions is given in Studies A, B, C, D, and E; notes concerning data sources and other studies are described in section F, Supplementary Notes.

Study A: Predicting Numbers of High School Graduates

Two methods were used. The live-birth method consisted in developing a simple regression of the numbers of graduates (as the dependent variable) on the numbers of live births eighteen years previously (as the independent variable). In the cohort method, regression technique was used to predict numbers of students in a particular grade, or numbers of graduates for a given year (as the dependent variable) from the numbers of students one grade earlier, or numbers of live births six years earlier for the first grade (as the independent variable). The approach here was novel in that the rate of movement from grade to grade was allowed to depend on time.

Study B: Predicting University Attendance

Several multiple-regression models were developed, the most successful using the numbers of students in attendance at the university as the dependent variable and the numbers of high school graduates and the net changes in the armed forces for several of the preceding years as the independent variables.

Study C: Transitions of Students Into, Out of, and Between Parts of the University

The 1960 data handling practices did not follow individual students through their educational careers. In an attempt to do so, a single punch card was prepared for each student who attended the university either in the fall of 1958 or in the fall of 1959. In this way the transition probabilities associated with students entering the university, changing colleges during a year, and leaving the university can be estimated by college and class. These transition probabilities can then be used for short-range prediction.

Study D: Relationships Between "Fall Quarter End of Second Week Attendance" and Other Important Variables in University Planning

The basic data used and predicted were the numbers of students in attendance at the beginning of the fall quarter. For planning purposes, however, it is necessary to know the numbers of students in the other quarters and the tuition income. It was shown that regression techniques yield very good estimates of these variables (as dependent variables) when the numbers of students in the fall quarter are used as the independent variable.

Studies A through D could be used in making predictions of numbers of students and tuition income from various parts of the university. From the 1960 data, these predictions could be made to the middle of the 1970s, since all students who will be at the university until then were already born. The most arbitrary decisions required in making these predictions were the fee schedule and the net changes in the armed-service personnel (in 1960, presumed zero through the decade).

Study E: College Attendance Expectations

A sample survey of attitudes of high school students toward their expectations of attending college was conducted by the Minnesota Poll.

Needs for Predictions

Interest in attendance patterns and in the prediction of them arises out of administrative decision making affecting both educational and fiscal policies. Such decisions must be made by many agencies although the distance into the future may vary.

In planning for the university, knowledge of attendance patterns alone is not sufficient, for the cost of operating the university is not proportional to attendance only: expansion of the medical school by twenty students is not comparable to expansion of the general college by the same number. Other activities of the university can be insensitive to attendance; for example, the main auditorium and stadium actually service the local community if not the whole state. Hence the need exists for detailed predictions of attendance as well as knowledge of the relations between attendance and other variables.

One of the major steps taken in these studies was to associate with a prediction, some measure of its possible error. These measures are helpful to anyone using the predictions for administrative purposes.

Finally, planning based on predictions resting on specific assumptions (either explicit or implicit) will not be satisfactory if the assumptions are violated. Throughout, it was assumed that the tuition and the academic level of the university will remain fixed compared to other available institutions. If the university administration should change the relative fee schedule or the academic standards, then plans based on the predictions of these studies would be suspect.

In making predictions we presumed that ten years into the future would suffice. Further, we presumed that predictions would be updated in a systematic manner as data accumulate or as structural changes occurred. Although one can be forced to live with decisions, one should not stick with his predictions when better ones can be made.

Comments on Methodology*

The educational process and the resulting attendance patterns reflect individual behavior. Data should be collected and treated so that an individual can be followed through time and several aspects of his behavior correlated. Study C

*A standard summary of techniques and bibliography for the prediction of educational patterns is by L. J. Linis, *Methodology of Enrollment Predictions for Colleges and Universities* (Washington, D.C.: American Association of Collegiate Registrars and Admissions Officers, March 1960).

makes a beginning effort to follow individuals over time and Study E yields several measures on the same individual at a particular time. But our work is far from our ideal. Most of the data were based on aggregates. The variables used were superficial (age, place in the educational system, and military status); our work did not use any deeper theory—educational, psychological, sociological, or economic. The predominant use of aggregate data reflects the weaknesses of the data system, and the lack of theory in choice of variables reflects our intellectual limitations.

Comments on specific techniques follow.

Cohort Method

The cohort method consists of keeping track of similar groups of individuals through life, that is, a cohort analysis uses aggregated longitudinal data. Enrollments by grade and year for the public schools of the state of Minnesota can be regarded as approximate cohort data (Study A): approximate, in that records of migrations in and out of the public schools and state, and deaths, are not coordinated. In the transition study (Study C) some cohort data for the university have been obtained and used.

Regression Analysis

The analytic tool frequently used here is regression analysis: specifically, linear models and least squares. In this method, it is assumed that the variable of interest—say, Y—can be expressed in the form $Y = a + bx + e$, where a and b are unknown coefficients to be determined, x is called an independent variable, and e is the error of the model, i.e., the model is not "perfect." The independent variable usually is chosen because it constitutes one that is known with greater precision than Y. If early knowledge (in time) of the x variable is available, the regression method can be used for predictive purposes with probability limits on the size of error in such predictions.

Sampling Methods

When attempting to learn something about a large number of individuals it is frequently sufficient to work with a sample (see Study E). When sampling is used carefully, precision of the answers can be assessed.

Persistence Forecasting

The simplest method of forecasting uses persistence, that is, the fact that tomorrow will usually be much like today. But when information becomes available from other sources than the phenomenon itself (e.g., births, eighteen years earlier) then other methods can produce more accurate forecasts or predictions.

Determination of Accuracy

So far as possible we attempted to evaluate the orders of magnitude of the errors of prediction as follows:

1. For some of the analyses (Study E), the errors can be determined by the data-collection method.

2. In fitting data by a particular linear model (Studies A and B), the mean of the squares of the differences (or average squared difference) between the observed series and the fitted series is given. When several methods are used for the same data, then the one with the smaller mean sum of squares promises to be more satisfactory for future data.
3. In working with several methods (Study B), the predictions have been plotted. This should help to determine roughly the differences between the methods of prediction as well as to assess the inherent variability of the predictions.

In several places we present predictions as intervals. These intervals are the least-squares prediction plus or minus two standard deviations of the least-square prediction. When these intervals are used, the probability is about .95 that the predicted quantity will be in the interval, provided the assumptions of the analysis remain valid.

STUDY A: PREDICTING NUMBERS OF HIGH SCHOOL GRADUATES

Several methods of prediction of numbers of public high school graduates are presented. The models consist of combinations of linear regressions of various ratios on time. These predictions of high school graduates were then used in Study B as independent variables to predict university enrollment.

For basic data, we used the numbers of live births for the calendar years 1921-60 plus public school enrollment figures for each grade and the number of public high school graduates for the years 1939-60.* The figures for grades are gross enrollments, i.e., students are counted more than once if they attend more than one school during a year.†

METHOD AI: PREDICTION USING LIVE BIRTHS

The following notation is used:

B_t = number of live births in calendar year t,
G_t = number of high school graduates in the school year *ending* in the calendar year t.

A simple method of estimating numbers of public high school graduates uses only the ratio of number of graduates to number of births eighteen years earlier.

*Live-birth data: For 1921-58 the values are from the Research Service, Minnesota Education Association, *Selected Statistical Trends Affecting Education*, No. 68, 1959. The 1959-60 values are from *Monthly Vital Reports*, U.S. Department of Health, Education, and Welfare, Washington, D.C. The data are closely related to the values in *Vital Statistics of the United States*, vol. 1, published annually by the same department.

Public school data were from Annual Minnesota Report of the State Department of Education, 1939-60.

†"Enrollment" refers to a gross count over some time period; "attendance" refers to a count at some instant.

Table 7.1
Method AI: Predicted Numbers of Public High School Graduates Using Live-birth Ratios, Minnesota, 1939–70

Year of Graduation	Method AI: Predicted Number of Graduates	Predicted Minus Actual Number of Graduates	Year of Graduation	Method AI: Predicted Number of Graduates	Predicted Minus Actual Number of Graduates
1939	27,924	73	1955	29,164	-490
1940	27,990	-801	1956	30,781	-425
1941	27,928	-1,675	1957	31,307	-530
1942	28,197	-1,002	1958	33,565	355
1943	27,561	694	1959	34,858	249
1944	27,333	2,938	1960	38,087 ± 1,507[a]	-909[b]
1945	26,922	3,535	1961	38,221 ± 1,555	-1,989
1946	26,561	2,488	1962	36,951 ± 1,550	-1,389
1947	25,426	280	1963	36,314 ± 1,573	-1,934
1948	26,703	-309	1964	45,672 ± 2,046	-201
1949	26,252	-454	1965	51,809 ± 2,402	-1,634
1950	26,364	-124	1966	50,458 ± 2,420	-2,074
1951	26,651	112	1967	51,988 ± 2,580	-2,636
1952	26,822	765	1968	53,471 ± 2,744	-1,815
1953	27,192	201	1969	57,482 ± 3,048	-2,161
1954	28,567	343	1970	57,498 ± 3,148	

[a]95% probability limits.
[b]Note that the figures for 1960–70 are projections based on data through 1959. The numbers of graduates prior to 1949 are also "predicted," in that the parameters for the model were estimated only from the 1949–59 data.

To avoid the disturbances of World War II and the postwar period, a straight line was fitted (by least squares) to the data from 1949 through 1959 (eleven years); the result was:

$$G_t = [.5601 + .0079\ (t - 1949)]\ B_{t-18}. \tag{7.1}$$

Using this straight line and the appropriate values of B, the number of high school graduates were predicted to 1978, since the values for B were available through 1960. See table 7.1.

Method AII: Prediction Using Transition Ratios

The live-birth method is suspect when making predictions too far into the future because straight lines are useful only for local approximation of what, in reality, must be a curvilinear trend. A more sensitive and more comprehensive description of changing school enrollments is attained by using available information on the changing tendencies of children to go on from one grade to the next. The following notation is used:*

*The value of t corresponds to the calendar year in which the school year *ends*. Accordingly, it is the live births for the calendar year $t - 7$ to which we compare enrollment in the first grade for the school year ending in the calendar year t.

g_{it} = the gross enrollment in the ith grade for the school year *ending* in the calendar year t,

$$r_{it} = g_{1t}/B_{r-t}, \tag{7.2}$$

$$r_{it} = g_{it}/g_{i-1,\,t-1}, \quad 2 \leqslant i \leqslant 12,$$

$$r_{13t} = G_t/g_{12t}.$$

The r_{it}, the *transition ratios*, were computed for each of the 12 grades and for the graduating class, for the years 1939–59. The ratios presented several interesting aspects: the effects of World War II were evident in *every* grade; in the lower grades, decreases in ratios in 1943 and 1944 must reflect migration out of Minnesota because of the war; a more marked decrease in the last several grades can be attributed to more students quitting high school to find jobs or to enlist in the armed services. The ratios also indicated that many students returned to high school after the war.

There was also a marked and steady decrease in the ratio of first-grade students to corresponding live births, from 1.01 in 1939 to .80 in 1959. The most plausible explanation of this phenomenon is that these figures, representing public school attendance only, evidence an increasing proportion of private school students in the state at the grade school and junior high level; at the ninth grade (r_{9t}) there was a correspondingly marked flow back into the public schools.

The change in the transition ratios was regular from 1949 on; accordingly, straight lines were used to fit the transition ratios for the years from 1949 through 1959:

$$r_{it} = a_i + b_i\,(t - 1949), \quad 1 \leqslant i \leqslant 13. \tag{7.3}$$

The least-squares estimates a_i and b_i, given in table 7.2, were used to predict enrollment in the ith grade, using the births of $i + 6$ years previously,* as follows:

$$g_{it} = B_{t-6-i} \prod_{j=1}^{i} r_{j,\,t+j-1}\,. \tag{7.4}$$

Discussion of Predictions by Methods AI and AII

Figure 7.1 compares the predictions of numbers of high school graduates for the 1960s made by Methods AI and AII and those made by H. M. Lokken in February 1960 for the Minnesota Department of Education. Now we can also supply the actual figures for the 1960s as a basis for comparing the methods.

Methods AI and AII correctly predicted a great increase in the number of high school graduates: from approximately 37,000 in 1962–63 to approximately

*An alternative would be to use the last observed grade enrollments as initial cohorts and to build on these by multiplying by the appropriate r_{it} values. This modification might be expected to yield slight improvements over (A.4.3), especially for very short-term predictions.

Table 7.2

Least-squares Estimates of the Regression Coefficients for Predicting Transition Ratios, Based on Observed Ratios from 1948–49 Through 1958–59

i	a_i	b_i, with 95% Probability Limits	i	a_i	b_i, with 95% Probability Limits
1	.9161	−.0139 ± .0047	7	.9853	+.0022 ± .0017
2	.9403	+.0020 ± .0019	8	.9734	+.0019 ± .0010
3	.9661	+.0017 ± .0014	9	1.0043	+.0102 ± .0026
4	.9731	+.0016 ± .0018	10	.9296	+.0043 ± .0017
5	.9797	+.0002 ± .0016	11	.9105	+.0028 ± .0014
6	.9750	+.0018 ± .0013	12	.9104	+.0007 ± .0016
			13	.9627	−.0011 ± .0013

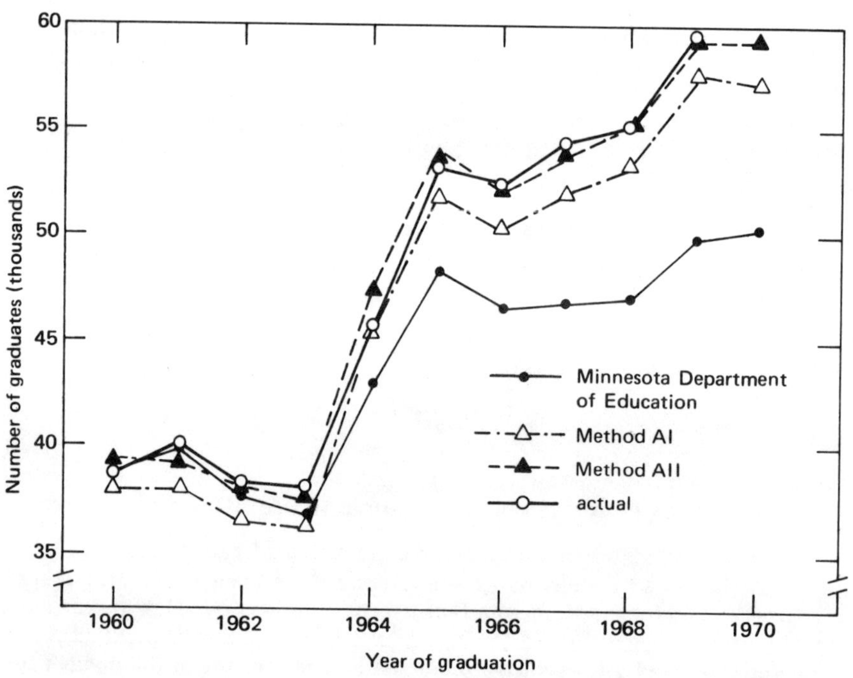

Figure 7.1

COMPARISON OF THREE SERIES OF PREDICTIONS OF NUMBERS OF PUBLIC HIGH SCHOOL GRADUATES, MINNESOTA, 1960–70

52,500 in 1964-65, or an increase of 40 percent. This increase was substantially higher than earlier predictions by other forecasters, and the reason lies, in part, in our assumptions of continued linear increase in several of the transition ratios as opposed to the customary assumption that the future resembles a composite (average) description of the past. Method AII seems a little more satisfactory than Method AI in forecasting the experience of the 1960s.

Problems

Methods AI and AII have the advantage of being simple to describe. The data used are readily available as well as relatively accurate, and the computations involve nothing more complicated than fitting straight lines to those data.

It might be possible to improve these methods by using additional information. Almost all observed transition ratios in a given year tend to deviate in the same direction from their respective best-fitting straight lines, and the problem is one of discovering what common causes operate in a given year to create such disturbances. When such causes are discovered, methods must be found to measure and predict them. Even if such causes cannot be predicted for future years, allowance for them should be made in examining past data in order to obtain prediction methods free from the specific effects of past years.

The use of more involved procedures presents several problems. Even for Method AII we lack an adequate method for forming probability intervals. Further, the computations for Methods AI and AII could be done on a desk calculator but a computer would be required for any more involved procedures. The additional detail and apparent superiority (in 1971) of fit of Method AII when compared to Method AI suggest that it would be worthwhile to develop experience and methodology to allow the evaluation of prediction errors with Method AII.

STUDY B: PREDICTING UNIVERSITY ATTENDANCE

Several methods of predicting attendance at the University of Minnesota are discussed in this study. The following criteria were established for developing prediction methods:

1. The method should be uncomplicated so that it can be easily and quickly explained and simple enough so that computations can be made on a desk calculator or with standard electronic-computer programs.
2. The model for any method should describe past data adequately; the average squared deviation of the observed values from the fitted model shall be the criterion of goodness-of-fit.
3. There should be grounds for believing that the model will continue to approximate events.
4. The data necessary for making predictions as well as for testing the model should be available in a satisfactory form at the desired time.

Table 7.3
Comparison of Fit and Forecasts for Four Methods of Predicting University Attendance

Year	Actual Attendance[a]	Error in Fitted Curve for Four Methods BI	BII	BIII	BIV
1921	7,637	608	2,753	-1,928	-300
1922	8,410	86	1,605	-1,445	1,210
1923	8,725	29	1,132	-863	1,042
1924	9,057	-37	738	-417	799
1925	9,502	-208	291	-127	454
1926	10,334	-758	-490	-259	-239
1927	10,913	-1,045	-804	-743	-214
1928	11,470	-1,303	-1,058	-1,328	-425
1929	11,676	-1,200	-1,135	-817	-886
1930	11,961	-1,166	-1,207	-594	-799
1931	11,560	-437	-587	451	-217
1932	10,700	761	378	2,998	265
1933	10,736	1,073	623	3,963	1,019
1934	11,712	456	49	3,263	898
1935	13,271	-734	-1,118	2,416	-512
1936	14,094	-1,176	-1,507	2,281	-853
1937	14,040	-729	-980	2,121	204
1938	14,436	-721	-861	3,371	-794
1939	15,122	-990	-943	4,256	-718
1940	14,986	-425	-191	5,049	669
1941	13,484	1,526	1,955	4,836	863
1942	11,672	3,788	4,322	5,151	1,461
1943	7,205	8,724	9,095	2,668	713
1944	8,917	7,496	7,575	3,951	-616
1945	11,505	5,407	5,316	3,608	-1,085
1946	27,103	-9,677	-9,688	5,090	-49
1947[b]	28,312	-10,356	-10,188	-8,332	-1,111
1948	27,243	-8,742	-8,321	-8,569	-638
1949	25,084	-6,021	-5,583	-6,795	-436
1950	22,080	-2,437	-2,099	-3,392	-557
1951	18,682	-1,557	1,565	-2,771	1,093
1952	18,806	2,049	2,110	-4,383	1,820
1953	19,074	2,414	2,666	-161	168
1954	20,399	1,742	2,304	-330	675
1955	23,393	-579	395	-2,130	132
1956	25,307	-1,800	-331	-3,363	112
1957	25,825	-1,603	32	-3,641	718
1958	26,568	-1,610	508	-3,109	810
1959[c]	26,538	-822	1,824	-2,269	1,936
1960[d]	28,277	-1,777	3,013	791	1,692

Table 7.3 (Continued)

Year	Actual Attendance[a]	Error in Fitted Curve for Four Methods BI	BII	BIII	BIV
1961	30,846	-3,546	1,314	-3,249	1,809
1962	33,616	-5,486	-1,316	-6,927	61
1963	35,112	-6,132	-2,382	-8,882	-1,598
1964	38,403	-8,543	347	-5,391	-4,939
1965	42,178	-11,408	1,092	-4,730	-2,110
1966	43,997	-12,287	-487	-7,551	944
1967	46,088	-13,408	-598	-8,569	1,068
1968	47,534	-13,864	-54	-8,987	-551
1969	48,592	-13,902	2,608	-7,210	444
1970[d]	48,921	-13,171	3,409	-7,602	3,760

[a]Source: Office of the Dean of Admissions and Records, University of Minnesota.

[b]State college at Duluth transferred to the administration of the University of Minnesota and its attendance is included in the university's total attendance.

[c]University of Minnesota, Morris Campus, established; attendance 238.

[d]The average squared error for each of the methods, measuring the fit over the years to 1960, is:

BI.	S^2 = 14,471,982	39 years	2 parameters estimated
BII.	S^2 = 15,009,465	39 years	3 parameters estimated
BIII.	S^2 = 14,116,867	39 years	3 parameters estimated
BIV.	S^2 = 893,578	39 years	9 parameters estimated

Of the four methods discussed below, Method BIV is the one that should be applied in practice. The first three methods illustrate the successive improvements arising out of the use of more variables and the consequent complications developing in the technique.

Method BI: Extrapolation

Table 7.3 presents the fall quarter, end-of-second-week attendance figures for the University of Minnesota from 1921 to 1970. The simplest prediction method (Method BI) consists of examining the series, mathematically fitting some simple function to the series over time, and extrapolating in time using this function. The data indicate that attendance is an increasing function of time, although there are noticeable disturbances in the mid-1930s and mid-1940s; nevertheless, the overall trend is a geometric increase with time. A geometrically increasing function can be fitted to these data by taking logarithms (base 10) and fitting a straight line:

$$y = \log \bar{a}_t = A + Bt, \tag{7.5}$$

where $\bar{a}_t$ is the estimated fall attendance in the year t ($t = 0$ corresponds to the year 1920). Least-squares estimation of A and B in equation 7.5, using the 1921–60 data, yields,

$$y = 3.9032 + .0130t; \tag{7.6}$$

or

$$\bar{a}_t = 8002\,(10^{.0130t}). \tag{7.7}$$

Equation 7.7 predicts a doubling of the university's attendance about every 23 years. The differences between these and the actual figures for the years 1921–60 and for the years 1961–70, not available when the forecasts were made, are given in table 7.3. Note that there are extended periods of six or more years with alternate over- and underestimation. The fit is extremely poor during and after World War II and the Korean War but for the rest of the period 1921–60 the discrepancies do not exceed 2,000 in absolute value. However, the extrapolations or forecasts for 1961–70 proved very poor, the 1970 estimate of 35,750 being an underestimate by about 25 percent.

Method BII: Use of Numbers of High School Graduates

Fitting attendance figures with time as the only independent variable does not take into account the fluctuations within the major factors affecting university attendance such as numbers of high school graduates and the tendency of high school graduates and university students to abandon education for employment or military service, or to suddenly flow back to the university from these sources.

The following function can be used to relate university attendance ($\bar{a}_t$) to the corresponding number of high school graduates (x_t):

$$\bar{a}_t = M + (A + Bt)x_t. \tag{7.8}$$

Note that the impact of high school graduates on university attendance (transition ratio) is taken to be a linear function of time. Thus, this model allows for increasing proportions of high school students to continue their educations.

Estimates of the constants M, A, and B were obtained by using the least-squares multiple-regression technique with x_t and $y_t = tx_t$ as the two *independent variables* (Snedecor and Cochran 1967).

$$\bar{a}_t = 13{,}065 + (-.3419 + .0201t)x_t \qquad (t = 0 \text{ for } 1920). \tag{7.9}$$

From equation 7.9 the percentage of high school graduates attending the university increases by 2.01 percent per year. This method (table 7.4) shows a poor fit during World War II and its postwar period (1942–49); several discrepancies are over 2,000, and many are over 1,000. The discrepancies are consistently of one sign over periods of five and six years.

The function 7.9 was used to forecast attendance in the 1960s. For this purpose we used the forecasts of high school graduates by Method AII (in Study A). The results are shown in table 7.3. It can be seen that although

Table 7.4
Net Changes in Military Personnel of the United States, 1941-70

Year	Net Change[a]	Year	Net Change
1941	-1,342,736	1956	128,666
1942	-2,057,690	1957	10,643
1943	-5,185,954	1958	195,217
1944	-2,406,974	1959	96,271
1945	-671,736	1960	27,875
1946	9,093,367	1961	-7,336
1947	1,447,089	1962	-324,048
1948	137,089	1963	110,130
1949	-169,450	1964	12,528
1950	155,099	1965	32,019
1951	-1,087,826	1966	-438,410
1952	-2,175,651	1967	-284,959
1953	80,845	1968	-170,918
1954	252,963	1969	88,006
1955	366,997	1970	298,776

Source: Statistical Abstract of the United States (Washington, D.C.: Bureau of the Census); 1960, 81st Annual Edition; 1962, 83rd Annual Edition; 1966, 87th Edition; 1970, 91st Annual Edition.
[a]A positive number denotes a decrease in the number of persons in the armed forces, i.e., a potential increase in university population. These figures are the net changes for the fiscal year ending in the indicated year.

Method AII did not yield a uniformly acceptable fit over the period 1921-60, the forecasts for the 1960s were surprisingly good. In our use of Method AII and further methods we used numbers of high school graduates as independent (exogenous) variables known without error. Although this is not the case, table 7.1 shows that the exogenous errors introduced in this way are rather small (Feldstein 1971).

Method BIII: Use of Numbers of High School Graduates and Net Changes in Military Personnel

Method BII can be extended. The flow of high school graduates into the armed forces caused by World War II and their sudden release after the war are clearly demonstrated by university attendance figures in table 7.3. Consequently, it would seem advisable to estimate the effect of high school graduates on university attendance *taking account* of the effects of changing military needs. Method BIII is a simple method for using both high school graduate data (x_t) and net changes in military personnel (v_t) to accomplish this. (The United States figure for v_t—see table 7.4—is used because the more relevant Minnesota figures are not available and it is assumed that Minnesota figures follow closely the pattern for the United States as a whole.) The function relating university attendance to number of high school graduates (x_t) and the net change in military personnel (v_t) is:

$\bar{a}_t = M + Ax_t + Bv_t$. (In computing, v_t is set to zero for the years 1921 through 1940 [Census 1960, 1962, 1966, 1970]). (7.10)

Estimates of M, A, and B were computed by least squares and the resulting equation was:

$$a_t = -107 + .6996x_t + .0017v_t. \tag{7.11}$$

This method yields substantial improvements in approximating actual university attendance during the years of World War II (see table 7.3), but no improvement is obtained for the years following the abrupt demobilization in 1946. Furthermore, the approximations for the periods 1921–40 and 1950–58 are noticeably poorer than those of Method BII.

If Method BIII equation 7.11 is to be used for prediction, high school graduate predictions must be available. The value of v_t would ordinarily be taken to be zero, and the prediction formula becomes,

$$\bar{a}_t = -107 + .6996x_t. \tag{7.12}$$

From table 7.3 it can be seen that Method BIII did achieve somewhat more satisfactory graduation of the fitted data, 1920–59. However, it can be seen in table 7.3 that the forecasts for the years 1960–70 were much too low. The setting of future v_t to zero is not the explanation, since substitution of the actual v_t of the 1960s (taken from table 7.4) makes little difference.

Method BIV: Use of Lags in the Numbers of High School Graduates and in Net Changes in Military Personnel

In predicting university attendance from high school graduate and military data, it is important to realize that several years are needed for a student to complete his education. Consequently, any large increase in the number of persons available for university attendance will affect the attendance figures for the year of enrollment as well as for several succeeding years.

One method of allowing for this lag in effect is demonstrated by the following function which relates university attendance to numbers of high school graduates and net changes in military personnel:

$$\bar{a}_t = M + [A + Bt]\, x_t + [C + D(t-1)]\, x_{t-1} + Ev_t + Fv_{t-1} + Gv_{t-2} + Hv_{t-3}. \tag{7.13}$$

The lag of four years for v_t (change in size of military force) as opposed to a lag of two years for x_t (high school graduates) was adopted because the military series contains marked discontinuities as compared with the much more regular changes in numbers of high school graduates.

Least-squares multiple regression (Snedecor and Cochran 1967) was used with x_t, tx_t, x_{t-1}, $(t-1)x_{t-1}$, v_t, v_{t-1}, v_{t-2} and v_{t-3} as the independent variables. The results, computed on data for 1921-59, are:

$$\bar{a}_t = 12{,}316 + [-.6119 + .013t]x_t + [.3828 + .0052\,(t-1)]x_{t-1} + .0015v_t + .0009v_{t-1} + .007v_{t-2} + .0004v_{t-3} \qquad (t = 0 \text{ for } 1920). \tag{7.14}$$

Equation 7.14 combines some features of 7.9 and 7.11, but now the increasing percentage of high school graduates is distributed over the current year (1.31 percent) and the preceding year (.52 percent). The effects of discharged military personnel are distributed over several years (15, 9, 7, and 4 per 10,000 from the current year, from the preceding year, and so forth). This gives a total high school effect about the same as in equation 7.9 but the total military-personnel effect is larger than in equation 7.11.

For forecasting purposes the values of v_t must usually be taken to be zero. Even if the values of several of the v_t's were of the order of 10^5 (as in 1954 through 1959) the effect on $\bar{a}_t$ would still be negligible. If v_t is disregarded, the prediction equation 7.14 becomes:

$$\bar{a}_t = 12{,}316 + [-.6119 + .0131t]x_t + [.3776 + .0052t]x_{t-1} \qquad \text{(where } t = 0 \text{ corresponds to 1920)}. \tag{7.15}$$

Table 7.3 shows the discrepancies in the fit for 7.14 to the data of 1920-59. The table also shows the agreement of the forecasts, using 7.15, with the actual attendance figures for 1960-70. The fit to both past and future data is quite good.

Discussion of Methods BI Through BIV

From table 7.3 it is clear that Method BIV graduates the attendance data of 1920-59 much better than the other three methods. Methods BI, BII, and BIII have estimated residual variances of about 15 million, whereas Method BIV has a variance under 1 million, even after taking into account the loss in degrees of freedom due to the greater number of parameters in the model for Method BIV.

In prediction of future attendance in the 1960s Method BII and Method BIV were substantially better than Methods BI and BIII. The estimated residual variances were:

Method	Residual Variance, 1960-70 (df = 11)
BI	106,931,905
BII	3,504,005
BIII	46,406,977
BIV	4,928,053

Table 7.3 and figure 7.2 show the details concerning errors for the four methods in forecasting attendance. We favored Method BIV at the time we did the fore-

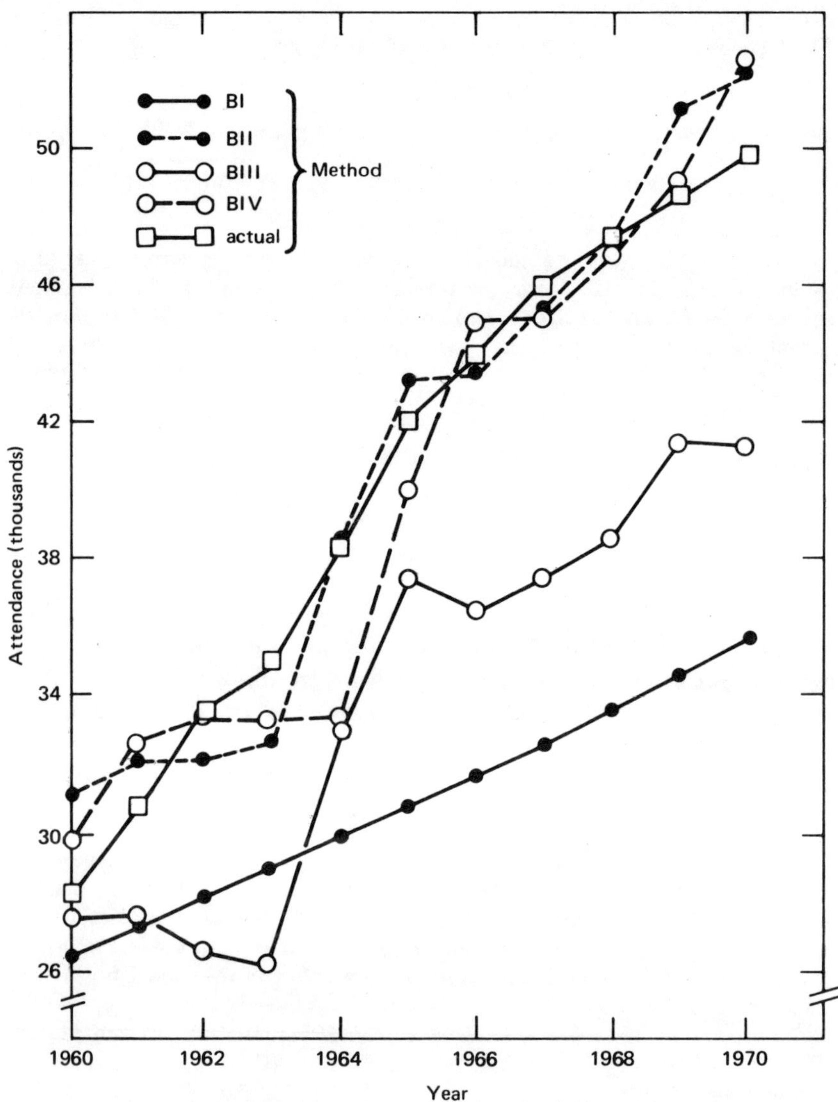

Figure 7.2

PREDICTION OF UNIVERSITY OF MINNESOTA ATTENDANCE FALL QUARTER, END OF SECOND WEEK, 1960–70

casting, because it graduated the past data well and because it spread the impact of changes in high school graduates and the military over several years, which seemed reasonable.

We are indebted to this book's editor for noting and asking why, in fact, Method BII did slightly *better* than our favorite. Indeed the difference is not striking, but Method BII *is* closer than Method BIV in 7 of the 11 forecasts and has an average absolute error of 1,511 compared with 1,725 for Method BIV. The editor asked if there might have been any way to anticipate this surprising superiority of Method BII over Method BIV.

On hindsight we can note that much of the 15 million residual variance during 1920-59 for Method BII was due to the tremendous distortions during and following World War II (see table 7.3). Barring changes in the military force of the magnitude experienced, the model might be expected to show a smaller residual variance, and, indeed, the residual variance during 1960-70 was 3.5 million, one-fourth the previous value. On the other hand, Method BIV used the military change data (v_t) and accounted quite readily for the World War II disturbances, to yield a residual variance of just under 1 million. However, in future predictions, one must expect some *increase* due to the uncertainty in the estimates of the parameters in the model *and* the fact that the values of v_t were set equal to zero. The residual variance for Model IV did increase, fivefold, to about 5 million for the 1960-70 predictions, and this was enough to make its performance on *forecasting* slightly worse than Method BII.

Thus, it could be concluded that it would have been better to use the simple three-parameter Model BII, ignoring the very poor fit over a period of admittedly unusual circumstances, rather than introducing a rather complicated model to graduate the series effectively through the whole period. We would argue that the more complicated model is to be preferred here because it furnishes more insight into the determiners of attendance, does practically as well as the simple model in ordinary circumstances, and would be superior to the simple model under more extraordinary circumstances, i.e., large, anticipated changes in the military.

It is clear that the choice of model is a matter of judgment and this choice can make a great deal of difference. Calculated standard errors of the forecasts under a variety of models will be only one consideration in the choice of model; the validity of the model itself and the weighing of extraordinary circumstances, past and anticipated, are even more important.

Prediction of Numbers of New Freshmen

Because of the success attained in fitting equation 7.13 to the total-attendance time series, the same type of equation was used to obtain a prediction equation for new freshmen. The numbers of new freshmen (b_t) were supplied by the Office of the Dean of Admissions and Records.

The least-squares method with independent variables x_t, tx_t, $(t-1)\,x_{t-1}$', v_t, v_{t-1}, v_{t-2}, and v_{t-3}, and the resulting prediction equation, based on data for 1921-58, is,

$$\bar{b}_t = 2{,}361 + (-.0935 + .0130t)\,x_t + [.0547 - .014(t-1)]\,x_{t-1} + .0003v_t - .0001v_{t-1} \quad (t = 0 \text{ for } 1920). \tag{7.16}$$

The terms corresponding to v_{t-2} and v_{t-3} were negligible. The total effect of high school graduates is greater and the total effect of changes in military personnel is less in 7.16 than in 7.14.

Table 7.5
Fall Quarter, End-of-second-week Attendance of Freshmen, 1921-58, and Errors in Fit for Method BIV, Equation 7.16

Year	New Freshmen	Error in Fit	Year	New Freshmen	Error in Fit
1921	1,826	-8	1941	2,752	188
1922	1,885	163	1942	2,802	-100
1923	1,896	188	1943	1,740	-117
1924	1,992	119	1944	2,402	13
1925	2,212	-71	1945	2,757	264
1926	2,489	-315	1946	5,855	-82
1927	2,363	-148	1947	3,451	119
1928	2,379	-126	1948	3,443	280
1929	2,467	-152	1949	3,732	-34
1930	2,480	-126	1950	3,537	164
1931	2,343	72	1951	3,079	114
1932	2,099	468	1952	3,619	-166
1933	2,106	477	1953	3,818	519
1934	2,627	-53	1954	4,243	271
1935	3,078	-376	1955	5,154	-419
1936	3,260	-478	1956	5,302	-383
1937	2,825	-120	1957	4,946	-196
1938	3,186	-54	1958	5,183	55
1939	3,204	55			
1940	3,070	121			

An interesting arrangement of this equation with $v = 0$ yields

$$\bar{b}_t = 2{,}361 + (.0378 + .0013t)(x_t + x_{t-1}) + (.3887 + .0117t)(x_t - x_{t-1}). \qquad (7.17)$$

Table 7.5 shows the actual values of $\bar{b}_t$ computed for 1921-58 and the differences between these and the fitted values, using 7.16. The fit is good, although for two years, 1932 and 1933, the prediction equation is in error by approximately 22 percent. In comparing the predicted values for the 1960s with the actual figures (not presented here) there was relatively good agreement though several forecasts early in the decade were much too small (approximately 30 percent). On the other hand, the estimates for 1967-70 were well matched by reality.

Predictions of Attendance for Three Campuses and Two of the Colleges of the University

The proportions of the total attendance for each of the three larger campuses and two of the larger colleges of the university were examined also for 1921-59.

Over recent years, relative proportions of total attendance at these campuses and in these two colleges have remained almost constant. Least-squares straight lines were fitted to each of the five series of ratios, over the last eleven years of the 1921–59 interval, and the results were as follows:

$$c_{1t} = (.8615 - .0013t)a_t$$

$$c_{2t} = (.0691 - .0006t)a_t$$

$$c_{3t} = (.0689 + .0020t)a_t$$

$$s_{1t} = (.2733 - .0006t)a_t$$

$$s_{2t} = (.0902 + .0005t)a_t$$

where c_{1t} is the Minneapolis campus attendance for the year t,
c_{2t} is the Saint Paul campus attendance for the year t,
c_{3t} is the Duluth campus attendance for the year t,
s_{1t} is the SLA college attendance for the year t,
s_{2t} is the Education college attendance for the year t,
a_t is the total university attendance and $t = 0$ corresponds to the year 1949. (7.18)

Forecasts of attendance on the three campuses and in the two colleges were made, based on 7.18 together with the forecasts of total attendance generated by Method BIV.

Discussion

The prediction models reported in this study can be improved in several ways. First, the high school data used should include all graduates, which would necessitate new prediction procedures, involving, probably, a separate treatment of public and private school data. Second, the data on the armed forces should be more closely associated with Minnesota men than is the time series on net change for the United States as a whole. Third, economic information should be used; note that in the models discussed above, some of the worst approximations to past attendance data were the figures for the depression decade. Fourth, instead of dealing with total attendance, each college should be handled individually. The results would be useful in planning, but more importantly, the accuracy of the total attendance prediction, which would be the sum of the individual college figures, might be improved. Fifth, the desirability of working on a transformed scale—for example, the logarithmic rather than the arithmetic—should be investigated. Sixth, the optimum length of past time series to be used in estimating the constants in the model should be investigated.

One important source of differences in the methods of prediction is the fact that some of the methods permit an increasing proportion of high school graduates into the university while others do not do this. Although such an increasing proportion is based on observation, one should reexamine this question in making long-range predictions. Certainly the rates of increase observed cannot continue for as long as twenty-five years. Recently, Stone (1971) published demographic models in which transition ratios were taken to be logistic functions of time, an especially appealing approach for longer-range fitting and forecasting, where the transition ratios might be expected to approach upper limits.

STUDY C: TRANSITIONS OF STUDENTS INTO, OUT OF, AND BETWEEN PARTS OF THE UNIVERSITY

Two objectives were formulated for this study: (1) to devise a feasible mechanical method for preparing and maintaining the records of individual collegiate students, and (2) to obtain specific data on rates of movements of such students between the various colleges and classes of the University of Minnesota for a recent year-to-year example (1958–59).

For the purposes of scientific analysis we solved the record linkage problem at a substantial cost.* For detailed presentation of the uses of the rates of movement in an educational system, see Stone (1971).

Caution should be shown in using the estimated transition probabilities from the 1958–59 data: first, because dependable comparisons are not possible with only one transition period and second, because the numbers involved in some of the categories are very small and hence, the resulting estimates are not very stable.

Preparing Transition Cards

A transition punch card was prepared for each student in attendance at the University of Minnesota in either the fall of 1958 or the fall of 1959. The cards were made up for all students attending all colleges at the Minneapolis, Saint Paul, and Duluth campuses. The information shown on the card consisted of basic data—the student's (1) name, (2) university file number, (3) sex, (4) decile rank in his high school class, and (5) year of birth; and educational data for the falls of 1957, 1958, 1959, and 1960—(1) if the student were new to the university in the fall quarter, his previous college or high school; (2) his residency status; (3) his designation, i.e., new freshman, new advanced standing, or previously registered student; (4) his class, i.e., freshman, sophomore, etc.; (5) college enrolled in; (6) degrees granted; and (7) if a new student, the time since he last attended school.

The procedure would require much space for description but it was straightforward work requiring meticulous care.

A great variety of summary tables were prepared from the transition cards. A few self-explanatory portions of such tables appear here.

Use of Transition Probabilities to Predict One Year Ahead

In Study B a prediction of 1,885 students was made for the College of Agriculture, Forestry and Home Economics for 1960. However, another predic-

*Our solution of the data linkage problem was not good enough for most operational purposes. Even in 1971, most colleges do not have rapid machine entry to individual student records.

tion could be made by multiplying the number of students in each college, fall of 1959, by the transition probability that a student of that college will transfer to the College of Agriculture, Forestry and Home Economics during the year and summing the results. The total, 912, is the number of students predicted for the college in 1960 who were in attendance at the university in 1959. To this sum should be added the number of students who will be in the college in 1960 but who were not in the university in 1959. This number was estimated by assuming that the number of new students in the college in 1960 would be equal to the number of new students in 1959. That number was 708 which, added to 912, gives a total prediction of 1,620 students for the College of Agriculture, Forestry and Home Economics in 1960. The actual figure was 1,753.

Study C is an example of the use of transition matrices based on individual data rather than the common use of aggregated data. Development of the methodology for statistical inference in transition matrix predictions is an important challenge for economists and demographers.

The prediction for the sophomore class of 1960 in the College of Agriculture, Forestry and Home Economics was 426; it was based on two components: the number of individuals who were freshmen in 1959 and who transferred to the college in 1960 and the number of new sophomore students in the college in 1960. The same method would be used to predict the junior and senior classes.

Use of Transition Matrices to Predict Attendance More Than One Year Ahead

Let A be the transition matrix for college-to-college transfers

$$A = (a_{ij}).$$

Let $x_t = (x_{it})$ be a (row) vector of the numbers of students in the ith college in year t, and $y_t = (y_{it})$ be a (row) vector of the numbers of new students of origin

Table 7.6
All Students, Transitions from College to College,[a]
University of Minnesota, 1958–59 (in percent)

College in 1958	College in 1959: AG	BA	ED	IT	GRAD	SLA
AG	51.72			.06	.51	.39
BA	.14	31.04	.56		2.39	2.11
ED	.12		40.94	.04	2.34	2.85
IT	.27	1.10	.60	56.84	2.39	4.80
GRAD		.03	.08	.14	46.18	.25
SLA	.21	2.76	4.43	.48	1.73	45.23
Totals	964	471	1,471	2,128	1,947	3,669

[a]Rows and columns of smaller units not presented; hence percentages will usually have a deficient sum. Totals include smaller units.

Table 7.7
Female Students, Transitions from College to College,[a] University of Minnesota 1958-59 (in percent)

College in 1958	College in 1959: AG	BA	ED	IT	GRAD	SLA	Not Registered	Total	*N*
AG	53.37					.52	45.60	100 -	579
BA		26.92	3.85		3.85		57.69	100 -	
ED	.17		41.02	.06	.74	2.50	54.03	100.01	1,760
IT			3.03	30.30		15.15	51.51	99.99	
GRAD			.35		33.80	.35	65.15	100.01	571
SLA	.24	.20	7.37	.04	1.38	45.06	40.53	99.99	2,470
Totals	319	13	934	12	241	1,192	3,687		7,329

[a]Rows and columns of smaller units not presented; hence percentages will usually have a deficient sum. Totals include smaller units.

Table 7.8
Male Students, Transitions from College to College by Class, University of Minnesota, 1958-59 (in percent)[a]

College in 1958	Class	College in 1959: AG	BA	ED	IT	GRAD	SLA	Not Registered	Total	*N*
AG	1	53.13						46.25	100.01	320
	2	63.37					.27	31.55	100 -	374
	3	74.78			.43	.43	.87	20.00	99.99	230
	4	10.30				2.58		86.70	100.01	233
		15.38				5.13		76.92	99.99	39
BA	3		61.67	.70		.70	3.83	31.71	100.01	287
	4	.27	9.70	.27		2.96	1.08	84.64	100 -	371
			3.57			10.71		85.71	99.99	28
ED	1			45.78			4.82	43.37	99.99	83
	2			71.96			6.54	19.63	99.99	107
	3			69.50		2.00	6.00	22.50	100 -	200
	4			17.61		10.21	2.11	70.07	100 -	284
				17.46		11.11		71.43	100 -	126
IT	1	.33	.22	.22	49.44		12.11	33.56	99.99	900
	2	.41	2.35	1.11	68.88		5.95	21.02	100 -	723
	3	.27	2.46	1.37	77.46	.41	1.50	15.85	100.01	732
	4	.15	.44	.15	73.37	8.88	.74	16.12	100 -	676
	5				8.94	3.25	.20	87.60	99.99	492
		1.10			14.29	8.79	1.10	73.63	100.01	91
SLA	1	.07	.34	.14	.89		56.12	36.84	100.01	1,463
	2	.46	11.69	6.21	.33		47.29	30.25	99.99	1,514
	3	.14	1.10	2.61	.41	1.37	58.10	27.75	100.01	728
	4		.14	1.96	1.40	6.73	15.29	70.13	99.99	713
				1.48	.99	15.27	12.32	65.52	100.01	203
Totals		645	458	537	2,116	1,706	2,477	8,045		18,871

[a]Classes are identified by number: 1 for freshman, 2 for sophomore, etc.; Business Administration (BA) admitted upper-classes 2 and 3.

Table 7.9
Predictions for Fall Quarter, End of Second Week, 1961, for Selected Colleges of University of Minnesota[a]

	1961 Students Present in 1959 $x_{1959}A^2$	1961 Students New in 1960 $y_{1960}BA$	1961 Students New in 1961 $y_{1961}B$	Predictions for 1961	Actual
Agriculture, Forestry & Home Economics	496.63	411.43	751	1,659	1,824
BA	268.74	169.72	123	561	570
ED	803.04	654.78	1,038	2,496	2,350
IT	1205.07	886.66	1,509	3,601	3,230

[a]Where B corresponds to transitions into the university and A corresponds to transitions between units of the university.

i in the year t. Let $B = (b_{ij})$ be a matrix such that a new student of origin i will be in college j with probability b_{ij}.

In making predictions for 1961 in the summer of 1960 we start with A, B, x_{1959}, and estimates of y_{1960} and y_{1961}. These data can be combined in the following manner:

$$x_{1961} = x_{1959}A^2 + y_{1960}BA + y_{1961}B.$$

Without details, we present some examples of transition matrices of type A in tables 7.6, 7.7, and 7.8. A transition matrix (B) was prepared, with the following rows and with the classes of the various colleges of the University as columns:

> previously registered but not in 1958; new fresh. or adv. stand. from Minn. public H.S.; new fresh. or adv. stand. from Minn. private H.S.; new fresh. or adv. stand. from non-Minn. H.S.; new from a Minn. public college; new from a Minn. Junior College; new fresh. or adv. stand. from Minn. Private College; new from non-Minn. college; origin unknown.

In table 7.9 the components of the 1961 forecasts for several colleges are shown, together with the actual figures recently retrieved for purposes of this report.

A serious shortcoming in these predictions is the lack of data for the vectors y_t.

STUDY D: RELATIONSHIPS BETWEEN FALL QUARTER, END OF-SECOND-WEEK ATTENDANCE AND OTHER IMPORTANT VARIABLES IN UNIVERSITY PLANNING

Throughout these studies the variable "Fall Quarter, End-of-second-week Attendance" at the University of Minnesota was treated as basic. The variable was clearly defined, meaningful in itself, readily available for the past, highly standardized, and becomes available early in each academic year. Of course there are other variables of interest in planning for the university. Using the relationship

$$y_t = ax_t + e_t$$

where $t = 1947, \cdots, 1959$, e_t is a random error in the prediction equation x_t is the "Fall Quarter, End-of-second-week Attendance" for year t, we obtained the following results:*

(a) if y_t represents "Fall Quarter, End-of-12th week Attendance" in year t, then the least-squares estimate of a is 1.018, the estimate of the standard deviation of the distribution of e_t is 526, the standard deviation of the estimate of a is .0061, and the standard deviation of the prediction of y_t, given x_t, is

$$526\left[\frac{x_t^2}{7.408 \cdot 10^9} + 1\right]^{1/2};$$

(b) if y_t represents "Net attendance at end of Fall Quarter" in year t, then the least-squares estimate of a is 1.025, the estimate of the standard deviation of the distribution of e_t is 216.71, the standard deviation of the estimate of a is .0025, and the standard deviation of the prediction of y_t, given x_t, is

$$217\left[\frac{x_t^2}{7.408 \cdot 10^9} + 1\right]^{1/2};$$

(c) if y_t represents "Net attendance at end of Spring Quarter" in year t, then the least-squares estimate of a is .9270, the estimate of the standard deviation of the distribution of e_t is 841, the standard deviation of the estimate of a is .0098, and the standard deviation of the prediction of y_t, given x_t, is

$$841\left[\frac{x_t^2}{7.438 \cdot 10^9} + 1\right]^{1/2};$$

(d) if y_t represents "Net total attendance for Academic Year" in year t, then the least-squares estimate of a is 1.1481, the estimate of the standard deviation of the distribution of e_t is 666, the standard deviation of the estimate of a is .0077, and the standard deviation of the prediction of y_t, given x_t, is

$$666\left[\frac{x_t^2}{7.438 \cdot 10^9} + 1\right]^{1/2}$$

Predicting "Income from Fees for Academic Year" is more complex. The prediction was done college by college since fees differ at each college, and where they happen to coincide for several years, they differ for other years. For each college, the following equation was fitted by least squares:

$$I_t = k(A_{rt}F_{rt} + A_{nt}F_{nt}) + e_t \tag{7.19}$$

*The estimates given in paragraphs (a) and (b) are based on data for the years 1947–48 through 1959–60, while the estimates in paragraphs (c) and (d) are based on data for the years 1946–47 through 1958–59. This is due to the fact that data for the end of the academic year 1959–60 were not available.

where

I_t = income from fees for the college in year t;
A_{rt} = resident second-week attendance for the college in year t;
F_{rt} = resident fee for full-time student in this college in year t;
A_{nt} = nonresident second-week attendance in year t;
F_{nt} = nonresident fee for full-time student in this college in year t;
k = constant to be estimated by least squares from the data for 1950-51 to 1958-59 (k differs for each college);
e_t = random error of prediction in year t.

The estimated values using this method were computed for each college for each year. The results estimated for the several colleges were added together to obtain estimated income for the year and a comparison was made with actual reported income. The percent errors were -7, -9, -3, 6, -4, -2, +1, -1, +1. Presumably, percentage errors of these sizes in predicted income would not interfere with university financial planning.

These techniques could be extended to make predictions several years in advance by using predicted values. For the independent variables, see Study B.

STUDY E: COLLEGE-ATTENDANCE EXPECTATIONS

Sidney Goldish of the *Minneapolis Star and Tribune* provided tabulations of data collected in a 1960 teen-ager study (Minnesota Poll ballot #192, "Truth From Youth" survey) involving personal interviews with 587 high school students enrolled in grades 9 through 12, all of them in the 15-18 age bracket. The questions dealt with college-attendance expectations. The interviewing period was April 9-16, 1960. All interviews were conducted by Minnesota Poll-trained interviewers, in respondents' homes.

The results of this survey are contained in our earlier report. However, the results were not used in any of our other work (due to our intellectual limitations, not the insignificance of the work). Here we present tabulations for two questions as an illustration of the nature of the survey.

Question 1. A. "What do you plan to do after you've finished high school?" (If "going-to-college" NOT mentioned):

B. "Do you plan to go to college within two or three years after you've finished high school?"

Respondent	Plan to Go to College		Do Not Plan		Total	
	N	%	*N*	%	*N*	%
All high school students	332	57	254	43	586	100
Boys	178	61	114	39	292	100
Girls	154	52	140	48	294	100

Question 1 (Continued)

Respondent	Plan to Go to College		Do Not Plan		Total	
Congressional						
districts: 1 and 2	79	53	69	47	148	100
3, 4, and 5	124	60	84	40	208	100
6 and 8	62	52	58	48	120	100
7 and 9	67	61	43	39	110	100
Minneapolis, Saint Paul, and Duluth combined	96	62	60	38	156	100
Smaller cities	96	63	57	37	153	100
Town	66	48	72	52	138	100
Farm	74	53	65	47	139	100
15–16 years	209	60	141	40	350	100
17–18 years	123	52	113	48	236	100
Catholics	85	51	82	49	167	100
Protestants	236	58	170	42	406	100
Upper-income households	81	81	19	19	100	100
Middle-income households	207	57	154	43	361	100
Lower-income households	40	35	75	65	115	100

Question 5. "Which college or university do you plan to attend?"

	N	%
University of Minnesota (including Duluth and Morris)	147	44
Macalester	11	3
Minnesota state colleges (Saint Cloud, Winona, etc.)	42	13
Big Ten universities other than Minnesota	8	2
Minnesota Catholic colleges	18	5
Other Minnesota (private) colleges	53	16
Out-of-state colleges other than Big Ten schools	31	9
Junior colleges in Minnesota	19	6
Other answers	11	4
Undecided, unsure	36	11
	376	113

NOTE: Columns total more than 332 teen-agers and more than 100 percent because of multiple answers by some respondents.

In our work (1960 and 1971) we have examined unpublished reports of several operating agencies at the state and university level in the United States. For predicting enrollments, our general conclusions are:

1. Standard statistical procedures (least squares) and standard statistical modes of inference (probability intervals) are seldom used.

2. The use of standard statistical procedures as modes of inference would be beneficial in enrollment prediction.

3. To make enrollment predictions, standard statistical procedures and modes of inference can be used and explicitly documented at reasonable expense.

4. Educational data, like many other areas of social data, are severely deficient because of ever-present aggregation which does not allow the researcher to follow the individual over time or to see the individual in detail. Enrollment prediction is a longitudinal problem but there is very little longitudinal data.

These conclusions were clear to us from our 1960 experience; our 1971 experience has supported them.

REFERENCES

Brown B. W., and Savage I. R. "Methodological Studies in Educational Attendance Prediction" (Department of Statistics, University of Minnesota 1960). Mimeographed.

Feldstein, M. S. "The Error of Forecast in Econometric Models When the Forecast-period Exogenous Variables Are Stochastic." *Econometrica* 39, no. 1 (January 1971): 55–60.

Middlebrook, W. T. "How to Estimate the Building Needs of a College or University" (Minneapolis, 1958). Mimeographed.

Snedecor, G. W., and Cochran, W. G. *Statistical Methods.* 6th ed. Ames, Iowa: Iowa State College Press, 1967.

Stone, Richard. *Demographic Accounting and Model-building.* Paris: OECD, 1971.

U.S. Bureau of the Census. *Statistical Abstract of the United States.* Washington, D.C.: U.S. Government Printing Office, 1960, 1962, 1966, 1970.

Donald B. Johnson and
Albert G. Holzman

8 A STATISTICAL DECISION-THEORY MODEL OF THE COLLEGE-ADMISSION PROCESS*

Total college and university enrollment is projected to increase from 6.1 million students in 1966–67 to 9.0 million students in 1975–76 (Vroman 1968). These figures represent a 49 percent increase. Despite this rise in college enrollment, demand for a college education in the 1970s will still exceed enrollment capabilities. Thus, formerly adequate admissions policies will come under increasing criticism from the community as well as from college and university administrators. New admissions policies must be developed and evaluated.

One example, medical school admissions, illustrates the severe problem facing college and university admissions departments. For the 1967–68 entering class of U.S. medical schools, 18,724 persons submitted 93,332 applications for 9,314 places (Mattson 1969), or 10 applications for each place. College and university admissions officers are faced with a similar problem yearly as they approach the task of selecting incoming freshmen, with the number of applications far exceeding enrollment capabilities. Admissions officers must consequently establish criteria on which individual accept/reject decisions are to be made. They must then use these criteria in conjunction with a selective admissions policy.

Regardless of the admissions policy used, several interacting restrictions must be considered. From a financial standpoint, enrollment must be adequate to support dormitory and faculty operations, yet not so large as to cause over-

*This chapter is based on the thesis of Donald B. Johnson in partial fulfillment of the requirements for the Master of Science in Industrial Engineering, University of Pittsburgh.

crowding in residence halls and classrooms; from an educational standpoint, the quality of instruction must not be sacrificed simply to fill classroom seats for efficient operation. In addition, colleges and universities have a responsibility to society, such as the responsibility of state-related schools to a particular region of the state in which they are located.

With a selective admissions policy, it must be assumed that by choosing certain individuals, certain other individuals will go without higher education. It has been estimated that one-third of the students graduating in the upper half of their high school class never go to college. In the past decade, approximately 1.5 million students who graduated in the upper half of their high school class never registered as full-time students (Vroman 1968). Of those students enrolling in college, a sizable percentage fail to graduate. Thus, the cost of admitting a student, who subsequently leaves college, is twofold: the cost of educating the "dropout" and the cost to society of not educating a person who had the potential for college work. With the increasing demand for higher education from all sectors of our society, and the resultant necessity for a selective admissions policy, it becomes imperative that those applicants selected for enrollment be capable of doing "adequate" college work. Considerable controversy exists, however, as to what constitutes "adequate" college work.

If it were possible to predict an individual's "success" at a given school, the savings in time, money, and emotional wear and tear on the student, his family, and society would be enormous. The value of predicting academic success has long been recognized; initial attempts in the 1920s to predict college success were based on correlating college grades with intellectual factors such as high school grades and class rank, aptitude tests, IQ and achievement tests. These early attempts at predicting college success yielded correlation coefficients between .45 and .55 (Stein 1963). Although a considerable amount of work has been done in developing more scientifically designed aptitude and achievement tests, standardized on a national basis (College Entrance Examination Board tests), correlation coefficients for predicting college success with intellectual factors have not changed significantly.

In a literature search of the 1950–59 period, 580 studies of the prediction of college success were identified; this was one of the most researched areas in the fields of education, psychology, and sociology (Fishman and Pasanella 1960). However, the low correlation of prediction equations of college success does not permit their equations to be used as the sole factor in admissions decision making. By comparison, very little work has been done in developing practical techniques for aiding admissions officers in establishing selection policies or making individual accept/reject decisions. The major concern in practical decision aids has been the development of "cutoff" scores. Applicants whose attributes place them above the cutoff point are accepted while those below the cutoff point are rejected. A cutoff score is established such that the desired enrollment is obtained. Cutoff scores, however, are dependent on obtaining precise information about the number of applications, probability of enrollment given acceptance, average "quality" of the applicant population, and an equation to consolidate applicant attributes onto a single scale (a predictor equation). Such precise information is not available.

The challenge is to bring together predictor equations, selection strategies, and other relevant information sources in order to develop an integrated, quantitative model of the admissions process. This model would be invaluable in evaluating the effect of different admissions policies on acceptance rates, subsequent enrollment, and the resulting academic quality for a given population of applicants.

ALTERNATE APPROACHES FOR COLLEGE-ADMISSION STRATEGIES

With the increasing demand for higher education and rising costs, admissions policies are coming under greater scrutiny. Choosing the best policy for a given situation has become a complex operation, particularly in the light of considerable uncertainty existing throughout the admissions process. The following factors, concomitant to the admissions process, vary and result in considerable uncertainty about which applicants to accept or reject:

1. When accept/reject decisions are made concerning applicants, the total number of applications that will be received can only be estimated since this number varies from year to year.
2. Since most prospective students apply to several schools, accepting an applicant does not always result in his subsequent enrollment. The ratio of enrolled freshmen to accepted applicants, the yield factor, also varies from year to year.
3. The "quality" of the total population of applicants, as defined by some arbitrary measure such as Scholarship Aptitude Test (SAT) scores, is not precisely known. The average total SAT score for all applicants may be 1,050 one year and 1,200 the next.
4. Attempts to predict college success from the information gathered from tests and interviews yield correlation coefficients ranging from 0.4 to 0.7. Thus, the academic performance of individual applicants cannot be predicted accurately.

The problem in college-admission decision making can be stated more specifically: What admissions policy will minimize the adverse effect of the following factors?

1. accepting a student who subsequently demonstrates inability to do adequate college work;
2. rejecting an applicant who had the potential to do adequate college work;
3. accepting too few students, so that the resultant enrollment is too low;
4. accepting too many students, so that the resultant enrollment is too high;
5. accepting an applicant early in application processing which may result in denying admission to a better-qualified applicant who applies at a later date.

As indicated earlier, the major work in developing quantitative aids for the college-admission problem has been the development of regression equations for predicting the college success of individual applicants. Limited accuracy in predicting college success negates the exclusive use of predictor equations in making individual accept/reject decisions. In addition, predictor equations do not address themselves to the whole college-admission problem because they deal solely with the ability of only one individual to do college work and neglect the problem of obtaining the necessary enrollment.

Predictor equations can be used in conjunction with a cutoff score. When using cutoff scores, applicants above a certain score are accepted and applicants below this score are rejected. A cutoff score can be set such that it yields the desired enrollment. This approach, however, does not cope adequately with the uncertainties about which applicants to accept and which to reject.

A third and more comprehensive approach to the college-admission problem could be obtained from the decision-theory format established by Cronbach and Gleser (1957) which, in fact, makes use of both predictive equations and cutoff scores. The elements of a decision-theory approach to college admission include: (1) tests (information about applicant), (2) treatments (accept or reject applicant), (3) costs for both tests and treatments, (4) outcomes (dropout or graduate), (5) conditional probabilities of the outcomes, and (6) the value of the outcomes. With these elements and with estimates about the applicant population, an admissions policy can be established to achieve the objectives of the institution.

It is important to be able to take into account the unique objectives of a particular institution when evaluating alternate admissions policies. For example, only a small penalty might be associated with enrolling 10–20 students more than the aim, while a much larger penalty would be associated with a final enrollment 10–20 less than desired. The relative magnitude of these costs, or other costs, can greatly influence the selection of the admissions policy.

The approach taken by the authors to problems created by the college-admission selection policy combines predictor equations, cutoff scores, and statistical decision theory with computer simulation techniques. The main thrust of this study is: (1) to combine cutoff scores with predictor equations so that the prediction of an individual applicant's success is coupled with the objective to obtain the desired enrollment; (2) to develop a decision theoretic format which addresses itself to the uncertainties associated with the cutoff scores and predictive equations; and (3) to establish a cause-effect simulation model which depicts the consequences of a given action which the director of admissions would like to have evaluated in his decision-making role.

To a large extent, the expected impact of computers on management decision making has failed to materialize. This failure is largely due to insufficient attention to the integration of the experience, judgment, and imagination of the responsible manager with the processing power of the computer (Jones 1970). It should be remembered that the manager or the admissions officer, not the model builder, must remain in control of the decision-making process. A cause-effect computer model on a time-sharing system could provide this integration of man's experience and the computer's power.

The decision maker could program a selection policy, and the computer would then simulate the processing of applicants for a year. The proposed model would present to the decision maker the consequences of taking a given course of action and thus permit quantitative evaluation of alternative policies. In addition, the proposed model would calculate the optimal admissions policy based on the institution's objectives. This approach also allows the decision maker to encode his subjective evaluations into the decision process as well as his estimates of the cost penalties associated with the various outcomes.

MODELING THE COLLEGE-ADMISSION PROCESS

Development Phases for a Decision-theory Model

The development of a decision-theory model generally proceeds through three distinct phases: a deterministic phase, a probabilistic phase, and an informational phase. In the deterministic phase the system of concern is modeled, the major state and decision variables are identified, and their relationships are explored. For the college-admission process, the model includes predictor equations and cutoff scores. The major state variables are the total number of applications, acceptance/enrollment ratio, and the overall academic quality of the class. The primary decision variable is the cutoff point, i.e., the point above which all applicants are accepted and the others are rejected. The deterministic phase also includes calculation of values for all possible outcomes of any decision. This corresponds to calculating the marginal costs associated with obtaining an enrollment either larger or smaller than desired.

In the probabilistic phase the major uncertainties are encoded and introduced into the analysis. In the model of the college-admission process these uncertainties include the year-to-year variation of the major state variables previously mentioned and the uncertainty associated with predicting academic performance of individual applicants.

An alternative decision to accepting or rejecting applicants is to gather more information about certain state variables. The expected value of the outcomes with and without this additional information can be compared, indicating the worth of the information being evaluated. In this informational phase, the cost associated with the uncertainty of each major state variable is calculated. For example, with the initial uncertainty in the acceptance/enrollment ratio, accepting 600 applicants could yield 250–350 enrolled students; reducing the uncertainty by 50 percent could reduce the range of the possible enrollment to 275–325. This decrease in uncertainty in the acceptance/enrollment ratio is thus very beneficial.

The three stages of implementing a decision-theory model will be illustrated using a much simplified method of selecting cutoff scores. Consider a cutoff score equation with only one state variable—total applications—and one decision variable—the percentage of applicants to accept. The resultant enrollment of any decision can be calculated as follows.

$$E = \frac{TOT \cdot P}{100 \cdot AE},$$

where

E = resultant enrollment
TOT = total applications
P = percentage of applicants to accept
AE = acceptance/enrollment ratio

After the decision variable, the percentage of applicants to accept, has been determined, the cutoff score can be obtained easily. The cutoff percentile at which the cutoff score should be set is given by the equation,

$$\text{Cutoff percentile} = 100 \left[1 - \frac{ED \cdot AE}{TOT} \right],$$

where ED = desired enrollment.

Historical data are used to translate the cutoff percentile to a cutoff score in terms of predicted QPA (Quality Point Average).

The cost of the resultant enrollment of any decision can be found from the following simplified objective function.

$$\text{Cost (Enrollment)} = 30 + (E - 100), \text{ for } 100 < E < 130$$
$$= 60 \text{ for other values of } E$$

The aim enrollment is 100. This objective function is depicted graphically in figure 8.1.

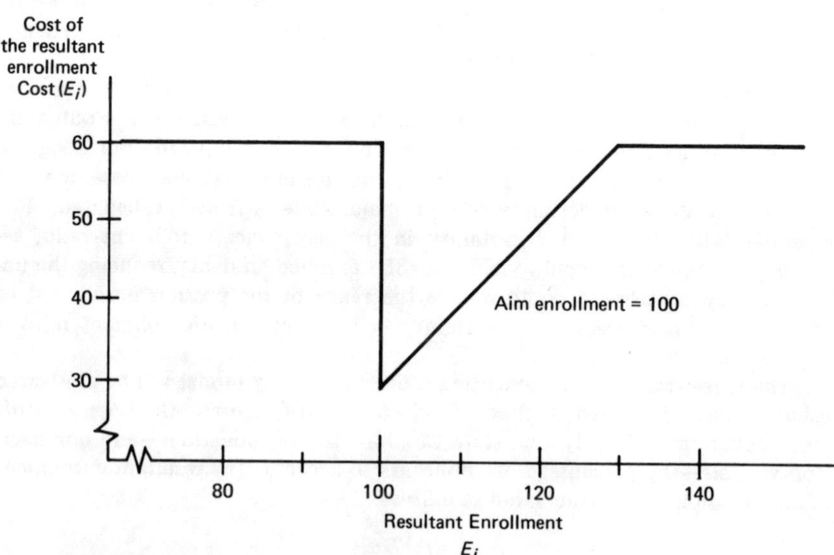

Figure 8.1
A SIMPLIFIED ENROLLMENT OBJECTIVE FUNCTION

Deterministic Phase

Knowing precisely the total number of applications and the acceptance/enrollment ratio, 400 and 2.0 respectively, accepting 50 percent of the applicants will yield an enrollment of 100 students. As shown in figure 8.1, this enrollment (100) minimizes the objective function.

Probabilistic Phase

Suppose total applications are not precisely known but are uniformly distributed in the interval (300–500), i.e., the probability of total applications,

$$p(TOT) = p, \text{ for } 300 < TOT < 500$$
$$= 0 \text{ otherwise.}$$

Since AE is still known precisely, for any percent of applicants accepted, P, the final enrollment, E_F, will be distributed according to:

$$p(E_i|P) = p, \text{ for } 300 \leqslant \frac{E \cdot AE \cdot 100}{P} \leqslant 500$$
$$= 0 \text{ otherwise}$$

Figure 8.2 shows the distribution of the enrollment for $P = 50$ percent. The expected cost, $\langle c \rangle$, of this decision can be calculated by multiplying the probability of each enrollment state, given the decision, by the cost of the state as determined by the equation for determining $p(TOT)$.

$$\langle c \rangle = \sum_i p(E_i|P = 50\%) \cdot \text{Cost}(E_i)$$

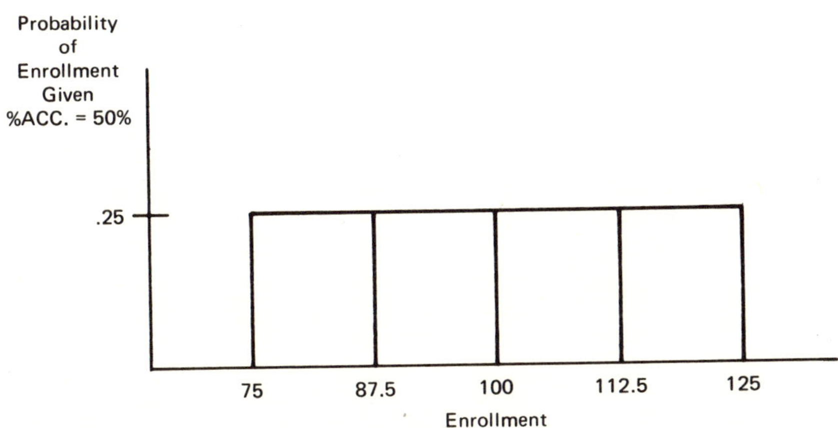

Figure 8.2

DISTRIBUTION OF ENROLLMENT FOR PERCENT ACCEPT = 50% AND *P(TOT)*

The expected cost of the objective function for $P = 50\%$ is calculated below:

$$\begin{aligned}\langle c \rangle &= .25 \cdot C(81.25) + .25 \cdot C(93.75) \\ &\quad + .25 \cdot C(106.25) + .25 \cdot C(118.75) \\ &= 15 + 15 + 9.06 + 12.19 \\ &= 51.25\end{aligned}$$

The enrollment of 81.25 is the midpoint of the cell interval 75 – 87.5, resulting from 300–350 applications; similarly, 93.75, 106.25, and 118.75, are midpoints of their respective cell intervals as shown in figure 8.2. The expected costs for the following decision were calculated in a similar manner.

Decision	Expected Cost
$P = 50\%$	51.25
$P = 52\%$	53.27
$P = 53\%$	53.72
$P = 53.4\%$	47.2
$P = 54\%$	48.3

Thus the objective function is optimized at $P = 53.4\%$, where $\langle c \rangle_{min} = 47.2$.

The effect of the uncertainty about total applications is thus twofold: the cost has increased from 30 (deterministic phase) to an expected cost of 47.2 (probabilistic phase), and the optimal percent of applicants to accept has increased from 50 percent to 53.4 percent.

Informational Phase

Suppose a better estimate of total applications could be obtained such that:

$$\begin{aligned}p(TOT) &= p, \text{ for } 360 < TOT < 440 \\ &= 0 \text{ otherwise}\end{aligned}$$

The enrollment resulting from a given decision is now given by

$$p(E_i|P) = p, \text{ for } 360 \leqslant \frac{E \cdot AE \cdot 100}{P} \leqslant 440$$

The expected costs of the following decisions were calculated using the equation to determine Cost (Enrollment).

Decision	Expected Cost
$P = 50\%$	47.5
$P = 51\%$	48.5
$P = 51.3\%$	41.3
$P = 52\%$	42.4

The objective function is now minimized at $P = 51.3\%$ where $\langle c \rangle_{min} = 41.3$. The information reducing the uncertainty about total applications from 300–500 to 360–440 has decreased the expected cost of the optimal decision from 47.2 to 41.3. Thus the information is worth 5.9 units.

Two-point Cutoff Score Policy

The model developed in the previous section was a much simplified method for determining the percentage of applicants to accepts; by the structure of this model it was easy to show the usual progression and to assess the relative impact of the various phases generally used to construct a decision theoretic model.

This section develops a more realistic and useful model; it is a two-point cutoff score policy. Many educational institutions today use a single-point cutoff score, but this procedure entails considerable risk: for example, setting a cutoff score of 2.16 (predicted Quality Point Average) could yield 300 acceptances on the average, but the enrollment could range from 180–420 students. A potentially worthwhile alternative is to delay processing and to obtain information reducing the uncertainty about the major state variables. An easy method of getting this information is to delay making any accept/reject decisions until all applications have been received. This would give precise information about total applications and applicant class quality, but the acceptance/enrollment ratio would still contain considerable uncertainty. A more practical problem with a delayed decision policy is that many of the better applicants might enroll elsewhere simply because they had been accepted earlier by the other schools. A secondary problem associated with a delayed decision policy is that all applications would need to be processed over a very short time, which requires a large, temporary, yet knowledgeable staff.

A third approach would be to accept only the best applicants and reject the worst ones. This would spread applicant processing over a longer period. Also, the "best" applicants would be accepted early, preventing losing them to another school. For an extreme example, applicants with a predicted QPA of 3.8 would always be accepted, while applicants with a predicted QPA of 0.8 would always be rejected. Note that this decision is based on a homogeneous applicant population and on a single admission factor, predicted QPAs, a simplification of the actual process.

Suppose it was determined, based on past experiences, that the cutoff score yielding an enrollment of 300 students would be in the range 1.8 to 2.4. The cutoff score would be as high as 2.4 only if an exceptionally large number of very well qualified applicants applied. If the correct cutoff score would be less than the cutoff used, the final enrollment will be larger than desired. The possibility of the final enrollment being too large is very slight if the accept point is set at 2.4. Very little chance exists of accepting applicants with QPAs above 2.4 who would not be accepted at a later date. A similar argument holds for rejecting applicants whose predicted QPA is less than 1.8. The cutoff score would be as low as 1.8 only if an exceptionally small number of applications were received and the overall quality of these applicants was very low. If the correct cutoff score turns out to be lower than that set, not enough applicants will be accepted and the enrollment will be low. There is very little chance of rejecting applicants with a 1.8 QPA who at a later date would be accepted.

The above logic implies that, initially, applicants above 2.4 should be accepted, applicants below 1.8 rejected, and applicants in between these points should not be processed until more accurate information is available. Note that the final cutoff score can be set anywhere in the interval 1.8 to 2.4. Thus this policy delays setting a final cutoff score until more accurate information becomes available. As applications are received, better estimates can be made of the total number of applications and of academic class quality. This reduction in uncertainty will correspondingly reduce the range of cutoff scores yielding the desired enrollment. For example, after one or two months of applicant processing, the range of cutoff scores yielding the desired enrollment may possibly be reduced to 2.0–2.2. At this point all applications on hand would be accepted if their QPA was above 2.2, rejected if below 2.0, and held for further action if between 2.0 and 2.2.

Statistical decision theory is used to calculate the two cutoff points, the point above which applicants are to be accepted and the point below which applicants are to be rejected, so that the school's objective function is optimized. Four factors are included in this objective function: (1) minimizing the risk associated with setting the cutoff score too low, such that too many applicants are accepted; (2) minimizing the risk associated with setting the cutoff score too high, such that too few applicants are accepted; (3) spreading applicant processing evenly over the processing period; and (4) obtaining more information about the acceptance/enrollment ratio by accepting applicants and sampling their response to the acceptance offer. The relative weight of these factors is set by the decision maker as he sets their cost coefficients, and thus the objective function becomes a cost-minimization criterion.

The Risk of Setting the Cutoff Score Too Low

When the cutoff point above which applicants will be accepted is set, there exists the possibility that the point was set too low and the resultant enrollment will be too large. This possible error exists since the cutoff point cannot be raised. To do this would be inconsistent. Note that no potential error is associated with setting this cutoff point too high, since this point can be lowered if need be. Figure 8.3 shows the effect on enrollment of a given cutoff score for accepting applicants. The risk associated with this action is indicated by the shaded area of this figure. This risk or expected cost of accepting applicants above QPA (AC) is given by:

$$R(\text{Large Enrollment}) = \sum_i \$E_i p(E_i | \text{QPA}(AC))$$

The probability of a given enrollment, E_i, given a certain selection policy, is considered to be normally distributed and is a function of the average enrollment and its standard error. The cost of a given enrollment is:

$$\begin{aligned} \$E_i &= A \cdot (E_i - E_{\text{aim}}), \text{ for } E_i > E_{\text{aim}} \\ &= 0 \text{ elsewhere} \end{aligned}$$

where

E_{aim} = aim enrollment

A = marginal cost per student over aim enrollment

This cost function is shown in figure 8.4.

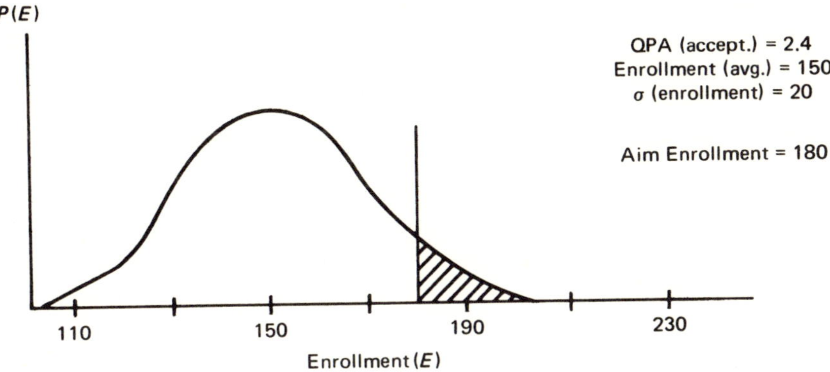

Figure 8.3
THE EFFECT OF AN ACCEPTANCE CUTOFF SCORE

Mathematical models have also been structured to determine the risk of setting the cutoff score too high, overtime required to process applications, and value of information that reduces the uncertainty of the acceptance/enrollment ratio.

Selection of the Optimum Two-point Cutoff Policy

The optimum two-point cutoff policy will minimize the total cost objective function consisting of:

1. the cost of enrolling too many students,
2. the cost of enrolling not enough students,

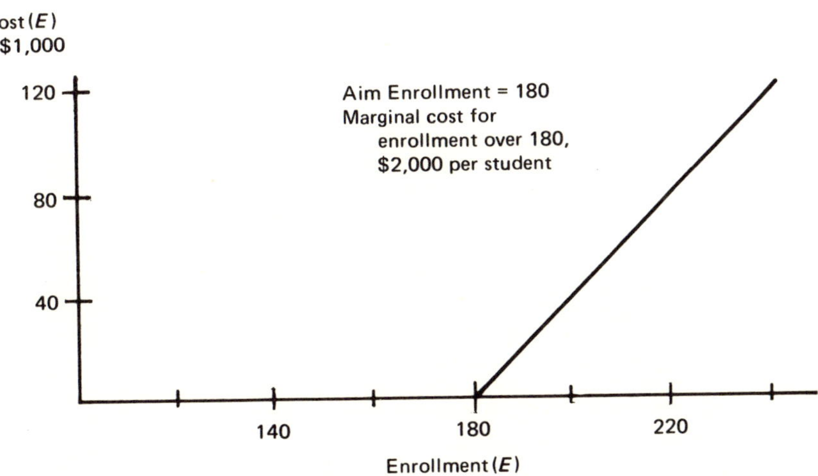

Figure 8.4
AN ENROLLMENT COST FUNCTION

3. the cost of uneven applicant processing,
4. the cost reduction resulting from reducing uncertainty about the acceptance/enrollment ratio.

Selecting the optimum to point cutoff or selection policy becomes complicated because we are dealing with two independent variables: (1) the point above which applicants are accepted; and (2) the point below which applicants are rejected.

The method of steepest ascent is used to map the response surface of these two variables and to locate the set of variables that minimizes the decision-maker's objective function.

The Box-Wilson method of steepest ascent is used to map the response surface of two variables and move from an initial point to the point on the surface of minimum or maximum response as quickly as possible. This method is based on taking a small number of observations and fitting a linear function or plane to these points. From these equations the contour lines of the surface are derived. Further observations are made along a line perpendicular to the contour lines.

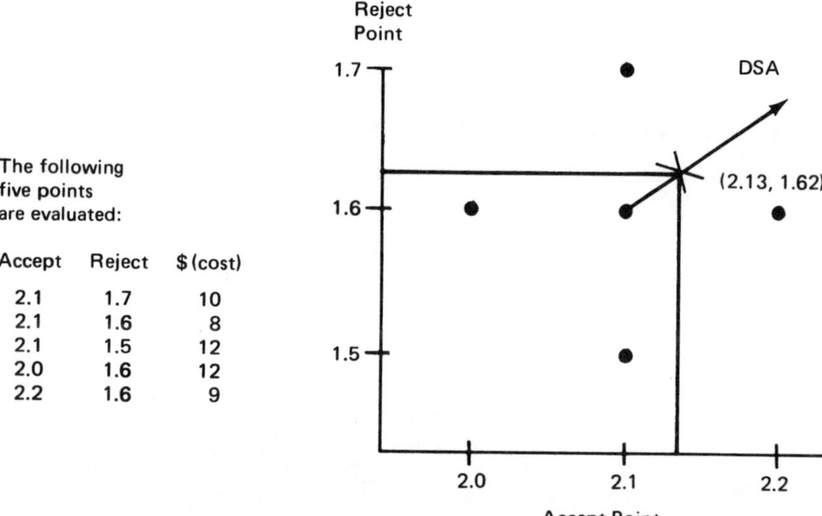

Numerical differentiation of:
(2.0, 1.6), (2.1, 1.6) and (2.2, 1.6) gives
(x min, 1.6) = 2.13

Numerical differentiation of:
(2.1, 1.5), (2.1, 1.6) and (2.1, 1.7) gives
(2.1, y min) = 1.62

The Direction of Steepest Ascent, DSA, passes from the origin (2.1, 1.6) through the point (2.13, 1.62).

Figure 8.5
CALCULATING THE DIRECTION OF STEEPEST ASCENT

Total Cost

QPA Accept \ QPA Reject		.65		.77		.90		1.02		1.15		
1.70	5505.	5505.	5505.	5506.	5506.	5506.	5508.	5508.	5508.	0.	0.	0.
	4228.	4228.	4228.	4229.	4229.	4229.	4231.	4231.	4231.	4232.	0.	0.
	2903.	2903.	2903.	2904.	2904.	2904.	2906.	2906.	2906.	2907.	2907.	0.
	1963.	1963.	1963.	1964.	1964.	1964.	1966.	1966.	1966.	1967.	1967.	1967.
1.90	617.	617.	617.	617.	617.	617.	617.	617.	617.	617.	617.	617.
	59.	59.	59.	59.	59.	59.	59.	59.	59.	59.	59.	59.
	-98.	-98.	-98.	-98.	-98.	-98.	-98.	-98.	-98.	-98.	-98.	-98.
	-76.	-76.	-76.	-76.	-76.	-76.	-76.	-76.	-76.	-76.	-76.	-76.
2.10	-68.	-68.	-68.	-68.	-68.	-68.	-68.	-68.	-68.	-68.	-68.	-68.
	-62.	-62.	-62.	-62.	-62.	-62.	-62.	-62.	-62.	-62.	-62.	-62.
	-55.	-55.	-55.	-55.	-55.	-55.	-55.	-55.	-55.	-55.	-55.	-55.
	-47.	-47.	-47.	-47.	-47.	-47.	-47.	-47.	-47.	-47.	-47.	-47.
2.30	-40.	-40.	-40.	-40.	-40.	-40.	-40.	-40.	-40.	-40.	-40.	-40.
	-35.	-35.	-35.	-35.	-35.	-35.	-35.	-35.	-35.	-35.	-35.	-35.

QPA Reject

Figure 8.6

COST MAP—TWO-VARIABLE SEARCH—BASED ON INFORMATION GENERATED UP TO NOVEMBER 30

When the gain in response along this initial path of steepest ascent begins to diminish markedly, further observations in this region are made and another plane and its contour lines are determined. This procedure of calculating contour lines of a region and its line of steepest ascent followed by continued observations along the line of steepest ascent until the response diminishes is repeated until a stationary point is reached. This method is most effective when the response surface is continuous and has no local minimum or maximum points.

The line of steepest ascent is proportional to the partial derivatives of the function, $\partial f/\partial x$ and $\partial f/\partial y$. These partial derivatives can be estimated numerically. Figure 8.5 shows how five points are evaluated in a region and the line of steepest ascent calculated.

A cost map is developed by exhaustive iteration to determine if any local minimum points exist. Figure 8.6 is a cost map for a particular stage in the college admission model. It should be noted that no local minima exist in this map, making the method of steepest ascent a feasible search technique.

Model Updating

Data from previous years are available for estimating the following system parameters: the total number of applications, distribution of the "quality" of the applicant population, and the acceptance/enrollment ratio. Because of the rapidly changing educational environment, however, data that is several years old frequently has little information value in establishing today's policies. Thus the uncertainty associated with this prior information is quite large.

As applications are received, new estimates of these parameters can be made. These estimates, however, based on small samples, also contain considerable uncertainty. Maximum accuracy in estimating system parameters results from using the two information sources: (1) prior information based on data from previous years, and (2) estimates based on sampled data from the current year. Two methods of combining these two information sources are used in the model: Bayes' equation and weighted averaging. Bayes' equation is independent of distributions being updated while the weighted averaging used assumes that the parameters being averaged are normally distributed. The latter technique facilitates the calculation process. In the model, both updating methods are used, depending on the need for accuracy and computing speed.

SIMULATION OF THE COLLEGE-ADMISSION MODEL

A simulation of the college-admission model was developed for two reasons:

1. Simulation is an effective method of evaluating many alternate college-admission selection policies.
2. For effective implementation of any operations research model, the decision maker must become intimately involved in the use of the model. A cause-effect simulation model showing the consequences of a given

action can bring about this necessary involvement of and communication with the decision maker.

Four major topics can be evaluated with this simulation model: (1) comparison of a fixed single-point cutoff policy with the sliding two-point cutoff policy, (2) calculation of the value of information corresponding to the reduction of uncertainty in system parameters, (3) determination of the sensitivity of selection policies to various cost factors, and (4) determination of the value or effect of more accurate predictor equations.

The simulation, which was developed in modular form, consists of ten functional subprograms and nine general subroutines, all directed by a main or executive program. These programs communicate through a large common area. This modular approach, patterned after a process control system, was taken to permit isolated changes to be made with minimum disruptions to the remainder of the simulation system.

The basic time unit of this simulation was a month. This system runs for a period of five months with applicant selection policies being evaluated at the beginning and end of each month.

The main program, in addition to directing the use of the major subprograms, provides for specifying the cost coefficients of the objective functions and establishing prior information on system parameters.

Examples of computer output from several subprograms are shown in figures 8.7, 8.8, and 8.9.

The subprogram PRIOR establishes probability distributions for the following system parameters: (1) total applications, (2) monthly rate of application arrival, (3) acceptance/enrollment ratio, (4) average-applicant class quality, and (5) standard deviation of applicant class quality. These prior distributions specify the range and the probability of occurrence of system parameters. If a parameter is normally distributed with a mean of 400 and a standard deviation of 30, this parameter will be in the interval 340–460 for 95 percent of the simulation runs. The prior information is summarized in the report shown in fig. 8.7.

GENPRO is another basic subprogram in this simulation. For each time unit, each month, this subprogram:

1. generates new applicants and their academic attributes according to predetermined arrival rates and an average and standard deviation of academic quality;
2. accepts or rejects applicants based on an established selection policy;
3. holds nonselected applicants in a queue for later processing;
4. generates the response of accepted applicants, i.e., enrolling or not enrolling, according to a predetermined acceptance/enrollment ratio;
5. generates the time of the above-mentioned response;
6. summarizes applicant processing to date, an example of which is shown in figure 8.8.

The selection policy used by GENPRO is provided by one of two decision subprograms: (1) the average number of applications that must be accepted to

```
TIME: NOVEMBER 1

                    THIS IS PRIOR INFORMATION BASED ON PREVIOUS YEARS EXPERIENCE

ESTIMATE OF APPLICANT CLASS CHARACTERISTICS

TOTAL APPLICATIONS TO BE RECEIVED                     340-  460
ACCEPTANCE/ENROLLMENT RATIO(YIELD)                   1.53- 1.87
AVERAGE QPA OF ALL APPLICANTS                        1.98- 2.26
QPA OF 95% OF ALL APPLICANTS WILL BE IN THE RANGE    1.48- 2.76


THESE CLASS CHARACTERISTICS ARE THE BASIS FOR RECOMMENDING APPLICANT PROCESSING POLICY FOR NOVEMBER
```

Figure 8.7
INFORMATION GENERATED IN THE SUBPROGRAM PRIOR

```
*********************************************************************************

TIME: END OF NOVEMBER

APPLICANT PROCESSING POLICY:
  ACCEPT APPLICANTS:PREDICTED QPA GREATER THAN    1.83
  REJECT APPLICANTS:PREDICTED QPA LESS THAN    1.83


NOVEMBER ACTIONS

   # ACCEPTED     89
   # REJECTED     28
TOT PROCESSED    117

SUMMARY OF ADMISSION ACTIONS TO DATE


         APPLICANTS    PROCESS     ACCEPT       REJECT   BACKLOG       HOLD
  TOTAL        117        117        89           28         0           0

*********************************************************************************
*********************************************************************************

TIME: END OF DECEMBER

APPLICANT PROCESSING POLICY:
  ACCEPT APPLICANTS:PREDICTED QPA GREATER THAN    1.83
  REJECT APPLICANTS:PREDICTED QPA LESS THAN    1.83


DECEMBER ACTIONS

   # ACCEPTED     80
   # REJECTED     17
TOT PROCESSED     97

SUMMARY OF ADMISSION ACTIONS TO DATE


         APPLICANTS    PROCESS     ACCEPT       REJECT   BACKLOG       HOLD
  TOTAL        214        214       169           45         0           0


                                              TOTAL
  RESPONSE OF ACCEPTED APPLICANTS              37
                           # ENROLLING         23
       #TURN DOWN OFFER TO ENROLL              14
                           NO RESPONSE        132
*********************************************************************************
*********************************************************************************
```

Figure 8.8
INFORMATION GENERATED IN THE SUBPROGRAM GENPRO

yield the desired enrollment; and (2) the cutoff score, in terms of predicted QPA, that will accept the correct number of applicants to yield the desired enrollment. This program also takes into account the uncertainty associated with the system parameters to calculate the standard error of the two above-mentioned values. The standard error is then used to calculate the range of the number of acceptances required and the range of the cutoff score.

The subprogram MINCUT, a decision-making program, calculates the single-point selection policy that minimizes the decision maker's objective function.

```
THE FOLLOWING 3 CASES ILLUSTRATE THE CALCULATION

OF THE RECOMMENDED APPLICANT PROCESSING POLICY


        ACC/REJ    NUMBER    AVERAGE    ENROLLMENT
        POINT      ACCEPT    ENROLLMENT   RANGE

          2.02      306.        185.        171-197
          2.05      296.        178.        165-190
          2.07      290.        175.        162-186
THE RECOMMENDED POLICY FOR MARCH     PROCESSING::
     ACCEPT APPLICANTS: QPA GREATER THAN  2.04
     REJECT APPLICANTS: QPA LESS THAN     2.04


TOTAL APPLICATIONS EXPECTED           401.
TOTAL APPLICATIONS RECEIVED           385.
      # ACCEPTED                255.
      # REJECTED                 55.
      # NO ACTION TAKEN          75.
APPLICATIONS TO BE RECEIVED            15.


APPLICATIONS ACCEPTED                 255.
      # ENROLL AS FRESHMEN       56.
      # TURNDOWN OFFER           35.
      # NO RESPONSE             164.


EFFECT OF RECOMMENDED POLICY
TOTAL APPLICANTS ACCEPTED             296.
TOTAL APPLICANTS REJECTED             104.
RESULTANT ENROLLMENT                  178.
AIM ENROLLMENT                        180.
RANGE OF POSSIBLE ENROLLMENTS      165- 191
```

FRESHMAN GRADES(EST) OF THOSE WHO ENROLL	NUMBER STUDENTS	FRESHMAN GRADES(EST) OF REJECTED APPLICANTS IF HAD BEEN ACCEPTED	NUMBER STUDENTS
0.0 -0.49	0.	0.0 -0.49	8.
0.50-0.99	1.	0.50-0.99	13.
1.00-1.49	6.	1.00-1.49	22.
1.50-1.99	30.	1.50-1.99	30.
2.00-2.49	57.	2.00-2.49	20.
2.50-2.99	48.	2.50-2.99	6.
3.00-3.49	23.	3.00-3.49	1.
3.50-3.99	10.	3.50-3.99	0.

Figure 8.9

INFORMATION GENERATED IN THE SUBPROGRAM MINICUT

This objective function consists of three costs: (1) the cost of enrolling too many students, (2) the cost of enrolling too few students, and (3) the cost of an enrolled student failing out of the school due to his inability to do adequate academic work. Refer to figure 8.9.

IMPLEMENTATION

Following is an approach for implementing this work on college admission selection policy evaluation:

1. *Applicant-selection criteria.* The first step is to establish one or two alternate general criteria for the selection of applicants. Two alternate criteria might be:
   (a) a predictor equation of college success utilizing considerable applicant data;
   (b) a ranking equation using only total SAT scores and adjusted high school rank.

   The predictor equation is developed by regression analysis. Because of the low correlation coefficient associated with these equations, however, an arbitrary ranking equation would be as satisfactory. If this ranking equation were accepted by all decision makers as the basis for most admissions decisions, then it might be preferred over regression-developed predictor equations. Examples of a predictor and ranking equation follow:

   Predictor equation

   Predicted QPA = −1.93 − 0.033 · SAT − *V*
   +0.143 · SAT − M
   +0.449 · Mean Ach
   +1.187 · High School Rank

   Ranking equation

   Rank = Total SAT Scores · 0.08
   + Adjusted High School Rank of Individual

   Adjusted High School Rank ranges from 20 to 100, 100 being the highest value.
2. *Prior information.* Prior information on relevant system parameters must be developed using at least several years of data. Initial parameters to be investigated should include:
   (a) total applications received,
   (b) acceptance/enrollment ratio, and
   (c) distribution of applicant class quality according to the selection criteria established.

   At this point applicants should be divided into subgroups if these subgroups have different characteristics. For example, the acceptance/enrollment ratio may be significantly different between in-state and out-of-state applications, thus warranting the development of completely separate statistics on each group. Other subgroupings could include:
   (a) sex;
   (b) overall applicant quality, i.e., excellent, average, or marginal;
   (c) financial need; and
   (d) time of application.

   Making calculations on subgroups becomes much more complicated than on a homogeneous population, but grouping can considerably reduce the uncertainties associated with the system parameters.

3. *Validating the predictor equation.* If regression-developed predictor equations are used, they should be validated each year by comparing the predicted QPA of accepted applicants with their freshman QPA.
4. *Revision of model to account for different information flows.* Information flows may differ from that used in the developed model. An example of this is that although applicants may apply to a school in November, their SAT scores and seventh-term grades are not available until January. A possible solution is to develop predictor equations (or ranking equations) based on junior year tests, etc. Thus the best applicants could be recognized and accepted early, a policy shown by simulation work to decrease uncertainty in enrollment projections.
5. *Develop conditional probabilities from sampling.* System parameters are monitored throughout the processing year by a sampling process. During this analysis, time trends should be looked for, i.e., are November and December applicants better academically qualified than those applying in January and February? Similarly, do acceptance/enrollment ratios differ between such groupings?
6. *Cost coefficients.* In the developed model, selection policies are chosen that minimize certain objective functions. The following cost coefficients must be developed:
   (a) the cost of enrolling too many students;
   (b) the cost of enrolling too few students;
   (c) the cost of a student failing out of school due to his inability to do adequate academic work;
   (d) the maximum number of applications the admissions staff can process each month and the cost (overtime, etc.) of processing each application over this maximum rate; and
   (e) the value of accepting applicants early.

   Certain of these costs may be negligible and additional costs may exist depending on the particular institution's procedures.
7. *Computer model development.* Having developed the prior information, methods to update this prior information with sampled evidence, system costs, and the general criteria for selecting applicants, a formal computer model can be developed. This model should be developed in modular form. In addition every attempt should be made to develop a cause-effect conversational model that can be used by the decision maker with minimum assistance from the model builder. After a computer model is developed, someone should be assigned to update this model on a regular basis. The person chosen should be completely familiar with the mathematics and programming features of the model.

REFERENCES

Cronbach, L. J., and Goldine C. Gleser. *Psychological Tests and Personnel Decisions.* Urbana: University of Illinois Press, 1957, pp. 48–60.

Fishman, Joshua A., and Ann K. Pasanella. "College Admission-Selection Studies." *Review of Educational Research* 30 (October 1960): 298.

Jones, Curtis H. "At Last: Real Computer Power for Decision Makers." *Harvard Business Review* 48, no. 5 (September/October 1970): 75–89.

Mattson, Dale E. "Use of a Formal Decision Theory Model in the Selection of Medical Students." *Journal of Medical Education* 44 (October 1969): 964.

Stein, Morris I. *Personality Measures in Admissions.* New York: College Entrance Examination Board, 1963.

Vroman, Clyde. "Problems and Issues Confronting the Admissions Community." Paper read at the Colloquium on College Admission Policies, Interlochen, Michigan, 18–23 June, 1967.

*Karl A. Fox**

9 PRACTICAL OPTIMIZATION MODELS FOR UNIVERSITY DEPARTMENTS

A typical department in a large public university operates in two principal environments: (1) the undergraduate programs, data systems, and administrative constraints of its own university; and (2) the graduate training, research, and publication system of its national scientific community.[†] Activity-analysis models of such departments can help to clarify many problems of resource allocation among levels of instruction and between undergraduate and graduate programs in general.

This chapter attempts to characterize these two environments on both conceptual and illustrative-empirical levels. The "prices" or objective-function weights applied to the outputs of a department may be given only ratio or index-number interpretations within that department, or they may be linked to systems of relative prices in other departments, or they may be linked to price systems (e.g., salary structures) in the national economy and treated as first approximations to dollar values (Sengupta and Fox 1969, Fox 1973, Fox and Van Moeseke 1973). The models presented should be useful in discussions of alternative instructional patterns within a given university and of alternative federal policies and funding levels for graduate training and university research within and among national scientific communities.

*The support of the National Science Foundation under research grant GS-2363 to Karl A. Fox and Erik Thorbecke at Iowa State University is gratefully acknowledged.

†The emphasis on *scientific* disciplines in this paper is for concreteness of reference; similar models are applicable to all other university departments and disciplines.

While the models and methods should be of wide applicability, the data and specific assumptions relate to the United States. We assume the department of primary interest to be part of a large state university located in a "university town" sufficiently far from the nearest metropolis to make it impractical for students to combine full-time employment there with enrollment at the university.* Some graduate students are employed by the university on a part-time basis as instructors, teaching assistants, or research assistants. To simplify the exposition, we assume that the university is made up of departments (i.e., we do not specifically include colleges as intermediate units of administration between departments and the university). The United States as a whole is assumed to be the relevant "market" area for graduate students, scientific publications and federally funded research grants, contracts and graduate fellowships. While we shall speak of a *national* scientific community as one of the environments of a department, the points we wish to make would not be substantially affected if we took cognizance of an *international* scientific community.

RELATIONSHIP TO PREVIOUS WORK AT IOWA STATE UNIVERSITY

From 1955 until 1972, I served continuously as head of a large and complex department in a major state university. Student enrollment at this university, as at many others in the United States, doubled during the 1960s; the expansion was somewhat larger percentagewise at the graduate than at the undergraduate level. Undergraduate enrollment at this university has been limited to students who graduated in the upper 50 percent of their high school classes. The dropout rate between lower- and upper-division levels has been moderate and a considerable percentage of the undergraduates has gone on for graduate or professional degrees at this or other universities. Under these circumstances, the use of selected graduate students as teaching assistants or part-time instructors has been compatible with the maintenance of a high-quality learning environment for both undergraduate and graduate students.

Most analysts who have modeled universities have used simulation rather than optimization techniques. The study by Koenig, Keeney, and Zemach (1968) is an outstanding example of the simulation approach. No objective function is specified by the model builders; in principle, the university president ponders a number of simulated futures and selects the one he prefers within the constraints he perceives or anticipates.

We have viewed optimization models from a different perspective. In the first place, we have been particularly interested in models of a university department in which we have played the role of a policy maker and have become familiar with the official university data systems. The structure of the department's teaching program can be represented in an activity-analysis format. As economists, the faculty members who have shared coordinating and policy-

*Part-time students and "adjunct professors" (if any) can readily be converted into full-time equivalents for statistical purposes.

making responsibility with us are also familiar with the implications and manipulation of activity-analysis models. We know that *relative* prices are sufficient to determine an optimal allocation of resources in such a model; also, the sensitivity of a particular solution to variations in the relative prices of the outputs can and should be investigated. We are also aware that some outputs of a university (e.g., the increases in career incomes expected as a result of various degree programs) can be at least roughly estimated. Knowing the crudeness of our present measures of relative and absolute values of university outputs, we should not be seriously misled by our assumed prices.

Work with optimization models at Iowa State University has included a large two-level planning or decentralization model by McCamley (1967); a collection of small expository models by Fox, McCamley, and Plessner (1967); a dynamic programming model by Plessner, Fox, and Sanyal (1968) in which, without presuming to put prices on research outputs, a department chairman transfers resources from teaching to research until he feels that a subjective optimum has been reached; a survey article by Fox and Sengupta (1968); an article by Sengupta and Fox (1970) on a computable approach to optimal growth for a university department; a chapter on models of resource allocation and planning in educational institutions by Sengupta and Fox (1969); some papers presented but not published by Fox (1969) and Fox, Sengupta, and Sanyal (1969); and an advanced monograph edited by Fox with contributions by himself, Sengupta, Kumar, and Sanyal (1972).

In the United States, most university departments that have significant graduate programs also have undergraduate teaching responsibilities. Before presenting optimization models of a university department, we will comment on the characteristics of the two environments in which such a department must operate, the local university and the national scientific community.

A DEPARTMENT'S ENVIRONMENT WITHIN ITS OWN UNIVERSITY

Many state universities have large undergraduate enrollments, ranging from 15,000 to 30,000 full-time equivalent students or even more. On most such campuses, the number of undergraduates is several times as large as the number of graduate students.

Such a university is dependent upon appropriations by the legislature of its state for a large proportion of its total income. Students from other states must pay substantially higher tuition fees than residents of the given state; hence, the undergraduate student body of a state university is usually dominated (to the extent of 80 percent or more) by residents of that state.

The financial support for a university by its state legislature evidently depends to a very considerable extent upon the perceived quality of its programs for undergraduates. In general, state legislators are not strongly committed to the support of graduate study and research in the sciences and humanities; such programs at a state university are rationalized partly on the basis of their complementarities with undergraduate teaching and partly by the fact that, directly and indirectly, much of their cost is borne by the federal government.

Thus, an effort to achieve an optimal combination of undergraduate and graduate programs implicitly involves an effort to strike an optimal balance between state and national concerns and sources of funds.

A few of the oldest and largest state universities have achieved strong graduate programs in almost every discipline. In some others, which were founded as colleges of agriculture and mechanic arts, graduate programs are strongly developed in the sciences (including agricultural sciences) and engineering but not in the humanities. We will give some attention later in this chapter to the situation of a university in which some departments have strong graduate programs and others have only undergraduate responsibilities.

Within a university, the resources-and-activity mix of a department with both graduate and undergraduate programs may be limited by various administrative constraints such as (1) a lower limit on the perceived quality of the department's undergraduate teaching program; (2) an upper limit on the dollars the department may be allocated per student quarter of enrollment, either unweighted or weighted by levels of instruction (lower division, upper division, and graduate); (3) a lower limit on student quarters taught per full-time equivalent instructor, unweighted or weighted by levels of instruction; (4) an upper limit on the percent of total resources allocated to the department by the university which may be devoted to graduate as against undergraduate programs; (5) quotas on the number of graduate students a department may admit; and (6) quotas on the numbers of full professors and associate professors a department may have. These points may be summarized by saying that the department must stay within reasonable bounds as reflected in the various measures used by the university's administrators as evidences of workload and performance.

THE RELATIONSHIP OF A DEPARTMENT TO ITS NATIONAL SCIENTIFIC COMMUNITY

For concreteness, let us assume that there are in the United States 50 departments in a given discipline that account for all acceptable Ph.D.s produced in that discipline and for all articles published in the professional journals sponsored by its members.

A few of the departments are in private universities that give top priority to graduate training and research. These universities limit undergraduate enrollment to a low level as compared with state universities; thus, considerations of the quality of their undergraduate programs have placed few restrictions on the development of their graduate programs. Some departments in the largest state universities have developed graduate programs rivaling those of the leading private universities; however, they and most others among the 50 departments must maintain a balance between their undergraduate and graduate programs.

If we examine a "community" consisting of the faculty members of our assumed 50 departments, we will find a number of systematic gradients (influence, prestige, professorial salaries, volume and quality of published research, number and quality of Ph.D.s trained) ranging downward from the top four or five departments. The general nature of such gradients is shown in table 9.1,

Table 9.1
Correlates of Quality in Graduate Education in the United States: Attributes and Performance Measures as of 1963-64 to 1967-68

Quality Attribute or Performance Measure	Perceived Quality Class of University's Graduate Faculty, 1963-64:[a] *A*	*B*	*C*	*D*
1. Ratio of doctorates to baccalaureates[b]	0.202	0.110	0.070	0.055
2. Index of library resources[c]	over 2.00	1.00-1.49	0.75-0.99	0.50-0.74
3. Average compensation of full professors (nine months)[c]	$18,838	$17,616	$16,600	$15,200
4. Professors as percent of all faculty members[d]	42	38	32	30
5. Number of full professors[d]	375	308	210	160
6. Federal obligations for academic research and development (1,000)[b]	$22,878	$10,898	$6,479	$3,447
7. Postdoctoral students in science and engineering (number)[e]	174	84	47	22
8. Selection of institutions by recipients of graduate fellowships (Number)[f]	362	62	26	10
9. Graduate students enrolled[g]	3,100	2,130	1,172	757
10. Number of doctoral awards per year[b]	316	205	102	56
11. Doctoral awards per graduate student[h]	0.102	0.096	0.087	0.074
Amounts and Numbers per Full Professor				
12. Federal obligations for academic research and development[i]	$61,000	$35,400	$30,900	$21,500
13. Postdoctoral students in science and engineering[j]	0.464	0.273	0.224	0.138
14. Graduate students enrolled[k]	8.27	6.92	5.58	4.73
15. Number of doctoral awards per year[l]	0.843	0.666	0.486	0.350

Source: Lawton M. Hartman, *Graduate Education: Parameters for Public Policy.* (Washington, D.C.: National Science Board, National Science Foundation, 1969.) See especially chap. 2, "Correlates of Quality," pp. 49-121.
[a]Classification made by NSB for the purpose of distributing 106 universities over seven class intervals. Only the top four classes, containing about 70 universities, are included in this table. [b]As of 1963-64. [c]As of 1967-68 (salary plus employee benefits, adjusted to a nine-month basis). [d]As of 1967-68. [e]Fall 1966. [f]Total, 1963-67. [g]Line 10 divided by line 11. [h]Doctoral awards in 1955-66 divided by graduate students enrolled (science and engineering). [i]Line 6 divided by line 5. [j]Line 7 divided by line 5. [k]Line 9 divided by line 5. [l]Line 10 divided by line 5.

which is based on figures and tables contained in a report prepared by Lawton M. Hartman (1969) for the National Science Board. Universities of the highest perceived quality (class *A* in the table) are characterized by large numbers of full professors and by higher average salaries for full professors than those in classes *B*, *C*, and *D* (in that order). Also, the class *A* universities rated higher *per full professor* in terms of federal research grant and contract funds, numbers of graduate students enrolled, and numbers of Ph.D.s awarded. A related study by Allan Cartter (1966) indicated that the perceived quality of the graduate faculties of different departments was highly correlated with the average salary paid to their "superior full professors" (the highest one-third by salary in the full-professor rank) and with their annual rate of publication in specified high-quality journals.

The gradients in table 9.1 refer to entire universities. Similar gradients among departments in individual disciplines are perceived by members of these disciplines, however, as illustrated by a recent survey of graduate programs in 36 fields by Roose and Andersen (1970). For example, 201 sociologists drawn from approximately 100 different universities rated graduate faculties in their discipline. Some 91 percent of the respondents characterized the top two departments as "distinguished" or "strong" and 4 to 6 percent said they had insufficient information to rate them. In contrast, only 20 percent of the respondents characterized the 21st ranking department as "distinguished" or "strong," and 28 percent said they had insufficient information to rate it. High quality was closely associated with high visibility. Similar results were obtained in the other 35 fields.

We will comment more formally about the structures and functions of national scientific communities later in the chapter.

AN ACTIVITY-ANALYSIS MODEL OF DEPARTMENT X

To assure realism and practicality in our illustrations in this section, we have based them upon data for a specific university department in a recent year. We have simplified the actual budget of the department by using average salaries (rounded) for each major category of personnel. The numbers of equivalent full-time positions shown in table 9.2 are identical with those in the department's budget except for slight rounding and other adjustments in the instructor, teaching assistant, and research assistant categories. The total budget shown in table 9.2 approximates the actual budget of Department X for the year in question within 1 percent.

Table 9.3 contains close approximations to the actual enrollments in courses taught by Department X in the academic year to which the budget figures in table 9.2 refer. In that year, almost without exception, the courses offered by Department X carried three hours of credit per student quarter, implying three hours of class meetings per week. The enrollments in column 1 of table 9.3 are in terms of student quarters of three credit hours each.

The unit of measure for the item called "dissertation research and comprehensive study" consists of one quarter in residence per full-time graduate student

Table 9.2
Department X: Budgeted Resources, Year 1

Type of Resource	(1) Equivalent Full-time Positions (number)	(2) Average Salary per Equivalent Full-time Position (dollars)	(3) Total Salaries and other Budgeted Resources (dollars)
All budgeted *positions*	*38.50*	*$13,466*	*$518,432*
Professors[a]	22.47	18,600	417,942
Instructors[b]	3.73	8,000	29,840
Teaching assistants[b]	5.00	6,400	32,000
Administrative assistants	0.30	13,500	4,050
Stenographers[c]	6.00	4,700	28,200
Research assistants[b]	1.00	6,400	6,400
Current expense (supplies, etc.)			13,500
Salaries plus current expense			531,932
Employee benefits[d]			62,212
Total, all items			$594,144

[a]Includes professors, associate professors, and assistant professors.
[b]Graduate students in Department X who work one-half time for the department and are paid amounts averaging one-half of the full-time salaries in column 2.
[c]Includes secretaries, stenographers, and clerk-typists.
[d]Twelve percent of total salaries.

seeking a degree in the department. This unit reflects, in addition to dissertation research, study for comprehensive examinations embracing entire fields of the discipline (as distinct from individual courses) and any other studies undertaken by graduate students outside the framework of an organized class or seminar.

Column 2 illustrates the use of relative (as distinct from absolute) measures of the values of outputs per unit at different levels of instruction. The figures in column 2 have been purposely rounded to focus attention on the concept rather than on the specific numerical values. The per unit figures shown for each level and kind of instruction are fairly close to the relative dollar costs of departmental budget resources used in a recent year.

If we provisionally accept the values of 1.000 and 2.000 per unit for lower- and upper-division instruction, we find that the average value per student quarter of all undergraduate instruction was 1.314, or 31.4 percent higher than that of an instructional program consisting exclusively of lower-division courses.

Similarly, if we accept the values of 3.500 and 10.500 for the two components of the graduate program, we find that the weighted average value per

Table 9.3

Department X: Expected Student Enrollments in Year 1 and Assumed Relative and Absolute Values of Outputs with Average Quality of Instruction, by Levels of Instruction

Level of Instruction	(1) Expected Enrollments (student quarters of 3 credit hours each)	(2) Assumed Relative Values of Outputs per Student Quarter (lower division = 1.000)	(3) Total Values in Assumed Relative Units: col. 1 X col. 2	(4) Total Values in Assumed Absolute Units: col. 3 X $400
Lower division	6,300	1.000	6,300	$2,520,000
Upper division	2,880	2.000	5,760	2,304,000
All undergraduate instruction	9,180	1.314	12,060	4,824,000
Graduate courses	870	3.500	3,045	1,218,000
Dissertation research, comprehensive study, etc.	300[a]	10.500	3,150	1,260,000
All graduate instruction	1,170	5.295	6,195	2,478,000
Total, undergraduate and graduate instruction	10,350	1.764	18,255	7,302,000

[a]The unit here is one graduate student in residence for one quarter and reflects dissertation research, study for comprehensive examinations, and other studies not associated with specific courses.

student quarter of all graduate instruction was 5.295, approximately four times as large as the weighted average for all undergraduate instruction. The final figure in column 2 implies that the weighted average value per unit of the department's instructional program was 1.764 times as large as the per unit value of its lower-division instruction.

To obtain column 3, the relative values in column 2 have been multiplied by the enrollment figures in column 1. Thus, column 3 contains "values" expressed in a particular currency which uses a student quarter of instruction at the lower-division level as its numeraire. In these units, the value of the upper-division program is only slightly smaller than that of the lower-division program. The sum of the values of the two components of the graduate program is nearly as large as that of the lower division and slightly larger than that of the upper-division programs.

In column 4 we take another step which converts the column 3 values into dollars. The value of output of the lower-division program is stated as $2,520,000 and that of the upper-division program as $2,304,000, a total of $4,824,000 for all undergraduate instruction. The two components of the graduate program are valued at $2,478,000, about as large as either the lower-division or the upper-division program taken separately. The combined value of output of all the instructional programs is stated as $7,302,000.

While the specific values in column 4 should not be taken too seriously, they should not be dismissed out-of-hand. The choice of $400 as a base enables us to make simple calculations using only one significant (nonzero) figure. Also, consider the fact that graduation from this university with a B.S. or B.A. degree requires a minimum of 192 credit hours, equivalent to 64 courses of 3 credit hours each. If half these courses are lower-division and half are upper-division, our $400 basic unit implies a value of $12,800 for 32 lower-division courses and $25,600 for 32 upper-division courses, a total of $38,400 for the complete four-year undergraduate program. If we view the $38,400 figure as the present value of a future income stream running over a forty-year period and discounted at an annual rate of 5 percent, the annual income stream implied is approximately $2,240.* This is not, we believe, an unreasonable estimate of the average net effect of a four-year college education as such upon students of given ability and motivation.† (Estimates of differences in average income between all college graduates and all high school graduates are considerably larger than this, but the average student actually graduating from college is at least more highly motivated, and probably more able, to enter occupations for which college graduation is a norm than is the average student who does not go beyond high school.)

Perhaps the chief advantage of the dollar figures in column 4 is a psychological one. They remind us that, as teachers or administrators of teaching programs, we are influencing the productivity of some very expensive human resources.

If we divide the total value of output in column 4 ($7,302,000) by the 38.50 full-time equivalent positions in Department X's budget, at first glance we seem to have a gross value of output per person approaching $190,000. However, we have left out by far the most numerous and important members of the relevant labor force, namely, the students. At 16 student quarters per student year in the lower- and upper-division programs and 12 student quarters per student year in the graduate program, the production processes supervised by Department X involved 394 student years at the lower division, 180 student years at the upper division, and 97.5 student years at the graduate level, a total of 671 student years. If we add to these the 38.50 full-time equivalent staff positions, we will attribute the output value of $7,302,000 to 710 (academic) man years, or roughly $10,000 per (academic) man year. The weighted average opportunity cost of the student input is probably on the order of $5,000 per student year.

Only three categories of the personnel listed in table 9.2 are directly involved in the instructional program, namely, professors, instructors, and teaching assistants. To bring out the essential aspects of substitution of different categories of personnel in an instructional program, we will omit several of the resources in table 9.2 (administrative assistant, stenographers, research assistants, current expense, and employee benefits) from our consideration in table 9.4.**

*If discounting is ignored (as it is in some popular expositions of the value of a college education), $2,240 a year over a working life of 45 years adds up to $100,000.

†The theoretical and empirical bases for estimating the economic value of education to an individual are presented by Schultz (1963) and Becker (1964).

**"Department X" is one of two major teaching and research divisions of a department which also includes an extension service faculty of 12.50 man years.

Table 9.4 shows the structure of Department X's instructional program in activity-analysis format. The instructional program must provide at least enough student places to accommodate the enrollment figures in column 1 of table 9.3. The array of activities in table 9.4 and the numbers of units of each closely approximate the actual instructional program of Department X in a recent year. The numbers of units of the various activities (shown immediately above the corresponding X_i, $i = 1, 2, \ldots, 18$) do *not* result from the optimization of an explicit objective function; rather, they reflect a program structure which was developed on a judgmental basis with successive modifications over a period of years. The enrollment of 6,300 student quarters in lower-division courses is handled by providing 8 units of activity 1, 9 units of activity 2, and 93 units of activity 3. As these activities accommodate 280,100 and 34 student quarters per unit respectively, the capacity of the lower-division program in table 9.4 is 8(280) + 9(100) + 93(34) = 2240 + 900 + 3,162 = 6,302 student quarters.

The numbers opposite lower-division teaching, upper-division teaching, and graduate-division teaching in the outputs section of table 9.4 are the numbers of students enrolled in a particular unit of the specified activities. For example, activity 1 involves two hours of lectures per week by a professor to audiences of 280 students; in addition, the students, in groups averaging 18 or 19 members, spend one hour a week in a discussion section with a teaching assistant. The conventional workload allowance given in Department X for these activities is 0.125 academic man years of professorial time and 0.500 academic man years of teaching assistants. (In a given quarter, each of three teaching assistants, working half-time, would meet with five of the small groups just mentioned, one hour per week for each group.)

Activity 2 involves a professor lecturing to a class of 100 students three hours a week; in addition, a teaching assistant grades examinations, reads term papers, conducts office visits with students, and arranges special small-group "help sessions" for students indicating an interest in or need for them. The teaching assistant's duties in connection with such a course are also rated as equivalent to 0.083 (academic) man years.

Activity 3 involves a part-time instructor (a graduate student with the equivalent of a Master's degree) who is wholly responsible for the instruction of a class of 34 students except for general guidance and advice from a designated professor.

Activity 4 involves lectures by a professor to a class of about 68 students; the professor is aided by a teaching assistant who performs duties of the kind indicated in connection with activity 2.

Activities 5 and 6 involve upper-division classes averaging 34 students each taught respectively by a professor or by an instructor. Activities 7 and 8 involve one undergraduate student majoring in the subject matter of Department X receiving advice concerning his academic program (selection of courses and so

---

An unpublished consistency model of the entire department as it might have been in 1972–73 under specified enrollment projections was prepared by Fox (1968) in connection with a planning effort involving all segments of the department. Many inputs and outputs in addition to those in table 9.4 were identified and rationales were given for the prices tentatively assigned to them. A more succinct description of these outputs, inputs and prices is given in chapter 9 of Fox (1972).

Table 9.4

Department X: Consistency Model of Instructional Program for Year 1

Assumed Relative Value per Unit of Activity, with Average Quality (3 credit hours of lower-division teaching = 1.00)	280	100	34	136	68	68	1.25	1.25	140	105
Number of Units of Activity	8	9	93	25	35	0	0	130	8	5
Activity Number:	X_1	X_2	X_3	X_4	X_5	X_6	X_7	X_8	X_9	X_{10}
A. *Outputs*										
1. lower-division teaching	-280	-100	-34							
2. upper-division teaching				-68	-34	-34				
3. undergraduate advising							-1	-1		
4. graduate-division teaching									-40	-30
5. dissertation research, etc.										
6. transfers										
7. faculty research time (residual)										
B. *Inputs of Budgeted Resources (man years)*[b]										
1. professors	0.125	0.083		0.083	0.083		0.005		0.083	0.083
2. instructors			0.083			0.083		0.005		
3. teaching assistants	0.500	0.083		0.083					0.083	
C. *Inputs of Student Time (man years)*[c]										
1. lower-division students	17.500	6.250	2.125							
2. upper-division students				4.250	2.125	2.125				
3. graduate students (courses)									3.333	2.500
4. graduate students (dissertations, etc.)										

[a]Student places available under this instructional pattern slightly exceed actual student enrollments.
[b]Assumes academic man years of nine months and work weeks of 44 hours.
[c]Assumes academic student years of nine months, 16 courses a year full-time load for undergraduates, and 12 courses a year full-time load for graduates. Courses are assumed to be on the quarter system and to carry three credit hours each.
[d]Excludes assumed 2.061 student years of time associated with academic advising.

on) from either a professor or an instructor. Serving as academic adviser to 50 undergraduate majors is regarded as one-fourth of a full-time work load.

Activity 8 involves a professor lecturing to some 40 graduate students, with a teaching assistant to grade problem sets, help with examinations, and so on. (The unusually large enrollments in some of Department X's graduate courses reflect the fact that Department X is one of two major teaching and research subdivisions of a larger department; the other subdivision also has approximately

									B_0	B_1	$B_1 - B_0$
70	52.5	35	10.5	0	0	0	0		Enroll-ments; Budget Resources and Student Time Available	Places Provided; Budget Resources and Student Time Used	Places Provided minus Enrollments; Resources Used minus Resources Available
10	4	14	300	2.009	0.860	0.341	3.623				
X_{11}	X_{12}	X_{13}	X_{14}	X_{15}	X_{16}	X_{17}	X_{18}				
								=	-6,300	-6,302[a]	-2[a]
								=	-2,880	-2,890[a]	-10[a]
								=	-130	-130	0
-20	-15	-10						=	-870	-870	0
			-1					=	-300	-300	0
				-1	-1	-1		=	-3.210	-3.210	0
						-1	-1	⩽	0	-3.964	-3.964
0.083	0.083	0.083	0.008	1.000	1.000		1.000	=	19.400	19.400	0
				2.325				⩾	3.730	8.400	4.670
					2.906			⩾	5.000	7.500	2.500
								=	393.750[d]	393.750[d]	0
								=	180.000[d]	180.000[d]	0
1.667	1.250	0.833						=	72.500	72.500	0
			0.083					=	25.000	25.000	0

100 graduate students in residence, all of whom take some required courses in common with graduate students in Department X.)

Activities 10, 11, 12, and 13 each involve a professor conducting a graduate course or seminar with the respective numbers of students indicated.

Activity 14 implies that each graduate student in residence requires 0.008 man years of professorial time *per quarter* over his entire period of residence. Thus, on the average, each student enrolled in the graduate program is estimated to require 0.024 professorial man years per academic year, or about 2.40 professorial man years for the group of 100 graduate students in residence. (The record system of Department X's university currently picks up only the role of the "major professor" for a graduate student who is actively working on his dissertation during a given quarter; in Department X's experience, this role accounts for perhaps 60 percent of the total professorial time involved in the graduate program over and above the conduct of organized courses.)

Activities 15 and 16 imply that "salary savings" resulting from leaves of absence without pay for some professors, or from their complete or partial transfer to research grants and contracts, are used to employ part-time instructors and teaching assistants over and above the number of such positions specifically budgeted. Thus, activity 15 "transforms" one professor into 2.325 instructors; activity 16 transforms one professor into 2.906 teaching assistants. Activity 17 becomes operative if activities 15 and 16 between them transfer less than 3.21 professorial man years out of the regular budget; any residual $(3.21 - X_{15} - X_{16})$ is "transferred" into faculty research time. The level of activity 18, faculty research time, is treated as a residual over and above the teaching activities (and transfer activities) in columns 1 through 17. (This does not mean that faculty research time is regarded as a residual in the basic value system of Department X; it is treated as a residual in this table to permit us to focus on the instructional program as such.)

It will be noted that in table 9.4 the number of professorial man years available is shown as 19.40 rather than 22.47 as in table 9.2. In order to emphasize direct instructional activities and inputs, we have omitted from table 9.4 some 3.07 professorial man years estimated to be involved in administration, coordination, committee work, national professional association activities, and the like.

The last two columns of table 9.4 indicate that the kinds and levels of instructional activities provided are sufficient to accommodate the expected enrollments at each level and to leave 3.964 professorial man years of faculty research time. The 19.40 professorial man years are used up precisely. However, the program requires 8.40 man years of instructors (as against 3.73 budgeted) and 7.50 man years of teaching assistants (as against 5.00 budgeted). To accomplish this, salary savings from 2.009 man years of professorial absences or transfers have been used to employ additional instructors (activity 15) and 0.860 man years of professorial salary savings have been used for additional teaching assistants (activity 16).

The inputs of student time in table 9.4 are obtained by dividing the corresponding enrollments per unit of activity by 16 for undergraduate and 12 for graduate students to convert student quarters into full-time student academic years. Thus, in activity 1, 280 student quarters of enrollment require 280/16 = 17.50 student years. The total lower division enrollment of 6300 student quarters requires 6300/16 = 393.75 student years.

We have stated that the pattern of resource allocation in table 9.4 was based on judgment and not upon the optimization of an explicit objective function. If the data in table 9.4 (apart from the row labeled "number of units of activity") were treated as an ordinary linear programming problem, the solution would probably include activities 1, 4, and 9 but not activities 2, 3, 5, 6, 10, 11, 12, and 13; all instruction at each level would be given in classes of the largest permissible size! In actuality, Department X offers some graduate courses which attract only 10 students a year and others which attract only 15 students a year; a "solution" which tells us to teach 870 student quarters at the graduate level in 21.75 classes of 40 does not meet all the practical requirements of Department X's situation.

In principle, the optimality of our choice of 8 units of activity 1, 9 units of activity 2, and so on could be checked against a much more detailed model. That model could include a separate activity, with an expected quality index, for each course in the department's offering if taught by each of a number of plausible instructors in each of a number of plausible class sizes. As Department X offers some 50 different courses and employs over 50 individuals, as many as 2,500 course-and-individual combinations, each replicated in two or more class sizes, would be theoretically possible. The great majority of these activities could be ruled out at once by the facts that teaching assistants are used only in conjunction with senior personnel, that instructors are not permitted to teach graduate courses, that professors specialized in one field might be of limited effectiveness in others, and that courses with small annual enrollments may be offered in only one class size. There would remain perhaps 200 course-and-individual combinations of reasonable prospective quality and some of these might be applied at two different class sizes; perhaps 300 activities would justify serious consideration in a formal model.

This model would include at least one restriction per professor and instructor (specifying a maximum teaching load) and one restriction per course (specifying the minimum enrollment to be accommodated)—perhaps 100 or more restrictions in all. The program in table 9.4 includes 211 units of teaching activities; as some individuals teach two or more units of the same course-and-class-size combination, the number of distinct activities represented is about 90. If 90 activities appeared in the optimal solution of a linear programming model, it would imply that 90 restrictions held with equality.

A formal model of the size indicated (perhaps 300 activities and 100 restrictions) could be used by a department chairman to test out the implications of his own estimates of the effectiveness of different individuals in specified activities. He could also test the sensitivity of the apparent optimal assignment pattern to uncertainties in his estimates of the quality indexes associated with various activities, to estimates supplied in confidence by other faculty members with coordinating responsibilities, or to estimates based on student feedback. Or, without revealing his own estimates of quality indexes, the chairman could ask one faculty member to act as a resource claimant for lower-division teaching, a second for upper-division teaching, and a third for graduate teaching; each would present the chairman with a proposed optimal-assignment pattern for his set of courses. Collectively, the three submodels would violate some restrictions which apply to Department X as a whole; the chairman, or the chairman and the three faculty members as a committee, could readjust the initial claims to arrive at a feasible (and nearly optimal) assignment pattern for the department.

Dissemination of the chairman's estimates of quality indexes for particular individuals in particular activities could, of course, be quite disruptive. The actual quality of an activity would depend on the motivation of the instructor and the amount of effort he put into it as well as upon his subject-matter competence and teaching skill. The enthusiasm of a professor for a given course might change considerably from one year to the next. In fact, the assignment problem could be approached by asking each professor to list in rank order the course-and-class-size combinations he would most like to teach in the coming year; the chairman might then work out an assignment pattern which minimized the sum of the ranks given to each activity by the individual who would be asked to teach it. If faculty members got maximum satisfaction from providing maximum benefits to students (within a specified total course load), faculty preferences should lead to approximately the same assignment pattern as student benefits. Encouragement and consideration of student feedback by each faculty member in each course should also promote the convergence of faculty preferences and student welfare.

Table 9.4 and more detailed models of the same type pose important questions concerning the utilization of departmental resources and pose them in a manner that invites quantitative answers. It would be unwise for a chairman to impose assignments based solely on the solution of a model. Nevertheless, a model sufficiently aggregated to eliminate invidious comparisons between individuals could be used effectively as a framework for faculty and student discussions.

UNIT COST AND WORKLOAD COMPARISONS FOR DEPARTMENTS X AND Z

Universities, like most other large organizations, pay careful attention to the details of financial accountability. While measures of workload and performance are poorly developed, the figures on dollar expenditures must add up and they must not exceed income received (plus perhaps, for short periods, some depletion of assets). Table 9.5 expresses the particular pattern of resource use in table 9.4 in terms of dollar expenditures. The activities in table 9.4 have been grouped into major program categories including lower-division teaching, upper-division teaching, undergraduate advising, graduate-division teaching, dissertation research and related studies, and faculty research supported from the regular departmental budget.

The first three lines in table 9.5 are obtained by multiplying the table 9.4 inputs of professors, instructors, and teaching assistants by the appropriate average salaries in table 9.2. Line 5 allocates an additional 3.07 professorial man years (not accounted for in table 9.4) to coordinating and administrative activities, committee work, national professional association activities, and the like specific to, or prorated over, the various program segments. Lines 4, 6, 7, 8, and 9 allocate those resources in table 9.2 (research assistants, administrative assistant, stenographers, employee benefits, and current expense) that were not included in table 9.4. Thus the total value of budgeted resources in table 9.5 is the same as that in table 9.2, namely, $594,144.

Once university policies concerning employee benefits have been determined, the resulting costs are not subject to modification by the department chairman. However, table 9.5 indicates that costs of $89,352 were incurred for salaries of

Table 9.5

Department X: Summary of Direct and Supporting Costs of Budgeted Resources, By Major Program Segment, Year 1[a]

Type of Resource	(1) Lower-division Teaching	(2) Upper-division Teaching	(3) Undergraduate Advising	(4) Graduate-division Teaching	(5) Dissertation Research, etc.	(6) Faculty Research	(7) Total Resources Used	(8) Transfers	(9) Original Budgeted Resources
Salaries of Personnel Used Directly	*$124,950*	*$106,333*	*$5,200*	*$67,817*	*$44,640*	*$80,140*	*$429,080*	*0*	*$429,080*
1. Professors	32,550	93,000	0	63,500	44,640	73,740	307,480	53,360	360,840
2. Instructors	62,000	0	5,200	0	0	0	67,200	-37,360	29,840
3. Teaching assistants	30,400	13,333	0	4,267	0	0	48,000	-16,000	32,000
4. Research assistants	0	0	0	0	0	6,400	6,400	0	6,400
Salaries of Personnel Used in Supporting Activities	*17,700*	*20,930*	*2,350*	*7,185*	*22,860*	*18,327*	*89,352*	*0*	*89,352*
5. Professors	9,300	14,880	0	6,510	15,810	10,602	57,102	0	57,102
6. Administrative assistant	1,350	1,350	0	675	0	675	4,050	0	4,050
7. Stenographers	7,050	4,700	2,350	0	7,050	7,050	28,200	0	28,200
Total Salaries	*142,650*	*127,263*	*7,550*	*75,002*	*67,500*	*98,467*	*518,432*	*0*	*518,432*
8. Employee benefits	17,118	15,272	906	9,000	8,100	11,816	62,212	0	62,212
Total Compensation	*159,768*	*142,535*	*8,456*	*84,002*	*75,600*	*110,283*	*580,644*	*0*	*580,644*
9. Current expense	3,000	2,800	200	1,500	4,000	2,000	13,500	0	13,500
Total Budgeted Resources	*162,768*	*145,335*	*8,656*	*85,502*	*79,600*	*112,283*	*594,144*	*0*	*594,144*
Approximate Opportunity Cost of Students' Time	$1,260,000	$1,152,000	$19,500	$696,000	$360,000	—	$3,487,500		

[a]Based on table 9.4 activities and on table 9.2 resources and average salaries. Opportunity costs of students' time per student quarter (three credit hours) are assumed to be $200, $400 and $800 for lower-, upper-, and graduate-division teaching respectively and $1,200 for dissertation research and related study.

personnel used in administration, coordination, committee work, other professorial activities, and stenographic support and another $13,500 for current expense (supplies, postage, telephones and tolls, rental of office machines, official travel, and so on). Together, the costs of support activities and current expense amounted to $102,852. This is nearly one-fifth of Department X's budget (after employee benefits are subtracted). Thus, studies of overall efficiency should cover the supporting activities as well as the direct teaching activities.

The allocations of administrative assistant and stenographic salaries among program elements are judgment estimates, though they could be refined on the basis of specific workload records during sample periods or for the year as a whole. The employee benefits add another $62,212 to total personnel costs, amounting in Year 1 to 12 percent of the combined salaries of all personnel used in the regular budget programs.*

The information in tables 9.4 and 9.5 obviously lends itself to calculations of costs per student quarter (three credit hours) of instructional programs at the departmental level. These calculations are summarized in table 9.6. The costs per student quarter in terms of salaries of direct teaching personnel are estimated at $19.83 for lower-division courses, $36.92 for upper-division courses, and $77.95 for graduate courses, and $148.80 for dissertation research and related activities. When the total budgeted resources of the department utilized in each program segment are considered (last line in table 9.5), the cost estimates rise to $25.84, $50.46, $98.28, and $265.63 respectively. If the total departmental cost per student quarter of lower-division instruction is taken as 1.00, the relative costs per student quarter of the other programs are approximately 2.00 for upper-division courses and 4.00 for graduate courses, and 10.00 for dissertation research and related activities. These ratios compare fairly closely with the ratios of 1.00, 2.00, 3.50, and 10.50 given in table 9.3.

The typical student course loads are 16 three-credit-hour courses per year at the undergraduate level (both lower and upper division) and 12 courses per year at the graduate level. Multiplying these figures by the program cost per unit in line 5 of table 9.6, we obtain estimates of total departmental costs per full-time equivalent student as follows: Lower division, $413.44; upper division, $807.36; graduate courses, $1,179.36; and dissertation research, comprehensive studies, and related graduate program activities, $3,187.56. As a graduate program in Department X consists of approximately three-fourths organized course and seminar work and about one-fourth dissertation research, it may be more in line with other estimates of the cost of graduate study to combine these last two figures using weights of 0.75 for graduate courses and 0.25 for dissertation research. The resulting figure is $1,681.41 per academic year per full-time equivalent graduate student.

To illustrate the possibility of comparing departments with and without graduate programs in the same university, we present in table 9.7 a hypothetical

*Many other costs are budgeted at the college and university levels (i.e., the university library, the computing center, building operation and maintenance, admissions and records, various other central services, and general administration).

Table 9.6
Department X: Student Quarters of Enrollment per Full-time Equivalent Instructor and Department Costs per Student Quarter, by Levels of Instruction, Year 1.

Item	Level of Instruction Lower Division	Upper Division	Graduate Courses	Dissertation Research, etc.
1. Expected enrollments (student quarters of 3 credit hours each)	6,300	2,880	870	300
2. Direct salary costs of teaching activities	$124,950	$106,333	$67,817	$44,640
3. Direct salary costs per student quarter	$19.83	$36.92	$77.95	$148.80
4. Total departmental costs	$162,768	$145,335	$85,502	$79,600
5. Total departmental costs per student quarter	$25.84	$50.46	$98.28	$265.63
6. Approximate relative departmental costs per student quarter (lower-division cost = 1.00)	1.00	2.00	4.00	10.00
7. Personnel used in direct teaching activities (full-time equivalents)	14.250	7.083	4.083	2.400
8. Student quarters per full-time person in direct teaching activities	442.1	406.6	213.8	125.0
9. Full-time equivalent instructors used in direct teaching and in supporting activities	14.750	7.883	4.433	3.250
10. Student quarters per full-time equivalent instructor in teaching and supporting activities	427.1	365.3	196.3	92.3
11. Total departmental costs per full-time student per year	$413.44	$807.36	$1,179.36	$3,187.56

Table 9.7
Department Z: Student Quarters of Enrollment per Full-time Equivalent Instructor and Departmental Costs per Student Quarter, by Levels of Instruction, Year 1 (hypothetical figures)

Item	Level of Instruction Lower Division	Upper Division
1. Expected enrollments (student quarters of 3 credit hours each)	7,200	3,168
2. Direct salary costs of teaching activities	$270,000	$171,600
3. Direct salary costs per student quarter	$37.50	$54.17
4. Total departmental costs	$346,496	$232,656
5. Total departmental costs per student quarter	$48.12	$73.44
6. Approximate relative departmental costs per student quarter (lower-division cost = 1.00)	1.00	1.50
7. Personnel used in direct teaching activities (full-time equivalents)	25.00	11.00
8. Student quarters per full-time person in direct teaching activities	288.0	288.0
9. Full-time equivalent instructors used in direct teaching and in supporting activities	27.00	13.00
10. Student quarters per full-time equivalent instructor in teaching and supporting activities	266.7	243.7
11. Total departmental costs per full-time student per year	$769.92	$1,175.04

department with undergraduate responsibilities only. To this department (let us call it Department Z), we have assigned almost exactly the same total number of student quarters of instruction as Department X (10,368 as against 10,350). Department Z's teaching load is about 70 percent at the lower-division level and 30 percent at the upper-division level. To simplify the arithmetic, we assume that the average class size at both levels is 24 students; that the lower-division courses are taught exclusively by instructors (who are not graduate students, as the university provides no graduate program in their field); and that all upper-division courses are taught by professors. We assume an average salary of $10,800 per academic year for instructors, whom we take to be experienced long-term teachers in their field either in Department Z or in high schools and junior colleges. We assume an average salary of $15,600 per academic year for all categories of professors (assistant, associate, and full professors). Given the strictly undergraduate teaching mission assumed for the department, research and writing by Department Z faculty members are regarded as free goods and average teaching loads of 12 hours are attributed to both professors and instructors. The average class size of 24 implies a tradition of participatory instruction; these class sizes and participatory patterns we understand to be characteristic also of liberal arts colleges. As the faculty members of Department Z do not publish extensively (if at all), they are not widely known among members of the graduate departments in their discipline; consequently, their alternatives to employment in Department Z would typically be found in other universities or colleges that do not offer graduate work in the field.

These not implausible assumptions, as expressed in table 9.7, lead to estimates of total departmental costs per student quarter (three credit hours) of $48.12 at the lower-division level and $73.44 at the upper-division level. If we assign an index of 1.00 to the lower-division cost, we obtain an index of approximately 1.50 per student quarter in the upper-division program. Assuming an average student course load of 16 per year at each of these levels, we obtain estimates of total departmental costs per equivalent full-time student of $769.92 at the lower-division level and $1,175.04 at the upper-division level. Including a reasonable complement of stenographers and current expense funds, the total budget of Department Z is identical with that of Department X at $594,144. Since research, if existent in Department Z, is treated by the university as a free good, Department X achieves a lower cost per student quarter of instruction than does Department Z despite the sizable volume of graduate teaching and dissertation research in its program. Department X's instructional program, as delineated in table 9.4, also leaves 3.964 professorial man years for faculty research, plus one man year of research assistants and $2,000 of current expense funds.

If we weight the index numbers in line 6 of table 9.7 by the numbers of student quarters of lower-division and upper-division instruction respectively, we get an average of 1.153. That is, the average cost per unit of Department Z's entire instructional program is 1.153 times that of its lower-division program.

For comparison, the average cost per unit of Department X's entire instructional program is 1.764 times as large as is that of Department X's lower-division program. This calculation is internal to Department X, just as the other calculation is internal to Department Z. The dollar cost corresponding to an internal index number of 1.00 is $25.84 in Department X and $48.12 in Department Z.

If we assign an index value of 1.00 to $25.84 in both departments, then the index of cost per unit of lower-division instruction in Department Z becomes 1.862 and that of upper-division instruction in Department Z becomes 2.842. The index of average cost per unit for Department Z's entire program becomes 2.147, compared with 1.764 on the same base ($25.84 = 1.00) for the combined undergraduate and graduate instructional programs of Department X.

On the surface, it would seem reasonable for a university to allocate its budget resources in such a way that the marginal costs per unit of any given level of instruction were the same in all departments. It would indeed be interesting to examine the implications of a set of departmental budgets which were determined in this fashion.

However, the production processes involved here include on the average 15 or 20 full-time students for each full-time professor or instructor. The outputs of these processes consist of changes in the behavioral capacities of the students. In the first place, we do not know whether the values of these behavioral changes per student quarter accomplished in Department Z are higher or lower than those accomplished at the same levels of instruction by Department X. Second, if we could measure the values of these behavioral changes per student quarter in the two departments and set them at identical levels, it is still possible that the optimal combining proportions of university budget resources and student effort would be different in the two departments. Thus, the marginal productivities of the university's resources should be equal in different uses, but the average quantities of university resources per unit of output in different programs could still be significantly different.

Such comparisons also raise questions about the accuracy with which the traditional currency of the registrar's office (student credit hours) measures either the outputs or the inputs of the educational process. Typically, minimum requirements for graduation are stated in terms of credit hours, for example 192 credit hours for a B.S. degree under a quarter system. Some students complain when the amount of time required to obtain a specified grade in one three-hour course is substantially larger than in their other three-hour courses. Hours spent in a laboratory (which may make homework unnecessary) are presumably offset against hours spent in the library or at home doing the assignments for non-laboratory courses. Thus, it would seem that the numbers of credit hours assigned to different courses should be roughly in proportion to the numbers of hours of student time required for equivalent grades. If so, student inputs per credit hour would tend to be equal in all courses at a specified level of instruction.

Although it would still not necessarily follow that the average dollar value of university resources per credit hour should be the same in all courses at a given level of instruction, it seems to us that the burden of proof should be placed upon those who would argue that the amount of university resources per credit hour (at a given level of instruction) should be substantially different in different departments. There is need for comparable information from departments in a given discipline in many different universities, so that "best current practices" may be disseminated and synthesized; practices used in different departments on the same campus should also be studied and compared.

UNDERGRADUATE PROGRAM QUALITY AND ENROLLMENT RESPONSE

Within the broad admissions policies of the university and the average level of resources per student available to it for undergraduate programs, each department is obligated to supply courses of reasonable quality to all qualified undergraduates who may seek to enroll in them. In the short run, the curricula of other departments may require their majors to take certain specified courses in Department X; alternatively or in addition, they may require their majors to select a stipulated number of credit hours from an array that includes two or three courses in Department X and several in other departments. University catalogs are prepared for at least one year and often two years in advance, so for a year or two Department X can count on not less than a certain minimum level of student enrollment in required or semirequired courses. Shifts in student demand will occur within a couple of years, however, if the quality of instruction in required courses is permitted to decline very much. Also, the courses required for some students are elective for others, so there is a possibility that enrollments in the sometimes-required courses will increase considerably if the quality of instruction is very good. An increase in its undergraduate enrollments relative to other departments in the university constitutes a reasonable claim for additional resources to be allocated to Department X.

Let us assume that an index of the attractiveness of each course in Department X which is available to undergraduates can be computed and all such indexes aggregated into a measure, v, of the overall attractiveness of Department X's "undergraduate program offer." The measure v may contain at least three components: (1) expectations of the students concerning the contribution Department X's courses will make to increasing their earning power and improving their employment prospects; (2) appraisals by students concerning the relevance of Department X's subject matter to their concerns as citizens and members of society; and (3) appraisals by students of the quality of teaching performance in Department X.

Suppose there are 70 departments in a university, each offering some undergraduate work, and that the sum of all enrollments in undergraduate courses in the university in a given year is a fixed number, n_u, resulting from the size of the student body. The prospective enrollments in the individual departments may be expressed by the following matrix equation:

$$n = a + Bv, \tag{9.1}$$

where n, a, and v are column vectors of 70 elements (departments) each and B is a square matrix of 70 rows and 70 columns. This set of 70 linear equations is assumed to determine the undergraduate enrollment in each department subject to the constraint that the sum of enrollments in all departments is equal to n_u, the total undergraduate enrollment in the university. In particular, suppose this constraint is satisfied when all the v_i ($i = 1, 2, 3, \cdots, 70$) are set at the previous year's values and consider the effect of an increase in v_1 for the given year.

An increase in v_1 (the attractiveness of Department 1's undergraduate program offer as perceived by students) will increase n_1, the number of student quarters of enrollment in Department 1's courses, if the other v_i remain constant ($i = 2, 3, \cdots, 70$). Since total university enrollment for the given year is assumed fixed, an increase in n_1 must be offset by decreases in some or all of the enrollments in other departments, n_2 through n_{70}. In principle, each student will try to reallocate his fixed "student quarter budget" among departments until the ratios of the perceived marginal utilities to him of the offerings of different departments are equal to the ratios of the corresponding v_i, and these ratios have changed in favor of Department 1. The matrix equation $n = a + Bv$ (together with the constraint $n_1 + n_2 + \cdots + n_{70} = n_u$) represents the aggregative consequences of such reallocations for the student body as a whole.

If the increase in v_1 is made known to potential as well as to actual students, it will tend to increase the number of applicants for admission to the university in the following year. In effect, the university competes with all other nonmarket and market activities for the allocation of human time.

LINKING DEPARTMENT X TO THE UNDERGRADUATE PROGRAMS OF THE UNIVERSITY AND TO THE NATIONAL SCIENTIFIC COMMUNITY

On pages 223–25 and particularly in connection with table 9.1, we described some gradients or correlates of quality among categories of universities and departments with nationally recognized graduate programs.

The reality of scientific communities is evidenced by the existence of national associations that sponsor journals and annual meetings, elect officers, and award honorific titles. In general, the salaries of members of such communities are substantially correlated with their perceived productivity and consequent influence within the community.

It must be difficult for many state legislators, parents, and undergraduate students to recognize the existence and appreciate the functions of such communities. Sociologists studying university communities some years ago characterized faculty members as either "locals" or "nationals." (In this context, "national" and "cosmopolitan" are interchangeable terms.) The "local" was said to devote his professional time and energy to the affairs of the university as such, including its undergraduate teaching functions. It was said of the "national" that he marched to a distant drum; to him, his national or international scientific community was the primary reality, and he produced research publications that would be valued by other members of that community.

In a department with major responsibilities at both undergraduate and graduate levels, few faculty members will fit either of these pure types. It is more likely that the faculty will constitute a continuum, with some members primarily involved in advanced graduate teaching and others in undergraduate and first-year graduate teaching; most will do some teaching at both graduate and undergraduate levels and will be involved to some extent in university affairs and also in national scientific activities. The department must allocate its regular budget resources judiciously, and if possible optimally, between its undergraduate (local) and graduate (national) programs.

The demand function for enrollment in the department's undergraduate courses must have a substantial downward slope, as its product is differentiated from those of other departments in the same university and the weighted average elasticity of demand for enrollment in all departments in any given year must be zero (as total university enrollment in a given year is assumed fixed). In contrast, the demand function for the department's contribution to the national output of graduate training and published research must slope downward very gently (as the department accounts for a small percentage of the national output of its discipline).

Now, suppose that the national demand function for graduate training and research rises sharply while the department's total resources remain fixed. Department X will tend to seek a new equilibrium at which a smaller proportion of its regular budget resources is used in the undergraduate and a larger proportion in the graduate program. Conversely, a sharp drop in the national demand function for graduate training and research would tend to result in the allocation of a larger proportion of its fixed resources to the undergraduate program and a smaller proportion to graduate training and research. The opportunity cost of regular budget resources used in the graduate program is their marginal productivity in the undergraduate program. This situation is replicated in each of the 50 departments in our hypothetical scientific community.

Assume now that an agency of the federal government recognizes (1) that the benefits of graduate training and research are diffused over the nation and not fixed in particular states and (2) that state legislatures will not appropriate sufficient funds to support the volumes of graduate training and research that may appear desirable from a national viewpoint. Assume further that the director (policy maker) of this federal agency has two major policy instruments, (1) an allocation of funds for research grants and contracts to be awarded to university professors and (2) an allocation of funds to provide fellowships for graduate students.* Suppose that the research grants and contracts may be used (1) to pay salaries of professors during the summer months, (2) to provide stipends for research assistants and associates who are graduate or postdoctoral students in the department, and (3) to pay some proportion of the academic year salaries of professors.

If federal funds for research are increased, some professors in Department X will transfer additional time to such funds, releasing salary savings which (under the circumstances) can and should be used for additional part-time instructors and teaching assistants. The total number of graduate students in the department may be expanded somewhat (on research assistantships even if the number of federal fellowships is held constant); also, the kinds of research performed by university professors are usually complementary with the preparation of dissertations by graduate students. In general, a moderate increase in the ratio of research assistantships to teaching assistantships in a department makes graduate students better off in terms of their own professional objectives.

The number of persons engaged in nationally oriented research and graduate training may also be expanded by adding temporary faculty members whose salaries are paid from research grants and contracts. Also, some persons who have recently completed Ph.D.s in a department may find it advantageous to accept a temporary teaching position in it to replace regular professorial teaching resources that are temporarily transferred to federally financed research.

The quality of the research output and the teaching programs of a department will depend partly on the quality of graduate students it attracts. Suppose that a specified number of graduate students, all of whom meet the admission standards of at least the less prestigious departments in the community, seeks admission to various of the 50 departments. Formally, the situation may be modeled in a manner much like that presented for undergraduate enrollment choices among departments in a single university. We assume that the total number of graduate students who will be admitted to the 50 departments in the coming year is a fixed number, m_T. Each department has an "offer" for

*Our references here and in subsequent pages to a federal policy maker using instruments to achieve (or approximate) specified targets are in the tradition of Jan Tinbergen's theory of economic policy as elaborated by Fox, Sengupta, and Thorbecke (1966 and 1973).

prospective graduate students, the attractiveness of which we will denote by u. This measure of the attractiveness of the department to prospective graduate students is closely associated with the rated quality of its graduate faculty which in turn is strongly correlated with the reputed effectiveness of its graduate program. These perceptions reflect the fact that graduate students in the most highly rated departments will usually be made aware of the most promising ideas and methods in their discipline, will engage in dissertation research reasonably close to the frontiers of their specialties, and will have considerably better than average employment opportunities.

The allocation of beginning graduate students among the departments in the discipline may be represented by the matrix equation

$$m = c + Du, \tag{9.2}$$

where m, c, and u are column vectors of 50 elements each and D is a square matrix with 50 rows and 50 columns. If u_1 is perceived as increasing while the other u_i remain constant, the number of students seeking to enroll in Department 1 will increase and (since we assume $\Sigma_{i=1}^{50}\ m_i = m_T$ is fixed) the numbers seeking to enroll in other departments will on balance decline.

The same model can be extended to the allocation of prospective graduate students among disciplines. Assume that the u_i for 50 departments in Discipline 1 can be combined into an aggregative measure, U_1, of the perceived attractiveness of obtaining a Ph.D. in Discipline 1. Suppose that similar measures, $U_2, U_3, \cdots, U_k$, are calculated for other disciplines requiring Ph.D.s or comparably long graduate training. Then a perceived increase in U_1 relative to the other U_i will tend to increase the number of potential graduate students seeking admission to Discipline 1. If total admissions to the 50 departments in Discipline 1 were held constant, the average quality of the graduate students admitted to them would rise.

One component of a vector of U_is ranging over disciplines would be the vector of expected salaries for persons with given characteristics who take their Ph.D.s in the various fields. A multiple-regression analysis of the salaries of scientists on the National Register of Scientific and Technical Personnel in 1966 was published by Emanuel Melichar (1968). Melichar's principal results are reproduced in tables 9.8 and 9.9.*

The net relations between salaries and years of experience in table 9.8 are presumed to be the same for all sciences. The salary differentials in the bottom portion of table 9.9 would imply that graduate students with the same ability and motivation could come out with very different salaries (ranging from 13 percent above to 15 percent below the average for all scientists) depending upon the particular science in which they earned their Ph.D.s.†

*A more elaborate framework for analyzing these data was outlined by Fox (1966) and may have conceptual interest.

†There is, of course, a wide variation in salaries of individuals within each discipline; the standard error of the residuals from Melichar's equation was approximately $\log_{10} = 0.114$. About two-thirds of the individual salaries in any given science lay within a range of 30 percent above and 23 percent below the corresponding regression estimates. A superior scientist in a low-salaried field still earned more than an average scientist in a high-salaried field as of 1966.

Table 9.8
Net Relationship Between Professional Salaries and Employer-experience Characteristics: All Professions, 1966 National Register

	Years of Experience						
Type of Employer	1 or less	2 to 4	5 to 9	10 to 14	15 to 19	20 to 29	30 and over
	Percentage difference from national geometric mean						
Educational institutions							
academic-year base	-36.6	-31.9	-25.7	-17.6	-11.5	-4.3	0.0
calendar-year base	-28.8	-23.4	-16.5	-7.3	-0.5	7.6	12.4
Government							
federal	-26.0	-15.8	-5.7	0.9	7.2	16.0	24.7
other	-36.5	-27.8	-19.1	-13.5	-8.0	-0.5	7.0
Other employer							
nonprofit organization	-20.9	-16.7	-9.0	-1.2	6.5	15.6	24.8
industry or business	-10.8	-6.0	2.7	11.5	20.2	30.5	40.8
self-employed	0.7	6.1	15.9	25.9	35.7	47.4	59.0

Source: E. Melichar, "Factors Affecting 1966 Basic Salaries in the National Register Professions," Study 2 in *Studies of the Structure of Economists' Salaries and Income*, Supplement (2) to *American Economic Review* 58, no. 5 (December 1968): 56–69.

We do not know the stability of the 1966 salary structure over time. As of 1971, the demand for persons with recent Ph.D.s in physics and chemistry had dropped sharply relative to the prospective supply. Ph.D. graduates in these and several other fields, if they succeeded in obtaining academic positions in 1971, secured them in departments with lower ratings in terms of graduate-program quality than they might have joined in 1966. Clearly, there is need for a future-oriented data system in the United States that will reflect the best available information and analysis concerning prospective career incomes and the probabilities of obtaining certain kinds of employment in the various disciplines over a time horizon of at least ten or fifteen years. Also, our practices relative to providing opportunities for periodic shifts of emphasis by individual scientists and scholars should be revised.

We return to our assumed federal policy maker who has the power to expand or contract the volume of research grants and contracts (and graduate fellowships) available to the 50 departments of our hypothetical scientific community. A given number of dollars allocated to university professors in the form of research grants and contracts will support fewer graduate students than the same number of dollars awarded as graduate fellowships. Thus, these two policy instruments should enable the policy maker to achieve (approximately) target values of two separate variables, (1) the number of graduate students trained and (2) the volume of published research. These two target variables would normally tend to move in the same direction, but the instruments (research grants vs. fellowships) could be manipulated to see that they changed

Table 9.9
Net Relationships Between Professional Salaries and Specified Characteristics: All Professions, 1966 National Register

Characteristic	Percentage Difference from National Geometric Mean, 1966	Percentage of Respondents in Class
Highest academic degree		
professional/medical	38.9	2.5
Ph.D.	15.5	41.5
Master's	-8.5	25.1
Bachelor's	-13.6	28.8
other or not reported	-18.3	2.1
Primary work activity		
management	14.9	23.0
research and development	-1.5	35.4
production and inspection	-5.5	7.9
teaching	-9.4	19.9
other or not reported	-2.3	13.8
Age		
under 30	-12.8	13.8
30-34	-4.2	17.6
35-39	1.9	19.2
40-44	4.7	17.0
45-54	5.9	22.0
55-64	2.7	8.8
65 and over	-2.8	1.4
not reported	-1.5	0.2
Sex		
male	1.1	93.4
female	-15.0	6.6
Field of science		
mathematics	13.3	9.6
economics	11.6	5.7
statistics	8.5	1.3
physics	7.9	11.0
anthropology	1.0	0.4
meteorology	-0.4	1.7
sociology	-0.6	1.5
psychology	-1.4	8.2
earth sciences	-2.7	7.9
chemistry	-4.7	27.2
biological sciences	-4.9	12.4
linguistics	-6.7	0.5
agricultural sciences	-15.5	4.8
other	3.7	7.7

Source: See table 9.8.

by different percentages. Under certain circumstances, the volume of published research could be caused to expand moderately at the same time that the number of graduate students completing Ph.D.s was moderately reduced, or vice versa.

Our policy maker should presumably use his two instruments with a view to approximating some "optimal" time paths of the two target variables. The optimal time path for numbers of graduate students enrolled or numbers completing the Ph.D. degree could hardly be chosen without some notion of the associated time path of salaries for Ph.D.s in Discipline 1 relative to salaries in other fields involving similar training and life styles.

COMPLEMENTARITIES BETWEEN GRADUATE AND UNDERGRADUATE PROGRAMS: COMBINING SUBJECT-MATTER QUALITY AND TEACHING PROFICIENCY

We have characterized the two environments of a university department with both undergraduate and graduate programs. Assume that each characterization has been validated and explained in detail to the chairmen of three departments, one with only an undergraduate program, one with only a graduate program, and one with both. How should they respond?

Evidently Chairman 1 should try to maximize the net revenue of his department's undergraduate program (i.e., the total net benefit accruing to its undergraduate enrollees) from any given set of university resources assigned to him. As a proxy for this, he might try to maximize v_1, the perceived quality (or value of output per student quarter) of his undergraduate program.

Chairman 2 should evidently try to maximize the net revenue of his department's graduate training and research program (i.e., the sum of the total net benefit accruing to its graduate students and the net excess of the value of its total research output, however funded, over the cost of regular university resources used) from any given set of university resources assigned to him. As a proxy for this, he might seek to maximize u_2, the perceived quality (or value of output per student quarter of his graduate program.

In theory, Chairman 3 might try to recruit two distinct faculties, one for the undergraduate and one for the graduate program. The undergraduate program would be a replica of Department 1 and the graduate program a replica of Department 2. The two faculties might benefit from interaction with each other but the benefits to students would be only indirect.

The values, u and v, of a department's offers to graduate and undergraduate students respectively, might each be viewed schematically as containing four components, as follows:

$$u = w_1(\lambda_1 t + \lambda_2 p) + w_2(\gamma_1 s + \gamma_2 r) \tag{9.3}$$

and

$$v = w_3(\lambda_3 t + \lambda_4 p) + w_4(\gamma_3 s + \gamma_4 r), \tag{9.4}$$

where t is an index of the quality of teaching techniques used, p is an index of the quality of subject matter learned, s is an index of the expected average salary of professional workers in the discipline, and r is an index of the expected riskiness of employment prospects in the discipline; the ws, λs and γs are weights such that $w_1 + w_2 = 1$, $\lambda_1 + \lambda_2 = 1$, $\gamma_1 + \gamma_2 = 1$, $w_3 + w_4 = 1$, $\lambda_3 + \lambda_4 = 1$ and $\gamma_3 + \gamma_4 = 1$.

The variables s and r are properties of the national market for professional workers trained in the discipline and cannot be significantly altered by the actions of a single department; they are matters of major importance to potential graduate students and substantial importance to undergraduates considering a B.A. or B.S. major in the field. The variables t and p are properties of the department's own program and can be influenced by choice of personnel, in-service training and learning opportunities, incentives, facilities and equipment, choice of course content, textbooks and reading lists, curriculum design, and other local actions. The quality of subject matter learned (including theory and methodology) is crucial at the graduate level and somewhat less so at the upper- and lower-division levels respectively; the quality of teaching techniques used is least important at the graduate level and progressively more so at the upper- and lower-division levels. Our hypothesis might be depicted as follows:

Level of Instruction	Relative Importance of Teaching Techniques: t	Relative Importance of Quality of Subject Matter: p
Graduate division	0.2	0.8
Upper division	0.4	0.6
Lower division	0.6	0.4

The specific figures are illustrative only.

The gradients in a national scientific community are dominated by productivity in the creation of new knowledge, which implies proximity to the frontier of the subject-matter field (and a high rating of the variable p in our equations). In contrast, the faculty of a strictly undergraduate department is in some danger of becoming detached from the national scientific community and teaching obsolescent subject matter (implying a low rating on the variable p). The undergraduate faculty may, however, take considerable pride in its teaching skills (leading to a high rating on t); a strictly graduate faculty may be impervious to advice on teaching techniques (leading to a low rating on t).

For numerical illustration of the potential leverage of t and p respectively in increasing program quality, we separate v into upper division (v_{ud}) and lower division (v_{ld}) components and supply values for all coefficients, as follows:

$$u = 0.5(0.2t + 0.8p) + 0.5(0.5s + 0.5r), \tag{9.5}$$

$$v_{ud} = 0.7(0.4t + 0.6p) + 0.3(0.5s + 0.5r), \tag{9.6}$$

and

$$v_{ld} = 0.9(0.6t + 0.4p) + 0.1(0.5s + 0.5r). \tag{9.7}$$

The following partial derivatives are of interest:

Index of Program Quality or Value	Partial Derivative with Respect to: t	p
u	0.10	0.40
v_{ud}	0.28	0.42
v_{ld}	0.54	0.36

Let us now relate the current discussion back to table 9.4, the display of Department X's instructional program in activity-analysis format, and particularly to the top row of figures labeled "assumed relative value per unit of activity with average quality." This implies that $v_{ld} = 1$ for activities 1, 2, and 3; $v_{ud} = 1$ for activities 4, 5, and 6; and $u = 1$ for activities 9, 10, 11, 12, 13, and 14. Suppose these are the values realized in Year 1. We would like to consider realistic ways of increasing these values. The values of s and r (salary and employment prospects in our discipline) are beyond our control and they are not of much concern to the lower division students anyway.

Our assumed values of the *w*s and λs imply that the partial derivative or "efficiency" of p in raising quality is about the same (from 0.36 to 0.42) at all three levels of instruction, while the "efficiency" of t appears to be twice as high at the lower division as at the upper-division level (0.54 as against 0.28) and to be quite low at the graduate level. Our search for ways to improve quality now becomes an examination of ways to increase t and p, and we are faced at once with the problem of specifying cardinal measures for each of these variables.

The problem with respect to p is researchable. In table 9.1, for example, we might assume that the median university (or department) in class *D* produces marginally acceptable Ph.D.s; the median university (or department) in class *A* is still half a class interval below the very best. The median for class *A* exceeds the median for class *D* by 24 percent on salaries of full professors, 38 percent on Ph.D.s awarded per graduate student enrolled, 75 percent on graduate students enrolled per full professor, 141 percent on doctoral awards per full professor per year, and 184 percent on federal obligations for academic research and development per full professor. (Another measure, not shown in table 9.1, is doctoral awards per member of the graduate faculty; the median for class *A* is 80 percent higher than the median for class *D*.) It seems reasonable to expect a range of p at the graduate level, within the top 50 or 60 departments, at least as large as the 24 percent range in salaries of full professors but no larger than the 80 percent range for doctoral awards per member of the graduate faculty.

The problem with respect to t should also be researchable by educational psychologists. Suppose that undergraduate students are invited to rate their instructors on a scale ranging from "excellent" through "very good," "good," "average," and "poor"; and that we assign a value of 1.00 to "average." If we assign values of 1.4 to "excellent" and 0.6 to "poor" as cardinal measures we imply that an "excellent" instructor causes his students to increase their behavioral capacities relative to the objectives of the course by 40 percent more than does an average instructor. How could this implication be tested? If we assume that an "excellent" instructor induces only 20 percent more increase in behavioral capacities than does an average one, the expected payoff to improvement in teaching techniques is only half as large as under our initial appraisal.

A department that has concentrated on maximizing u may already have achieved a high value of p in its graduate program and its graduate students are being attracted and benefited by this. If so, a combination of graduate faculty members and graduate students (teaching assistants and instructors) should be able to achieve a high value of p in the upper and lower divisions also. Further, if teaching skills have been largely ignored, there should be a potential for large increases in t at the lower-division level through imparting such skills to instructors and teaching assistants; moderate increases in t would be possible at both lower-division and upper-division levels through improved teaching techniques on the part of professors.

A systematic attempt at program improvement in a department with both undergraduate and graduate responsibilities might be guided by an objective function with six components as follows:

$$W_{total} = W_l + W_u + W_{adv} + W_g + W_{gsq} + W_{r(s+gc)}, \tag{9.8}$$

where the subscripts l, u, adv, g, gsq, and $r(s + gc)$ refer respectively to lower-division teaching, upper-division teaching, advising undergraduate majors, graduate teaching, dissertation research and related graduate study, and research involving regular university budget resources (s) and/or grants and contracts (gc) typically from federal sources. The Ws are scalar-valued objective functions; let us assume for the moment that they are expressed in dollars, as in column 4 of table 9.3. (This would mean that each figure in the top row of table 9.4 should be multiplied by \$400; for example, the value of output of one unit of activity 1, a lecture-plus-recitation-section pattern involving 280 lower-division students, would be rated at \$112,000 with average quality, i.e., with v_{ld} equal to 1.00.)

In table 9.3, the sum of the first five components of W_{total} for Department X in Year 1 was stated as \$7,302,000. On certain assumptions the sixth component $W_{r(s+gc)}$ amounted to \$700,000, so the resulting value of Department X's total gross output in Year 1 would be about \$8,000,000. A first approximation to the production possibilities frontier for the department as of, say, Year 5 might be stated as a series of conjectures by the chairman and faculty members most knowledgeable concerning each of the six program segments. For example, the value of output of the lower division program in Year 1 was stated as \$2,520,000. Maximum feasible gains in the value of output of this program by Year 5, and the prospective sources of such gains, might be conjectured as follows: (1) better teaching materials, 10 percent; (2) better instructors and teaching assistants in terms of basic ability and motivation, 10 percent; (3) better training and supervision of instructors and teaching assistants in their teaching functions, 10 percent; and (4) better preparation and performance in lecture groups of 280 and 100 students respectively by existing faculty members,

10 percent. The importance of the various sources would differ substantially from one program segment to another.

The conjectural magnitudes might provide a starting point for advice by experts in educational technology, motivation, and learning theory for supporting and directing the department's efforts in the most "profitable" directions. Similarly, the figures could serve as a starting point for discussions among teaching assistants, graduate student instructors, and the faculty members most involved in their supervision and training as teachers. The conjectures as to means of increasing the values of output of the lower-division and upper-division programs could provide starting points for discussions between faculty members, undergraduate majors in Department X, and other students who are taking, or have taken, courses in Department X.

Note also that estimates of the quality indexes expected and resource inputs required (including students' time) for any proposed activity could be inserted in an activity analysis model similar to that underlying table 9.4. Detailed sensitivity analyses could be performed at the levels of individual courses, clusters of courses or major program segments to observe the consequences of alternative estimates of relative values of the quality indexes associated with different activities.

SOME ELEMENTS OF AN EQUILIBRIUM SYSTEM

We have outlined the components of a system that could be further integrated conceptually with some additional work.

For example, if there are k disciplines and J universities we may write

$$v = (w_1 \lambda_1 t + w_1 \lambda_2 p) + (w_2 \gamma_1 s + w_2 \gamma_2 r) \tag{9.9}$$

and

$$u = (w_3 \lambda_3 t + w_3 \lambda_4 p) + (w_4 \gamma_3 s + w_4 \gamma_4 r), \tag{9.10}$$

where all variables are column vectors with k times J elements. Further, assuming that linear relations exist over relevant ranges of the variables, we may write

$$n = a + Bv \tag{9.11}$$

and

$$m = c + Du, \tag{9.12}$$

where n, m, a, c, v, and u are column vectors with k times J elements and B and D are square matrices with k times J rows and k times J columns. Substituting, we obtain

$$n = a + B[(w_1 \lambda_1 t + w_1 \lambda_2 p) + (w_2 \gamma_1 s + w_2 \gamma_2 r)] \tag{9.13}$$

and

$$m = c + D[(w_3 \lambda_3 t + w_3 \lambda_4 p) + (w_4 \gamma_3 s + w_4 \gamma_4 r)], \tag{9.14}$$

where B consists of J diagonal blocks of k rows and k columns, each block representing the enrollment preference matrix of undergraduates in a particular university, and D consists of k diagonal blocks of J rows and J columns, each block representing the enrollment preference matrix of graduate students in a particular discipline. The variables s and r each take k distinct national average values, one for each discipline; their time paths should be predicted, analyzed and if need be modified as a matter of federal responsibility for national manpower data, analysis and broad policy. The variables t and p are subject to influence in each of k departments in each of j universities; this is the level at which activity analysis models may be used and attempts made to achieve optimal relationships between graduate and undergraduate programs.

While the chairman of each department might reasonably try to maximize v_{ij} for his own undergraduate program, the university president (once he has designated a total dollar amount e_j for undergraduate instruction in the university) should evidently try to maximize $\bar{v}_j = \sum_{i=1}^{k} (n_{ij}/n_j)v_{ij}$, where $n_j = \sum_{i=1}^{k} n_{ij}$ is total undergraduate enrollment in the university and each v_{ij} is a function of the amount of budget resources, e_{ij}, allocated for the undergraduate program of department i. Formally, the e_{ij} should be allocated in such a way that

$$\frac{\partial \bar{v}_j}{\partial e_{1j}} = \frac{\partial \bar{v}_j}{\partial e_{2j}} = \frac{\partial \bar{v}_j}{\partial e_{3j}} = \cdots = \frac{\partial \bar{v}_j}{\partial e_{kj}}, \tag{9.15}$$

and $\sum_{i=1}^{k} e_{ij} = e_j$.

Similarly, while the chairman of each department might reasonably seek to maximize u_{ij} for his own graduate program, our hypothetical federal policy maker with a constructive interest in the national scientific community of discipline i (once a total dollar amount f_i has been designated for federally financed research grants, contracts and graduate fellowships) might aspire to maximize $\bar{u}_i = \sum_{j=1}^{J} (m_{ij}/m_i)u_{ij}$, where $m_i = \sum_{j=1}^{J} m_{ij}$ is total graduate enrollment in the discipline and each u_{ij} is a function of the amount of federal resources, f_{ij}, made available (through whatever mechanisms) for the graduate training and research program of department i. Evidently, the f_{ij} should be allocated in such a way that

$$\frac{\partial \bar{u}_i}{\partial f_{i1}} = \frac{\partial \bar{u}_i}{\partial f_{i2}} = \frac{\partial \bar{u}_i}{\partial f_{i3}} = \cdots = \frac{\partial \bar{u}_i}{\partial f_{iJ}}, \tag{9.16}$$

and $\sum_{j=1}^{J} f_{ij} = f_i$.

Federal policy makers must (should) also be concerned about the allocation of total federal resources for research and graduate training among disciplines, $f = \sum_{i=1}^{k} f_i$. The equilibrium conditions at this level would evidently be

$$\frac{\partial \bar{u}}{\partial f_1} = \frac{\partial \bar{u}}{\partial f_2} = \frac{\partial \bar{u}}{\partial f_3} = \cdots = \frac{\partial \bar{u}}{\partial f_k}, \tag{9.17}$$

where $\bar{u} = \sum_{i=1}^{k} (m_i/m)\bar{u}_i$. To the extent that complementarities existed and were realized between program quality at undergraduate and graduate levels in each department, there would be multiple links between the undergraduate program equilibrium system of each university and the graduate program equilibrium system within and between national scientific (and scholarly) communities.

UNIVERSITY SCIENCE

Our approach in this paper is one of provocative quantification. Some may regard it as ill advised or premature. However, universities in the United States are confronted with a challenge which is itself premature—i.e., it has arrived before we were ready for it in terms of concepts, measurements, and data systems.

Leo Rogin once remarked that the hottest arguments are based on different preconceptions as to what is self-evident. It is self-evident to many older persons that a college education is transmitted by a professor to a student in a classroom and that this is the only way in which the education can get into the student. It is implicitly assumed that the knowledge got into the professor originally in the same way.

University professors know there are other ways. However, most of us operate without much scientific knowledge of the learning process, with a limited awareness of the range of learning aids available, and without a common vocabulary and set of measures to compare the effectiveness of alternative patterns of instruction in different disciplines.

If the outputs of different departments are truly incommensurable, all possible patterns for allocating a given number of dollars among them are (on logical grounds) equally defensible. In practice, we believe university presidents try to allocate resources in an optimal manner "all things considered," including faculty and student morale and the need for public support. In principle, an optimal allocation implies the existence of at least one set of relative prices and constraints such that no other feasible allocation increases the value of an objective function for the university as a whole. ("Prices" are taken in a generic sense to include what Van Eijk and Sandee [1959] called "barter terms of trade" between competing goals or outputs which may not be stated in dollar terms; the objective function attributed to a university president is of the type made famous by Jan Tinbergen [1952, 1956] in his theory of economic policy.)

Tinbergen's policy maker was responsible for the stability and growth of a national economy; for these purposes he needed an econometric model. This model linked the relevant measures (national income, employment, wages, prices, production and others) into a set of equations describing the technological and behavioral structure of the economy at an appropriate level of aggregation. Theil (1958) showed that this set of equations (i.e. the structure of the economy) could be viewed as a set of constraints subject to which the policy maker seeks to optimize his objective function (i.e., a weighted combination of employment, rate of inflation, federal budget deficit, and other variables reflecting the performance of the economy). Plans were formulated using published economic data available to any interested person; the model itself was published, criticized, improved, and updated as the structure of the economy changed (in most respects cumulatively or gradually) over time.

Our inference is unflinching. Within the university we need models that display the actual program structures of different departments and incorporate all the inputs and outputs (a) which are attributed to them by official university records and (b) which are required by, or contribute to, the recognized objectives of the university. At the department level, an activity-analysis format identifies the variables that need to be measured and the precision with which they must be measured if proposed improvements in the programs are to be validated as such. Such data, in such formats, for all departments in a university, should be made widely available to members of the university community along with whatever caveats may be justified about their numerical accuracy and conceptual adequacy at each successive stage in their development. Any interested person could criticize, or suggest improvements in, any concept, measurement, or instructional pattern in any part of the university as reflected in these models.

If many universities develop such data systems and departmental models, concepts can be clarified, knowledge transferred, and data aggregated or pooled across universities. Clarity and comparability in the internal data systems and models of universities would stimulate improvements in the corresponding data for national aggregates. The development of econometric models of the higher education sector and its components at the national level would be facilitated. Weights and coefficients of the kinds included in our various equations could be estimated from empirical data. Data, concepts, and models could be criticized in appropriate journals and conferences and would be improved over time as in the case of data and models relevant to economic forecasting and stabilization.

We see no threat to higher education in these developments. The production processes of higher education are legitimate subjects for scientific inquiry. The efficiency of departments and universities (according to clearly specified criteria) is a legitimate subject for analysis; so is the effectiveness of federal policies with respect to the support of graduate training and research. We need to develop a small community of "university scientists"—i.e., scientists who specialize in the study of universities. The science they apply or synthesize should be the best that the relevant pure sciences can bring forth.

Operations research, management science, economic theory, and econometrics are necessary to university science but by no means sufficient. Cognitive psychology, ecological psychology, transactions analysis, and sociology are also needed, perhaps in new combinations. The university is an environment for human behavior. This environment consists of an array of behavior settings (Barker 1968) in which people perform roles, engage in transactions, make contributions, and receive rewards. But all other environments of human behavior can be characterized in these same terms. The university is an integral component of the society; its outputs are part of the total output of the society; and the values of its outputs are determined as part of the general reward system of the society which includes reputation, influence, recognition, response, affect, and other media of social interchange (Parsons 1968) in addition to money income.

There need be no alienation between the university and the surrounding society.

REFERENCES

Barker, R. G. *Ecological Psychology: Concepts and Methods for Studying the Environment of Human Behavior.* Stanford: Stanford University Press, 1968.

Becker, G. S. *Human Capital: A Theoretical and Empirical Analysis, with Special Reference to Education.* New York: Columbia University Press, 1964.

Cartter, A. M. *An Assessment of Quality in Graduate Education.* Washington, D.C.: American Council on Education, 1966.

Fox, K. A. "Economists' Salary and Income Relationships." Memorandum dated 25 May 1966, prepared for use of the American Economic Association Advisory Committee on Studies of the Structure of Economists' Salaries and Income, Department of Economics, Iowa State University, Ames, Iowa.

Fox, K. A. "A Framework for Appraising the Consistency of 1972–73 Plans for Various Department Programs." Memorandum dated 15 November 1968, Department of Economics, Iowa State University, Ames, Iowa. Cyclostyled.

Fox, K. A. "Optimization Models for University Planning." Paper prepared for the Conference on University Planning and Management Models, Directorate for Scientific Affairs, OECD, Paris, 21–24 April 1969. Cyclostyled plus appendix.

Fox, K. A. "Combining Economic and Noneconomic Objectives in Development Planning: Problems of Concept and Measurement." *Essays in Honor of Jan Tinbergen*, edited by Willy Sellekaerts. New York: Macmillan International, 1973.

Fox, K. A., ed. (with contributions by K. A. Fox, J. K. Sengupta, T. K. Kumar, and B. C. Sanyal). *Economic Analysis for Educational Planning: Resource Allocation in Nonmarket Systems.* Baltimore, Md.: Johns Hopkins University Press, 1972.

Fox, K. A.; McCamley, F. P.; and Plessner, Y. *"Formulation of Management Science Models for Selected Problems of College Administration."* Mimeographed. Final report submitted to U.S. Department of Health, Education and Welfare, 10 November 1967.

Fox, K. A., and Sengupta, J. K. "The Specification of Econometric Models for Planning Educational Systems: An Appraisal of Alternative Approaches." *Kyklos* 21 (1968): 665–694.

Fox, K. A.; Sengupta, J. K.; and Sanyal, B. C. "On the Optimality of Resource Allocation in Educational Systems: Problems Posed by Fixed, Semi-fixed, Divisible or Semi-divisible Resources." Paper presented at the annual meeting of the Operations Research Society of America, Miami Beach, Fla., 10-11 November 1969. Mimeographed.

Fox, K. A.; Sengupta, J. K.; and Thorbecke, E. *The Theory of Quantitative Economic Policy: With Applications to Economic Growth and Stabilization.* Chicago and Amsterdam: Rand McNally and North-Holland Publishing Co., 1966. See also 2nd ed., rev. Amsterdam: North-Holland Publishing Co., and New York: American Elsevier, 1973.

Fox, K. A., and Van Moeseke, P. "Derivation and Implications of a Scalar Measure of Social Income." To appear in a volume in honor of Jan Tinbergen, edited by H. C. Bos. Amsterdam: North-Holland Publishing Company, forthcoming.

Hartman, Lawton M. *Graduate Education: Parameters for Public Policy.* Washington, D.C.: National Science Board, National Science Foundation, 1969.

Koenig, H. E.; Keeney, M. G.; and Zemach, R. "A Systems Model for Management, Planning and Resource Allocation in Institutions of Higher Education." Final report under National Science Foundation Project C-518, Division of Engineering Research, Michigan State University, East Lansing, 30 September 1968.

McCamley, F. P. "Activity Analysis Models of Educational Institutions." Ph.D. dissertation, Iowa State University Library, 1967.

Melichar, E. "Factors Affecting 1966 Basic Salaries in the National Register Professions." Study II in *Studies of the Structure of Economists' Salaries and Income*, supplement 2 to *American Economic Review* 58, no. 5 (December 1968): 56–69.

Parsons, T. "Systems Analysis: Social Systems." In *International Encyclopedia of the Social Sciences*, vol. 15. New York: Macmillan Co. and Free Press, 1968, pp. 458–73.

Plessner, Y.; Fox, K. A.; and Sanyal, B. C. "On the Allocation of Resources in a University Department." *Metroeconomica* 20, no. 3 (Sept–Dec 1968): 256–71.

Roose, K. D., and Andersen, C. J. *A Rating of Graduate Programs.* Washington, D.C.: American Council on Education, 1970.

Schultz, T. W. *The Economic Value of Education.* New York: Columbia University Press, 1963.

Sengupta, J. K., and Fox, K. A. "Models of Resource Allocation and Planning in Educational Institutions and Systems" and "Operations Research and Complex Social Systems." Chapters 7 and 9 in *Economic Analysis and Operations Research: Optimization Techniques in Quantitative Economic Models.* Amsterdam: North-Holland Publishing Co., 1969.

Sengupta, J. K., and Fox, K. A. "A Computable Approach to Optimal Growth of an Academic Department." *Zeitschrift fur die Gesamte Staatswissenschaft* (January 1970): 97–125.

Theil, H. *Economic Forecasts and Policy.* Amsterdam: North-Holland Publishing Co., 1958; 2nd ed., 1961, pp. 431–43.

Tinbergen, J. *On the Theory of Economic Policy.* Amsterdam: North-Holland Publishing Co., 1952; 2nd ed., 1955.

Tinbergen, J. *Economic Policy: Principles and Design.* Amsterdam: North-Holland Publishing Co., 1956.

Van Eijk, C. J., and Sandee, J. "Quantitative Determination of an Optimum Economic Policy." *Econometrica* 27, no. 1 (January 1959): 1–13.

Jati K. Sengupta

10 COST AND PRODUCTION FUNCTIONS IN THE UNIVERSITY EDUCATION SYSTEM: AN ECONOMETRIC ANALYSIS*

Empirical studies of production functions have played a very important role in economic research in the study of problems of resource allocation. For an individual firm in a competitive market framework, cost minimization under a production function offers a useful criterion for specifying an optimal input mix and the associated output responses specified by a supply curve. Under such conditions the cross-section data for firms comprising a more or less homogeneous industry would reveal cost and production relationships that are fairly stable and meaningful. The existence of an aggregate production function and the associated cost function may be given a meaningful economic interpretation in this case, although the data are in aggregate quantities.

A university can in many ways be viewed as a multiproduct firm and the higher-education sector as an industry. The university produces tangible outputs, e.g., degrees and contract research, and uses scarce inputs, e.g., teaching and research faculty, library and other supporting facilities, plant and equipment. Although most outputs and inputs of a university have market values (e.g., returns from additional degrees and skills and the costs of additional faculty and other inputs) they have some aspects of the externalities of a "public good," not internal to the tangible market system, e.g., benefits of academic noncontract research (Sengupta 1973). A second important feature of the university education sector (industry) comprising individual universities as firms is that it may not be fully competitive in a situation where conditions of entry

*Work done under the National Science Foundation research project 420-21-13 at the Iowa State University.

are very significantly affected by financial supports available and other regional factors.

These two qualifications, though important for any analysis of the university education sector in its aggregative production and cost relationships, cannot be adequately appraised unless these relationships are quantitatively specified and econometrically estimated. Our first topic here is to attempt alternative specifications of aggregate input-output relations in the university education system and their estimation from cross-section data.

A second topic to be considered is the study of the various linkages between econometric and control theory models that can be introduced for purposes of dynamic planning of the growth of an educational institution, and for that matter, of a large academic department.

A UNIVERSITY AS A MULTIPRODUCT FIRM

In the analysis of a multiproduct firm it is assumed that it produces n products $y_i (i = 1, \ldots, n)$ with m inputs $x_j (j = 1, \ldots, m)$, some of which may be fixed, some variable. Each output is assumed to follow a production function

$$y_i = f^i(x_{1i}, x_{2i}, \ldots, x_{mi}),$$

with the condition $\quad (i = 1, \ldots, n) \qquad (10.1)$

$$x_j \geqq \sum_{i=1}^{m} x_{ji} \qquad (10.2)$$

where x_{ji} denotes the amount of input x_j used to produce output type i. If we knew the exact proportion λ_{ji} of input x_j used in producing y_i, i.e.,

$$\lambda_{ji} x_j = x_{ji}, \qquad (j = 1, \ldots, m)$$

$$\sum_{i=1}^{n} \lambda_{ji} = 1, \lambda_{ji} \geqq 0 \qquad (i = 1, \ldots, n) \qquad (10.3)$$

then the production function 10.1 can be written in a simpler form

$$y_i = f^i(x_1, \ldots, x_m) \qquad (10.4)$$

where the parameters (e.g., marginal productivity coefficient for a linear function) would now include the combined effects of allocation ratios (λ_{ji}) and their physical productivity. Whereas for an individual firm production function 10.1 may be used to generate an activity-analysis model for determining the allocation ratios λ_{ji} which are in some sense optimal for the firm, it is impossible to do so with aggregative cross-section data, where only the form 10.4 can be estimated. It is clear that the cross-section data we utilize assume not only a particular procedure of aggregation but a specific way of preassigning a set of values of the allocation ratios mentioned above.

The estimation of the production function for a single university in the form 10.4 rather than 10.1 may be justifiable if either sufficient data are not available within the university or a comparison is intended with the average input-output relationships in the education industry as a whole. Of course, for purposes of national educational planning, aggregate production function 10.4, if it is reasonable, may be useful for planning in advance the scale of expansions and contractions in the various inputs given a target (or forecast) rate of growth of the various outputs.

If the average university for which production function 10.4 appears reasonable could be assumed to behave like a multiproduct firm under competitive market conditions, then one would naturally impute profit-maximization objectives to such an institution, where profits z are defined as follows by the difference between revenue (R) and cost (C) functions:

$$\begin{aligned} z &= R(y_1, \ldots, y_n) - C(x_1, \ldots, x_m) \\ &= \sum_{i=1}^{n} p_i y_i - \left(\sum_{j=1}^{m} q_j x_j + F(x_1, \ldots, x_m) \right). \end{aligned} \tag{10.5}$$

Here p_i and q_j are the prices of outputs and inputs and F denotes the part of fixed costs which allow divisibility and transferability between different outputs only in a very limited sense (Tolles and Melichar 1968). Note that the prices of inputs x_j are available in case of universities, although these are proxy estimates in the form of financial cost measures (e.g., teaching costs measured by salaries of teaching staff). Note also that the process of maximizing profits z defined by 10.5 subject to the production function 10.4 can be decomposed into two distinct stages. At the first stage it is assumed that the output vector y is preassigned (say, $y = y^0$), so that profit maximization becomes equivalent to minimization of total costs (C),

$$\begin{aligned} &C = \sum_{j=1}^{m} q_j x_j + F(x_1, \ldots, x_m) \\ &\text{subject to } y_i^0 \leqq f^i(x_1, \ldots, x_m) \qquad (i = 1, \ldots, n). \end{aligned} \tag{10.6}$$

apart from other reasonable restrictions such as nonnegativity of inputs and outputs and so on. At the second stage the preassigned output vector $y^0 = (y_i^0)$ is parametrically varied in its domain, thus inducing a parametric variation of minimal costs $C = C(y^0)$ and the associated revenue functions $R = R(y^0)$ and finally we select that vector $\bar{y}$ to be the optimal which maximizes the profit function defined in 10.5. It is clear that the first-stage problem does not require any knowledge of the vector of output prices and hence it is most suitable for applying the econometric estimates of a production function like 10.4, which is considered in 10.6 as an inequality for providing slacks to the decision makers.

Two important features of the first-stage optimization model 10.6 may be worth emphasizing. First, the parametric variation of the preassigned output vector y^0 may be done in a consistent fashion by ranking the cross section of universities in terms of the ratio of graduate to undergraduate enrollment, since the latter reflects in some sense the weightage given to two major outputs (e.g., undergraduate and graduate degrees) produced by the universities. This approach will be used in the statistical analysis.

Second, the framework of cost minimization in 10.6 would have dynamic components due to the presence of the fixed costs $F(x_1, \ldots, x_m)$, which in the short run for given plant and equipment could vary only marginally in the sense of capacity utilization rates (i.e., user costs); but in the long run the capacity variations may have significant economies of scale (e.g., library costs, computer costs may have scale effects due to size variations) and in this sense there is the well-known problem of specification of optimal expansion of capacity given the projected trend of student enrollment. Mathematical solutions to such problems are available in the literature (Sengupta and Fox 1969), except that most of these solutions are restricted either to single-product firms or to a case where the capacity variable is a scalar.

The university system, however, is unlike the profit-maximizing firm in that its output prices p_i are not observable as market quotations; however, these prices may be related partly to the goals of a university (e.g., the relative emphasis on graduate vs. undergraduate teaching) and partly to the various "satisficing" (rather than maximizing) objectives which are implicit in the production and distribution of public goods (Sengupta 1972). Approximating these prices in terms of discounted lifetime earnings from receiving additional degrees (Fox, McCamley, and Plessner 1967) provides a partial answer but only at the cost of ignoring the fact that these imputed earnings cannot be internalized by the university. Assuming a full-cost pricing principle and applying a markup rule to the observed costs provides another approximation which, however, underemphasizes and sometimes distorts the opportunity costs of academic resources (Fox, Sengupta, and Sanyal 1969). Methods of simulation have some valid scope of application here, particularly when output prices are viewed as relative weights (i.e., ranks). An approach that can be used in this case is the one mentioned before, i.e., to rank the cross-section sample of universities in terms of the ratio of graduate to undergraduate enrollment. Then we might ask how to expand the present input level and its mix, if the expansion of a university from one rank to another is planned. Planning for optimal expansion becomes a valid problem in this case.

FRAMEWORK FOR THE STATISTICAL ANALYSIS

The input-output relations in the university system may be specified at three different levels depending on the purpose of specification: (1) at the level of a single university and its components (departments or colleges); (2) at the aggregate level, comprising a cross section of universities; and, (3) at the level of a single department, across the cross section of universities that are similar in some sense. The first type of specification leads to an activity analysis formulation for allocating resources within a university and its components and problems of modeling and optimizing in this area have been emphasized by a number of authors (Fox, McCamley, and Plessner 1967; Fox, Sengupta, and Sanyal 1969). The second type of specification leads to aggregate production and cost functions which can be estimated from suitable cross-section data. The third type of specification is suitable for analyzing the demand-supply behavior of particular specialties (Tolles and Melichar 1968, Sengupta and Fox 1970), e.g., the economists' salaries, the supply of engineers, and so forth.

Our objective in the analysis below is to consider the second type of specification. We have the same starting point as Southwick (1969), who uses time-series statistical data on the various inputs and outputs over the period 1956–67 to 1962–63 for 68 land-grant colleges and universities as published by the U.S. Office of Education (Lind 1959–65, Lindsay 1959–60) to estimate the cost functions and their various components, such as teaching costs, costs of research, cost of net investments in plant and equipment, and the like. This is perhaps one of the first econometric attempts at analyzing the trend of increases in the social costs of educating students, graduate and undergraduate. From a purely econometric viewpoint, one may raise three basic questions about this attempt. First, the specification of the linear cost function (e.g., cost as represented by senior teaching staff) as a function of the three major outputs, undergraduate and graduate enrollment and research (measured by expenditures on research, i.e., research contract without any intercept terms) is admittedly one of several possibilities, as long as the production basis of the model along with its optimizing conditions are not explicitly spelled out. Second, the single-equation least-squares estimates mentioned by Southwick do not indicate either the significance or the stability of the estimates, insofar as the presence of multicollinearity and the effects of heterogeneity of samples are concerned. The aggregative data of 68 land-grant universities may be too heterogeneous to validate the specification and estimation of aggregative cost functions. Grouping the data into two or more subgroups depending on the ratio of graduate to undergraduate enrollment would enable us to analyze the effects of heterogeneity on the estimates of individual regression coefficients. Third, even if the estimates of the aggregate cost functions are found reasonable, its specific usefulness in national educational policy and planning on the level of the individual university would very much depend on the way the other parts of the complete decision model are set up, e.g., on the level of the individual university, allocation or resources between the different divisions, or departments using an activity analysis model (Fox, Sengupta, and Sanyal 1969), may incorporate as a boundary condition the national trends in overall costs; at the national level the pattern of growth of the structure of the overall economy might include the educational sector as one of the branches that produces skills and research knowledge.

In order to find partial answers to these basic questions, we have attempted to obtain econometric estimates of cost and production functions despite the fact that, from a statistical estimation viewpoint, two factors are favorable to estimating a cost rather than a production function in the cross-section framework of the higher education sector. First, the output measure considered here in terms of the enrollment data is largely exogenous in a given year; hence, for two or more outputs the cost function would more nearly satisfy the assumptions required to validate the least-squares method of estimation. By the same reasoning, the problem of multicollinearity among independent variables would be much less important for cost rather than production functions. Second, the cost data are in a basic sense decomposable by activities, so that the concept of a minimum supply price to sustain a particular activity at a certain level may be easily introduced; while in the case of a production function the problems of disaggregation are more complicated. In other words, an aggregate cost function, which admits of comparison with individual cost functions in specific universities under suitable frameworks, may imply more easily a supply function, e.g., the response of output to price variations when prices are assumed to equal marginal costs.

The data to be used in the estimation of the cost and production functions come from a cross-section sample of 25 universities for the year 1961–62. The selection of the samples is primarily based on the enrollment data and its trend. The following inputs are considered: senior teaching staff, defined in the original data as the full-time equivalent number of teaching faculty with rank of instructor and above (x_1); junior teaching staff, i.e., those who do not fit the definition of senior teaching staff, e.g., graduate students with teaching duties (x_2); professional staff for organized research (x_3); administrative staff, i.e., professional persons acting as administrators as reported by the institutions (x_4); professional library staff (x_5); and a measure of capital represented by the dollar value of net investment in plant and equipment at the end of the fiscal year without considering depreciation and the book value of land (x_6). Four types of output measures are constructed from the published data: undergraduate students in full-time equivalent units measured by considering all part-time students as equivalent to half of a full-time student (y_1); graduate students measured by total graduate enrollment (y_2); combined enrollment y^* formed in the following way: y_1 was regressed into y_2 for the whole 25-university sample obtaining a regression function $y_1 = 27.6598y_2$. The combined variable y^* is obtained from $y^* = \hat{y}_1 + y_2$ where $\hat{y}_1$ is the computed value obtained from the regression above. The fourth type of output measure is research, as evaluated by research contracts, which naturally exclude individual academic research that is unsponsored (y_3). Below, the logarithm of a variable will be denoted with the corresponding capital letter, e.g., Z denotes the logarithm of z.

Note that none of the four output measures above represents outputs in a direct sense; for instance, the production of degrees like B.S., M.S., or Ph.D. are outputs, but the variables y_1 and y_2 denote the total enrollment of undergraduates and graduates to which we have to apply correction factors due to dropouts, failures, and the like; similarly, the value of research may be reflected only partly in the variable y_3, since much unsponsored academic research has externalities in terms of benefiting the national and international scientific community. Likewise, some of the above input statistics are only approximate and sometimes proxy measures. In this sense the production and cost functions based on these input-output statistics should be considered as "surrogate functions" and not as direct physical relationships characterizing the technology of production of knowledge at the universities.

As observed above, for several reasons it is useful to classify the sample to be studied in terms of the ratio of graduate to undergraduate enrollment. The cross-section sample of 25 universities considered will be divided into two groups, depending on whether their graduate/undergraduate ratio falls short of (group I) or exceeds (group II) the value 0.15. It is clear that the universities in group I, emphasizing undergraduate teaching more than graduate instruction and research, would have a different pattern of input-mix than those in group II.

Preliminary regression analyses showed that it is also useful to homogenize the data by expressing each variable (except the output variable y_1) in terms of 100 undergraduate students. These modified data will be called below *normalized*, and will be denoted with an apostrophe, i.e., z' is the normalized value of z. With the normalized data, the input structure appears very homogeneous, except for two outlying observations represented by the University of California and Massachusetts Institute of Technology (MIT). By adopting the currently accepted statistical theory of rejection of outliers (Ferguson 1961), we decided to exclude these two observations when we divided the whole sample into groups I and II.

COST-FUNCTION ESTIMATES

For the statistical analysis, the simplest possible definition of cost function is adopted, i.e., inputs as a function of outputs. Two types of specifications are considered in analyzing each of the two groups into which the data is divided: linear and logarithmic. These two specifications are used with both the normalized and the nonnormalized data. Finally, preliminary statistical analysis showed that the regression equations without intercept gave better results. Only these results are presented in table 10.1 and commented on below.

The regressions with x_1 or X_1 as dependent variable show that when teaching staff are all lumped together, as in the definition of senior teaching staff with no separate divisions (such as assistant professors, full professors, and so on), then graduate enrollment y_2 is statistically unimportant in explaining the trend of senior teaching staff as defined here. It is of some importance for junior teaching staff, but this is largely a spurious relationship in that it very likely involves double counting in some sense (e.g., graduate students may also be part-time junior teaching staff). This suggests that for improvement of statistical precision of these estimates, more detailed data on the teaching staff by rank or salaries are probably required; this would, of course, increase the number of independent variables, but would reduce the bias in estimates due to heterogeneity.

The equations in which X_3 is the dependent variable suggest the following conclusions: (1) it is evident that the student elasticity of demand for research inputs is very high and definitely greater than unity; and (2) research expenditures (y_3) is far more important as an explanatory variable for group II universities than for group I universities (the respective regression coefficients are significant here at 10 percent level).

The result obtained with respect to the influence of graduate-enrollment input on research output is somewhat puzzling. To study this topic further, the following regressions are presented:

$$\begin{aligned}
&\text{(a) Group I: } x_3' = 25.7741^* \, y_2' + 7.4982 \, y_3' \; (\bar{R}^2 = .8886)\\
&\text{(b) Group II: } x_3' = 19.6605^* \, y_2' + 20.3492 \, y_3' \; (\bar{R}^2 = .7795) \qquad (10.7)\\
&\text{(c) Southwick's estimate (pooled date, } N = 68\text{):}\\
&\qquad x_3 = 23.083 \, y_2 - 0.220 \, y_3 \; (\bar{R}^2 = .695).
\end{aligned}$$

Table 10.1 **Cost-Function Regressions**

Dependent Variable	Group I Samples			$\bar{R}^{2b}$	DW Statistic	Group II Samples			$\bar{R}^2$	DW Statistic
	y_1	y_2	y_3			y_1	y_2	y_3		
x_1	6.51*	9.70	-.28	.978	2.73	9.41	-15.3	21.0*	.976	1.704
x_1 (S)[a]	5.99	10.32		.945						
x_2	4.47	-18.1	.84	.813	1.43	5.48	-7.69	17.60	.881	2.170
x_2 (S)	2.86	10.04		.851						
x_3	6.51*	-25.8	3.57	.924	1.504	13.38	-49.0	30.1	.793	1.407
x_3 (S)		23.1	-.22	.695						
x_4	.158	1.21	-.04	.536	.905	.48	-1.13	.60	.562	1.488
x_4 (S)	.542	1.24	.92	.895						
x_5	1.10*	-5.43*	-.72	.938	3.09	.24	.008	2.06	.785	1.380
x_5 (S)	.43	-.48	.87	.886						
x_6	.81*	-1.09	-.25	.966	2.78	.54	-.31	2.88*	.935	1.599
x_6 (S)	.53	.93	.61	.920						
	Y_1	Y_2	Y_3	$\bar{R}^2$	DW Statistic	Y_1	Y_2	Y_3	$\bar{R}^2$	DW Statistic
X_1	1.63*	-.33	-.06	.999	2.79	2.18*	-1.31	.25*	.999	2.46
X_2	1.53*	-.66	.05	.994	1.59	1.34*	-.28	.33*	.997	2.40
X_3	1.67*	-.82*	.15	.997	1.25	1.67*	-.94	.62*	.994	1.84
X_4	.24	.78	.09	.965	.95	1.24	-.80	.11	.961	2.35
X_5	1.23*	-.69	-.21*	.992	2.91	.78	-.13	.23	.983	1.98
X_6	.997*	-.12	-.07	.997	2.46	.999*	-.30	.29	.994	2.02

[a] $x_i(S)$ denote Southwick's estimates based on 68 samples all pooled ($i = 1, 2, \ldots, 6$) and the values reported in the $\bar{R}^2$ column. Southwick's estimates are only R^2 which is not adjusted for degrees of freedom.

[b] Coefficient of multiple correlation is denoted by R, whereas $\bar{R}^2$ denotes $1 - (1 - R^2)\,[(N-1)/(N-k-1)]$, N = number of observations, k = number of independent variables.

*Significant at a 5 percent level of significance. **Significant at a 1 percent level of significance. DW = Durbin-Watson statistic.

Equations (10.7) show that the results in table 10.1 are due in part to multicollinearity between y_1 and y_2 and the heterogeneity of the data. Once these two problems are avoided, a reasonable result is obtained for the relationship between y_2 and x_3.

To explore further the effect of multicollinearity, the combined output variable y^* is used. In this case the results in table 10.2 are obtained. All these results present fairly high $\bar{R}^2$ and marginal cost coefficients, all significant at a 1 percent level of significance.

It is worthwhile to observe that regressions not presented here showed that with the cost functions specified in table 10.2 the presence of the intercept term affects the estimate of marginal input cost, particularly in cases of junior teaching inputs (x_2), research (x_3) and administrative staff (x_4). Forcing the intercept term zero has in general the effect of improving $\bar{R}^2$ and stabilizing the regression coefficients.

In the results being analyzed, the difference in cost-function parameters for groups I and II is much less than it would appear otherwise. However, the application of Chow-test statistic (Chow 1960) to test the difference in estimates of marginal cost between the two groups shows that cost functions are significantly different between the two groups at 1 percent level insofar as the teaching and research inputs are concerned. It is clear that this suggests that even for a purely forecasting exercise (e.g., estimating the future national requirements of various inputs such as teaching and research staff) there would be a considerable amount of improvement in statistical precision if the cross-section sample of universities is first grouped into two or more groups and then the cost parameters estimated. This would also ensure the stability of the parameter estimates when cost functions are regressed for different years.

Table 10.2
Cost-Function Regressions with Combined Input Variable

Dependent Variable	Group I Samples y^*	$\bar{R}^2$	DW Statistic	Group II Samples y^*	$\bar{R}^2$	DW Statistic
x_1	2.234**	.955	1.895	1.522**	.941	2.118
x_2	.670**	.696	1.274	.998**	.860	2.570
x_3	1.072**	.719	1.479	1.178**	.729	1.015
x_4	.088**	.616	.789	.058**	.620	1.290
x_5	.101**	.808	1.582	.721**	.753	2.049
x_6	.185**	.934	2.156	.130**	.890	2.017
	Y^*	$\bar{R}^2$	DW Statistic	Y^*	$\bar{R}^2$	DW Statistic
X_1	1.147**	.999	2.206	1.066**	.998	2.380
X_2	.960**	.993	1.632	.975**	.995	2.778
X_5	.623**	.986	2.021	.595**	.985	2.415
X_6	.729**	.996	2.528	.690**	.992	1.975

See Notes to table 10.1.

Another important characteristic of the logarithmic cost function in table 10.2 is that inputs such as senior teaching staff (x_1) or both senior and junior teaching staff show very clearly increasing marginal costs, which imply that as output requirement rises, input requirements for teaching rise at a faster rate, and vice versa when output requirement tends to decline. As long as the teaching cost forms the most important element of the aggregate cost of the university, this broad tendency would still be valid. Since by equating marginal costs (where all costs are aggregated) to output price we may define a condition of competitive equilibrium, however, an aggregate supply function showing the response of university outputs to price variations can be derived, and in the case of increasing marginal costs the price elasticity of supply will be positive. This suggests that in a programming framework an optimal mix of supply can be estimated by the optimizing criterion of minimizing total costs, provided a set of projections of demand (e.g., enrollment data by fields or colleges) is available.

PRODUCTION-FUNCTION ESTIMATES

As in the case of cost function, the two main sources of sign instability and low $\bar{R}^2$ in the case of production functions were the presence of the intercept term (which incidentally turned out to be statistically insignificant in most cases) and some intercorrelation among the various input variables which appear now as explanatory variables. The analysis below will be limited to that of the regressions in table 10.3 in which a specification with no intercept is used. In our production function estimates the research input did not appear to be very significant, and hence its estimates are not mentioned in table 10.3 but this is quite expected in view of the specific definitions of research used in the calculations. In a conventional production function the research inputs affect technological efficiency through developing and applying new knowledge, and these are reflected in augmented productivity of other inputs such as labor and capital (e.g., neutral, capital-augmenting and labor-augmenting technical progress). In the empirical analysis of the production function for industries, the role of research and diffusion of knowledge as agents of technical progress have been amply evidenced in the literature (Brown and Conrad 1967). In the higher-education system, the quality of graduate teaching, and also senior-level undergraduate teaching to some extent, is greatly influenced by the experience and research of the faculty members, but in the cost functions above these qualitative effects are ignored almost completely. This suggests the need of building more quantitative data so that research inputs and outputs can be defined more appropriately, particularly with reference to the effects of research on the quality and efficiency of teaching. In contrast with these results, the research output had the appropriate significance in the estimates of the cost function.

It should be observed that if all inputs other than x_1 and x_2 are either fixed in the short run, or jointly proportional to $(x_1 + x_2)$, then the estimated coefficient of the production function in table 10.3 would indicate short-run input elasticity of output as a whole. It is clear from the estimated coefficients that the hypothesis of diminishing or constant returns to scale cannot be

Table 10.3
Production-Function Regressions

Dependent Variable	Group I Samples					Group II Samples				
	$x_1' + x_2'$	$x_1' + x_2'$	x_5	$\bar{R}^2$	DW Statistic	$x_1' + x_2'$	$x_1 + x_2$	x_5	$\bar{R}^2$	DW Statistic
y_2'	.011*			.953	1.48	.013**			.899	2.30
y^*		.317**		.920	1.49		.364**		.918	2.17
y^*		.297**	.566	.912	1.52		.566**	-6.71	.938	2.65
		$\log(x_1 + x_2)$	X_5	$\bar{R}^2$	DW Statistic		$\log(x_1 + x_2)$	X_5	$\bar{R}^2$	DW Statistic
y^*		.833**		.998	1.58		.880**		.998	2.61
y^*		.853**	-.040	.998	1.56		1.01**	-.24	.998	2.77

See Notes to table 10.1.

rejected in this case. Also, the application of Chow-test (Chow 1960) to the equations $y^* = a \log (x_1 + x_2)$ showed that in terms of input-elasticity of output, the two groups do not significantly differ at 5 percent level of significance.

These regressions also show diminishing returns to scale for the inputs $x_1 + x_2$. As a consequence, the short-run supply function that they imply specifies a positive price-response of supply. In other words, the usual demand-supply model, demand having a negative slope and supply having a positive slope, may provide a reasonable working hypothesis for the university sector. For an individual university, the production functions being analyzed imply some kind of industry-supply curve (e.g., the hiring of teaching inputs may be constrained by such an industry curve, since competition in the professional field would tend to determine equilibrium input prices). Given the industry-supply curve, the individual university has to adjust its use of inputs in the short run so that input costs tend to equal the value of marginal product. Again we get back to the problem of determining an optimal input mix given the existing marginal productivity estimates for individual inputs. It is clear that in principle the production functions above may be estimated for single departments within a university over time, and such estimates would be helpful in showing the divergence from the national cross section. However, it is only through a more detailed and careful econometric technique that one can build estimates on marginal costs and returns from using specific types of inputs, and it is only then that a design for optimal policy making for the resources of the university system can be built and appraised.

To complete the analysis, a brief comparison of the estimates for the cost and production functions will be made. The cost function estimated by single regressions in the form

$$x_j = a_j y^* \qquad j = 1, \ldots, 6$$

and presented in table 10.2 implies a limitational production function of the form

$$Y^* = \min \left[\frac{x_1}{a_1}, \frac{x_2}{a_2}, \ldots, \frac{x_6}{a_6} \right]$$

which is quite different from the production functions used in neoclassical theory and estimated in table 10.3. However, it is well known from growth theory based on neoclassical models (Burmeister and Dobell 1970) that at the optimal point the neoclassical production function attains an input-output equilibrium which may be identical with that postulated by a Leontief-type limitational production function as mentioned above.

Indeed, if we use the cost functions

$$x_1 = 1.665^{**} y^*$$

and

$$x_2 = .938^{**} y^*$$

obtained with the total sample of 25 universities, it is possible to obtain the composite cost function

$$(x_1 + x_2) = 2.60 y^*$$

and write it as a production function by inversion. In this case we get the output/input ratio of 0.38, whereas the production function also estimated from the sample of 25 universities, i.e.,

$$y^* = 0.349^{**}(x_1 + x_2)\,(\bar{R}^2 = .953),$$

gives a value of 0.35 for that ratio. Indirectly, this shows relative stability of the estimates of marginal costs from our specifications used in table 10.2.

GROWTH ANALYSIS AND PLANNING

This section presents the outline of mathematical models for university planning in which the cost and production functions estimated before could be used.

Granted that the cost function estimates in table 10.1 do not reflect the opportunity costs of research vis-à-vis other inputs as they affect the three outputs (y_1, y_2, y_3), they are nevertheless useful as a first-stage approximation of the educational administrator's problem of planning the changes in scale and mix of various inputs in future. Given a valid projection of enrollment data and for that matter a projection of the total (potential) output vector, the requirement of the input vector which is in some sense optimal can be computed on the basis of these estimates (Nordhaus 1969). For instance, if the outputs can be imputed their prices or weights at every point of time t, then an instantaneous value of output, can be defined as

$$z(t) = w(y_3) \cdot y_1(t) + (1 - w(y_3))\, y_2(t)$$

with its cumulative value (δ being the exponential discount rate);

$$Z(T) = \int_0^T \exp(-\delta t) \cdot z(t)\, dt$$

where the weight coefficient $w = w(y_3)$ indicates that its value is affected by research and its quality. Maximization of $Z(T)$ subject to the following input-output restrictions

$$\sum_{i=1}^{n} a_{ji} y_i(t) \leqq x_j(t)$$

$$y_i(t) \geqq 0,\ x_j(t) \geqq 0; \quad t = 1, \ldots, T$$

$$i = 1, \ldots, n; \quad j = 1, \ldots, m$$

where (a_{ji}) indicates the input-output coefficients, as in (10.3) above, would define a valid decision problem for the educational policy maker. If we were to evaluate the impact of research expenses over time, then we can introduce Lagrange multipliers $u_j(t)$ to form a transformed objective function

$$\bar{Z}(T) = \int_0^T \exp(-\delta t) \cdot \left[z(t) - \sum_{j=1}^{m} u_j \left(\sum_{i=1}^{n} a_{ji} y_i(t) - x_j(t) \right) \right] dt \qquad (10.8)$$

and interpret this as the discounted value of net output (net benefit over costs) produced by the system. When the output prices cannot be used to reflect the influence of research, as in $w(y_3)$, we have to analyze whether the input-cost coefficients (a_{ji}) can be suitably modified to reflect this interdependence. This would raise questions, e.g., whether the opportunity cost of teaching a graduate course ought to differ as between faculty members who are either active or passive in research. Problems of data requirement and the need for some quantification by separate disciplines are worth analyzing in this framework.

The model just presented can be extended for the analysis of a dynamic policy situation. The outline to be presented of the dynamic framework differs basically in two ways from the optimizing model presented before. First, there was no dynamic difference or differential equation before, since the question of time lags and stock-flow relationships are ignored. In the dynamic policy situation to be presented, some inputs are characterized as stocks, others as flows, and the growth of the system is determined in part by the rate at which addition to certain stock inputs affecting the capacity of the system is made. In this sense our dynamic framework is very close to the concepts of optimum growth theory. Second, the costs and prices implied by the econometric estimates of cost and production functions are expost, since they use realized past data; in a dynamic policy framework the prices and costs should reflect the shadow prices (or true opportunity costs) of scarce resources. The divergence of shadow prices and market (or imputed) prices may be either in direction or in magnitudes or both. The dynamic policy model presented in this section seeks to show the impact of such divergences in future, assuming that in the initial period the divergence is either zero or fixed at a certain level. It is in this sense that the shadow prices used here are assumed flexible as in the neoclassical theory.

It is clear then that we start with the following question in the dynamic framework:

Assuming that a reasonable estimate of the production function can be made on the basis of statistical data, cross-section or otherwise, how are we to use it for purposes of planning and growth problems? This question arises naturally at the national and the individual university levels and we attempt here an outline of the decision problem at the university level, where it is presumed that an aggregate production function, which is plausible can be built up from its past trends and other data. The decision maker in this case may be the president and/or the deans of the respective constituent colleges of the university system (Simon 1967). It will be presumed that the overall decision problem of planning in such a framework arises in two interrelated stages: (1) in the first stage the problems of optimal expansion of basic inputs such as the stock of faculty and research staff are analyzed in the context of a long-run horizon, given the constraints of an aggregate production function and a projected trend of student enrollment; (2) in the second stage we consider the short-run problem in a detailed disaggregative form, preferably in an activity-analysis framework since it allows the most generalized specification of production relations in the university system (Fox, Sengupta, and Sanyal 1969). If the first-stage problem is interpreted as one of growth, the second stage could be compared with the analysis of short-run imbalances and deviations from the long-run path of growth. The linkages between the two stages offer an interesting field for designing appropriate policies; the various techniques known as the decomposition algorithms and methods of coordination (Sengupta 1971) are applicable here.

A possible specification of the first-stage model that can be easily estimated on the basis of available statistical data would proceed as follows:

$$\begin{aligned}
&\text{(a)}\ \ Y = D_1 + p_2 D_2 + p_3 D_3 && \text{(composite index of output);} \\
&\text{(b)}\ \ Y = f(K, L, R) && \text{(production function);} \\
&\text{(c)}\ \ \dot{K} = aD_2 - bK && \text{(growth of the stock of faculty);} \quad (10.9) \\
&\text{(d)}\ \ \dot{R} = c\dot{K} && \text{(growth of research inputs);} \\
&\text{(e)}\ \ \max W[U(D_1, D_2, D_3)] && \text{(objective function).}
\end{aligned}$$

Here D_1, D_2, and D_3 are the three aggregate output measures in terms of undergraduates (e.g., undergraduate degrees), graduates (e.g., graduate degrees) and research (e.g., index of research sales) with their prices denoted by p_i ($p_1 = 1$ as a numeraire); the aggregate production function 10.9 has three types of inputs, the stock of teaching faculty (K), the stock of professional research staff (R) and other basic inputs as a composite index (L) comprising plant and equipment etc., the time rates of growth of inputs K and R are denoted by $\dot{K}$ and $\dot{R}$, where in (10.9d) it is assumed for simplicity that the changes in research inputs are proportional to those in the faculty stocks; the specification (10.9c) assumes that changes in faculty stocks are induced by the trend of graduate enrollment (i.e., graduate students acting as junior teaching staff) and the depreciation due to retirement or dropout among faculty stocks. The objective function specified implicitly in (10.9e) assumes that the instantaneous utilities derived at time t from the output mix $U(D_1, D_2, D_3)$ have to be combined in some sense to arrive at an objective functional $W[U(\cdot)]$ defined over a planning horizon.

By assuming research outputs (D_3) proportional to D_2 and research inputs proportional to the faculty stock, the two variables D_3 and R can be subsumed in the aggregative variables D_2 and K respectively and the equations above may be further simplified as follows:

$$\begin{aligned}
&\text{(a)}\ \ Y = D_1 + p_2 D_2 \\
&\text{(b)}\ \ Y = f(K, L) \\
&\text{(c)}\ \ \dot{K} = aD_2 - bK \qquad (10.10) \\
&\text{(d)}\ \ \max W[U(D_1, D_2)]
\end{aligned}$$

The mathematical form of the educational growth model is now very similar to the formulations in the general theory of optimum economic growth (Sengupta 1970, 1972). Note, however, that in this case the capacity creating effects of capital accumulation are introduced through variables like research and graduate students augmenting the flow of teaching man hours. Assuming linearity where necessary a specific example of the above formulation (10.10) would proceed as follows in terms of a linear programming model over time:

$$\text{(a)}\ \ \text{maximize } W = \int_0^T \exp(-\delta t)\,(wD_{1t} + (1 - w) D_{2t})\,dt$$

subject to

$$\text{(b)}\ \ a_{11} D_{1t} + a_{12} D_{2t} \leq K_t$$

$$
\begin{aligned}
&\text{(c)} \quad a_{21}D_{1t} + a_{22}D_{2t} \leqq L_t \\
&\text{(d)} \quad D_{it} \geqq \bar{D}_{it}, \quad (i = 1, 2) \qquad (10.11)\\
&\text{(e)} \quad c_1K_t + c_2L_t \leqq \bar{C}_t \\
&\text{(f)} \quad \dot{K} = dK/dt = aD_{2t} - bK_t \\
&\text{(g)} \quad K_0, L_0 \text{ given at } t = 0;\ D_{it}, K_t, L_t \geqslant 0. \\
&\qquad (\delta : \text{discount rate}; w, a_{ij}, c_i, a, b : \text{parameters})
\end{aligned}
$$

Here $\bar{D}_{it}$ is the projected demand for output (enrollment) $\bar{C}_t$, the total projected cost with c_1, c_2 as the cost coefficients and w denotes the weight (price) given to the output D_1 such that by varying it within the range (0, 1) one can generate the whole spectrum of optimal solutions to this model. This model is an adaptation of the discrete capital model due to Bruno (1967), and since this is in linear programming terms, it is easily computable by the simplex algorithms.

In order to characterize the optimal solution of this model, where D_1, D_2 are the control variables and K the state variable we introduce the Hamiltonian function H following the Pontryagin principle (Tintner and Sengupta 1972)

$$H = \exp(-\delta t)\,[wD_{1t} + (1 - w)D_{2t} + p_6(t)(aD_{2t} - bK_t)]. \qquad (10.12)$$

As in the theory of economic growth, the Hamiltonian function H can be "interpreted" as the net output produced by the university system assuming that investment in the form of additions to the stock of faculty is valued at the price of $p_6(t)$. Following Pontryagin's maximum principle (Pontryagin et al. 1962), we might say that if an optimal program defined by the sequence $(D_{1t}, D_{2t}, K_t, L_t; 0 \leqslant t < T)$ exists, then there must exist a continuous function $p_6(t)$ such that the following canonical relations hold:

$$\dot{K} = aD_{2t} - bK_t \text{ with } K(0) = K_0 \qquad (10.13a)$$

$$\dot{p}_6(t) = (b + \delta)p_6(t) - p_1(t) - c_1p_4(t) \qquad (10.13b)$$

where $p_1(t), p_4(t)$ are the Lagrange multipliers associated with (10.11a) and (10.11e) respectively. Also, at each moment of time t, the following linear programming (LP) problem must be solved to

$$\text{maximize } z(t) = wD_{1t} + (1 - w)D_{2t} + ap_6(t)D_{2t}$$

$$\text{subject to 10.11b through 10.11g, excluding 10.11f.} \qquad (10.14)$$

Also, the adjoint variable $p_6(t)$ must satisfy certain jump conditions (i.e., corner conditions) and the transversality condition for the terminal time T (Bruno 1967, Pontryagin 1962). Note that since the system 10.14 defines a LP model, it has a dual price system, where the dual variables may be interpreted as suitable prices in the sense of opportunity costs.

There are two distinct advantages of the above formulation for allocation of resources within a university system and its planning problems, apart from the computing ease and convenience. First, the model would show the relative costs of imbalances to the allocation system, caused by budget cuts (e.g., $\bar{C}_t$ lowered) and excessive enrollment (e.g., $\bar{D}_{it}$ increased under fixed budgets) in the form of the altered values of the dual variables defined in the LP model which is dual to 10.14. Similarly, the problem of updating the parameters (a_{ij}, c_i, a, b) and the variation of the relative weights (w) may be easily incorporated. Second, once an optimal program denoted by the sequence ($D_{1t}^*, D_{2t}^*, K_t^*, L_t^*; 0 \leqslant t < T$) is computed, one might proceed to construct a short-run activity-analysis model, where each of the aggregative variables D_1, D_2, K, L, etc., are decomposed into several activities. An example of such a short-run detailed activity-analysis model is given in Fox, Sengupta, and Sanyal (1969). It is clear that the short-run model by going into the details of activities within several specific departments would introduce several new control variables, which may be amenable to the control of the hierarchical decision makers, e.g., deans, departmental chairmen, etc. Denote the set of these new control variables by the vector u. The decision problem in the short run would then be to choose the control vector u by means of a short-run model (specified by e.g., $F(x, u) = 0$, where (x, u) are the set of activities) subject to a set of short-run constraints such that the short-run deviations from the long-run optimal path ($D_{1t}^*, D_{2t}^*, K_t^*, L_t^*; 0 \leqslant t < T$) are in some minimized. The linear decision rule approach of the theory of economic policy (Sengupta 1970, 1972) may also be applied in such cases.

CONCLUDING REMARKS

The econometric estimates of cost and production functions, which have been based here on cross-section data of selected universities, ought to be considered provisional at this stage, since the existence of an aggregate cost and production function has been presupposed and not tested empirically. In addition, as noted before, the estimates of marginal costs and productivities in the university sector are much affected by the presence of aggregation and multicollinearity. One should, therefore, explore further before accepting a specific set of marginal cost estimates derived from the overall data. The empirical estimates may also be affected in this case by the presence of simultaneity in the input-output relationships, which is not taken into account by our single equation estimates. It is clear, therefore, that the marginal cost estimates obtained by Southwick may be of doubtful validity to a far greater degree since they ignore the structural differences between universities completely. It appears that more work is needed on the econometric estimates, which must be based on more disaggregative data for individual universities, before we can say something meaningful about the aggregative cost functions applicable in groups of universities.

In principle, it should be possible to estimate disaggregated and microeconomic production and cost functions for several specific departments of a university, and this ought to be helpful in providing reasonable estimates of marginal costs and productivities of inputs. How could such estimates be used in a static and dynamic framework? This question has been partially answered by providing illustrative models, one static (comparative-static) and the other dynamic.

The static (comparative-static) model seeks to compute a consistent set of input requirements, given a set of projected demands in terms of future enrollment. This provides in a sense a balanced growth path of input-provisions, provided the base year is considered to be under a demand-supply equilibrium. As in a typical open-static Leontief-type input-output model, changes in demand mix can lead to change in input mix; otherwise deviations from equilibrium prices and costs are to be incorporated into the framework. In the dynamic model, which in its control-theoretic framework is illustrated by the LP model (10.11), the deviations from an equilibrium or balanced growth path are analyzed in some detail in terms of shadow prices, stability of optimal path in different zones or phases and in terms of the controllability of the set of instrument variables that can be potentially used by the policy maker. Here the production functions are constrained by prior allocation of inputs by the policy maker, and such allocation decisions may be arrived at in the short run through a more detailed activity-analysis type model. Note that the specific formulation such as 10.11 is intended to provide an illustrative example of a simple computable framework; several other variants of the control model may be easily constructed and empirically implemented.

REFERENCES

Brown, M., and Conrad, A. H. "The Influence of Research and Education on CES Production Relations." In *Empirical Analysis of Production*, vol. 31, Studies in Income and Wealth. New York: National Bureau of Economic Research, 1967.

Bruno, M. "Optimal Accumulation in Discrete Capital Models." In *Essays on the Theory of Optimal Economic Growth*, ed. by K. Shell. Cambridge, Mass.: MIT Press, 1967.

Burmeister, E., and Dobell, A. R. *Mathematical Theories of Economic Growth*. London: Macmillan Co., 1970.

Chow, G. C. "Tests of Equality Between Sets of Coefficients in Two Linear Regressions." *Econometrica* 28 (July 1960): 591–605.

Ferguson, T. S. "Rules for Rejection of Outliers." *Review of International Statistical Institute* 29 (1961): 29–43.

Fox, K. A.; McCamley, F. P.; and Plessner, Y. "Formulation of Management Science Models for Selected Problems of College Administration." Final report (cyclostyled) submitted to U.S. Department of Health, Education, and Welfare, 10 November 1967.

Fox, K. A.; Sengupta, J. K.; and Sanyal, B. C. "On the Optimality of Resource Allocation in Educational System: Problems Posed by Fixed and Semi-fixed, Divisible or Semi-divisible Resources." Paper presented at the Annual Meeting of the Operations Research Society of America, Miami Beach, Fla., November 1969.

Lind, G. "Statistics of Land-Grant Colleges and Universities (1959–1965)." Circulars 541, 612, 639, 689, 702, 734, and 763; U.S. Department of Education, Washington, D.C.

Lindsay, F. H. I. *Financial Statistics of Institutions of Higher Education, 1959-1960.* Washington, D.C.: U.S. Office of Education.

Nordhaus, W. D. *Invention, Growth and Welfare: A Theoretical Treatment of Technological Change.* Cambridge, Mass.: MIT Press, 1969.

Pontryagin, L. S., et al. *The Mathematical Theory of Optimal Processes.* New York: Interscience Publishers, 1962.

Sengupta, J. K. "Optimal Stabilization Policy with a Quadratic Criterion Function." *Review of Economic Studies* 37 (January 1970): 127–45.

Sengupta, J. K. "Economics of Decomposition and Divisionalization under Transfer Pricing." *Zeitschrift fur die Gesamte Staatswissenschaft* 127 (1971): 50–71.

Sengupta, J. K. "Economic Policy Simulation in Dynamic Control Models under Econometric Estimation." In *Essays in Honor of Jan Tinbergen.* New York: Macmillan Co., 1973.

Sengupta, J. K. "Economic Problems of Resource Allocation in Nonmarket System" and "Quantitative Models of Planning for Educational Systems." Chapters 6 and 3 of *Economic Analysis for Educational Planning*, ed. by Karl A. Fox. Baltimore, Md.: Johns Hopkins Press, 1972.

Sengupta, J. K., and Fox, K. A. *Economic Analysis and Operations Research: Optimization Techniques in Quantitative Economic Models.* Amsterdam: North-Holland Publishing Co., 1969.

Sengupta, J. K., and Fox, K. A. "A Computable Approach to Optimal Growth of an Academic Department." *Zeitschrift fur die Gesamte Staatswissenschaft* (January 1970): 97–125.

Simon, H. A. "The Job of a College President." *Educational Record*, Winter 1967.

Southwick, L. "Cost Trends in Land-grant Colleges and Universities." *Applied Economics* 1 (1969): 1967–82.

Tintner, G., and Sengupta, J. K. *Stochastic Economics.* New York: Academic Press, 1972.

Tolles, N. A., and Melichar, E. "Studies of the Structure of Economists' Salaries and Income." *American Economic Review*, supplement 58 (December 1968): 1–153.